ZEW Economic Studies

Publication Series of the Centre for European Economic Research (ZEW), Mannheim, Germany

ZEW Economic Studies

Vol. 1: O. Hohmeyer, K. Rennings (Eds.)
Man-Made Climate Change
Economic Aspects and Policy Options
1999. VIII, 401 pp. ISBN 3-7908-1146-7

Vol. 2: Th. Büttner
Agglomeration, Growth, and Adjustment
A Theoretical and Empirical Study
of Regional Labor Markets in Germany
1999. XI, 206 pp. ISBN 3-7908-1160-2

Vol. 3: P. Capros et al.
Climate Technology Strategies 1
Controlling Greenhouse Gases.
Policy and Technology Options
1999. XVIII, 365 pp. ISBN 3-7908-1229-3

Vol. 4: P. Capros et al.
Climate Technology Strategies 2
The Macro-Economic Cost and Benefit
of Reducing Greenhouse Gas Emissions
in the European Union
1999. XIII, 224 pp. ISBN 3-7908-1230-7

Vol. 5: P.A. Puhani
Evaluating Active Labour Market Policies
Empirical Evidence for Poland During
Transition
1999. XVI, 239 pp. ISBN 3-7908-1234-X

Vol. 6: B. Fitzenberger
Wages and Employment Across Skill Groups
An Analysis for West Germany
1999. XII, 251 pp. ISBN 3-7908-1235-8

Vol. 7: K. Rennings et al. (Eds.)
Social Costs and Sustainable Mobility
Strategies and Experiences in Europe
and the United States
1999. VI, 212 pp. ISBN 3-7908-1260-9

Vol. 8: H. Legler et al.
Germany's Technological Performance
2000. X, 191 pp. ISBN 3-7908-1281-1

Vol. 9: O. Bürgel
The Internationalization of British Start-up Companies in High-Technology Industries
2000. XIV, 230 pp. ISBN 3-7908-1292-7

Vol. 10: J. Hemmelskamp et al. (Eds.)
Innovation-Oriented Environmental Regulation
Theoretical Approaches and Empirical
Analysis
2000. VI, 348 pp. ISBN 3-7908-1313-3

Vol. 11: K.L. Brockmann, M. Stronzik (Eds.)
Flexible Mechanisms
for an Efficient Climate Policy
Cost Saving Policies and Business
Opportunities
2000. VIII, 130 pp. ISBN 3-7908-1314-1

Vol. 12: W. Smolny
Endogenous Innovations
and Knowledge Spillovers
A Theoretical and Empirical Analysis
2000. VIII, 277 pp. ISBN 3-7908-1320-6

Vol. 13: M. Lechner, F. Pfeiffer (Eds.)
Econometric Evaluation
of Labour Market Policies
2001. X, 242 pp. ISBN 3-7908-1372-9

Marian Beise

Lead Markets

Country-Specific Success Factors of the Global Diffusion of Innovations

With 29 Figures
and 8 Tables

Physica-Verlag
A Springer-Verlag Company

ZEW
Zentrum für Europäische
Wirtschaftsforschung GmbH
Centre for European
Economic Research

Series Editor
Prof. Dr. Wolfgang Franz

Author

Dr. Marian Beise
Centre for European Economic Research (ZEW)
L 7, 1
68161 Mannheim
Germany

ISBN 3-7908-1430-X Physica-Verlag Heidelberg New York
D 83

Cataloging-in-Publication Data applied for
Die Deutsche Bibliothek – CIP-Einheitsaufnahme
Beise, Marian: Lead Markets. Country-Specific Success Factors of the Global Diffusion of Innovations / Marian Beise. – Heidelberg; New York: Physica-Verl., 2001
(ZEW economic studies; Vol. 14)
ISBN 3-7908-1430-X

Physica-Verlag Heidelberg New York
a member of BertelsmannSpringer Science+Business Media GmbH

Cover design: Erich Dichiser, ZEW, Mannheim

SPIN 10848719 88/2202-5 4 3 2 1 0 – Printed on acid-free paper

Dedicated to the reconciliation of BWL and VWL

Es kann der Einbildungskraft vielleicht verziehen werden, wenn sie bisweilen schwärmt, d.i. sich nicht behutsam innerhalb den Schranken der Erfahrung hält, denn wenigstens wird sie durch einen solchen freien Schwung belebt und gestärkt, und es wird immer leichter sein, ihre Kühnheit zu mäßigen, als ihrer Mattigkeit aufzuhelfen.

I. KANT, PROLEGOMENA, § 35

Foreword

Ever since I began studying the determinants of the international allocation of R&D by multinational firms in the early 1990s, statistical analysis as well as interviews with executives of multinational firms indicated the importance of different market characteristics of countries as nation-specific location factors for R&D. They felt that there are regional markets where "the music plays", where the worldwide "bandwagon" begins, where users are "most advanced" and demanding and employ technology, which would later be adopted worldwide, where the global standards are set and the most fierce competition makes new worldwide trends most visible. These are all attributes of lead or leading markets. Over time I became fascinated with the phenomenon of lead markets and the great advantage they could bear for multinational firms.

In reviewing the literature related to the regional influences on global innovations, I found a surprising gap between global marketing strategy, product development and the location of R&D activities. Global marketing is preoccupied with how to introduce an innovation in a foreign country with cultural or other differences in demand preferences. Product development takes less account of cultural differences between countries and treats the market as *initially* global and homogeneous or aims at global innovations regardless of where (at which R&D site) the innovation is going to be designed. On the other hand, literature on international R&D strategies focuses on supply factors such as regional centres of science excellence.

This thesis presents a theory of the lead market. It is suggested as a theory of the international diffusion of innovations that brings all three subjects together by showing how a firm can leverage national markets to create innovations that can be commercialised worldwide through local R&D activities. The rather new concept of lead markets is theoretically founded and structured to be applicable in multinational companies. Yet, this study does not provide all the empirical validation and proofs that are necessary. I hope, this task will be completed in future.

Mannheim, May 2001 Marian Beise

Acknowledgements

This thesis was written during my employment at the Centre for European Economic Research (ZEW), Mannheim. I received help and support from many colleagues and scholars. In this thesis I have wrestled to reconcile arguments and methods of both management and economic sciences, an approach that runs the risk – at least in Germany – of being disapproved by both professions. All the more grateful am I to those who encouraged me. First of all, I am grateful to Prof. Hans Georg Gemünden for his inspiration, indulgence and the courtesy with which he has criticised each chapter of the thesis. His pleasant nature made the work with him and writing the thesis delightful. It was he who finally encouraged me to put the lead market phenomenon at the centre of my thesis. His further guidance was equally helpful and enriched the thesis tremendously. I thank Dietmar Harhoff, Nikolaus Franke, Joachim Henkel, Mark Lehrer, Hariolf Grupp, Martin Möhrle and several anonymous people at conferences in Portland/Oregon, Manchester (UK), Charleston/South Carolina, and Cottbus where I had the opportunity to present the argument of my thesis and benefited from valuable comments and constructive criticism.

I thank my colleagues at the ZEW, at IBU and TIM for their support, their critical comments and their indulgence. In particular I would like to thank Prof. Wolfgang Franz for his support and encouragement. As an economist who specialises in labour economics he nevertheless let management scientists feel appreciated. I thank Thomas Cleff, with whom I loved collaborating, for his friendly support and his strong spirit of team-work. Katrin Cremers, Christian Rammer, Norbert Janz, Georg Licht, and Bettina Peters have generously read parts of the thesis and made valuable comments. They all made the main argument of the thesis more focused.

The last chapter was written when I was a visiting researcher at the Centre for Technology Policy at the Multimedia University, Cyberjaya, Malaysia. I am grateful to Prof. Dr. Mohd Ismail, the Dean of the Faculty of Management, and Dr. Avvari Mohan for graciously hosting me. I thank Paul Townsend, Heide Crawford and Johanna Bollinger for making the English of this thesis more readable.

I am grateful for the willingness of many firms' officials to share their riches of knowledge about markets and technologies, among whom I would like to thank Werner Irler, Karl Kammerlander, Hans-Jürgen von der Neyen, Heinz Blanckenfeld, Friedhelm Hillebrand and Markku Saari in particular. I am especially indebted to Manfred Böhm for discussing the lead market concept, reading a draft of the case study and drawing my attention to flaws and misleading formulations. I thank Michael Kokes and Walter Titz of DaimlerChrysler AG for their openness to the lead market concept and their willingness to co-operate with us on a pilot study of the lead market concept. Their comments gave me new insights into the value of the lead market concept.

Contents

1 Introduction

1.1 Summary

This thesis intends to answer three questions: First, what is a lead market; second, what constitutes a lead market, and third, how companies can harness lead markets to generate global innovations. Considering the international, cross-border diffusion of innovations one can observe that a particular technological design such as the facsimile machine, the personal computer or the mobile cellular telephone is often adopted by one country or region much earlier than by other countries which subsequently follow this country, which I will call the lead market. A lead market is defined as a country that adopts an innovation that is subsequently adopted worldwide. When different designs of an innovation compete internationally, the design preferred in the lead market becomes the global dominant design. The study suggests a theoretical explanation for the phenomena of lead markets and collects empirical evidence from a detailed case study of the cellular mobile telephone industry. The international diffusion of an innovation design adopted first by the lead market, i.e. subsequent adoption of an innovation design preferred in the lead market by other countries, can be put down to the special market context in the lead market. The market context includes demand preferences, the environmental condition and the degree of competition.

Multinational firms are often confronted not only with varying market acceptance of new products and processes from country to country, but with national preferences for particular specifications of an innovation, i.e. nation-specific *innovation designs*, and various technological design alternatives on the one hand, and the necessity of global standardised innovations on the other. This thesis outlines how international corporations can cope with the international divergence by harnessing lead markets for the development of globally standardised innovation designs. The thesis suggests that in order to develop global standardised innovations, companies could follow a lead market concept. According to the lead market concept firms can develop global innovations when they focus their innovations on market conditions and demand preferences in the respective lead markets.

The lead market concept is based on three hypotheses: (1) market opportunities for an innovation are nation-specific because market contexts vary from country to country; (2) particular characteristics of a nation's market context increase the probability that innovation designs that are initially adopted in this country are adopted worldwide; and (3) nation-specific demand and the national market context needs can be perceived more efficiently by domestic firms. The second hypothesis represents the core of lead market theory and is the focus of the theoretical (chapter 3) and empirical (chapter 4) work of this thesis. The first hypothesis is a prerequisite and will be based solely on literature (chapter 2), while the third hypothesis aims at lead markets as the locus of companies' innovation activities, in the last consequence the location of R&D (chapter 5).

The first hypothesis asserts that lead markets exist because demand preferences and market contexts vary from country to country and not because the availability of technological knowledge and the capability necessary for the development of the innovation differs internationally. Although globalisation of markets is epitomised by the apparent homogenising of national demand preferences, apart from the convergence in per-capita-income there are still national differences in the economic, industrial, environmental, political and social structures which determine initially varying national demand preferences when a new technology first emerges. At the same time, in many technologies there are no international technological gaps – at least between industrialised countries -, because new knowledge is diffusing internationally very rapidly in an early stage of the innovation process. Global innovation capabilities and varying market contexts lead to a variety of nationally preferred technological designs. Localised technical change occurs not only because of initially varying demand preferences but differences in relative factor prices, varying stages of availability of complementary assets and different degrees of competition. These differences give way to varying incentives for local users to adopt particular designs and firms to develop them, thus resulting in internationally different innovation designs. Accumulation of knowledge on a particular design over time, local network effects and other externalities reconfirm and reinforce the national technological choice. As a result, countries follow varying technological trajectories which firms perceive to be worth pursuing.

When markets vary in their demand preferences and market contexts, how can one particular innovation design be successful internationally and even squeeze other nation-specific designs out of their home markets? The second hypothesis suggests that characteristics of national demand and market conditions exist that render the locally adopted innovation designs international competitive compared to innovation designs preferred by other countries. Basically, an internationally standardised innovation emerges when either the demand conditions of other countries converge to the demand conditions of a country that adopted an innovation or the differences of preferences to other countries can be compensated with lower prices, information advantages, or with increases in the benefit of an innovation. Based on these convergence and compensation mechanisms five groups of national advantages can be derived. First of all, the market that leads an international trend of changing demand preferences and contexts is a lead market (anticipatory demand advantage). In this instance, a lead market is a regional market that foreshadows future global needs. Second, international price differences cause different national adoption rates. Countries leading an international factor price trend lead penetration rates of an innovation using (price decrease) or economising (price increase) this factor and thus become lead markets of the innovation. Furthermore, relative prices reductions of the innovation design preferred in the lead market can compensate differences of preferences between countries (price advantage). Third, information on the real benefit of an innovation and the international transfer of preferences can raise the worldwide attractiveness of nation-specific designs (transfer advantage). Fourth, if there are no differences in preferences internationally but the preferences are not precisely known, information on the real user preferences can vary internationally (market structure advantage). In the lead market the global demand preferences become known earlier; because of a higher level of local competition, for instance. Finally, differences from country to country can be taken into account with dual-usability or built-in compatibility of an innovation design (export advantage). In this instance, a lead market sets incentives for local firms to enhance the usability of national innovations for users in foreign countries. These are the principles of lead markets that will be shown first in a simple theoretical model of consumer demand (3.1) and later for reasons of practicability in a system of five lead market advantages (3.2). When alternative technological designs compete on the world market, eventually only one prevails on the world market. The lead market advantages support the reduction of the international variety of technological designs towards the worldwide adoption of the lead market design as the globally dominant design.

In order to be applicable for firms, the system of lead market advantages derived from theory has to correspond to real cases. There are a number of examples showing that the market opportunities of new technologies and products that have achieved global dominance first emerged regionally bounded. The emergence of worldwide mass application is often initiated in one country or region. In this thesis, the case of the cellular mobile telephone industry is studied in detail (chapter 4). Mobile cellular communication was widely used in Nordic countries in the 1980s, whereas in other European countries and the United States it was regarded as a niche market only being appreciated by businessmen. The huge demand in Nordic countries pushed forward a new European standard (GSM), which was designed to fit the special European context. After GSM service was introduced into other European countries, the demand in those places grew at an unexpectedly rapid rate, and it became adopted by countries outside Europe as well. Other designs for mobile telephony, such as pagers and cordless access systems, that had been highly successful in certain countries in the past, were rapidly squeezed out even in the markets that favoured them before. The study finds that the derived system of lead market factors is capable of explaining the international success of an innovation design that was preferred by one country or region before it became the global dominant design.

Multinational firms are still faced with different demand preferences and market conditions from country to country, inhibiting the success of globally standardised innovations. At the same time, firms in high-tech industries are pressured to introduce global products onto the world market in order to reap economies of scale in production and justify the vast R&D investments for new innovations. This study suggests that multinational firms can harness lead markets for the generation of global products. Firms that align their innovation activities towards the lead market context can subsequently introduce their innovations successfully in other countries as well. Firms can react at several levels to lead markets: from locating sensing resources in the lead market to assigning R&D tasks to affiliates located in the lead market. By locating R&D units in the lead market to develop and refine innovations in close interaction with its local environment, a firm can focus on a narrow range of feedback, lowering the risk of locking-in to idiosyncratic environments and generate true global innovations through locally-leveraged innovations. Yet, lead markets are not only important for multinational firms but also for national governments. The last chapter of this thesis addresses the relationship between national technology policy and lead markets.

1.2 Methodological Approach

This study is mainly based on theoretical reasoning and a detailed case study. The aim of the study is, first of all, to introduce a theory of the mechanisms of the global diffusion of innovations. Second, it shall derive a applicable concept of national advantages of countries leading the international diffusion of innovations (lead markets). In the end, a multinational firm should be helped to identify potential lead markets for the development of global innovations of multinational firms. The main practical idea is that firms leverage the demand and market conditions of lead market countries in order to generate innovations that can be commercialised worldwide. The lead market is a rather new concept of the international diffusion of innovations. Literature discusses aspects of the lead market phenomenon, but a comprehensive model of lead markets is still missing. This thesis embarks on developing a theory of lead markets. Since a range of internationalisation mechanisms of innovations can be found in literature, the suggested theory of lead markets is eclectic taking advantage of a various theories and arguments. Yet, I first present a formal model based on traditional consumer behaviour theory. Albeit a simple comparative static model, it exhibits the basic mechanisms that explain the global diffusion of innovation designs that were first adopted by a single country, a lead market. A simple formal model is important for clarifying the main ideas behind the lead market concept. However, it proves unsuitable for identifying lead markets in practice. The parameters of the theoretical model are either unobservable (latent) or data required by the model is generally not available for new innovations. In order to develop a practical method of explaining lead markets, a system of nation-specific lead market factors is derived from the theoretical discussion. These lead market factors allow the derivation of indicators which approximate the theoretical lead market parameters. The practicability of the system of lead market factors is then evaluated in a detailed case study on the cellular mobile telephone industry. The case study was prepared on the basis of existing studies, data available on the lead market factors and interviews with key persons involved in the development of cellular telephone systems. In these interviews the specific influence of the lead market factors for the international success of the innovation were discussed with the interviewees.

From the lead market analysis I conclude that firms can harness lead markets for the development of global innovations. The lead market concept is a normative concept. This thesis does not claim that firms already take lead markets into consideration in their innovation process. Yet, literature as well as existing data show at least that the international allocation of R&D follows a market-oriented pattern: firms locate R&D in markets that are important for them to penetrate. The common explanation for this is that in order to fully penetrate a large foreign market, a firm must at least adapt existing products and processes locally to the varying demand preferences if not develop locally specific innovations. This reflects the traditional responsiveness approach to nation-specific preferences as well as the firm's strategy for the outcome that a variety of country-specific innovation designs will prevail and no global standard emerges. Yet the observed pattern of efficiency of proximity of R&D to markets is used for the normative assertion that if lead markets exist, it is most effective for a multinational firm to develop global innovations in concentrating its R&D activities in the innovation-specific lead markets.

1.3 Concept of the Study

The thesis follows the traditional structure of analysis: analysis of existence of lead markets, analysis of contingency of lead markets and analysis of efficiency of lead markets. The hypothesis of existence is that there are lead markets for a broad range of innovations. The hypothesis of contingency is that several systematic nation-specific demand and market conditions can be identified that facilitate the international diffusion of innovation designs domestically preferred. These are combined in five lead market factors. The hypothesis of efficiency is that multinational firms can promote the global success of their innovations in concentrating the innovation development activities in the respective lead markets.

The first chapter explains the motivation, the main problem and the aim of this study. It sets the demand advantage of nations within Porter's diamond of national competitive advantages as the point of departure. A detailed and extended definition of lead markets is given and compared with varying definitions given in literature for lead or leading markets. In the second chapter, the prerequisites of lead markets in the literature are discussed. Three strands of literature lay the foundations of lead markets: how national market contexts shape the preferred innovation design, the theory of competing technologies and dominant designs and the theory of the diffusion of innovations. The existing literature on these three subjects will be summarised. In particular, it is shown that in a setting of competing technologies induced by varying national market contexts, several forces exist that can subsequently reduce the variety of technologies towards a globally dominant design. The theory of user-producer interaction is the link between market conditions and the international success of domestic firms. The classical home market theory explains internationally successful innovations with national demand preferences of the country-of-origin. The chapter ends with the main historic explanation of the international success of national demand induced innovations. The international product life cycle theory gives a first complementary explanation as to the international success of one particular innovation induced by a country's demand: a lead in per-capita-income of a country.

In the third chapter the theory of lead markets is developed. A simple model shows that growth of national per-capita-income is not the only mechanism of international diffusion of a particular innovation design. In the Chapter the mechanisms found in the model and in literature are re-formulated and arranged in a new typology of lead market factors which explain why the national context can support national innovation designs becoming globally dominant designs. Some aspects of lead markets such as time persistence and the regional width are further discussed in this chapter. Chapter 4 attempts to evaluate the practicability of the suggested system of lead markets in a detailed case study on the cellular mobile phone industry. It shows that the factors derived theoretically can be singled out and analysed for a particular innovation and finally be related to its international success.

In the fifth chapter I present how firms can harness lead markets for their innovation projects. First, I review the advantage of globally standardised innovations. Second, I discuss that firms can utilise the lead market to learn about future global needs and the coming dominant technological design. Since R&D is the core innovation activity of a firm, I examine the main hypothesis on the drivers of foreign R&D activities. This is based on a review of the literature. It shows that the local market interaction potential is still considered as one of if not the most important reasons for conducting R&D abroad. Together, the importance of proximity between markets and R&D and the existence of lead markets lead to the conclusion that firms should locate their R&D resources for particular product or process innovations in the respective lead markets of these products or processes. In order to focus innovation development in the lead market a firm must first identify a lead market. The chapter offers a tentative approach for predicting lead markets for new innovation ideas.

Chapter 6 summarises the counter arguments to the lead market theory and the limitations of the lead market concept. Not all counter arguments can fully be refuted and some further research has to be done in order to fully evaluate the lead market concept. In addition, it shows that lead markets do not exist for all innovations but only for a fraction of innovations. In the last chapter technology policy issues are briefly addressed. The lead market concept can lead to conclusion that governments are able to increase the likelihood of a country becoming a lead market. In the discussion, however, I question the ability of governments to create lead markets in their countries. Governments may aim to allocate their public R&D funds to industries in which a country has the potential to become a lead market. But if a country has a genuine lag market environment, a government may rather support the domestic firms to adopt the lead market technology quickly. An example for lead market policy is given for the newly industrialised countries in Southeast Asia.

1.4 Porter's Concept of the Competitive Advantage of Nations

The analysis of the study on the lead function of country markets is closely related to the extensive and insightful study of Michael E. Porter on the competitive advantage of nations (Porter 1990). Porter asks the question of why firms of a particular nation gain a competitive advantage in a particular industry over firms residing in other nations. Porter (1990) concludes that the international competitive advantages result not only from technical excellence but from the ability to commercialise innovations worldwide. This ability results from the characteristic of the national market context for achieving high and rising levels of productivity and innovations that are demanded worldwide. Porter's aim was to identify and systemise the determinants of the national advantage of firms' home countries. He identified four basic factors of national competitive advantage: (1) national factor conditions, (2) market rivalry, (3) demand and (4) domestic suppliers and related industries. Porter stresses that the four location advantages are also strongly reinforcing each other.

Besides Porter and the classic studies of Vernon (1966) and Linder (1961) there has not been a great amount of attention drawn towards the factors of national *demand* on the generation of internationally successful innovations compared to the technological factors such as scientific excellence. In the latter models nations compete internationally solely on technical factors.[1] Yet, it is often observed that there is no gap in technological abilities and scientific knowledge between highly industrialised countries. Rather, innovations are highly related to the national

1 The finding of neo-classical economics that national economic growth is mostly based on technical progress led to extensive studies explaining differences of national growth with nation-specific technical knowledge accumulation and the factors allowing countries to catch up through international technology transfer, see Romer (1990), Fagerberg (1994), Abramowitz (1986), Barro (1991), Verspagen (1993).

environment but cannot be differentiated by technological superiority. These national-specific innovations compete on the world market and the aim of the study is to find national demand characteristics which support the international competitiveness of the innovations that are induced by the national demand and market context.

In this thesis the attributes of a national market that support the commercialisation of innovations worldwide other than scientific excellence are studied. They constitute part of the demand conditions and domestic firms rivalry described by Porter (1990). Porter suggests three main attributes of home demand advantage: the composition, the size and growth of home demand and the mechanism by which a nation's domestic preferences are transmitted to foreign markets. This thesis intends to further elaborate these demand factors, reformulate and extend the attributes of national markets and shift the focus from competitiveness of a nation's firms to the competitiveness of multinational firms reaping the benefits of the lead market. Ultimately, a different and extended typology of lead attributes of national markets based on theoretical considerations will be introduced.

1.5 Definition of Lead Markets

The term 'lead markets' appears in the literature with varying meanings. Three main groups of definitions are given by literature: (1) the country of the invention of an innovation[2], (2) the country where a subsidiary of a multinational firm takes over responsibility as global coordinator of marketing activities[3] and (3) the country where an innovation is first widely adopted and accepted. In this thesis only the last definition will be followed. The reason for this choice is that the most innovations (e.g., PC, Fax) are available in many countries when diffusion first takes-off in one country and that this country is often not the country of the invention or innovation. Furthermore, as will be argued, innovation activity as well as

---

2 For instance, see Yip (1992, p. 43): Innovations are prone to take place in just one or few countries, which are called lead countries; the lead market is the market where the innovation was first developed.

3 In marketing literature as well as in firms the lead country concept is a firm's organisational concept of global marketing (Bartlett, Ghoshal 1986, Raffée, Kreutzer 1989, p. 50, Schröder 1996, p. 182). In this concept a subsidiary develops a global marketing strategy for a single new product which is the basis for all marketing activities in any other country. Often, the product is introduced in the lead country as a test market (Schröder 1996, p. 183). The lead country is supposed to be selected according to resource advantages of the subsidiary as well as country-specific factors such as the firm's country-market shares, the market size, global reputation of a country (country-of-origin effect), degree of domestic competition. Similarly, in economic studies of diffusion of innovation such as in Griliches' (1957) seminal work, the country sequence of the adoption of innovations are considered determined by the decision of firms to enter the country market. The starting point of diffusion within a country is therefore the availability of the innovation not the decision of adopters.

the decision of firms to enter a country market first are caused by nation-specific factors. Albeit not frequently mentioned in standard marketing literature, a lead market in the third definition is a country where the diffusion process of an innovation first took off.[4] An innovation has to diffuse through many country markets and is normally accepted differently from country to country. Often there are countries in which an innovation has been accepted earlier and diffused more rapidly or thoroughly than in other countries, regardless of when the innovation has been introduced in these country markets. The term "lead" in lead markets means that most other countries follow the first country in adopting an innovation widely. Lead markets are therefore markets which adopt an innovation before it becomes adopted by most other countries. Figure 1-1 exhibits the stylised international diffusion pattern of an innovation by typically s-shaped diffusion curves of several countries.

Bartlett and Ghoshal (1990) use the term lead markets in the context of the ability of these markets to stimulate global innovations. Lead markets are "the markets that provide the stimuli for most global products and processes of a multinational company" (Bartlett, Ghoshal 1990, p. 243). Lead markets exist, they suggest, because "local innovation in such markets become useful elsewhere as the environmental characteristics that stimulated such innovations diffuse to other locations" (Bartlett, Ghoshal 1990, p. 243). The definition of lead markets by Bartlett and Ghoshal (1990) is the starting hypothesis for the analysis of this thesis. Based on my analysis, the following important refinement is added. The term of the innovation *design* is central to understanding lead markets. If countries have varying market contexts, users prefer different innovation designs from country to country. An innovation design is a specification or configuration of an innovation idea. Different designs of an innovation have the same function but different modes or specifications (see Utterback 1994, p. 18) or a different mix of attributes such as size, quality performance, precision, technology, energy consumption etc.[5] In economic terms, different designs are characterised by a high substitution elasticity in consumption. Since countries adopt different designs of an innovation several innovation designs compete on the world market. Often, one globally dominant design emerges. A dominant design is defined as a design that is adopted by a majority of users (Utterback 1994, p. 24).

---

4 E.g. Kalish et al. (1995), Kotabe, Helsen (1998). The take-off phase or breakthrough is the point of time when the number of adopters suddenly increases rapidly (Link 1997, p. 81). Rogers (1995) locates the take-off phase between 10-25 % of all potential adopters. Ever since Griliches (1957), it has been commonplace to calculate the diffusion lag of a country as the number of years from the time when an innovation is first adopted to the point when it reaches a 10 % penetration level in the country (Antonelli 1986).

5 For instance, the facsimile machine is an innovation design of a communication device transmitting written information. An IBM and an Apple computer are different designs of a personal computer. The GSM cellular telephone and pagers are different designs of mobile communications.

Figure 1-1: An international diffusion pattern of an innovation design

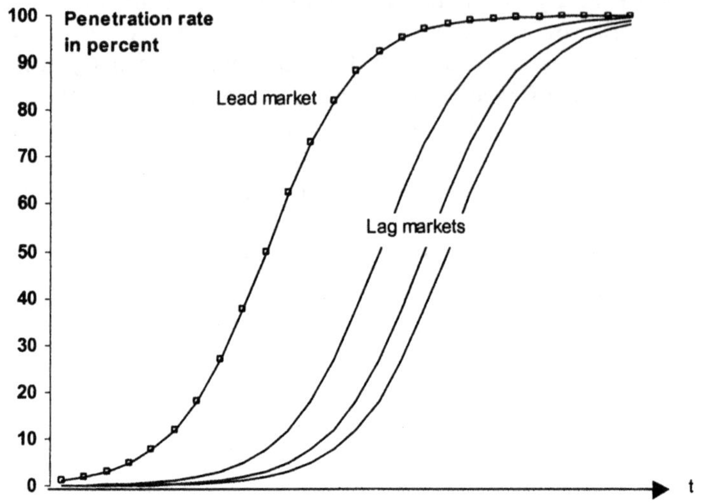

Figure 1-2: An international diffusion pattern of competing innovation designs

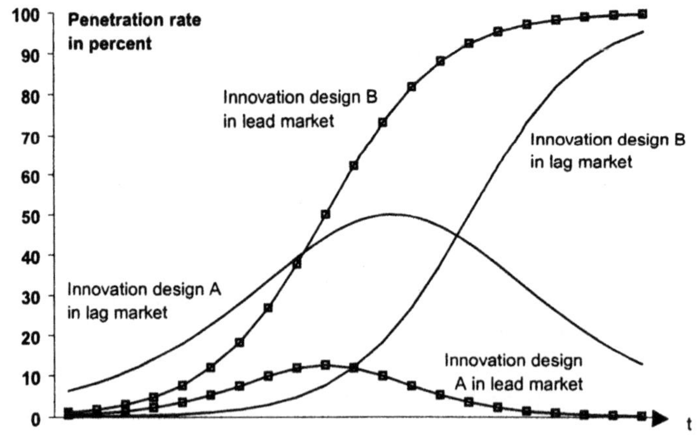

A global dominant design is the design that is adopted by most countries, in contrast to national dominant designs, that are only widely adopted within a country. Lead markets have the characteristic that product or process innovation designs adopted early become the globally dominant design and supersede other innovation designs initially adopted or preferred by other countries. Figure 1-2 exhibits the extended stylised pattern of the international diffusion of an innovation design. If only the innovation design B is observed, the pattern of Figure 1-1 is derived. In Figure 1-2 the lag market adopts a different innovation design A even before the lead market adopts the design B, but later switches to B, which becomes the globally dominant design. This refinement leads to the following hypothesis of the existence of lead markets:

There are nation-specific demand and market conditions (market context) that support the adoption of an innovation design that is subsequently adopted by other countries as well, even if the other countries have preferred or adopted different innovation designs before.

In addition to the definition, the following clarifications can be made. (1) A country can be said to have "adopted an innovation" when the innovation reached the take-off phase of diffusion. (2) The definition of a lead market does not include the regional origin of the invention or of the technology used for the innovation design. A lead market is not necessarily attributed initially with an international technological lead in the tradition of technological gap theories of international trade. It is possible that the innovation was invented and designed in another country, but first accepted in the lead market. While the regional origin of the development of the innovation does not matter for the definition of lead markets, invention and acceptance are often interrelated, since many innovations are developed in response to local demand. The lead country is often the country of innovation because the demand for the innovation is most likely to be perceived first by firms in the country. The local interaction of demand and innovation activities are discussed in the next chapter. It explains why domestic firms in the lead market can gain an international advantage. (3) A specific design could have been rejected in countries unless it is introduced in a country that has a lead advantage over other countries. (4) A lead market need not be the first country to adopt any design among various alternatives of an innovation, but the country that first adopts an innovation design that becomes the global dominant design. Lead markets are not necessarily the most "innovative" countries, witness the innovative Japanese customers in the telecommunications sector who adopt new technologies early, but failed to *lead* the world in most telecommunications equipment.[6] The term 'innovativeness' of a country does not require that other countries adopt the same innovation design. Innovative countries adopt innovation designs early without regard to other countries' choices.[7] Porter (1990) finds that country demand

---

6 See the detailed studies by Fransman (1992, 1995) on the Japanese telecommunications industry. For instance, Japanese telecom early adopted digital switching technology and Japan was the first country to introduce mobile cellular telephony, see chapter 4. Only the facsimile machine was an international success led by Japan.

7 In consumer research 'innovativeness' has been defined as "the degree to which an individual makes innovation decisions independently of the communicated experience of others" (Midgley, Dowling 1978, p. 235). On the contrary, Lee (1990, p. 40) defines 'national innovativeness' as the "degree to which a country adopts an innovation relatively earlier than the rest of the other countries". This relative-time-to-adoption definition, however, includes a selection bias. It considers only internationally successful innovation designs. As a result, countries that early, compared to other countries' adop-

for innovations can be idiosyncratic or anticipatory. Demand is idiosyncratic if users prefer innovation designs that will not be demanded in other countries, while countries with anticipatory demand prefer innovation designs which are subsequently demanded worldwide. These are simple ex post definitions without regard to the rationale. Countries could be defined as *idiosyncratically innovative*, if they adopt new ideas early which no other country ever finds worthy of adopting. In this thesis, these countries are called *idiosyncratic markets*. The lag market in Figure 1-2 is an idiosyncratic market because it adopts an innovation design A which is not adopted by other countries. The lead market in Figure 1-2 is *anticipatory innovative* although it adopted its specific innovation design later than the lag country. The lead market hypothesis suggests that anticipatory innovativeness of a country is constituted by a nation-specific market context and not by discoveries or inventions, the decision of firms or simply by chance. Anticipatory demand does not necessarily mean that the users consciously forecast that other users will have the same needs in the future or even care about other users' needs at all. It is not assumed here that users decide strategically in their adoption process and include possible decisions of other users and nations but base their technology decision on their own situation.[8] Although Porter (1990, p. 91) adds that "anticipatory buyer needs may arise because a nation's political or social values foreshadow needs that will ultimately emerge elsewhere", this statement does not imply that one nation has particular prophetic abilities or manipulates the needs of other nations. In this thesis anticipatory demand for innovations is defined simply as a demand for a particular innovation design that emerges in some nations earlier than in other countries. (5) The lead market hypothesis assumes that lead markets are product- or process-specific. The lead market for one product or process innovation can be a different country than the lead market for another innovation. (6) In addition, it is not assumed that a lead market pattern exists for each innovation that becomes internationally successful. This thesis shall formulate the conditions for the existence of lead markets.

Hitherto, literature does not supply a systematic explanation of lead markets, never mind a theoretical model. Instead, most authors offer lead market definitions that already include explanations for the leading role of a market. Takeuchi and Porter (1986, p. 129) define lead markets as country "markets with the most demanding buyers or those buyers most likely to adopt innovations". Johansson and Roehl (1994, p. 142) define lead(ing) markets as countries of demanding and sophisticated customers which compete fiercely and demand "a continuous flow

---

tion of similar innovations, adopt an innovation design that are not adopted by other countries later on would be considered as countries with a low national innovativeness, which would actually be not correct.

8 Although strategic games of adoption behaviour of firms and standardisation within oligopolies have been proposed starting with Farell and Saloner (1985), see Tirole (1988, pp. 401-409) for a review, strategic behaviour is mainly excluded from the discussion in this thesis.

of new product introductions incorporating state of the art technology". Here, competition is added as a characteristic of lead markets. Gerybadze et al. (1997, pp. 209-210) name several characteristics for lead markets without elaborating them in great detail: high per capita income, low price elasticity of demand, demand for high-quality products and innovations, fast learning processes of producers, lead-user marketing of producers, specific demand for problem-solving innovations, approval procedures accepted by other countries, and a regulation[9] that is open to innovations. Although the analysis in this thesis will confirm most of the attributes of lead markets given by the authors my *definition* avoids to already include an explanation for the phenomenon under consideration. The analysis in this thesis will derive the national lead attributes from the theoretical discussion in Chapter 3.

For the economic analysis of lead markets it is important to distinguish between the lead effects of markets themselves and features of markets which support the lead function of a country. The lead or leverage effect is a mechanism by which a design adopted by the lead market supersedes initially preferred alternative designs in lag markets and becomes the globally dominant design. In chapter 3 the basic lead mechanisms will be outlined first theoretically. These mechanisms and the variety of factors supporting these mechanisms will be refined into a system of lead market factors for better practicability.

The facsimile machine is a good illustration for the pattern of the international diffusion presented in this thesis. In Chapter 4 the case of the cellular mobile telephony will be assessed as a lead market phenomenon. In the history of the facsimile machine the diffusion pattern of a lead market is clearly visible (Figure 1-3). The fax machine was a failure in the US and Europe untill it was adapted to the Japanese market. The fax machine, although invented in principal in 1843 and since then improved continuously in many advanced countries such as Germany and the United States, was stuck in niche applications until a mass market emerged in Japan in the early 1980s (Peterson 1995, Coopersmith 1993). However, this mass application was not confined to the Japanese market for long, spreading over to the United States and later to Europe within a few years. Today, the fax machine is seen worldwide as an indispensable means of text communication. Previously competing technologies like telex which was favoured by European firms, were referred to minor applications. At the moment the facsimile became a success in Germany it squeezed out the telex system, which was the design widely adopted before in Germany but not much in Japan (Figure 1-4).

9 Regulation "includes the full range of legal instruments by which governing institutions, at all levels of government, impose obligations or constraints on private sector behaviour. Constitutions, parliamentary laws, subordinate legislation, decrees orders, norms, licenses, plans, codes and even some forms of administrative guidance can all be considered as regulation" (OECD 1997c, p. 9).

Figure 1-3: The international diffusion of the facsimile machine

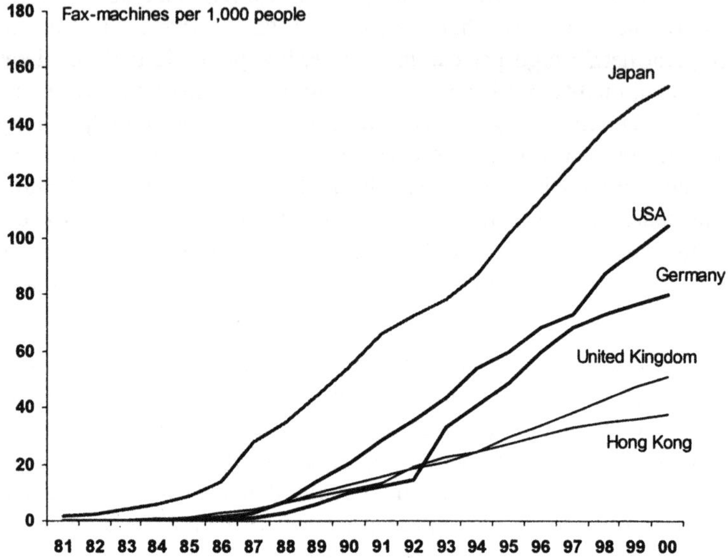

Source: International Telecommunications Union

Figure 1-4: The success of the facsimile machine and the demise of telex

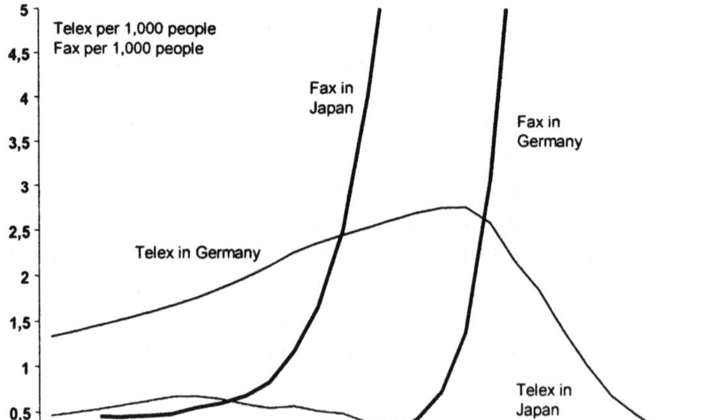

Source: International Telecommunications Union, estimations based on Scherer (1992) and Yoffie (1997).

2 International Diffusion of Innovations: Overviews of Literature

The so-called "technological gap" may, in fact, be an experience gap
BRUCE D. HENDERSON (BOSTON CONSULTING GROUP)

2.1 Introduction: From Technological Gap to Adoption Lead Theory

A nation is considered to be able to gain a competitive advantage – among others – by generating product and process innovations.[10] As knowledge about these innovations leaks out of the country and is used by firms of other countries as well, the country loses its competitive advantage. The national competitive advantage is therefore based on a *temporary technological knowledge monopoly*. Trade between advanced countries can occur even if factor prices are equal but the national "scientific and technological capabilities" (OECD 1968) differ. This is known as the technology gap theory in international trade. The technological gap hypothesis was first introduced by Posner (1961) and evaluated in a case study of synthetic materials by Hufbauer (1966). Posner (1961) assumes that consumer

[10] A rich strand of literature discusses this assumption of technological performance of nations as a determinant of international trade performance of nations, see e.g. Dosi, Pavitt, Soete (1990) and Fagerberg (1988). Because the international diffusion of technological knowledge is not instant but takes time, a national competitive advantage is not based on factor prices alone as the traditional trade theory suggests, rather on knowledge leads. The possibility of gaining a competitive advantage through innovations increases with the innovation intensity of industries. Innovation intensive industries are traditionally considered as R&D intensive industries. R&D intensive industries are industries in which the R&D intensity, e.g. R&D expenditures per sales, is above the average of the manufacturing sector (see e.g. Gehrke, Grupp 1994, pp. 35-47). Innovations, however, are not only generated by R&D activities but also by various other activities such as design (OECD 1997b).

preferences are equal worldwide. A country can gain a technological lead over other countries through pioneering innovations occurring either randomly by chance, out of entrepreneurial effort[11], or they are correlated with former innovations and investments, which also stabilises the technological lead of a country. In contrast to popular interpretations of the technology gap theory, scientific advances and basic inventions are not assumed to be facilitating a technological gap.[12] Instead, a technology lead is assumed to be based mainly on knowledge accumulated during the production (called learning-by doing, see Arrow 1962b).

Posner (1961) calls the lag in the adoption of a new product by other countries the *demand lag*.[13] Since preferences are assumed equal internationally and information on new products and processes flows quickly from country to country, a demand lag is considered unimportant for the theory (Hufbauer 1966, p. 79). Yet, it will be argued in this thesis that an adoption lag can occur when countries initially adopt different designs of an innovation, for instance, because entrepreneurs in each country offer different incompatible designs generating local externalities or when user preferences vary from country to country internationally. Thus a demand lag can lead to an international technology gap. Indeed, case studies such as Tilton (1971) find that in the semiconductor industry a technology gap is caused by a demand gap rather than vice versa (see 2.4.6).[14] Early demand in a country

---

[11] The entrepreneurial "failure" of countries to generate innovations has been discussed widely and especially made responsible for the decline of the British industry in the 20th century, see Thirtle and Ruttan (1987, p. 125).

[12] Knowledge generated by "pure technical progress" is regarded by Posner (1961) as being available to all countries and does not lead to international technological gaps. It is very well known that the scientific advance in Europe was not behind that in the US, see e.g. Freeman, Soete (1997), Vernon (1971), Franko (1976). For instance, US firms were the product pioneers in the machinery industry although many inventions were first conceived in Europe. Hufbauer (1966, p. 86) shows that new synthetic materials were often discovered in countries other than the country first producing them commercially. Shockley based his theory of semiconductors on the surface theory developed by Shottky at the German firm Siemens, see Plettner (1994, p. 186). The OECD notes in a 1968 study that not inventions but the ability of turning inventions into commercially successful products is a main determinant of an international technological gap between the US and Europe (OECD 1968, p. 17). Differences between OECD countries in the scientific capabilities are less marked. Many fundamental scientific findings and inventions originate in Europe. The OECD study argues that the homogeneity and size of the US market proving the necessary economies of scale is the main cause of the technological gap between the US and Europe.

[13] This lag occurs because users in other countries have to be aware of the new product or process and "new foreign products may not be regarded, for some reasons, as perfect substitutes for home-produced goods until some time elapses" (Posner 1961, p. 333).

[14] Even the early technology gap studies find that demand factors influence the invention effort of firms. Poser (1961) notes that "complementarities in consumption may lead to pressure for innovations in products jointly demanded with that just innovated" (Posner 1961, p. 338).

leads to innovations of domestic firms and the production and adoption experience subsequently to a technological lead.

If a country is and remains the only country that demands and uses the innovation, then the firms responding to the national demand garner no international competitive advantage from the generation of innovations. I will argue that firms of a country that first adopts an innovation design can gain a competitive advantage if other countries follow in adopting the same innovation design. The ability to commercialise innovations abroad can even be sufficient for creating a national competitive advantage without having invented the innovation or generated the technological knowledge used for it. Normally, the time elapsing between the invention of an innovation until it starts to get widely adopted (take-off) is often long[15] compared to the time producers outside the country-of-invention need to learn to produce an innovation based on the invention. The international pattern of invention therefore does not necessarily determine the international pattern of adoption. Firms in the country that first adopted the innovation design can build a competitive advantage on the same basis Posner (1961) already mentioned for firms in the country of origin of the innovation: learning-by-doing effects, static economies-of-scale and access to additional knowledge generated during usage (called learning-by-using, see Rosenberg 1982). Here, the national competitive advantage is based on an adoption lead that causes a technological knowledge lead, which I call an *adoption knowledge lead*, because domestic firms accumulate knowledge which is generated in the adoption process (technological, market intelligence). The main concern of this thesis is to explain why innovations first adopted by a country, called the lead market, diffuse to other countries, called the lag markets. It has to be explained more precisely than technology gap theory does why other countries adopt an innovation design preferred in the lead market before, i.e. why there is an demand lag for a specific design. International diffusion of an innovation includes the eventual superseding of innovation designs previously adopted by other countries. This substitution effect has to be explained as well.

In this chapter, the literature and basic models related to the lead-market phenomenon will be summarised. The chapter is organised by strands of literature. The chapter exhibits the different perspectives on the diffusion of innovations that can be found in the literature and discusses their relevance to the international diffusion of innovations. First, I will briefly describe the different nation-specific incentives for innovations (2.2). The literature draws a line between technology choice models and diffusion or adoption models, although both are closely related. Models of competing technologies (2.3) explain why standardisation processes occur that lead to all user adopting the same, dominating innovation design. The

[15] For most of the innovations studied by Gort and Klepper (1982), the first phase between invention and market take-off was the longest phase in the whole life cycle. The mean of the first phase for 46 products studied was 14.4 years.

next section summarises the existing literature on the international diffusion of innovations (2.4). The literature on technology choice, diffusion and adoption is reviewed in this thesis in addition to the existing studies on the international diffusion of innovations, because many additional conclusions can be derived from the related literature for the theory of lead markets. The traditional international diffusion models are based on the technology gap model or general supply side models, assuming an international lag in the national availability of an innovation. In this thesis, the international diffusion of innovations is interpreted as the convergence of different regionally-induced innovation designs towards a global dominant design. As a primer for the application of lead markets to the innovation strategy of firms, section 2.5 reviews literature that suggest that nation-specific innovations are developed predominantly by domestic firms and are traded to a small extend. This chapter ends with a historic view on lead markets. The international product life cycle theory gives a first complementary explanation as to the international success of one particular innovation induced by a country's demand: a lead in per capita income of a country. Thus the United States were long regarded a universal lead market until the 1970s when their lead in per-capita-income marginalised and other countries gained lead market roles.

This chapter assesses a broad range of literature for the theory of lead markets. Chapter 3 will build on the wealth to develop the lead market theory as a new approach to leads of countries in the international diffusion of innovations.

2.2 International Variety of Innovation Designs

This section reviews the literature on factors that explain why varying national market contexts induce different innovation designs. If countries present different market conditions, different innovation designs are offered in and selected by the market. Market conditions include demand preferences formed by customers, budgets constraints of customers, entrepreneurial possibilities, degree of competition, standard-setting mechanisms and regulation imposed by governments. The role of demand for innovations and technical change has been stressed since the work of Schmookler (1962). This and subsequent studies assert that demand stimulates and directs innovation activities.[16] Purchases of consumer good designs are based on preferences, the relative prices of goods and a budget constraint, the personal income (Deaton, Muellbauer 1980). Purchases of investment good de-

16 From these studies a controversy on demand-pull vs. technology-push arose (Mowery, Rosenberg 1979). However, the regional variation of technical change is independent from the model of technical change itself, whether the innovations offered in the market are induced mainly by demand ("demand-pull") or pushed-trough by scientific findings ("technology push"). The *selection* of innovation designs offered in the market always depends on (or at least is biased by) the preferences of users, the conditions of the local market and the country-specific technical path.

signs are based on their profitability which is based on projected sales and the price and cost of goods produced with the capital goods, local prices of input factors and compatibility to the existing local capital stock. When prices of goods and factors vary internationally, users adopt different consumer and capital goods from country to country, even if preferences are equal. The next section summarises the factors ensuing from internationally varying preferences, the following section discusses the hypothesis of international convergence of demand preferences. The last two sections review the effects of price changes on innovations and explain why countries temporarily follow different paths of technical change.

2.2.1 International differences of demand preferences

International differences in preferences are reflected by international differences of goods purchased and capital goods employed. On the part of technological innovations, Terpstra and David (1991) suggest three basic groups of determinants for regional differences of technological designs employed by national users: material, cultural, and motivational factors. The material determinant of the demand of a country is expressed by the geographical, ecological, environmental and climatic factors of a country. These factors affect the performance of machines, instruments, vehicles and materials. In addition, when climate and other geographical attributes vary regionally they induce different needs. Therefore, nations demand different innovation designs to satisfy domestic needs. For instance, air conditioning is a vital feature of every vehicle in humid countries but not in countries with a mild climate. In general the technology most appropriate for the environment will be employed. The higher the environmental specificity of technology, the higher the differences in product design demanded in national markets.

The cultural determinant, which was stressed by Max Weber at the beginning of the century as a main determinant of capitalism, is today mainly deviated from religion, traditions and values. Values are priorities concerning social goals. Culture includes the demographic system, kinship, political and legal system. Since cultural factors are frequently suggested as a main determinant of the demand for innovations, they will be discussed in detail in the next section. The third factor, the motivational factor, is known from work-related studies (Maslow 1970, Hofstede 1980). They are determined mainly by the reward system. Motivation can be derived from personal success, personal security and group affiliation (Terpstra, David, 1991, p. 165). Hofstede (1980) finds that motivational factors vary from country to country. In addition, motivational factors such as the prestige of entrepreneurs and inventors are reinforced by the religious system.

These three groups of determinants form the preferences of customers in a country. Since the determinants vary from country to country, customers in different countries have different preferences and therefore demand (or select) different innovation designs. In addition, markets vary in their media availability, distribution systems, legal restrictions, competition, transportation and communications (Buzzell 1968, Takeuchi, Porter 1986). International differences often require modifications and adaptations of existing products or lead to the development of different product designs.

2.2.2 Cultural factors of the demand for innovations

Cultural factors of demand for innovations have recently attracted a range of studies.[17] The sociological strand of diffusion research represented and summarised by Everett Rogers since the early 1960s stresses the importance of the cultural background of a society, or in sociological terms of a social system, for the timing and speed of adoption of innovations. The adoption of innovations is suggested to be affected by cultural factors such as norms, religion, and general education (Rogers 1995). For instance, Mansfield (1989) comes to the conclusion that the reason why Japanese firms adopted robots more widely than firms in the United States (where the robot was invented) was the long-term orientation of Japanese firms and not economic profitability factors such as scale economies, factor prices etc.

Marketing literature has taken up the effects of cultural factors on the adoption of innovations because cultural differences often inhibit the global diffusion of new products (Kreutzer 1989, p. 278). Keegan and Green (1997) define culture as "ways of living" or conscious and unconscious values, ideas, attitudes and symbols that shape human behaviour and that are transmitted from one generation to another" as distinct from fashions. Terpstra and David (1991) define culture as the problem-solving mode of nations and therefore relate innovation activities of countries directly to culture. That means that different cultures generate different solutions, i.e. innovation designs, to "problems that all societies must solve if they are to remain viable" (Terpstra, David, 1991, p. 6).

In the late 1980s the Academy of Sciences of Berlin prepared an extensive study on culture and innovation under the auspices of Horst Albach. Albach (1993, p. 68) defines culture rather broadly comprising all institutions in a "system of norms, behavior, expression and values shared by a group of people" and confines the analysis on observable behaviour avoiding general anthropological considerations, which leading cross-cultural scholars like Hofstede (1980) base their cultural management analysis on. Albach (1993) attributes the innovative society to four main cultural factors: progress orientation, risk-taking, failure tolerance and heterogeneity of lifestyles.[18]

---

17 Such as Albach (1993), Albach et al. (1989), Steenkamp et al. (1999), Herbig, Palumbo (1994). More authors, however, study the relationship between culture and new product development, see e.g. Nakata, Sivakumar (1996) for a review.

18 These attributes seem very general and not consistent with observations. For instance, the United States are characterised with failure tolerance, despite the fact that the exten-

One important part of culture is religion. Religion forms peoples attitudes towards problems and their solutions. It has been suggested that religion has a general impact on the willingness of people to adopt innovations (Robertson, Wind 1980, Lee 1990). In contrast to most religions that suggest to get on with the status quo, Protestantism is said to be less resistant to change and more responsive to innovations (Terpstra, David, 1991). Besides these general impacts of religion, there are important nuances in the relationship of religious norms and innovation designs. For instance, abortion is strongly sanctioned morally in the catholic doctrine. Countries in which Catholics form the majority are expected to be more reluctant towards contraceptives and pharmaceuticals supporting abortions.[19] Many soft drinks originate from the southern States of the US caused by the south's hot climate as well as its strong religious culture, which frowned upon harder beverages (Economist 1999a, p. 81). Since Shintoism disapproves of organ transplantation, there is not much demand in Japan for this medical treatment.[20] Hindus in India, not supposed to hurt even the smallest creatures on the basis of "ahimsa" (non-violence), adopted nylon gill early, because the fish suffered less with these nets (Terpstra, David, 1991, p. 14), and demanded an innovative insecticide which had a built-in time delay[21].

Literature does not, however, so far theoretically explain the ability of a country to lead the adoption of an innovation design to its cultural origins. The internationalisation mechanisms of nationally preferred innovation designs are still not clear. Terpstra and David (1991) remain focussed on phases of economic development of countries (national income, infrastructure, R&D expenditure) to explain international differences in technology employed by countries. In this framework, a lead market is the most developed market in economic terms. Cross-national diffusion research in marketing on the other hand remained committed to evaluating the impact of Hofstede's cultural dimensions on national attitudes towards adopting innovation (innovativeness) (e.g. Gatignon et al. 1989, Lynn, Gelb 1996,). In these studies cosmopolitanism, mobility, individualism and uncertainty avoidance have a positive effect on the early diffusion (as indicated by the p parameter of the Bass diffusion curve, see section 2.4.2). Cultural and motivational factors, however, are unsuitable to explain lead markets sufficiently, because of their generality. First, while studies suggesting a general "innovativeness" of countries discuss a wide range of factors that render a country more innovative and national characteristics more conducive to innovations, they seem unable to differentiate between idiosyncratic and anticipatory country-specific innovation designs.

---

sive jurisdiction in the US on product liability of firms delayed the adoption of innovations such as the airbag.

19 A comparison within European countries could not confirm the influence of religion on the usage of contraceptives (Unger, Lachnit-Fixson 1993).

20 I owe this example to Hariolf Grupp.

21 Personal communication with official from Bayer AG, 1993.

Second, the characteristics of innovativeness of countries are supposed to influence the demand for innovations in general. Yet, the lead market role of countries varies from innovation to innovation. Lead markets are not explained by a country ranking of general innovativeness. A country could be first in adopting a global innovation design and late in adopting another one. Third, cultural factors give no explanation for the internationalisation mechanism of nationally induced innovation designs and the substitution effect of other nation-specific designs.

2.2.3 The theory of induced innovation

Besides demand preferences, the technological design employed by users depends on local factor prices. Factor prices are determined by the local scarcity of factors. The regional variation of factor prices itself depends on transportation costs, e.g. for raw materials, energy etc., and factor mobility, e.g. of labour and capital. When factor prices vary regionally, the technological designs employed vary regionally. In a country where a factor is relatively more expensive than in other countries, the technology employed there would use that factor relatively less than the technology employed in other countries. Under additional assumptions, innovation designs in a country are expected to be more directed at reducing the factor that is relatively more expensive than in other countries. For instance, a country with higher labour costs compared to other countries would adopt innovation designs that reduce the labour input in the production process than other countries. A country with high fuel costs adopts more fuel-efficient motor vehicles than a country with lower fuel prices.

To regard relative price changes as the source of technical change is known as the induced innovation theory (see Thirtle, Ruttan 1987 for a review). Innovations respond to factor price changes. Factor prices change relatively to each other when a factor becomes more scarce or more available and this change does not affect all input factors to the same extent. The induced technical change hypothesis was originally suggested by Hicks (1932). The theory assumes that a change in relative prices of the factors of production is an incentive for innovations directed at economising the use of a factor which has become relatively expensive. The simple version of the theory assumes that the innovation possibilities are factor neutral, i.e. it is not easier to save a specific factor through innovations activities. The direction of technical change is then only biased in such a way as to save the factor that becomes more expensive.[22] Since changes in factor prices can, again, vary regionally, the induced innovation theory explains why demand for innovation designs can differ from country to country.

[22] For a review of empirical evidence and the critique, see Binswanger, Ruttan (1978), Thirtle, Ruttan (1987) and Ruttan (1997). In particular, the assumption of the innovation possibility function was criticised.

While no longer viewed as an important contribution to the theory of technical change and growth, induced innovation can contribute to the understanding of the historical process of technical change across countries (Ruttan 1997, p. 1521). The examples named by Freeman and Soete (1997, p. 199) to demonstrate the importance of demand side factors for technical change also demonstrate that the stimulation of innovation is often country-specific. In Germany, demand for artificial materials to substitute natural materials was high, because Germany lacked the same access to raw materials in foreign colonies of firms in the UK, the Netherlands and France (Franko 1976, pp. 36-44). German chemical firms invested in R&D intensely to meet this local demand. On the other hand, countries use the material being in plentiful supply more than countries where the material is scarcer, not only due to low prices but also by pressure from suppliers. For instance, electric ovens were used early on in Switzerland and Norway because of the scarcity of fuels and abundance of water power generating electrical energy, whereas in Germany gas suppliers tried to block the diffusion of electric ovens (Siemens 1961).

The relationship between local induced innovation and the international competitiveness of nations has rarely been discussed as yet (Ruttan 1997). If relative factor prices vary internationally, trade would be low since each country employs a local specific technological design matching local factor price relationships. Yet, induced innovation theory offers a mechanism for the international diffusion of innovation designs. In section 3.1 it will be theoretically shown that a country can become a lead market that anticipates global factor price trends, i.e. experiences factor price changes earlier than other countries.[23]

2.2.4 Intra-industry trade

According to Grubel and Lloyd's theory of intra-industry trade, countries would specialise in alternative designs of the same product line depending on their physical environment, their history and culture, the quality of products demanded by the average consumer and the market size for technically-sophisticated goods (Grubel, Lloyd, 1975). For example, the US automobile industry is committed to large automobiles for long-distance driving. Due to low prices, fuel consumption is a minor choice parameter for buyers than in countries with high fuel costs. In addition, a general speed limit also confines the car's performance needs. In Europe, conditions are most suited for smaller cars and in Germany users demand high-performance automobiles to take advantage of high-speed highways. High fuel

23 In addition, Binswanger and Ruttan (1978, p. 69) note that countries that are willing to close a technical gap often transfers technology from developed countries, that is shaped by factor price relationships in the developed countries, and experience factor-saving biases that overcompensate any simple price effects.

prices make fuel consumption an important product attribute.[24] But even if nations prefer different designs, there is trade between countries. Products are not exclusively demanded by domestic users. Heterogeneous demand within countries enables small market shares for foreign products as well as exports. For instance, there are consumers in Europe who prefer US automobiles and vice versa. This explains why there is sometimes a large variety of differentiated products in one product line with some trade, that is called intra-industrial trade, but strong regional preference of demand for each alternative.

Intra-industry trade theory provides an explanation for the trade of nation-specific goods, but fails to explain the global dominance of nation-specific goods. Firms would export extremely differentiated products leading to intensive intra-industrial trade. Hitherto, no real lead market exists because exported innovations are not likely to totally supersede the local innovations of foreign markets which fit these foreign environments much better. Lead markets only exist if an innovation design first preferred by a country has an advantage over foreign market innovations in their home markets, which can over-compensate the home-advantage of foreign firms. Such an over-compensation reduces the initial variety of innovations mirroring the variety of global environments.

2.2.5 Global convergence of markets

It is a common hypothesis that the international homogenisation of cultural and economic factors reduces the international variety of technology demanded. At first glance, the hypothesis of globalisation challenges two lead market conditions: homogenous demand could mean that there is no demand lag for innovations and that there is no variety of demand preferences for innovation designs. In the early literature, such as Linder (1961) and Vernon (1966), which will be reviewed in section 2.5.1 and 2.6.1 respectively, international differences in demand preferences were mainly put down to the economic stage of development, indicated by the per-capita-income (see 2.3.1 and 2.6.1). As per-capita-income converges within a large group of countries (industrialised and newly industrialised), preferences would converge. Yet, the preceding section showed that preferences are not only determined by income. There are trends of international divergence of demand preferences, that have often been neglected (Kreutzer 1989, p. 38). As Freeman and Soete (1997) note, for most of the products and services the differences in demand between countries are large. "While there are certainly some products and services where there is indeed a demand which is global in nature and where local variations in taste, regulation, climate and other circumstances can be largely ignored, there are far more products and services where such varia-

---

[24] Altshuler et al. (1984)'s study on the automobile industry elaborates that different prices and environments create different mixes of demand in the US, Europe and Japan which lead to different designs and technological knowledge and skills within the triad.

tions certainly cannot be overlooked without dire consequences." (Freeman, Soete 1997, p. 308). Other studies find diverging trends as well (Craig et al. 1992, Douglas, Wind 1987, Bartlett, Ghoshal 1990, p. 220). Another counter argument to the globalisation hypothesis is that the higher the per-capita-income the more self-conscious are users and the more unwilling to adopt foreign products without adaptations to national conditions (Kreutzer 1989, pp. 55-56). Livingston (1989) suggests that the homogenisation process of consumption until the 1970s was merely a convergence of other countries on the American pattern. Doubts in many countries about the desirability of American lifestyle have added divergence trends since (see section 2.6.2). The hypothesis of the globalisation of markets has therefore to be qualified.

The globalisation of markets merely means that, increasingly, specific innovations are diffusing internationally very rapidly, are available and adopted subsequently worldwide. In his seminal article, Levitt (1983) suggests that technologies such as telecommunications, television and transport also lead to the convergence of demand preferences and in particular of demand for innovations. Technology equalises the availability of information on innovations. Through worldwide communication, transport and travel, "almost everyone everywhere wants all the things they have heard about, seen, or experienced via the new technologies" (Levitt 1983, p. 92). Information availability and the demonstration effect is indeed a main factor of the diffusion of innovation (see 2.5.2). Once an innovation has been adopted somewhere it is rapidly known and made available elsewhere. Globalisation of markets is first and foremost the disappearance of information deficits about innovation designs among countries and the international availability of nation-specific innovation designs. The globalisation of markets does not imply that the same innovation design is *initially demanded* in all countries. In contrast, users in all countries can select from among a variety of innovations designs induced by national market conditions. Regionally varying material and cultural factors still differ from country to country inducing country-specific innovations and local technical change.

Yet, the dominance of an innovation design can emerge even if demand preferences differ, the dominance of a worldwide innovation design can emerge. A apparent convergence of adopted designs should not be interpreted as the homogenisation of preferences. Levitt (1983) himself points out that the relative lower price of one product design can lead to global adoption of a national product despite varying preferences. Levitt (1983) asserts that global producers "attract customers who previously held local preferences and now capitulate to the attractions of lesser prices". In this case, differences in demand preferences are compensated through a relative price reduction (see section 3.2.1). It makes clear that the globalisation of markets, e.g. the emergence of globally dominant designs, is not necessarily based on global homogenous demand. Although homogenous demand is a driver of the international diffusion of innovations, it is not a *conditio sine qua non* of the pattern exhibit in Figure 1-2 of the international adoption of one technological design. Other mechanisms as well can either explain the homogenisation of demand after a variety of designs are induced by national demand and market conditions or compensate for the international differences in demand preferences. On the other hand, even if preferences of consumers are seemingly equal internationally, incentives for adopting a specific innovation design can still vary internationally, for instance because of internationally varying prices of complementary factors, of the innovation itself and of other products, with which the innovation can be substituted. Local externalities can lead to regional islands of standardised innovation designs (2.3.4).

2.2.6 Localised learning and path dependency

Dynamic theories of technical change have stressed the learning processes of technical change and its path dependency. This offers an explanation for regionally varying technology employment and considerable time delays in the adoption of a global dominant technology as well. Regionally localised technical change contrasts with a global shift of techniques and products by *exogenous* technical change assumed by the neo-classical theories. According to localised learning theories countries follow different nation-specific technical paths. On these paths, learning processes continuously improve the products and processes along the path or technical trajectory. Among the variety of paths one country happens to follow the most profitable source of innovation trajectory. In other countries the adoption of this technology is delayed because they initially chose a different technical path and later had to switch to the more profitable technology. The switch to the better technological path is more delayed the higher the switching costs are. These dynamic theories of technical change should be briefly reviewed.

The evolutionary theory of technical change points to the dynamic persistence effect of region-specific technical change. Evolutionary theory of technical change has been established by Nelson and Winter (1982) and refined by several authors since. The two processes of the Nelson-Winter model are the search for better techniques and the selection of successful innovations by the market (Ruttan 1997). In this model the market's role is, first, the motivator for innovations, in that a firm can gain monopoly rents from innovations (for a review see Scherer, Ross 1990, pp. 630-644). Based on Schumpeter's notion of rivalry-driven innovations, fiercely competitive markets or contestable markets, i.e. markets with low entry barriers, are expected to generate a higher *variety* of innovations. Second, the market *selects* innovations that are offered on the market. Even when technical development is generated by scientific discoveries, market forces modify the rate and direction of technical change. When country market conditions are different it is likely that markets will select different innovations.

The induced innovation theory and the evolutionary theory led to the theories of localised learning. Localised technological change results from the interplay between factor substitution and learning processes (Antonelli 1998). Localised learning means that technical progress of a country depends on the technology employed by the country ("Localized") through learning processes. In order to capitalise on the competencies by exploiting learning-by-doing (knowledge derived from the production process) and learning-by-using (knowledge derived from using an innovation), a firm's R&D activities would be focussed on the products and processes (input factor relations) already employed. Learning processes occur during the diffusion process. Part of the diffusion process is the refinement process of an innovation, which can change the design and the benefit of a product. When an innovation is first introduced into the market it is not perfect, often lacks reliability and is full of "teething" troubles. The feedback from its users will pressure the firm that produces the innovation to improve the innovation and adapt it to environmental conditions that could not have been simulated during the test phase in the laboratory. This process was first called learning-by-using by Rosenberg (1982). He observed that the design of turbines is gradually improved upon after introducing the product in the market. The refinement process occurred in an interactive communication with the first users, the airlines in Rosenberg's case. Freeman and Soete (1997, p. 355) note that, "as diffusion proceeds the specific user's demands become more stringent" and that "performance, quality and reliability of the innovation will increase substantially" as a result.

In addition, after an innovation is offered on the market, users do not only become educated and learn to use the innovation more efficiently but often find new applications for the innovation. Christensen (1997) strongly supports the importance of learning during the diffusion process for the final design of an innovation. New technologies often have to be tested in the market to discover their benefits, applications and how to alter and improve them to maximise their benefit. He observes that in emerging technologies, neither manufacturers nor customers know how the applications of a new technology will finally be used. The final utilisation of a new technology is to be found in a process of mutual discovery by customers and manufactures (Christensen 1997, p. 135). This incremental improvement and refinement is part of the technological trajectory.[25]

The specific technological design adopted can be initiated by historical events and persists because the countries' resources are committed to this technology. On the firm level, there are two explanations for the path-dependency of technical change. First of all, firms accumulate knowledge and competencies on the products they produce and processes they employ. Second, established firms are embedded in a network of long-standing suppliers and customers. Christensen (1997, p. 31) calls this a 'value network' and observes that firms allocate their internal resources according to the benefit of their most important customers. The direction

[25] Dosi (1982) combines the concept of technical trajectories by Nelson and Winter (1982) with scientific paradigms as a model for path dependence of technical change. A trajectory is the direction towards which the problem solving activities moves which a paradigm defines as relevant.

of the technical change of firms are determined by their most important customers in that they determine the firm's perception of the economic value of a new technology. The most profitable new technology for the established firm is the one which is of most benefit for its important long-standing customers.

The firm-level effects of path dependency can be easily translated onto the country-level. Most firms are more embedded in a domestic network than in an international network. Second, regional spillovers, technical information derived from other firms located in the same region[26], make it more profitable for firms to follow the technological trajectory of the other firms in the region (David et al. 1998). As a result, nations can follow different national paths of technical change (Lundvall 1993).

The technological paths are stable over a long time because the change of the path is hindered by switching costs. Switching costs occur because producers and users build up competencies in the nation-specific context. The transition of a country from one technical path to another occurs only when one technical path emerges to be a dead end and progress is no longer possible, while another technical path offers continuous progress. Large factor price changes are another trigger to escape locking-in to a nation specific path. Ruttan (1998) offers a case for this switch of paths by a country:

"From the 1870s to the 1930s, German leadership in the organic chemical industry was based on coal-based technology. Beginning in the 1920s with the rapid growth in the demand for gasoline from automobiles and trucks in the United States, a large and inexpensive supply of olefins become available as a by-product of petroleum refining. By the end of World War II, the US chemical industry has largely shifted to petroleum-based feedstock. In Germany this transition – locked in by skills, education and attitudes that has been developed under a coal based industrial regime – was delayed by more than a decade. By the 1960s, however, Germany was making a rapid transition to the petroleum-based feedstock path of technical change in heavy organic chemicals".

In evolutionary models, the initial selection of technological designs are based on market conditions and previously employed technologies, the switch from a "domestic" technology/design/path to a foreign technology/design/path is caused by different potential of progress of technological paths. As soon as a technological path leads to a superior technological level compared to other technological paths that can overcompensate the switching costs of other countries, countries adopt the superior technology. Learning processes can therefore explain, why countries switch to a design adopted in another market before. In section 2.3.2 formal models of technology choice under learning economies shall be discussed.

---

26 These regional spillover effect were already mentioned by Marshall (1920, pp. 222-231). They lead to agglomerations of specialised industries.

2.3 Competing Technologies and Dominant Designs

How can the emergence of one international dominant technology amongst an initial variety of alternative technologies be explained? There are two types of standardisation procedures: de-facto and de-jure standardisation. While international de-jure standardisation is achieved by inter-governmental or non-governmental standardisation bodies, de-facto standardisation denotes the selection of one global design within several product versions by market forces. I will first explore de-facto standardisation and then move on to de-jure.

The degree of international standardisation of goods depends on the degree of advantages and obstacles of standardisation. Advantages of standardisation are economies-of-scale in production, the necessary volume of R&D investments, consumer mobility and the role of multinational firms as customers. Whitlock (1987) assigns industrial goods to the most standardised end of the standardisation continuum and consumer non-durables (food) to the other end of low degree of standardisation. Yet, international standardisation of goods is a process, which takes time and frequently includes an initial variety of non-standardised goods.

The pattern of variety in the early phases of a new technology and the continuous reduction to one single alternative can often be observed. Klepper (1996), Utterback and Suárez (1993) and Tether and Storey (1998), drawing on a number of studies, describe the long-term pattern of the industry life cycle. Once a major innovation is established, a large number of new firms enter the market, various product versions are developed and introduced in the market in the early phase of a new industry. [27] In time, the number of entrants declines and the market selects a small number of advantageous product alternatives, separating "the wheat from the chaff", while more and more firms exit the market. It is often the case that the surviving product versions equal each other in terms of basic features. The succeeding technical variant has been called the 'dominant design' (Abernathy, Utterback 1978, Anderson, Tushman 1990), which has been already used in the lead market definition in this thesis. First, the concept of the dominant design is reviewed. Utterback (1994, pp. 26-29) suggests several factors as to why a dominant design can occur: user-producer interaction, complementary goods, standardisation, and strategy at the firm level. I will discuss the relevance of these factors for the emergence of *global* dominant designs. Complementary goods are, however, just one type of *increasing returns of adoption* that can cause the emergence of a dominant design and which will be addressed in the following section. The role of international de-jure standardisation will be discussed in 2.3.5. Firm strategy can be shaped by country-specific factors as well, caused by the local environmental context such as degree of competition, import restrictions, and general export

---

[27] I follow Utterback Suárez (1993, FN 2) in defining 'industry' as a "group of similar products that serve the same need and thus compete directly in the market-place". The facsimile machine and the telex thus share one industry.

orientation of domestic firms. I will discuss export orientation of firms as a lead factor of markets in chapter 3.2.4.

A lead market was defined as a market that adopts an innovation design that succeeds internationally as a globally dominant design. An important question is whether the standardisation process first leads to country-specific dominant designs or immediately leads to an internationally dominant design without a transition phase of standardisation on the national level. Differently formulated, does the adoption of an innovation within a country precede the cross-border diffusion? This question is important because in the former setting, the lead market selects an innovation as the globally dominant design, in the latter the globally dominant design and the global dominant design would emerged from regionally unbiased adoptions in an interspersed pattern. If the lead market selects the technological design that subsequently conquers the world market and drives out other technologies on foreign markets and in particular foreign dominant designs, the lead market concept would be much more powerful. Several models suggest that there is indeed a convergence on the national or regional level before a globally dominant design emerges. In section 2.3.4 it will be shown that in the occurrence of local externalities, such as network effects national dominant designs are to precede the emergence of globally dominant designs.

2.3.1 Dominant designs

In studying pattern of innovations, Utterback and Abernathy (1975) observe that many new industries can be characterised by a standardisation process from basic product innovations towards domination of process innovations. In the first phase a variety of product designs is tested in the market. A performance maximisation process of product innovation leads in addition to a better understanding of user requirements. Once a product design that best matches user needs is found, cost-minimising process innovations are starting to dominate the innovation process. The product design is only improved on and altered slightly. Abernathy and Utterback (1978) term the remaining product design on both the firm and the industry level a *dominant design*.[28] The persistence of a dominant design is explained simply by that it is hard to find better designs, that users develop loyalties and that the firm functions such as production and marketing demand standardisation. The emergence of dominant designs has been confirmed in several case studies (Utterback 1994) and supported by related concepts of technological trajectories (Dosi 1982), product design hierarchies (Clark 1985) and technological guideposts (Sahal 1981). Anderson and Tushman (1990) build an evolutionary framework around the emergence of dominant designs. They suggest that successive genera-

[28] For instance, Abernathy and Utterback (1978) call Ford's T-model a dominant design among variants tests in the Ford workshop as well as designs that are used by all firms of an industry, such as the diesel locomotive.

tions of technologies often start with a technical breakthrough, called a technical discontinuity, inducing a variety of new technical designs that compete against the old technology and later converge into a dominant design.

In view of these models, the emergence of a dominant design is user-need driven, the process of standardisation a result of the "reduction of market need uncertainty".[29] The selection of a design is not based on technical advance but on a package of features that "found favor in the market" through socio-political processes (Anderson, Tushman 1990, p. 617). It follows from the model that the locus of a dominant innovation design is the "individual or organisation that is intimately familiar with needs" (Utterback, Abernathy, 1975, p. 643). Although there is not even an allusion to the geography of innovation in the models of dominant designs, one could conclude that a global dominant design emerges where there is the best knowledge about global user needs, if needs are somewhat globally homogenous. This knowledge could either be generated by discovery processes driven by competition or by users representative for global needs. In the lead market theory presented in Chapter 3 the first will be called *market structure advantage* of a country and the second *export advantage*.

Anderson, Tushman (1990) present appropriability of innovations as another factor that supports the emergence of a dominant design. In industries of low appropriability, a dominant design would emerge more easily than in industries in which firms can appropriate all innovation returns, because low appropriability spurs imitation by other firms. A successful design can thus become adopted by competitors, which increases its advantage to become a dominant design. The IBM PC, which was cloned subsequently by other computer companies because the main components (CPU, software) were available to all firms, is considered as a main success factor of the IBM compatible design to become the dominant design in the personal computer industry (Utterback 1994, pp. 14-16).

The weak point in the Abernathy-Utterback type of model is the performance-maximising process that leads to a dominant design. First of all, heterogeneity of users, especially international heterogeneity, is not dealt with. If there is user heterogeneity the variety reduction requires strong increases in product performance to compensate for international environmental differences. Second, the best performance rule of a dominant design contrasts with the observation that *inferior* designs have been selected as dominant designs, not only technically inferior but inferior performance-wise – witness the shortcoming of facsimile machines to transfer Latin letters and numbers used in the western world; a cellular mobile

---

29 Anderson, Tushman (1990) further suggest that a dominant producer could set a dominant design through its market power. It is possible that a firm such as Microsoft, that owns the proprietary rights of a dominant design, can more easily set another dominant design given the compatibility to former dominant designs, its market share, its worldwide distribution system and reputation. However, the origin of the market dominance has still be explained in the first place.

telephone is not the optimal mobile telecommunication technology for cities like Hong Kong. Yet, these two inappropriate designs were used in these places and became dominant within their industry. Theoretically, a much better explanation of the market-led standardisation process towards a dominant design that includes the selection of inferior designs is given by the theory of increasing-returns of adoption which will be elaborated in the next section. Although Anderson, Tushman (1990) explicitly argue that economies of scale and learning effects are *enabled* by the emergence of a dominant design and do not lead to a domination of the design.[30] At least for the purpose of explaining global dominant designs that can emerge among national dominant designs it is important to include learning and cost effects as the driving factors towards *global* dominant designs.

2.3.2 Economies of adoption and complementary goods

Dominant designs are often simply the most useful designs for users (Utterback 1994). However, economies of scale and economies of adoption can also drive a technological variety towards standardisation and the selection of a dominant design. Increasing returns of adoption occur if the benefit of a product increases indirectly or directly with the number of users. If the additional benefit resulting from the adoption is not compensated in a price increase, the returns of adoptions are an positive externality for subsequent users. The growing literature on the standardisation of technologies explains increasing returns of adoption by learning effects (Arthur 1989), network effects (Farell, Saloner 1985, Katz, Shapiro 1985), the availability (Teece 1986) and increasing returns of scale in the production of complementary assets (Chou, Shy 1990).

For most technical innovations the benefit is not a constant but increases after market entry. Post-invention improvements result not only from learning in the production but also from learning about how to increase functionality of an innovation during the usage. For products with complex and interacting components the benefit cannot be predicted before such products are used. The more a product is used, the more knowledge is generated about how to alter the design for more reliability and to enhance the benefit. These learning-by-using effects have been described in section 2.2.6. The importance of learning-by-using should even increase nowadays with increasing complexity of new technologies and share of software content that has to be used in order to correct for the "bugs" included in all new software programmes (Littlewood, Strigini 1992). As has been noted above, the close interaction with users enhances the payoff of an innovation. While learning effects increase with the cumulative number of adopters, the utility of network services are often positively correlated with the number of network

[30] For Anderson, Tushman (1990), the emergence of a dominant design by the tendency of late adopters to select a design by cost considerations would be artificial. In contrast, I will call it a cost advantage of a country that prefers a design that becomes globally dominant because it is cheaper than other designs.

participants at the present time. This increasing return of adoption is called network effect. In contrast to learning which is an indirect effect of adoption, network effects can also be direct (Woeckener 1995). A network has direct increasing returns of adoption if the benefit of the participation in a network such as a telecommunication network depends directly on the size of the network. The number of people a telephone user can call is the main benefit of a telephone network and thus the more adopters, the higher the benefit. Economies of adoption can be high compared to the core benefit of a product, especially in network usage. In a telecommunications network there is no benefit of a product, e.g. a facsimile machine, until the persons with which one wants to communicate adopt the product too, but it increases rapidly with the number of adopters.

An indirect effect of a network or of the adoption of an innovation besides learning effects is the increasing availability of complementary goods. Collateral or complementary assets are a feature of many high technology industries where bundling of devices into systems is common. If a product is normally to be utilised in conjunction with other devices or services, the benefit of a product increases with the availability and variation of these complementary goods. A microprocessor for instance is embedded in a system of computer devices and increases its value with the broadness of available software that runs on the machine. Teece (1992a) suggests that the new "product" is not merely the newly invented device, rather the device compounded by all its complementary goods. Training can also be a complementary asset. Operation of a new technology, such as typing on a typewriter, writing a programme in a programming language or using a NC-machine, mostly requires training. Investments in training for a particular machine are mainly sunk costs: once the machine is not used anymore, the knowledge gained through training is worthless, if it cannot be used with the newly adopted technology (David 1985). The switching of technology employed is thus connected with additional cost of training, reorganisations etc., which is called the switching cost (Klemperer 1987). A new technology which is not compatible with the old can only substitute a technology in use if the benefit of new technology exceeds the benefit of the old one plus the switching cost.

The availability of complementary goods usually grows with number of adopters, since the increase in the population of adopters increases the market for the suppliers and distributors of complementary goods and lowers their risk to invest in a technology that fails to be accepted broadly. High development costs for complementary goods such as software must ensure a large market of the hardware good. Chou and Shy (1990) present a model in which network effects are substituted by increasing returns to scale in the production of complementary products, which are high in the production of software because fixed development costs are high while marginal production costs are almost zero.

Increasing returns of adoption can explain why technologies that are inferior[31] can become a dominant design. Even the intervention of a government cannot prevent the lock-in to an inferior good if the path of post-invention improvements by adoption are not totally predictable. These conclusions have been shown in a detailed case study of nuclear reactors by Cowan (1990)[32] and a formal model by Cowan (1991a). The dominance of one nuclear reactor type, the light-water reactor, despite its technical inferiority, is at the same time an example of an international diffusion of a nation-specific design. Cowan (1990) studies the forces which drove the world market to select the light-water reactor as the global dominant design for civil nuclear reactors. Cowan identifies two learning-factors leading to a global dominant design. First, learning about uncertain payoffs to technological designs can shift the preference of users towards a more-used foreign design compared to untested designs especially designed to fit the domestic environment best. Second, learning-by-using increases the payoff of a design with adoption. Cowan observes that the decision concerning the global dominant design in nuclear technology was apparent when US utilities ordered 13 nuclear reactors of one type between 1962-1965 indicating a 'bandwagon market' in the US. In other countries such as Germany (Keck 1980), utilities and manufacturing preferred the standardised US design of a light-water reactor through licenses from the US producers, instead of designing their own national reactor type.

Cowans's insightful case study reveals three other important factors of the *international* successful diffusion of a technical design. In contrast to common export restrictions of high technology due to national security arguments, the US administration was firmly export orientated in the case of nuclear reactors. Fear of the Soviet Union setting nuclear standards "led to the desire to have US technology spread throughout the world" (Cowan 1990, p. 563). Large subsidies were granted to Europe. Second, in contrast to governments, which try to support domestic technologies, private users and producers try to avoid adopting designs that make them technically isolated internationally. Third, relative factor prices can change when a design is increasingly adopted. In the case of nuclear reactors, relative prices of enriched uranium used for the light-water reactor dropped considerably after the US adopted this type of reactor.

---

31 An inferior design is a technology that has a lower benefit when broadly adopted than another design that would yield a higher benefit if it would have been adopted instead (Arthur 1990, p. 119 and Cowan 1991b, p. 510). This means that the standardisation process by adoption dynamics under increasing returns is not always efficient.

32 The design of nuclear reactors originally selected by the US navy to power submarines became the standard civil design as well, although other types (in particular the gas graphite design) were seen as technically and economically superior for a civil power station. Taking the high risk of nuclear power into consideration, the proven and standardised reactor design was still advantageous.

2.3.3 Technical choice under global externalities

First theoretical models of increasing returns have been suggested by Arthur (1989) and Cowan (1991a) for technology adoption with product improving learning and by Farell and Saloner (1985) and Katz and Shapiro (1985) for network externalities. The basic Arthur model considers a sequential choice of an infinite number of potential adopters between two technologies A and B. Heterogeneity of users is assumed in that there are two different users which have different benefits from each of the two technologies. In each period a new user adopts a technology which will maximise his payoff. The sequence of the two types of users is random. The payoff of each technology increases with the number of previous adopters. This stochastic model and other related models exhibit that under many circumstances there will be a reduction in the variety of designs and a standardisation towards a single design (Cowan 1991b). The differences between preferences of users are compensated by post-invention improvements of the learning-by-using type.

Based on the conclusion from the case study on nuclear reactors, Cowan (1991a) models the adoption process as a stochastic movement along the learning curves of two technologies (stochastic increasing returns). Each adoption increases the payoff of the technology selected. In addition, the model includes another aspect of adoption besides increasing returns that leads to the selection of a dominant design: uncertainty reduction about the benefit of an innovation. An adoption reduces the uncertainty of the benefit of the adopted technology. There is therefore Cowan's (1991a) model exhibits that a government cannot prevent the dominance of an inferior technology. Despite the advantage that it could support the adoption of technologies according to the criteria of what can be learned about the benefit of each technology for future adopters (a private user would not take this selection criteria into account), it increases the benefit with each adoption and thus increased the benefit of an actually inferior technology as well. Because it becomes more and more costly to shift away from the more-used technology, a country would stick with an inferior technology if it was used early. This result further limits the option of an international agreement on a standardised technological design (see next section). On the other hand, both case study and model suggest that in a technological field in which the benefits can only be revealed when designs are actually tested, an international dominant design can emerge simply from the adoption of a pioneer user.

Formally, increasing returns of adoption can be written as the payoff P of technology A for user i

$$P_A = f(a_i, n_A) \quad \text{with} \quad \partial f / \partial n_A > 0 \tag{2.1}$$

and n_A as the number of previous adopters of technology A. In the Arthur model a is a constant while in the Cowan model a random parameter with an unknown distribution. The index i denotes the heterogeneity of potential adopters. In the

Cowan model the more adoptions of A exist, the more is known about the real distribution of *a*. Even under constant returns ($\partial f / \partial n_A = 0$), lock-in to one technology would occur and the better-known technology has an advantage over the unknown technology regardless of its real inferiority if its expected benefit is sufficiently high and the early implementation of the superior technology accidentally failed.

The Arthur-Cowan models of competing technologies are criticised for the assumption of one *irrevocable* technology choice by each user (An, Kiefer 1995), an infinite number of users, that the increasing returns are global and only based on learning. Irrevocable choices are only realistic for long-lived physical infrastructure such as nuclear reactors (David, Foray 1994, p. 67). A firm or consumer can normally switch from one technological design to another one albeit at the cost of switching. In addition, in the context of international diffusion of innovations the models are too simplistic, because the world is not a homogenous field of users. National barriers are impediments to increasing returns. Externalities are thus often national or local. Local externalities mean that the additional benefit of each technology from the adoption is not always the same for all potential users (global externalities) but only for a sub-group of users (local externalities). Often the adoption of a technology only benefits other users in the country but not users in foreign countries. This follows from the localised learning hypothesis, which suggests that improvements will focus on the domestic context, e.g. factor prices, local preferences (see 2.2.4).[33] Therefore increasing returns of adoption are more likely to lead to *national* dominant designs inhibiting the emergence of global dominant designs.

Below (2.3.4) I will review models that incorporate network externalities and switching of users from one design to another design. If countries begin selecting a technology with a different starting configuration they can lock-in to a different technology. If switching costs are high there have to be large global externalities to compensate local externalities as well as switching costs. If not, some countries are finally locked-in to nation-specific technologies. A second argument for the initial emergence of national designs is that firms and governments can successfully promote the adoption of a new technology, for instance through subsidising a product or complementary assets such as infrastructure during the launch period of an innovation. Since governments are prone to intervene in favour of domestic technologies and more and more governments are to intervene if one government starts to subsidise a domestic technology, different national dominant designs are a likely outcome.

33 For instance, continuous improvements of automobiles are directed to local conditions. In the US, air-conditioning and comfort is improved while in Germany handling characteristics of cars at high speed levels are optimised.

The main conclusion from this section is that increasing returns of adoption can be a strong mechanism of standardisation. But the learning type of increasing returns has to be strong and must affect global users to compensate international heterogeneity as well as national lock-in effects in order to lead towards a globally dominant design. Other country-specific factors supporting economies of adoption seem to be more promising as mechanisms of *international* standardisation such as the economies of scale based on the size of a country, the domestic growth of adoption, uncertainty reduction through pioneering adoption of technologies, relative prices of factors needed for different designs, public influence of the technology choice, a country's export orientation and complementary assets. Complementary assets can vary from country to country, because they are part of the infrastructure or because they are nation-specific such as software in the native language. If complementary assets are only built up in one country, no other country follows in adopting the innovation. A lag in the availability of complementary assets from country to country induces an international lag in the benefit of an innovation and thus the international order of adoption of an innovation. National differences in complementary assets can therefore be a national advantage for setting the national dominant design as a globally dominant design. These lead factors will be discussed in Chapter 3 as well.

2.3.4 Technology choice under local externalities

As mentioned above, positive externalities to adoption can lead to the diffusion of innovations, because the utility of an innovation increases with the number of adopters making the innovation profitable for more and more adopters. Positive externalities can also lead to the adoption of a dominant design because relative increases in profitability of a design compared to other designs can lead to the substitution of the other design by a design that became relatively more beneficial. The early standardisation and competing technologies models assume global externalities, additional benefits that are the same for all adopters. For instance, post-invention improvements increase the intrinsic utility of an innovation. By contrast, local externalities increase the benefit of an innovation only for a group of users, for instance within a region or a (regionally dispersed) special community of users.[34] Local externalities in a geographical sense are common in regional economics.[35] Arthur (1990) considers local increasing returns in the choice of locations of new firms. The establishment of a firm increases the attractiveness of the region in the form of knowledge spillover for other firms. This opens a self-

---

[34] The adjective 'local' does not imply geographical proximity but only differentiates between user groups whether they are regionally defined or by other criteria such as sharing the same language or profession.

[35] In the field of regional economics local externalities have been observed since Marshall (1920), who explained industrial agglomerations with local spillovers, for a review see Harhoff (1995).

reinforcing mechanism leading to agglomerations in knowledge-intensive industries such as in Silicon Valley (see also 2.4.5).

In technology adoption externalities are often local, because individual decisions are rarely based on the selection of all adopters but only on the selection of members of a sub-group, a reference group (David 1993). Within the reference group the communication is most intense (Cowan, Cowan 1998b). For instance, the adoption of a PC standard depends much more on the choice of friends and colleges than on the global market share of the different standards (An, Kiefer 1995, p. 104). In particular, technologies that are based on communication are adopted according to the choice of the communication partners. Furthermore externalities are mostly local in a geographical sense (national), because the reference group is often formed by cultural and physical proximity. For instance, the adoption of communications equipment such as the facsimile machine by Japanese users increases the attractiveness of the equipment for most users in Europe only to a small extent, because telephone communication between Europe and Japan is rare. In addition, learning, observability á la Rogers (2.4.3) and the spread of information vital for the diffusion of innovations as described above can be facilitated by close cultural or physical proximity (2.5). The adoption of a technological design by a firm enhances the pool of specialised employees in the regional labour market and increases supply of other specialised factors, thus raising the attractiveness of the technological design for potential adopters within the region. As a result, local externalities induce correlated choices among neighbouring users. Besides the demonstration and knowledge effect in the epidemic diffusion model (2.4.2), local externalities arise, for instance, if the participation at a network is only possible for customers in the same region.

More broadly, local externalities are more pronounced compared to global externalities, if externalities are based on personal contacts, local complementary assets or technological improvements that reflect adaptations to local environmental conditions. The need for compatibility does not only increase with proximity because of contact intensity but because the profitability of technical interfaces between networks of different standards can increase with distance. The telecommunications industry is a typical network industry, but network externalities are mainly national. International calls are easily emulated from one national standard to a foreign standard at international switching centres. This explains the feasibility of the variety of national standards in the telecommunication industry still apparent today. Complementary assets are often local- or nation-specific, such as infrastructure and software or videos in a national language. Local externalities become more important compared to global externalities the more the national preferences differ and the less users of various countries interact. Including the distinction between local and global externalities the formal model of the payoff P of technology A for user i becomes

$$P_{Ai} = f(a_i, n_A, n_{Ai}) \tag{2.2}$$

where n_{Ai} denotes the number of local users of technology A of user i. Cowan and Miller (1998), David and Foray (1994), David, Foray and Dalle (1998), and An and Kiefer (1995), study the adoption of technologies with local externalities.[36] In a dynamic model, David and Foray (1994) simulate the spread of two technological designs exemplified by Electronic Data Interchange (EDI) standards, the electronic transmission of business documents. They assume that a finite number of potential users choose a standard sequentially according to the proportion of the neighbours' choices of standards and not according to the total market share of standards. The restriction of earlier models of technology competition (e.g. Arthur 1989) is avoided in that adopters can switch from one standard to the other one when it is profitable despite the switching cost. These revisions can lead to one standard prevailing in a constant population. Choice revisions are additionally a feature of the lead market phenomenon, which includes the possibility that countries switch from a domestic standard to a global dominant design. Their simplest stochastic adoption model – choices of an agent at random time interval depending on the prevailing standard among neighbouring agents without switching costs – always leads to a global standard determined by an initial head-start of one design. However, Cowan and Miller (1998) argue that pure local externalities do not necessarily lead to global standardisation if users have switching costs. Although they present a 1-dimensional general static model of technology selection (each user decides one time only), they argue that the main problem is that users at borders between standardised areas do not improve their payoff by switching to the other standard if the two technological designs have symmetric payoffs and switching bears some cost.

David, Foray and Dalle (1998) confirm the persistent multi-standard outcome through simulations of a more complex model of stochastic adoption decisions incorporating Marshallian externalities, switching costs and interaction between neighbouring adopters. In this model, spatial enclaves of different standards can emerge and persist for a long time. The outcome is undetermined resembling the historical-events argument by the Arthur-type models of competing technologies. In the multi-dimensional model of An and Kiefer (1995) an infinite potential of adopters make technology recurrent decisions on the basis of price and quality of each technology and the choice of neighbouring users. They find that two tech-

36 The methodologies of these studies will not be described in detail. Models with global externalities are mostly based on a Markovian process, in which the probability of adopting a technological design increases with the number of previous adopters. Local interaction processes originate from Markov random field theory (David, Foray 1994) or physical models of particle interaction in space (David et al. 1998). In principle, all potential users are arranged on a d-dimensional lattice, each having 2d neighbours which positively influence their recurrent choices of technology. In a 1-dimensional model the users can be visualised as arranged on a circle and each having two neighbours (Cowan, Miller 1998). More than one dimension can be interpreted as different reference groups such as friends, colleges, relatives (An, Kiefer 1995).

nologies can co-exist unless one technology has a slightly better quality or if the complexity of local externalities exceeds two interaction dimensions.

Local-externality models hitherto do not take post-invention improvements (global externalities), complementary infrastructure or goods (software) into account; they merely model the social interaction process of adoption decisions. An even bigger problem of these models in the context of the international diffusion of innovations is that the separating impact of national boundaries is not taken into account. If several designs of a technology are introduced in countries, it is likely that in the presence of switching costs and local externalities the regional diffusion process will lead to national or regional enclaves of different dominant designs. Since the communication within countries is more intense than between countries, these geographical zones are likely to be congruent with country borders.

Cowan and Cowan (1998b) present a model in which both local and global externalities are present. In addition, the model includes idiosyncratic inherent benefits of the competing designs to each adopter and pre-defined boundaries so that no user in one region interacts with users in other regions. The results of this model are: 1) large user heterogeneity inhibits any kind of spatial structure of standardisation; 2) if global externalities are strong, the same choice of technology is guaranteed across regions but historical events determine which technological design is chosen; 3) if global externalities are weak, different regions standardise on different technologies. The results are intuitively and easily interpreted in the context of international diffusion of innovations. Here, user heterogeneity means that the benefit of a design differs between countries, but the benefit is equal for users within countries. This applies if the benefit depends on the regional environmental context. National dominant designs can emerge from pure local externalities, but it is unlikely that global dominant technological designs will emerge within national competing designs from pure local externalities without any global externalities. The international spread of technology designs by "word-of-mouth" could be expected to be limited for instance to a pan-European standard or a standard in North America and Mexico. Therefore the relationship between global and local externalities effects the global prevalence of a dominant design as well as sustainable variety of national standards. It is straightforward to conclude that strong local externalities lead to local or national dominant designs and are able to inhibit the emergence of a globally dominant design whereas strong global externalities are a force towards global dominant designs. If there are no local but global externalities (and demand preferences are equal globally), an innovation will diffuse in an interspersed pattern, i.e. regionally unbiased. If local externalities are strong and global externalities are weak (and switching costs are high), then either a global dominant design emerges within local (national) dominant designs or local enclaves of standardisation can become permanent. The latter represents the frequently observable situation among national standards where no nation switches to a global design because it loses more than it gains.

The question relevant for a lead market theory is, what are the factors which are strong enough to transfer a technological design across national borders leading to one globally prevailing design (standard) and whether these factors are at all country-specific. The global diffusion of information via a communication network like an epidemic disease would require that all parts of the world be connected as intensely as users within countries. Otherwise a domestic user would have no incentive to adopt or switch to a foreign technology. However, some local externalities are conceivable – this time not in a geographical sense – that have a positive effect on the internationalisation of an innovation design. International reference groups of experts of a specialised high technology industry in which learning from experience is important in the adoption decision, such as nuclear reactors or biotecnology, could play the role of such 'local' externalities. In the next chapter, possible *international 'local'* externalities on the basis of international information exchanges will be elaborated as transfer advantages.

The problem of models of local and global externalities for the aim of a comprehensive lead market theory is that they are still focussed on specific diffusion mechanisms and sensitive to their assumptions (switching costs, interaction across regions, user heterogeneity, benefit of competing designs), limiting economic insights (David et al. 1998, p. 178). The models do not exhibit the country-specific conditions leading to globally dominant designs. At least from the cultural and institutional homogeneity and conformity pressures within countries it is clear that, besides asymmetric *inherent* post-invention improvements, the relative strength of the global network effects represent the internationalisation mechanism of a technological design that tends to prevail globally. The success of the Internet is a case of global network effect, forcing France to switch from its own domestically successful online-service Minitel to the globally dominant Internet standard. The formal models reviewed in this section are, however, of limited benefit for the purpose of modelling the lead market phenomenon with all ramifications, which is needed to estimate the lead market potential of countries. In the next chapter, a simple static two-period model is used instead, because it offers the broadest flexibility to incorporate a multitude of mechanisms of the choice and revision of technological designs by countries. Before I present the model, the literature on *de jure* and *de facto* standardisation processes is very briefly reviewed.

2.3.5 International standardisation

Often, international compatibility standards are recommended by international organisations, such as the ISO, the International Standardisation Organization, and the ITU for telecommunications. This *de jure* standardisation of products and processes lowers uncertainty and are supposed to spur the adoption of new technology. This is especially important in the case of increasing returns. For manufacturers and industry users, it increases the probability that other companies will adopt and offer the same technology, thus raising the market share of the technology. It signals to early customers that the technological design is compatible with products of other suppliers, so that the customer does not have to stick with the sole supplier. Compatibility indicates that the technology will diffuse rapidly. As Utterback (1994) points out, in the early phase of a new technological path it is mainly technologies – and not firms – that compete, and the firms are even pleased by any market entry because it raises the probability that a particular technology will be established on the market. Technical specifications that are accepted by the market as dominant designs among several alternatives are called *de facto* standards (EITO 1997, p. 89). Examples are the IBM compatible personal computer employing Intel processors and Microsoft software. De facto standardisation is an outcome of the competition of designs on the world market.

De jure standardisation is often only a precondition and does not guarantee the success of an innovation. When network effects are in place, a standard is a precondition for the utilisation of a product. In telecommunications, a standard that lays down the technical specifications for sending and receiving data, called a protocol, has to be established first before a product can be developed for the market. The facsimile machine was first standardised internationally in 1968, though it took 15 years for its worldwide success. Moreover, de-jure standards are often set for several alternative technological design which still have to fight it out in the market place. While the facsimile technique was uniquely standardised, it still competed against other means of telecommunications such as telex, voice, television, and traditional mail. International standard-setting bodies, such as the ITU and ETSI in telecommunications, certainly reduce the variety of alternative technical designs. At the same time, this worldwide standardisation spurs the international competition between competing technologies in a design oligopoly.

Although facilitating the diffusion of a technology, it is observable that standards often *follow* and do not *lead* the industry. Already it is said that the importance of *de facto* standards increased and is now as important as *de jure* standardisation for the prevailing of a technological design (e.g., Jung, Warnecke 1998, p. 6-28). The dynamic process in the first phase of the life-cycle of a new product type has to prop up designs, configurations, and applications that later be standardised. Standardisation does not pre-empt the market selection process but supports the unambiguous and industry-wide formulation of a standard in the final phase. The final standardisation of the facsimile machine in the 1980s by the ITU ensued compatible design and thus increased price competition (Coopersmith 1993, p. 48). With the increasing emergence of *de facto* standards standardisation bodies are changing, with quicker acceptance of *de facto* standards as an "intercept strategy" (EITO 1997, p. 90).

International *de jure* standardisation faces several problems that adds to its limited role in setting a globally dominant design. First of all, the international heterogeneity of demand preferences induces that standardisation is a compromise leaving all countries with an inherently inferior design. This inherent inferiority is likely to be compensated by the advantages offered by worldwide compatibility. Yet it could leave parties with the feeling that the standard is better suited to other countries' environments than the domestic one, which would give these countries a competitive advantage. Second, even if user preferences are equal, under uncertainty of the real merit of technologies nobody would definitely know the best technology before it has been widely adopted. Governments would be obliged to argue in favour of their domestic technologies and publicly support the domestic technology in order to yield pioneer advantage from uncertainty reduction. Third, the US authorities adopted an attitude of "letting the best standard win". The market should decide which technology to choose in a competing technology setting. This is most prominently the case in the mobile telecommunications industry, in which standards are defined but no standard is publicly subsidised in the process of allocation of spectrum to the standards (see chapter 4). As a result *de facto* standards play an important role in the *international* standardisation process, because national standardisation bodies are normally better suited to the usage of a standard than international bodies. International standardisation committees mostly recommend the adoption of a standard but have no power to impose the standard on all users.

2.4 Diffusion of Innovations

2.4.1 Diffusion theory in an international context

The diffusion of an innovation is a process of adoption of an innovation by the potential users. Since an innovation is not adopted immediately by all users who can benefit from the innovation, there is a time period of diffusion, starting with the market introduction and ending with all potential users having adopted the innovation. In order to understand the international diffusion of an innovation, the adoption process has to differentiate between the diffusion within a country and the diffusion across countries. Dekimpe et al. (1998b) label these two processes the *depth* and *breadth* of adoption, respectively. As I will show in Chapter 3, these two adoption processes are fundamentally different, evoked by different questions and require different models of diffusion.

In model-building and estimation, the within-country diffusion is concerned with the diffusion pattern, the diffusion curve. The cross-border diffusion analysis pursues the question of the international order of adoption of innovations and the time-lag between the first adoption of an innovation by a (lead) country and the following adoption by other (lag) countries. Traditionally, diffusion theory and empirical studies have considered the diffusion process within a country and neglected to explain the national order of adoption of an innovation (Audretsch 1996, p. 110, Dekimpe et al. 1998b, p. 5). Even marketing studies which took the order of countries adopting an innovation into consideration were mainly focussed on the effects of the time lag on the form of the diffusion curve, for instance whether lag countries have a steeper diffusion curve due to a learning effect.[37] Only few studies analyse what factors drive a country to adopt an innovation earlier than other countries. [38] In these studies, however, the operationalisation of national innovativeness as relative-time-of-adoption of an internationally successful innovation design suffers from the adoption-bias as noted in section 1.5. The innovations studied are seen as product categories comprising several technical standards (such as cellular mobile telephony, colour TV). Therefore, they omit the fact that nation-specific designs compete against each other on the world market to become the global dominant design. Lead markets do not have to be the first countries that adopt an innovation as a category; other countries could have adopted different designs earlier or at the same time as the lead market, but later prefer the lead market design to their own nation-specific designs. No study as of yet has focused on the question followed in this thesis, i.e. what country-specific demand-side factors cause a country market to lead the international diffusion of a specific design or standard of a product category in the way that other countries subsequently adopt the specific design of an innovation.

In addition to the marketing-related diffusion research, the international diffusion of innovations was analysed by economists in order to explain the different growth and catching-up process of countries (see Fagerberg 1994). In these models, however, a technological gap is assumed to explain the lead of a country based on R&D activities, science and human capital investments. A country first achieves an absolute technological advantage because, for instance, it discovers new technological knowledge, but loses its advantage when the new technological knowledge "leaks out" to other countries. The main question pursued by these economic diffusion studies is, why the lag countries adopt the innovation at different times and not why they are following a particular country. Although it is assumed that technological knowledge diffuses equally rapidly from inventing countries to other countries, countries adopted a new technology with differing time lags. The economic studies therefore focus on the question of what facilitates an absorptive capacity, that is what factors render a country able to adopt an innovation adopted by other countries previously. They differentiate between the followers and not between the first and the following countries. The following sections briefly review the main diffusion and adoption models and assesses what can be used to explain the international diffusion of a dominant design.

---

37 For instance, Redmond (1994), Chen, Takada (1994) study inter-regional variance of the pattern of diffusion, Helsen, Jedidi, DeSarbo (1993) international differences of diffusion curve parameters. For studies that considered the national order of adoption see Gatingnon et al. (1989), Dekimpe et al. (1998a), Poznanski (1983), Takada, Jain (1991), Antonelli (1986) Ihde (1996), Ganesh et al. (1997). In some of these studies the effect of the lag on the diffusion rate is found positive in others negative (see section 3.2.1).

38 See e.g. Lee (1990), Dekimpe et al. (1998b) and the following sections.

2.4.2 Diffusion of innovations

The diffusion of innovation is the process of adoption of an innovation by users. The diffusion begins when the innovation is already introduced in the market. Diffusion studies therefore do not consider the innovation process explicitly. The fact that the adoption of innovations by users does not happen at the same time but instead requires a considerable amount of time is explained by three distinct phenomena: first, the diffusion of information on innovations; second, changes in the preferences of users after the adoption of the innovation by other users, and third, changes in the adoption stimuli such as post-invention improvements of the innovation when user needs are heterogeneous.[39]

The most common diffusion model, the epidemic model, assumes that the dissemination of information on the usefulness of an innovation is the main mechanism in the spread of an innovation. The diffusion of an innovation is a transition process between the market equilibrium before the innovation is introduced in the market and the new market equilibrium after the new product or process is offered and all users know about the benefits of the innovation. Information about the innovation is not only awareness of an innovation but includes certainty about the benefit of an innovation. The adoption of an innovation is associated with risk evoked by the uncertainty surrounding the value of the innovation for the user (Mansfield 1961, Mansfield 1989, p. 186). Potential adopters seek input from others prior to making a purchase to gain credible and objective product information, particularly when products are technologically complex. Positive experience of preceding adopters with the innovation lowers the uncertainty for potential adopters. The demonstration effect and communication between adopters and potential adopters transfer the knowledge on the usefulness of an innovation and thus determine the spread of the innovation. Since personal contact or possibility to watch other adopters using the innovation is facilitated by regional and cultural proximity, the diffusion will be spread locally like an infectious disease. The epidemic model leads to an s-shaped (logistic) diffusion curve of the cumulative number of adopters and a bell-shaped distribution of the number of adopters by time-to-adoption (density function of the logistic frequency distribution). The model can be formulated by the differential equation

$$\frac{dn_t}{dt} = q\frac{n_t}{N}(N - n_t) \tag{2.3}$$

---

[39] There is another possible reason for the diffusion of innovations on the supply side that often retard the adoption process: an innovation is not available for all potential users at the time of introduction. Normally, the production of a new good is started slowly until full capacity is reached. The larger the demand from the beginning, the larger the delivery period. Only seasonal goods such as Christmas gifts require that the supplier produces in stock to supply all potential adopters at one particular point of time.

where n_t is the number of adopters at time t, N is the maximal number of adopters (market potential) and q is a variable for the speed of diffusion. The first adopters (about 2.5 % of all users) have been (confusingly) called innovators (Rogers 1995) followed by the early adopters (13.5 %), who are most influential in their communities, whereas the last adopters are laggards (16 %). The number of adopters at time t is a function of the number of preceding adopters, "so that the basic characteristic of the process is imitative behaviour, or a bandwagon effect" (Thirtle, Ruttan, 1987, p. 80). A "bandwagon process" describes the effect that when the profitability of an innovation is difficult to estimate, users adopt an innovation that a large number of users has already adopted (Mansfield 1961, p. 8). Bass (1969) introduced a generalised form of the diffusion curve, which includes the non-epidemic mass market information effect and avoids the symmetry property of the simple form and allows skewness of the diffusion pattern. This model is frequently used in marketing studies. It can be written as

$$\frac{dn_t}{dt} = (p + q\frac{n_t}{N})(N - n_t) \tag{2.4}$$

where p has been called the propensity to innovate and q the propensity to imitate, because the former increases with the gradient or thickness of the left tail of the diffusion curve (early adopters) and the latter determines the speed of the take-off of the diffusion curve, i.e. the speed of adoption of the majority of adopters (Mahajan et al. 1990). Epidemic diffusion models presented in this section point to the importance of the demonstration effect (3.2.3). An international demonstration effect shall be suggested in Chapter 3 as a national *transfer advantage*.

Yet, international diffusion studies focus on cross-border differences in the national within-country diffusion curves (differences in the coefficient of innovation p and imitation q, see Dekimpe et al. 1998c). Yet for the question of lead markets this is not relevant, because it does not matter what diffusion pattern certain countries develop. Second, most studies follow the tradition of social science diffusion research (Hofstede, Rogers) in testing a general set of societal characteristics like cosmopolitanism, masculinism, individualism, mobility, heterogeneity, isolationism, etc. on the timing of adoption of an innovation by a country or the penetration rate – assuming that higher penetration rates means earlier adoption, see Lee (1990). The problem with this approach is that it tries to estimate the "innovativeness" of a country in general and not the international adoption process of particular innovation designs. The examples given above show that the country of the first adopters of an innovation vary from innovation to innovation. Therefore a model of the international diffusion of innovations must be innovation-design-specific and not only country-specific. For the lead market study it is sufficient to study what country adopts a specific innovation first and why are other countries following despite not adopting it earlier and even relinquishing the previously preferred design. This cannot be explained through a general "innovativeness" of a country.

Diffusion models describe the behaviour of firms in aggregate. Diffusion models are very limited in explaining technical change, because they only describe successful innovations *ex post* and are silent about innovations that failed in the market. Furthermore, they cannot explain why some users adopt an innovation earlier than other users (Thirtle, Ruttan, 1987, p. 101).[40] In contrast, adoption models model the time of adoption of an individual firm depending on firm and innovation characteristics. The aggregation of all dates of adoptions by all firms leads to the diffusion curve. On a country level the date of adoption of all countries describes the global diffusion of an innovation. Individual adoption theory can additionally provide us with valuable information about possible factors driving the global diffusion of innovations. In the next section the literature on adoption of innovations will be briefly reviewed.

2.4.3 Adoption of innovations

The distribution of time lags of adoption by users determines the rate of adoption of an innovation. Micro adoption theory can be divided into two main strands of literature, namely studies in the sociological tradition focussed on individuals such as consumers, and economic studies concerned with the adoption of technologies or products by firms. The first strand of literature provides a rich collection of adoption-decision processes and factors influencing the adoption of innovations by individuals. Rogers (1995) summarises the large body of adoption studies by marketing and sociologists. He stresses the role of change agents and opinion leaders, which change the preferences of potential adopters. The rate of adoption of innovations by individual human adopters has been explained by perceived attributes of an innovation, the Rogers-Criteria. Rogers (1995) distils five attributes of innovation responsible for the rate of adoption from the rich body of diffusion literature: relative advantage, compatibility, complexity, trialability, and observability. The benefit-price relationship or profitability of an innovation for the adopter compared to the product it supersedes, the relative advantage, is identified as the dominant economic determinant of adoption. Mansfield's (1961) seminal work on the imitation of innovation and other economic diffusion studies stress the profitability as the salient factor of adoption. Lead users formulised by v. Hippel (1986) (see section 2.4.4), as well, adopt innovations because they benefit most from an innovation. Compatibility is defined by Rogers as the degree to

[40] Diffusion models are even limited in forecasting and estimating the influence of product attributes on the diffusion growth, the main purposes of estimating diffusion curves (see Albers 1999). Traditional approaches to diffusion models such as the Bass-model are that these models assume that the innovation does not change during the diffusion period. Yet, it is more likely that the innovation will change during the diffusion process because of price changes or increases of utility due to continuing improvements and external effects like network effects. Therefore, a diffusion curve over time derived from real data on sales is merely a sequence of small diffusion curves each depicting the time between changes (see e.g. Karshenas, Stoneman 1995).

which an innovation is consistent with values, experiences and needs of an adopter. Together with the rather objective profitability, this subjective factor forms – in economic terms – the preferences of an individual adopter. The compatibility factor emphasises the location-specific character of an innovation in that the innovations are valued differently from country to country depending on the degree of differences in the physical environment, the products used previously (path-dependency), taste and culture. Rogers notes that innovations are sometimes incompatible with the context in other countries, inhibiting global diffusion, such as an IBM barcode that can store prices up to $10,000 but is not useful in Italy where most goods start at 10,000 lira.[41] International compatibility is therefore the degree of which a innovation design preferred in one country is consistent with the needs of adopters in another country. I will include international compatibility in the lead market theory in section 3.2.4 as an *export advantage* of a country.

The other three factors take account of the imperfect information about the benefit of an innovation. Because the adoption of an innovation is associated with risk of failure, Rogers (1995) calls the diffusion an uncertainty-reduction process. Alternative innovations are not only valued by potential adopters by the promised benefit but also by the risk of failure to deliver the promised benefit. Complexity of an innovation increases uncertainty, whereas observeability, the degree to which the result of an innovation is visible to others, and triability, the degree to which an innovation can be experimented with, reduce uncertainty for potential adopters. Uncertainty is able to disparage the expected value of benefit, whereas relative certainty can compensate a lower utility of a variant. It can be expected that these attributes support the international diffusion of an innovation as well. A country has therefore an international advantage if other countries have better access to information on innovations adopted there.

---

41 A concept suggested by international management literature that seems to be similar to Rogers' compatibility criteria is that of psychic distance between countries (Johanson, Vahlne 1977). Psychic distance comprises differences in "business" and native languages, legal and administrative systems as well as Hofstede's cultural dimensions. Differences in cultural dimensions have been called cultural distance. Cultural distance has even been used as proxy for psychic distance (O'Grady, Lane 1996). In practise, psychic distance include all factors disturbing the flow of information between producers and foreign users (see also section 2.5.1). It has been shown that firms start their internationalisation process with entering new markets that are not psychically distance to their home countries, because the level of uncertainty about the new market context is lowest in psychically close countries. Psychic distance can be overcome by exporters by experience and learning about foreign market contexts. However, there is a difference between psychic distance and compatibility. The concept of psychic distance does not explicitly assumes that innovations that fit the home market are compatible with the market context in a psychically close foreign country but that firms have less *uncertainty* about the foreign market context and therefore less problems of adapting the existing products to the foreign context. I will argue in section 3.2.4 that when firms know about the foreign market context they can include requirements of foreign markets already in their innovation equipping these innovations with an international advantage.

The second strand of literature models the adoption decision of firms. Pioneering studies such as Mansfield (1963, 1968) identified the profitability and the size of firms as the main determinants of time of adoption. Larger firms are more suited to taking the risk of adopting a new technology. Empirical studies have indeed found that the larger the firm and the higher the profitability, the earlier the adoption of an innovation. The impact of price of an innovation design, price changes and the prices of factors that are used by a design are especially valid. Empirical evidence on the role of market structure and other firm characteristics on adoption time is inconclusive (Thirtle, Ruttan 1987, Karshenas, Stoneman 1995). In the context of the international diffusion of innovation, profitability and the size distribution of firms are expected to exert an effect on the time of adoption of process innovations. Since the structural environment determines profitability and varies from country to country, profitability of a new technology varies and thus the incentive to adopt the technology (Edquist, Jacobsson 1988, p. 9). In the early models, the spreading mechanisms of an innovation diffusion, i.e. the question of why firms follow others in adopting an innovation, are unclear, however. These spreading mechanisms are especially important, when each nation initially adopts a different technological design that has the highest profitability in a country's environment.

Diffusion mechanisms are developed in the more recent economic adoption models other than the epidemic models. The mechanisms of the spread of innovation are either *learning effects*, i.e. changes in the prior beliefs of potential adopters of the profitability of an innovation, or changes in the stimuli of adoption over time (threshold models) (Thirtle, Ruttan 1987, p. 108). First, different beliefs of firms about the value of an innovation can explain a variance in the date of adoption. Firms then learn about the true profitability of an innovation over time, modify their beliefs and either adopt or reject an innovation (Stoneman 1980). Firms that have a better understanding about the prospect of a profitable innovation would adopt a subsequently successful innovation earlier than other firms.

Second, when the stimuli of adoption change over time and reach a threshold, additional potential users adopt an innovation. Increasing returns of adoption are changes of adoption stimuli as well. Adoption models of diffusion have been extended decisively by incorporating post-innovation technology improvements (Davies 1979, Gruber 1992, Stoneman 1989), price and adoption cost changes, network effects (Schoder 1995), strategic firm behaviour (Fudenberg, Tirole 1985) and standardisation (David, Foray 1994) during the diffusion process (see Karshenas, Stoneman 1995 for a review). These changes of adoption stimuli cause the diffusion of an innovation across a group of heterogeneous users. Continuous changes of adoption stimuli mean that the maximum potential of adopters increases gradually (Edquist, Jacobsson 1988, p. 13). The diffusion process is no longer a move to an equilibrium in which information about the innovation disseminates to all potential adopters over time (epidemic model). In contrast, perfect information is assumed but the profitability of an innovation varies among firms (rank models, see Davis 1979). When users adopt an innovation, prices or other attributes change and the other users start to adopt the innovation. While theoretical studies assume that the gross profit of adopting an innovation (by a producer of the innovation) declines with an increasing number of adopters (stock effect models, e.g. Reinganum 1981), improvements in technology, network and scale economies and standardisation suggest that the utility of an innovation increases with number of adopters and the price of the innovation and additional cost of adoption declines, making an innovation profitable for more and more users. Asymmetric increases in the attractiveness of innovation designs during the diffusion process can explain why one design finally prevails against other designs (see e.g. Stoneman 1991). Evolutionary theory, too, has addressed the question of competition among a variety of innovation designs with improvements in profitability leading to a design becoming dominant in the diffusion path (Metcalfe 1995). However, these studies lack the complexity and formalisation of price-benefit changes occurring during diffusion. Some of the formal models of competing designs reviewed in section 2.3.4 are applicable to the international diffusion context, because it can be assumed that users are internationally heterogeneous, i.e. gain a different profit from each innovation from country to country, which leads to the country rank model of cross-border diffusion pattern (i.e. a lead market pattern).

In the next chapter, the Rogers criteria as well as the conclusions from the learning and threshold models will be adapted to an international context. Tentatively, we can conclude from the adoption theory that several mechanisms lead to the diffusion of innovations. First, information about an innovation disseminates in space through interaction. Furthermore, learning mechanisms explain diffusion. Learning processes of how to use an innovation raise the propensity of others to adopt. Other adopters follow more rapidly the more they can observe the results of an innovation, the more complementary to their needs and the less risky it is. Third, adopters yield different returns of an innovation. While the first adopter of an innovation is the one who can yield the highest profitability from an innovation, profitability of the adopted innovation design can increase relatively to other designs when the utility rises or the price of adoption drops, making a specific design relatively more attractive to adopt for additional users. For consumer products the level of disposable income also determines the date of adoption of an innovation. For instance, when income of households increases more and more households can afford to buy a superior good such as an automobile (Deaton, Muellbauer 1980, p. 370). Increasing normal distributed incomes thus lead to the s-shaped diffusion pattern of innovations. Analogous, when the adoption stimuli changes across countries, more and more countries adopt an innovation.

A special application of the adoption theory is the lead user model of Eric von Hippel. In the next section I discuss the relevance of the lead user model for the lead market theory, before turning to the literature on the geographic dimension of the adoption process.

2.4.4 Lead users in the diffusion process

The relationship between early adopters of innovations and followers is addressed in the lead user model developed by Eric von Hippel (1988). In analysing the sources of innovations in the industry of professional instruments, Hippel (1976) discovers that a majority of the innovations were invented not by manufacturers of the respective product line but by users of instruments. Hippel explained these user inventors with different benefits of new products for manufactures and users. Sometimes users can yield a higher benefit of a new product than manufactures, for instance if manufactures cannot gain market share with a new product but would instead cannibalise their existing products. If users profit more from innovations they have a higher incentive to innovate.

Although the lead user model is basically a model of innovation and not a model of diffusion, the question that is important for the international diffusion – why other users follow in adopting the innovation -, is addressed by the lead user theory as well. First, Hippel (1988, p. 107) assumes the existence of lead users, because the s-shaped diffusion curve of new products can regularly be observed. He then explains the adoption of the lead user innovation by other users with a second condition (the first condition is that users have the highest profit from an innovation). Lead users are users who "face needs that will be general in the marketplace – but face them months or years before the bulk of that marketplace encounters them" (Hippel 1986, p. 786). In essence, Hippel's diffusion mechanism is a change in the adoption stimuli.

Based on his findings, Hippel (1986) develops a strategy of how manufacturers can use lead users in order to get new innovations. Users with extreme demands, v. Hippel argues, exist that have either already invented a technology themselves or have some experience and ideas as to what a new technology should look like. According to Hippel (1987), in order to identify a lead user, there must be a trend, for instance continuous improvements of a technical characteristic such as precision, size etc., on which lead users are found at the front. Urban and Hippel (1988) showed in a case study that lead users could indeed be identified.

The condition of high benefit of early adopters has already been mentioned in the previous section. The concept of heterogeneity of users and the utility rank was used before to explain the diffusion process: the first adopters are the users which gain the greatest benefit from an innovation. In contrast to the learning or improvement models presented above, Hippel suggests trends of environmental conditions or technology as the diffusion mechanism. The trend is considered as explaining why other users follow the early users in adopting the innovation. It is not clear, however, whether the trend is a *conditio sine qua non* of lead users or simply a condition of identifying lead users. Hippel does not further elaborate as to why some users "are familiar with conditions that lie in the future for most." (Hippel 1988, p. 107) as well as what actually generates "the trend". The trend explanation would be a tautology if the trend merely reflects the process of diffusion. Nevertheless, the lead user model is valuable in explaining the diffusion of innovations. Translated in terms of diffusion theory, a trend changes the stimulus of adoption, causing more and more potential users to adopt it. In the context of the international diffusion of innovations, a trend can be a driver of the international diffusion of an innovation as well. If there is an *international trend* and there are countries in which users profit more from an innovation than users in other countries, then the adoption of an innovation starts in that country and diffuses to other countries. That is the main conclusion of the lead user model for the theory of lead markets (see 3.2.2).

2.4.5 The spatial diffusion of innovations

Studies on spatial diffusion of innovations has been concerned mainly with the regional diffusion within a country. In his classic paper, Griliches (1957) studied the diffusion of hybrid corn across several US states. He found a diffusion pattern of Figure 1-1 with Iowa as the core of the Corn Belt leading the diffusion within the USA towards the fringes of the Corn Belt (Figure 2-1). The time of take-off of the adoption of hybrid corn in each state, however, is not interpreted as acceptance – which is actually indicated by the *slope* of the diffusion curve – but as a supply side factor: the *availability* of the innovation in each state. Availability is the result of the decision of seed suppliers to adapt the seed to the local conditions in each state, which depends on the attractiveness of the local market.[42] The attractiveness of a market is the *profitability* of a market entry, indicated by market sizc[43], and the *adaptability* of an innovation design to the special environmental conditions of a market. This model of the diffusion of innovations, in which cross-region diffusion is determined by the profitability of market entry whereas within-regional diffusion is determined by country-specific factors of *innovativeness*, has been used by most of the diffusion studies since then. Consistent with adoption theory, the first country of adoption is the country where the innovation is most profitable. In the international context this model of a market entry determined national take-off can still be viable for firm-specific products and brands but not in the context this thesis studies: in technologies in which several designs are offered in different country markets and in which one design finally becomes dominant worldwide.

In a spatial context of diffusion, the geographical reach of externalities is a determinant of the spatial pattern of diffusion. In a spatial model, externalities are therefore physically local. In general, spatial diffusion theory stresses the impact

---

42 Interestingly, Thirtle and Ruttan (1987, fn. 97) note that hybrid corn was not *invented* in Iowa but in Connecticut. The supply side factor was therefore independent from the location of invention of the innovation.

43 However, Griliches (1957) admits that a market "may be entered because it is a springboard to other areas rather than on its own ground" and suggests that the "market potential", including the adjunct markets, should have been taken as an indicator for profitability of market entry.

Figure 2-1: Diffusion curves of Griliches' study on hybrid corn in several US states

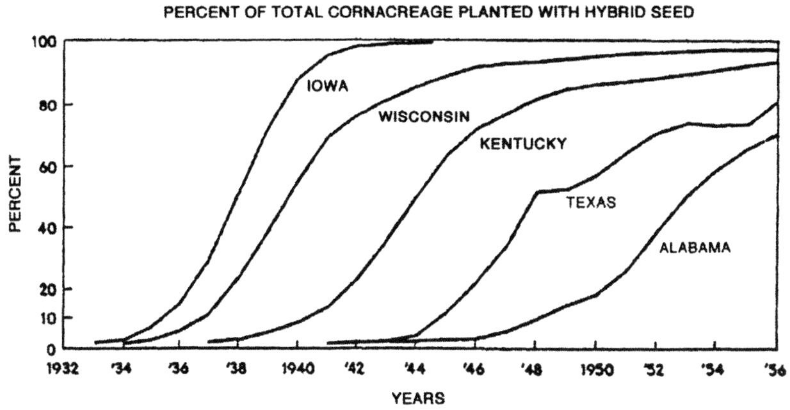

Source: Griliches (1957)

of communication links between first adopters and potential adopters. Since communication links are expected to decrease with increasing distance between adopters, the spatial diffusion of innovations is considered as a flood covering a growing regional area. This hypothesis is known as the *neighbourhood effect*.[44]

The model is based on private information dissemination and therefore limited to adoption processes in which private information is the decisive determinant. A second spatial diffusion model is based on the physical infrastructure that is complementary to innovations. Infrastructure and diffusion agencies such as distribution networks are suggested to facilitate the diffusion of innovations (McIntyre 1988). When infrastructure is an important complement it can also be an important factor for international diffusion (section 3.2.2). Formal spatial diffusion models incorporating local externalities have been reviewed in section 2.4.3. As has been noted there already, the problem of a spatial model is its simplification that the diffusion of innovation is modelled *only* as a spatial process. The assumption of information dissemination seems not to be as relevant for the international diffusion process as for the within-country diffusion because of international differences in national preferences and other environmental contexts.

44 The common observation of similarities of cultural features within regions such as house types and music is interpreted as a spatial diffusion of innovation. In a seminal study, Hägerstrand (1973) documented the spatial continuity of acceptance of tuberculosis controls in Swedish farms. The dominant feature of the diffusion process was the dissemination of private information (face-to-face) supported by proximity, the neighbourhood effect (Hägerstrand 1973, p. 165). The centers of the adoption process and exactly why other persons follow a particular center – besides awareness of an innovation - were not explained, however.

2.4.6 The international diffusion of innovation

The cross-border diffusion of innovations has received relatively little attention in the literature yet. There are few studies on the international diffusion of innovation that regard not only the national diffusion pattern but the lag between the adoption from country to country as endogenous.[45] Most authors study the international diffusion of production techniques; there are fewer studies on the diffusion of industrial or consumer goods. The first study on the international diffusion of a specific innovation is by Maddala and Knight (1967). They study the diffusion of a new steel-making process, the top-blown oxygen converter. Steel technologies have since received much attention but with little additional insight (see Poznanski 1983 and the literature cited there). Maddala and Knight (1967) assume that after the invention, the knowledge of the new technique has spread throughout the world at a fast rate and that differences in the extent of adoption between countries must depend on factors other than knowledge gaps, such as factor price differences, economies of scale and age of existing capital. They suggest that the time lags occur because of varying factor prices (e.g. electricity), growth of production (the higher the growth the faster new techniques are employed), rigidities in the planning process, ineffective planning and barriers to international competition. Poznanski (1983) adds "a lack of communication links with the world economy" to the factors of low national diffusion rates.

Detailed studies on the diffusion of production techniques have been published by Nabseth and Ray (1974). In reviewing the national diffusion of ten process innovations in the 1960s, Ray and Nabseth (1974) present detailed insights into the question of why countries adopt new processes earlier or later than other countries. First of all, *information availability* on innovations varies in line with the epidemic model of diffusion. Furthermore, the *growth of domestic markets* correlates positively with incentives for new investments. Third, *factor prices* differ internationally making innovations more or less profitable. For instance, the price of scrap influences the profitability of the oxygen steel production process. Fourth, financial sources are said to vary internationally. However, the (supply) factor of financing is likely to depend on the local demand for the good being produced and is therefore endogenous. The relation between the time of adoption and the firm size distribution of countries is inconclusive. The expectation that larger firms adopt new techniques earlier than smaller firms could not be confirmed. For instance, the oxygen steel process was adopted earlier by smaller firms. The studies reviewed by Nabseth and Ray demonstrate furthermore that the origin of invention does not determine the adoption lead of a country. By contrast, in his study on synthetic rubber, Swan (1973) follows Posner in that he assumes that the lead

[45] Most cross-border diffusion studies regard the lag as exogenous, depending on the market introduction. Another reason for the neglect is the lack of diffusion data on an international basis.

country is the country where the invention is made.[46] He studies the determinants of how quickly other countries follow in substituting natural with synthetic rubber. The matter of how fast a country follows the leader, says something about why it follows suit. Swan (1973) suggests that adoption of other countries occurs earlier the more adaptable and suitable the new products are to the local conditions and preferences, the lower the *barriers to trade*, and the more two countries are connected through *communication channels*. Suitability of a foreign innovation to domestic conditions can be indicated by *similarity of demand structure* (Tilton 1971), which is the generalised argument of Linder, who considered demand similarity as a function of per-capita income.

Although Swan (1973) calls for more research on the nature of international diffusion, not many scholars have followed. Studies that focus on the lag of adoption are confined to the pharmaceutical industry (Andersson 1992) and information technologies (Antonelli 1986). One of the most insightful studies on the international diffusion of a new technology to date is Tilton (1971). He qualified the technology gap theory in international diffusion through an in-depth case study on the international diffusion of the production of semiconductor devices. Tilton (1971) finds two factors for the international diffusion pattern. First, demand for semiconductors in Europe and Japan lags several years behind the United States. Second, start-ups react to demand for new technology faster than established firms. The technological knowledge gap is localised in the production experience induced by early demand. The technical knowledge of semiconductors and the ability to produce semiconductors diffuses fast and few differences between advanced countries can be observed.[47] The diffusion process he observed starts with early demand for semiconductors from the US-military "where performance takes over costs" (Tilton 1971, p. 35). Start-up firms react to this small volume demand. Subsequently, cost of production of the device decreases dramatically, so that the devices become cheap enough to compete in the industrial and consumer market against alternatives such as tubes. When costs decreased sufficiently, large-volume demand for industrial and consumer applications arose in Europe and

---

[46] See discussion in section 2.1: Hufbauer (1966, p. 39) already noted that the most widely used rubber today was invented in Germany in the 1940s to counteract the British blockade during the First World War. True synthetic rubber, a polymer of isoprene, was achieved almost simultaneously in 1955 by several major rubber manufacturers (internet information from J. Plambeck). This means that the international lead in the demand for synthetic rubber (in the US) cannot be explained by the origin of invention.

[47] "All [countries considered] have modern research facilities and well-trained scientists and engineers in the semiconductor field. Moreover, the nature of the technology makes industrial secrecy difficult to maintain, the major innovating firms follow liberal licensing policies. Competent semiconductor firms can normally duplicate new devices within six to twelve months. Thus, supply considerations, aside from demand-dependent learning economies, rarely delay diffusion in Europe and Japan at the producer level by more than a year; the relevant constraint in these countries generally comes from the demand side." (Tilton 1971, p. 37).

Japan as well, served by established European and Japanese electronics firms and European subsidiaries of US firms. The early demand of the US military and lead-users[48], together with preferential treatment of domestic suppliers, brought American firms a lead in unit cost reduction. A continuous stream of new semiconductor innovations has maintained the competitive advantage for decades. Tilton (1971) generalises his findings in accord with the lead market construct of this thesis: "Because of differences in demand conditions arising from variations in the size and composition of national markets certain countries enjoy a comparative advantage in the introduction and initial diffusion of new technology in some industries." Tilton (1971, p. 171). In Tilton's model, the large cost reduction of a new technology is the driver of the internationalisation of a lead-market technology. Cost reductions of semiconductors enable firms serving early demanding users in the lead market to follow the military-industry-consumer pattern of demand. In the lag markets, there is only the industry-consumer part of demand, which causes a demand lag between lead and lag market. In addition, low entry barriers in the lead market support early reaction to demand. When demand arises in lag markets multinational firms of the lead market can gain a large market share in the lag markets.

Multinational firms have been frequently regarded as one of the main actors transferring technology internationally.[49] Consequently, Antonelli (1986) regards that *multinational firms* are able to disseminate their own product innovations internationally. Countries in which large multinational firms are deploying new technologies and introduce new products are possibly able to impose their innovations internationally, overcoming national varying preferences. In his econometric estimation of the diffusion lag in the adoption of modems, however, US multinational firms' activity in a country surprisingly extends the time lag of adoption. Several studies on international differences in the date of introduction of new drugs have found that there is a lower average delay of introduction in the UK than in other countries (see Andersson 1992 for a review). Pharmaceuticals are considered as "science-based or "science-driven"[50] and an industry in which demand is ho-

---

48 The first semiconductor was developed by AT&T as an alternative to tubes in switching equipment. Although the military is no (inventing) lead-user, it is a user that demands technical developments later adopted by civilian applications.

49 Especially process technologies are transferred by multinational firms to production facilities abroad. The hypothesis of the importance of foreign direct investment for international technology transfer goes back to Vernon's (1966) product life cycle theory. Teece (1977) studied how multinational firms transfer process technologies abroad and found that firms with higher R&D-intensity, larger manufacturing experience and size are more likely to transfer their technology abroad. Models on FDI and technology transfer such as Findlay (1978) are based on the technology gap theory, see Wong (1995, pp. 618-624) for a review.

50 In science-based industries technical progress is said to be stimulated intensively by scientific advance (Pavitt 1984), indicated by a high ratio of R&D expenditure per sales that exceeds 8 % (Gehrke, Grupp 1994, pp. 39-40). Although technology does stimulate

mogenous worldwide. At first glance, a lead market effect is not expected. The adoption of drugs is, however, dependent on the process of clinical research, which is in effect a research cooperation with users, and national approval procedures. Reger and Hinze (1999) found that clinical research is supported by hospitals differently internationally. Many UK hospitals have special study nurses attracting pharmaceutical firms to introduce drugs into the UK first. This is an example for the global impact of efficient user-producer interaction on the timing of market introduction of an innovation (2.5.2).

The review of literature on the international diffusion reveals that although some factors have been identified determining the adoption lag between countries, there is no theoretical concept of the mechanisms of the international diffusion of nationally induced innovations. International adoption models have rarely been combined with models of local or global externalities described in section 2.3. Furthermore, in these studies the link between early adoption and the competitive advantage of companies is only stressed by Tilton (1971). This link is especially the main contribution of the international product life cycle proposed by Vernon (1966). To conclude this review, I now turn to the historical assessment of the home market advantage of multinational firms.

2.5 User-Innovator Proximity and Regional Innovation Design

Regional demand for regional specific innovations leads to region-specific innovations if firms respond to the demand by developing region-specific innovations or adapting innovations to region-specific conditions. This responsiveness and the development and refinement of region-specific innovations requires an interaction between users and producers. If this interaction is supported by geographic proximity, it can be expected that region- or nation-specific innovations are developed by domestic firms. The international competitiveness of firms is therefore linked with a regional lead market role. The national interaction-based theory of technical change was first introduced by Staffan Burenstam Linder in the 1960s and later refined by the Nordic research tradition. This section reviews the interaction literature.

2.5.1 The home market theory

The global success of firms is traditionally explained by an advantage of the home country, whether it be low factor costs, a technological lead or a market advantage. These home market advantages can be used as a lever to enter foreign markets (Porter 1986, Porter 1998, Krugman 1994). While cost advantages correspond

---

scientific progress as well (Kline, Rosenberg 1986; Brooks 1994; Stephan 1996), it is not yet clear whether these industries are *based* on scientific knowledge. This is why Freeman and Soete (1995) call these industries "science-related" rather than "science-based".

to the comparative advantage in trade theory, a demand side advantage is suggested by the home-market theory for explaining a competitive advantage of nations. The home-market theory, which Linder (1961) originally introduced, asserts that companies develop and introduce new products mainly to fit demand conditions in their home market. There are two reasons for this. First of all, firms have better information on local customer needs and consumer preferences.[51] These information asymmetries of local demand conditions are explained in innovation theory by the need of close contacts between producers, customers, suppliers and industrial services in the introduction phase of innovations and thus regional proximity and low cultural distance such as language or societal rules (e.g., Anderson et al. 1981, Fagerberg 1992). In marketing theory it is well known that a marketer's perception of market needs is framed by his own cultural experience and thus biased by local market needs even if new products are aimed at foreign markets. Terpstra and David (1991) counter the possible argument of easy access to information on foreign demand preferences for innovations with the observation that culture includes standard ways of doing things which members of the culture are not willing to share with outsiders, which are for instance regarded as shameful. They call these elements of a culture the backstage culture.[52] Second, even if firms perceive foreign needs, the corresponding product that fills it might not be fully conceived or may eventually not be adapted to unfamiliar conditions without additional cost (Linder 1961, p. 90). A lack of home testing ground causes heavy costs overseas, where the necessary information has to be found. Domestic firms will thus be more effective if they first react to changes in local demand and will get faster and better feedback from the first applications of their innovations which will have been introduced into the local market for refinement. This interactive learning process standardises innovations for widespread application.

2.5.2 User-producer interaction

A rich strand of literature in management science has pointed to the importance of innovation as an interactive process between user and producer ever since Linder's work.[53] Various studies have found user-producer interaction a significant success factor of new products (Rothwell et al. 1974, Cooper, Kleinschmidt 1987,

---

51 The generation of economically valuable information through "on-the spot" information-exchanging interactions has been already stressed by Hayek (1945). The local market interaction discovers the knowledge dispersed over market participants.

52 Lee (1966) introduced the term 'self-reference criterion' to refer to the unconscious tendency of people to resort to the own cultural experience and values to interpret a market opportunity. Furthermore, management of multinationals with a strong home base is prone to consider its own culture as leading the world trends, a tendency called ethnocentrism in this context by Perlmutter (1969).

53 One of the fundamental articles cited is Lundvall (1988). Even earlier, Gemünden (1981) empirically studied different types and efficiencies of interaction processes between producers and customers in the computer industry.

Gruner, Homburg 1997). The interaction theory has been extended to the network model of the firm (Håkansson 1987). In this model a firm's innovations are embedded in the network of customers and suppliers (Gemünden, Heydebreck, Herden 1992). These interaction models refer primarily to business-to-business relationships. To assess the importance of proximity between users and producers for all users, firms and consumers, the whole range of user-producer interaction shall be considered. Brockhoff (1998) differentiates five roles customers can play during the innovation process. First of all, customers formulate their needs (need perception); second, customers can participate in the innovation process (launching customers); third, they can be innovators themselves (lead users)[54]; fourth, customers are a source of knowledge of applications (reference customers) and finally, customers can act as support for overcoming internal resistance of the producer. For the first four roles of users it is assumed that proximity between users and producers is a success factor of communication and cooperation. Distance includes spatial distance, cultural distance, economic distance, and distance in needs (Törnross 1991). The first and the fourth roles, those of a source of information about needs and applications, represent the main function the home market thesis assigns to users. Although consumers are less actively involved in the process of innovations, producers of industrial and consumer products require information on current and potential users. Producers learn about consumer preferences through successive rounds of product testing and reformulation in the local market (Cornish 1997, p. 148). User-producer interaction is even seen as a market creation activity because it is capable to provide a link between non-articulated local needs of firms and external sources of supply (Teubal et al. 1991). The main hypothesis is that distance between producers and markets reduces the quality and quantity of consumer market intelligence. The other roles of users refer more to industrial goods, where the interaction between users and producers is intense during the innovation process.

While an extensive body of studies have strengthened the user-producer proximity hypothesis since Linder's theoretical reflections, the globalisation of firms and new communication technologies have been made responsible for the weakening of the impact of geographic proximity on innovation success (Fagerberg 1992). In addition, high export shares of technology intensive firms and their inter-regional access to technological knowledge and market intelligence suggest that regional sources are not as important anymore (Cornish 1997).

Yet, interaction theory still regards face-to-face communication as the most effective means of communication (Nohria, Eccles 1992). A the high share of uncodified, tacit (Polany 1966) or "sticky" (Hippel 1999) knowledge of innovative ideas make face-to-face communications more efficient, especially in cooperations in the innovation process between users and producers that have since increased dramatically (Licht 1994). A greater distance between users and producers reduces

[54] See section 2.4.4.

the amount of face-to-face communication and learning-by-interaction (Gertler 1995). Assuming that geographic proximity facilitates the information exchange and the interaction between users and producers, regional networks are expected to generate innovations that are most adapted to local market needs (Camagni 1991, Porter, Sövell 1998). Lundvall (1993) values culture distance and thus national boundaries even higher than spatial distance (regions) and introduces the notion of *national* systems of innovation. This model suggests that innovations are embedded in a national, cultural context.

The question of why firms adopt innovations that have been developed in close interaction with other users, and therefore adapted to their specific needs, has rarely been explicitly addressed. The lead user concept by Eric v. Hippel, however, points directly to this crucial link (see 2.4.4). The model suggests it is not the interaction itself that is the success factor, but the selection of the right user to interact with. Besides the empirical evidence on the firm level and within countries, the relationship between user-producer interaction and exports or the competitive advantage of nations is less clear. Fagerberg (1995, p. 244) admits that the positive effect of a high degree of integration between users and producers on the international competitive position still lacks a theoretical explanation. For Linder (1961), the economic level of development measured by per-capita-income is the only rational for the globalisation of nation-specific innovations. The other scholars who suggest the importance of regional networks for the international competitiveness of firms seem to largely refer to the quality or utility enhancing effect of regional network-based innovations ("perfection of innovations"). They rather neglect the international differences of internationally varying user preferences and environmental contexts that inhibit exports. Furthermore, improvements tend to focus on locally preferred attributes of the innovation and do not have to include attributes preferred abroad (localised learning, see footnote 33). Porter (1990) is an exception and his findings of the effect of the quality of national demand on the international success of innovations will form the nucleus of the theory of lead markets elaborated in the next chapter. In particular, it must be theoretically explained why customers would prefer foreign products as opposed to domestic products, which would be expected to fit domestic needs much better. Or to put it another way: how do foreign users profit from domestic user-producer interaction?

2.6 Historic View: Home Markets of Multinational Firms

As Takeuchi, Porter (1986) states, presence in lead markets has particular advantages for companies, because lead markets supply them with the latest information on customer needs, technological developments and competitive moves. The effect of proximity highlighted in section 2.5 couples the market context with the international competitive advantage of domestic firms. The lead role of a market will affect all domestic companies and give them an international competitive advantage. It is therefore reasonable to investigate lead functions of markets by exploring the home markets of international competitive companies. In the past, the United States used to be the lead market for most industries, which gave US companies an international competitive advantage. Since the 1970s, it became more apparent that other countries too ascended to lead markets in particular product lines. The lead role of the United States has been investigated most comprehensively since the 1960s. In the 1980s, Porter (1990) studied the home market advantage of countries more systematically.

The strength of the US firms in the postwar era has been explained predominantly by the home market advantage of large market size.[55] The largeness of US market justifies the immense investments for high-tech innovations that were not profitable for European markets. In addition, the large US market enabled economies-of-scale that made US innovations more price competitive compared to innovations adopted in European countries. Another theory that comprises both the local innovation adoption and the international diffusion of innovations is the *international-life-cycle theory*. This theory will be reviewed briefly.

2.6.1 The international product life cycle as a theory of lead markets

The international product life cycle hypothesis originally suggested by Vernon (1966) can be described as the first theory of lead markets. Vernon (1966) introduced a version of the home-market theory in his product life cycle theory of trade and international direct investment of US multinationals. According to the theory, beginning with the second half of the nineteenth century, the emergence of a middle-class in the United States initiated mass demand for innovative consumer products. In turn mass producers demanded sophisticated capital goods and process innovations. As time passes, new products get standardised. Foreign demand is subsequently served through exports and later through local production in these markets in order to react to the threat of domestic producers gaining the ability to produce the then standardised product cheaper locally. Vernon (1971) considers the environment in the United States responsible for the advantage US firms gained over European firms and not a scientific lead. While innovations in the United States were pulled by a rising high-income middle class demanding convenience products and the high cost of skilled labour inducing new processes for mass manufacturing[56], European firms' innovations were shaped by high costs of

---

[55] For instance, Nelson, Wright (1992) explain the long standing dominance of US firms in mass production industries with their favourable access to the world's largest domestic market.

[56] This labour scarcity hypothesis, first introduced by Rothbarth (1946), is an early example of the induced innovation theory of technical change. Even the adoption of the computer was explained by shortage of clerical labour (Franko 1976, p. 27). For a survey of the labour scarcity hypothesis to explain the supremacy of the US, see David (1975).

materials and a high availability of skilled (artisan) workers.[57] When the per-capita-income and the cost of skilled labour in Europe converged to the pattern prevailing in the United States, "products generated in response to the special conditions of the US market became even more appropriate to the European market" (Vernon, 1971, p. 84) and the US conditions proved to be a more rewarding path for globally successful innovations in many product fields than the European.

On the other hand, Vernon (1971) does not exclude other countries from developing special conditions for innovations, which after time emerge in other countries as well. He remarks that Germany gained a lead in dyestuffs and artificial fertilisers, because it had no access to natural raw materials like Britain did. Germany held a lead in pharmaceuticals immediately after the second World War due to the first compulsory health insurance introduced in 1889, which created a major market for drugs in Germany. In line with the product life cycle theory, German chemical and pharmaceutical firms invested in the United States as early as in the nineteenth century (Wilkins 1989, pp. 390-392). In a study on European multinationals following Vernon's landmark study, successful European innovations are found to be focussed on material saving due to the scarcity of raw material and political autarky policies (Franko 1976, pp. 24-44). Especially German firms excelled in 'Ersatz' products from rubber and fertilisers to margarine and coffee. When the prices of natural products increased worldwide while economies of scale lowered prices of synthetic products, other countries shifted consumption to synthetic products as well laying the foundation of the international success of the German chemical industry.

However, besides these successful European innovations, on the whole, high per-capita-income, scarce artisan labour, large internal market including military purchases, all generated innovations in the United States that would later be wanted abroad. The special conditions in the European market rather encouraged innovations which less fitted the future international demand (Vernon, 1971, p. 109). With increasing income, demand for innovations responding to the low income segment became less pronounced. In essence, the product life cycle hypothesis explains the international success of multinational firms with the lead effect of their home markets.

---

57 Since the 19th century US innovations are aimed at the raising middle class demand for convenience that emerged in Europe and Japan decades later such as motor vehicles, home appliances, personal computers. European innovations responded either to necessities of the working class, e.g. margarine, or to luxury demands, e.g. Mercedes motor vehicles (Franko 1976, pp. 33-36). Even earlier, Dichter (1962) associated the world consumption trend with the raising middle class in contrast to the proletarian class.

2.6.2 The demise of the United States' dominant lead-market role

By the 1970s the dominance of the United States as a market which generates innovations for the global market seemed to be losing its main ground (Vernon 1979). Among the ten new processes reviewed in Nabseth and Ray (1974), only a few were first adopted by the US; no country could be characterised as a general leader, rather each of the industrialised countries studied occasionally led the adoption of an innovation. One reason for this international disorder is the global convergence of per capita income. Linder (1961) and Vernon (1966) see home demand for a particular product mainly as a function of per-capita-income.[58] As per-capita-income of the industrialised countries in the triad converged up to a marginal difference, the US demand lost its dominant high-income-induced innovation lead.

Other components of the leadership of the United States in terms of the adoption of innovations are eroding as well. Livingstone (1989) observes that Western and other countries did not adopt US demand preferences automatically with increasing per-capita-income anymore and puts it down to an emerging contemplation in Western societies about the desirability of the American cultural pattern leading to new trends of divergence adding to convergence in demand preferences. An MIT study on US competitiveness (Dertouzos et al. 1989) points to a decline in the lead role of customers in the United States as being responsible for the waning competitiveness of US manufacturing. For instance, the early user of semiconductors was mainly the military, demanding designs which could be later commercialised in civil applications as well (Tilton 1971, Langloise, Steinmueller 1999). Not only did the weight of military procurement for semiconductors decrease by the mid-1970s, but defence needs ceased to foreshadow civil applications and "technology sought by the Department of Defense began to lag rather than lead commercial use" (Dertouzos et al. 1989, p. 255). Lack of user demand for product innovations has been identified as a key contributor to the decline of the US machine-tool industry (Dertouzos et al. 1989, p. 239). In addition, users were not involved in the development of new equipment. In contrast, German and Japanese users were much more demanding, eager to catch up on the leading US industry with the newest technology, developed in close cooperation with them. For instance, the automobile industry is the largest and most demanding user for steel mills. In Europe and Japan higher fuel costs induced more incentives for steel producers to invest in R&D for low weight bodies and frames than in the US, making its steel industry more competitive in the long-run, as weight decreases became a global trend in the automobile industry. In all industries examined, the MIT study stresses the importance of demand for innovations for international

[58] Therefore, studies testing the home market theory (e.g. Anderson et al. 1981) take GDP per capita as a proxy for the similarity between demand preferences. The other argument for its impact of international successful innovations is that per-capita-income is a proxy for the middle-class income.

competitiveness and supplier customer linkages, These linkages provide information on customer preferences and leads to product and process innovations.

In addition, global trends are turning to towards the traditional European and Japanese context of scarcity of input factors. For instance, energy-saving innovations are developed in Europe and Japan because energy is more scarce there than in the US (Harrigan 1984). The Council on Competitiveness (1998, p. 131), a forum of chief executives of US-companies, calls it an innovation dilemma of the US-automobile industry that US-firms must innovate to become globally competitive, but that its home market is not at the front of the global trend towards energy efficiency. Because of lower energy prices in the United States "customer demand for innovation for fuel-efficient or alternative fuel vehicles is not particularly strong". As a result, "the market pull for advanced technology and alternative design vehicles is coming primarily from overseas". On the other hand, the US computer industry managed to stay ahead of foreign competitors, although foreign competitors often dominate their (often protected) home markets. It could be suggested that US computer firms remained competitive because the United States remained a lead market for computers. Penetration rates of personal computers are still the highest in the United States worldwide (Source: ITU).

Does the diminishing of the dominate lead market role of the USA, described in literature, together with the convergence of per-capita-income and technological capabilities among a growing number of industrial countries, mean that lead markets no longer exist at all? I have argued that technical innovations are still localised and market contexts vary internationally. There are drivers of globalisation other than raising per-capita-income that facilitate the emergence of a globally dominant design. As will be summarised in the next chapter there are several lead mechanisms which can support a localised innovation becoming globally dominant. The United States certainly lost its almost exclusive lead role but at the same time globalisation enhances the group of countries that are able to step into their footsteps, depending on a multitude of factors which make it hard to foresee the lead market for a particular innovation.

The next chapter describes all possible lead effects of a market. Each of these are only possible mechanisms and are neither sufficient nor necessary conditions. They demonstrate that there are a variety of reasons which explain why lead markets can exist.[59]

[59] This, too, is the conclusion of Thirtle and Ruttan after reviewing historical evidence, that in the context of international diffusion of innovations "aspects of technical change such as induced innovation, the effect of market structure, appropriate technology, diffusion, and technology transfer interact in a complex manner" (Thirtle, Ruttan, 1987, p. 120).

3 Foundations of Lead Markets

Leaders need followers and followers need leaders
JAMES MACGREGOR BURNS (LEADERSHIP, 1978)

The last chapter demonstrated that a variety of technological designs could, over time, be reduced to a dominant design. If preferences vary among nations dominant designs for each country emerge. Examples show, however, that the convergence of the variety amongst technical alternatives does not stop at national borders despite internationally varying demand. Instead, the variety on an international level can also be reduced and the world market becomes more and more homogeneous. It is often the case that one alternative drives other product versions or technologies out or confines them to niche markets. Or competitors simply give up the race on the international market and start producing the competitor's design as was the case in VCR standards (Rosenbloom, Cusamano 1987). Whereas Utterback (1994) only looks at the emergence of a dominant design (normally the United States), one has to explain when and how a globally dominant design emerges among national favourites. Often, several national or regionally specific dominant designs co-exist for a while before one dominant design emerges on an international level.

The lead function of a market implies that the adopted country-specific dominant design becomes the globally dominant design. The lead market hypothesis assumes that local demand or market conditions are responsible for the adoption of a design that diffuses internationally and is able to supersede other nation specific innovations. A globally dominant design emerges among nationally dominant designs that are each designed and refined in different countries. This chapter will explain this international diffusion process. Literature, as reviewed above, has offered several possible mechanisms that can be applied to this international process. These approaches must be integrated in a system of lead market mechanisms. I will start with a simple formal model and transfer the theoretical argument into a practical system of lead market factors. At the end of this chapter, I will discuss several additional attributes of lead markets such as geographical extent or time persistence.

3.1 A Simple Model for Lead Markets

In this chapter I will embark on modelling the fundamental lead effects of a market. Theoretical modelling is an abstraction of the main ideas. Abstraction is necessitated by the need to communicate ideas and information. Although less useful in the practical task of applying the lead market concept to particular products, which is the main purpose of the case studies in Chapter 4, a theoretical model will help in the comprehension of the fundamental logic behind the concept and can allow further statistical tests if a broader data set can be made available. The model I propose is a static consumption model that looks at two points in time when a dynamic process changed the conditions of consumption. As described in Chapter 2, several conditions change constantly during the diffusion process. First, products are improved by learning-by-using and economies of adoption. Second, the communication-based diffusion model suggests that most of the potential users adopt the innovation only after other users have adopted it, i.e. they change their preferences depending on penetration rates. At first glance, a simple consumption model just seems inappropriate for modelling dynamic innovation processes. Yet I am only interested in demonstrating the lead market effect, that is the mechanism of why the consumption pattern in one country, the lag market, converges to the consumption pattern in another country, the lead market, after innovation designs have been developed and offered in the countries. The user-producer interaction has already led to nation-specific innovations. For the single purpose of explaining the lead effect, I prefer the simplicity of the two-country model (one lead and one lag market) presented here. I also found it sufficient to relax the transitory axiom by allowing indifference curves to change over time due to changes in tastes by habit formation (Deaton, Muelbauer 1980, p. 53) and due to the utility enhancement of the goods between two points in time.

To support the existence of lead markets, one must clarify why a country adopts an innovation in the first place that subsequently becomes adopted globally or why a nation-specific innovation design becomes globally adopted and other nation-specific are abandoned. For a lead market concept to be viable in practise the theoretical discussion must be exhaustive because a firm must take all cases into consideration. As the model demonstrates, national markets can be lead markets for several reasons. In other words, a lead market theory is an eclectic theory like the theory of international production by Dunning (1979). The advantage of the theoretical model presented here is that all different lead effects can be demonstrated.

Let us assume that the two products q_1 and q_2 can be easily substituted and combined continuously within a country. It does not matter where the products are produced, there are no transportation costs. The model should be focussed on the adoption process of an innovation competing against other innovation designs or against an established product. In this context the traditional consumer theory (the consumption of goods) and the Lancaster approach (the consumption of attributes) are congruent. The two goods are alternative technical designs with the same functions and have the same product attributes but in different proportions, i.e. they belong to one group of goods (Lancaster 1981). The two goods are consumed in different quantities from country to country if different properties are preferred nationally, e.g. if the environmental context differs between countries. The two goods represent either an established older good and an innovation or they represent different designs of an innovation, each induced by demand for innovations with nation-specific properties.[60] The former case describes the simple situation of the adoption of an innovation that substitutes an established product. The latter case describes two nation-specific innovation designs competing for the globally dominant design with the possible result that one is a lead country and the other an idiosyncratically innovative country.[61] This is the situation, for instance, where there are two technologies for verbal communication: a fixed line telephony (q_1) and a mobile telephony (q_2). Consumers can select the amount of telephone calls they make via their mobile and fix line phones. There are neither fix costs of access to networks nor are there costs for phones for the user since service providers subsidise phones for long term contracts with users. An example for the case of competing designs is a country where two different mobile telephone services have been introduced. The users can choose between the services. The quantities of consumption are equivalent, for instance, to the number of subscribers to the two services.

Consumers form their preferences for the two goods according to the properties they possess. The individual preferences of users determine the relative weights given to the various characteristics in making choices. Indifference curves of the collective consumption of users of one country for the two goods have the usual property of strict convexity and can hit axes, i.e. the products are not essential.[62] The model assumes that both goods are offered in all countries.[63] I confine the

60 An innovation design can be induced by nation-specific demand either when the innovating firm knows user preferences, or when firms offer different versions of an innovation in the market and users select the version that is most suitable to their preferences. The model is therefore not limited to innovations actively demanded by users.

61 In the lead-lag market context the first case is the situation of an innovative country adopting an innovation first and other non-innovative countries adopting the innovation later (Figure 1-1). In the second case, all countries are innovative but the lag market demands idiosyncratic innovation designs, whereas the lead market demands an innovation design that later becomes adopted by the lag markets (Figure 1-2).

62 An indifference curve is a group of combinations of goods with the same utility, so that any combination on the curve is preferred. In this context I understand preferences as an ordering of choices of goods according to a utility function (Deaton, Muellbauer 1982, p. 25).

63 The model would even allow varying availability of innovation designs in countries, if potential preferences are introduced. The model would reflect the potential consumption pattern and not the real consumption pattern. For innovations that are not offered, preferences could be reconstructed by consumer research tools such as conjoint meas-

model to two country markets: one that leads the adoption of a dominant design and one lag market that initially prefers a different innovation design (or the old product) but later follows the lead market in adopting the design preferred in the lead market. The two countries have the indifference curves I_{lead} and I_{lag} respectively and budget constraints P_{lead} and P_{lag}. The budget constraint represents the collective purchasing power of the countries' users. Both the preference system and the budget constraint are aggregates of the individual preferences and budgets of all consumers of a country (the problem of the aggregation of budgets of users is discussed further in section 0). Per-capita-income shall be taken as the main proxy for the national budget, because only the relation between q_1 an q_2 are important for the national penetration rate and not the total volumes, which are a function of size of countries as well.

The lead effect, i.e. the emergence of a dominant design of consumption, occurs between two points in time, t_0 and t_1. At t_0 one country, the lead country, prefers q_2 and the other country, the lag market, q_1. 'Prefer' means that the good has a higher market share in the country market. Because the two goods are preferred differently by the countries, they are characterised as nation-specific or nationally preferred designs. Different consumption patterns in the countries can be a result of (1) different preferences, i.e. different properties of goods are preferred because of varying environmental context or tastes, (2) different budget constraints and (3) different prices of each good in the two countries. At the point in time t_1 both the lead and the lag country prefer the good q_2. There are three reasons for the lag country to change its consumption pattern: (1) the relative benefit of q_2 for users in the lag country could have increased, (2) the available budget of users in the lag country could have increased and (3) the relative price of q_2 in the lag country could have decreased. Based on this typology of changes of adoption stimuli, three basic lead market mechanisms can be derived. First, a time lag between the average income of consumers in the lead and the lag markets causes the consumption of a superior good in the lead market to emerge earlier in the lead market than in the lag market even if preferences are equal. I call this the income-lead effect. Second, the lead market yields a high relative benefit of an innovation design that later emerges for users in other countries as well and drives these lag countries to adopt the design as well. This can be called *anticipatory demand* or the demand-lead effect. And third, a relative price reduction of the design preferred in the lead market for users in the lag market shifts consumption in the lag market away from the previously preferred design towards the design preferred in the lead market. This price mechanism can be further divided into two sub cases. If the price of the lead market design has been lower in the lead market in the past than in the lag market, the mechanism can be called the price-lead effect. If the price of the design preferred in the lead market decreases relative to the prices of designs pre-

urement, in which potential adopters reveal their preferences about a non-existing new product through simulated choices between pairs of product variants (Green, Wind 1975).

ferred by other countries it will be called the price reduction effect. These mechanisms shall now be discussed further.

3.1.1 The income-lead effect

The first case is the main explanation given in the classical international product-life-cycle theory by Vernon. The consumption of an expensive luxury good is low in countries with low per-capita-income but increases with higher per capita income. In the traditional framework, the lead market is simply the country market with the highest per capita income. Users in the country with the highest per-capita-income consume the highest amount of a superior good when preference systems and prices do not vary from country to country. In the simple model with two countries and two alternative designs, if one design were more superior to the other, countries with low income would concentrate on consuming the less expensive design.

In general, if per-capita-income in all countries increases over time, the lead market will be the first market to reach a per-capita-income that triggers the take-off of the adoption of the innovation.[64] As a result of user-producer interaction and feedback, users in the lead market will shape the new product design and the improvements of the refinement process of the innovation design until per-capita-income in the lag market increases to such a degree that the demand for the innovation design takes-off there as well.

The demand function for good q_i can be written as a function of income y

$$q_i = g_i(y) \tag{3.1}$$

which is the well-known Engel curve. The income elasticity β_i of good q_i is

$$\beta_i = \frac{\partial q_i}{\partial y_i}\frac{y_i}{q_i} \tag{3.2}$$

A possible functional form of the share of the consumption w_i of good q_i can be written as (Leser 1963)

$$w_i = \alpha_i + \gamma_i \log y \tag{3.3}$$

---

[64] The take-off in the diffusion curve within a country depends not only on the per-capita-income but also on the income distribution $\sigma(y)$ within a country. A large variance of the income distribution can slow down the diffusion within a country and therefore weaken the income-lead market effect. For instance, there are several countries especially in the developing world with a small segment of people with very large incomes. This segment increases the per-capita-income but does not facilitate a mass market. As Franko (1976, p. 35) points out, the reason that per-capita income was a good proxy for the lead role of the United States after World War II is that it reflects the emergence of the middle-class that induced the emergence of a mass market for convenience products and became the centre of the success of US multinational firms.

The income-lead effect proposes that consumption good q_2 in the lag market exceeds the consumption of q_1 with increasing income (t_0: $w_{1lag}>w_{2lag}$, t_1: $w_{2lag}>w_{1lag}$) It is clear that in the two product case ($w_{1lag}+w_{2lag}=1$) lead markets of the budget-lead type exist for luxury goods only, which by definition take up a larger share of the budget of wealthier nations, whereas the consumption share of necessities and inferior goods decreases with an increasing income. Therefore good q_2 is a luxury good (share of consumption grows with income: $\gamma_2>0$) and q_1 is a necessity (consumption share declines: $\gamma_1<0,\ 1>\beta_1>0$) or an inferior good (total consumption declines: $\gamma_1<0,\ \beta_1<0$). The income lead effect therefore can explain the global replacement of a necessity or an inferior good with a luxury. Product q_2, however, could finally squeeze out the other innovation design or older product q_1 only if q_1 is an inferior good. Innovation designs that respond to demand from low-income segments can be inferior goods. These innovation designs are prone to be superseded by more superior designs when income of the low-income segment increases. An example could be margarine, which was invented in responds to the low income in Europe. Increasing income worldwide can lead to falling demand for margarine and increasing demand for more delicious spread. In a multiple product model, the observation that demand for good q_2 will exceed the demand for good q_1 over time requires that $\beta_2>\beta_1$, allowing that both goods are luxuries.[65] In the fixed-line vs. mobile telephone example, the income-lead model is plausible if mobile telephony is more a luxury as fixed-line telephony.

A graphic representation of the income effect is depicted in Figure 3-1. The indifference curve system reflects the consumption patterns of the two goods with a higher income elasticity for good q_2 than for good q_1. The indifference curve system is equal for both countries, meaning that for a given income users have the same preferences.[66] Prices are the same in both countries and are constant over time but the two countries have different budgets. As a result q_2 is almost not demanded at all in the country with low per-capita-income (A), expressed by the budget curve P_{lag}, and almost entirely demanded in the country with high per-capita-income (B), expressed by the budget curve P_{lead}. When income in the lag market grows over time it follows the consumption pattern of the lead market and consumes more and more q_2.

The prevalence of q_2 over q_1 will first occur in the country for which the budget constraint is most advanced to the right. This depends on a high per-capita-income of the potential user group. Total size of the country, however, can matter as well. The national demand for an innovation is the sum of demand from users with an income that exceeds a certain threshold depending on the superiority of the inno-

---

65 Demand for one design, however, would totally extinguishes only if $\alpha_i = 0$. The model also requires that prices of the two goods are constant and no function of demand, for instances, because marginal costs are constant or prices are set by the world market.

66 This is the traditional assumption of Linder's home market theory, Vernon's international product life-cycle theory and Stigler and Becker (1977).

Figure 3-1: Lead market through higher income

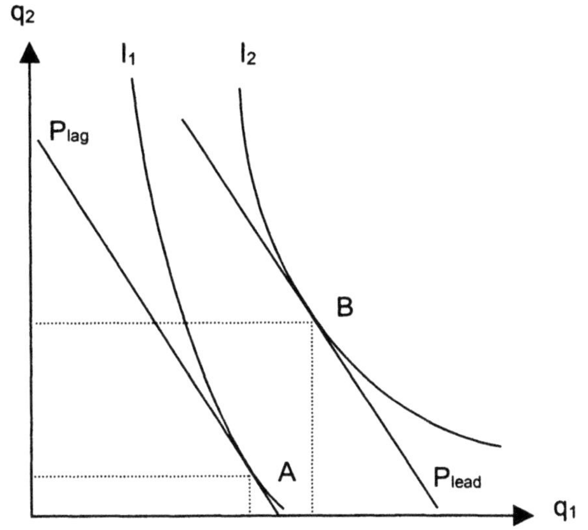

vation. If the introduction of an innovation depends on the market size, the lead market is the country where the innovation is first offered and that is the country with the largest market for the innovation.[67] That means that a very small country, e.g. Luxembourg, is not always the lead market even if it has the highest per-capita-income. For innovations that are associated with large market entry costs (e.g., product approval procedures for each country market entry) a country has to have a necessary total market size to justify the investment of market entry. In the example outlined above, for instance, investments in the mobile network are so large that they require a minimum market size.

The income-lead effect requires that the per-capita income of the user group in other countries grows over time and that preferences are equal internationally.[68]

---

67 This size argument corresponds to the explanation of the diffusion process of hybrid corn across US states given by Griliches (1957).

68 The model implies that the group with the highest income adopts superior products first and therefore shapes the design of the innovation. At first glance, there is a parallel to the innovation strategy of offering innovations to high-income users, for instance testing new features in luxury sedan cars first (e.g. airbag, anti-lock braking system) before adopting them in medium and low class cars as well. Consumers have the same preferences regarding the new feature (e.g. safety) regardless of what car they choose, but have different budgets at their disposal. In order to transfer the innovation to lower class cars, however, the relative cost of the new feature must decrease (or preferences must change), allowing middle-income consumers to adopt the new feature. Increasing budgets alone would lead to the substitution of medium class cars with luxury class cars that have the new features.

The model suggests that the likelihood of the existence of lead markets increases with the income elasticity of an innovation ($ß_i$), the larger the difference between the income elasticity of competing innovation designs and the larger the lead of a country in terms of per-capita-income and the larger the cost of entry in a country market.

3.1.2 The price-reduction effect

The second type of lead effect is a simple price mechanism. The preference systems are now different in the lead and the lag market. If the relative price of the good that was previously preferred by users in the lead market, but for some reason not by users in the lag market, decreases for users in the lag market, they shift consumption from the previously preferred good to the good preferred initially by the lead market. There are two sub-cases: one is discussed in this section, the other in the next section. First, I assume that two countries have the same budget, for instance they are two advanced countries with the same per-capita-income. Prices of the two goods are the same in the two countries at the time of market entry ($p_{ilead}=p_{ilag}$). This is reasonable when transportation cost and trade restrictions are low. The two products, however, have a different potential of price reduction.[69] Price changes can be caused by cost reductions due to dynamic and static economies-of-scale, price changes of factor inputs or when the market power of producing firms changes, e.g. new firms enter the market with imitations and end the monopoly of the innovating firm. Relative price changes of goods lead to the substitution of the one good that became relatively more expensive for the other good that became relatively less expensive. As a result of large relative price changes, the good with the largest price reduction (or lowest relative price increase) prevails in both countries and becomes the globally dominant design. The adoption process of the innovation design q_2 in the lag country is actually a substitution process. Figure 3-2 depicts different indifference curve systems for the two country markets that cause different designs to be preferred in each country. The initial budget curve P_0, equal for both countries, leads to the prevailing consumption of q_2 in the lead market, while the lag market favours the good q_1. When the cost advantages of q_2 turn the budget constraint to the right toward P_1, the lag country shifts its consumption in favour of the now cheaper good q_2 up to a level where the preferred good switches from q_1 to q_2.

This price mechanism is the centrepiece of Levitt's (1983) globalisation hypothesis, in which the consumers "capitulate" to the attraction of lower prices of foreign products and abandon their initially preferred innovation design. Consumers in the

[69] Different price increases of the two goods can occur as well and result in the same mechanism but this case should be an exception as a mechanism of the international diffusion of innovations.

Figure 3-2: Relative price reduction effect

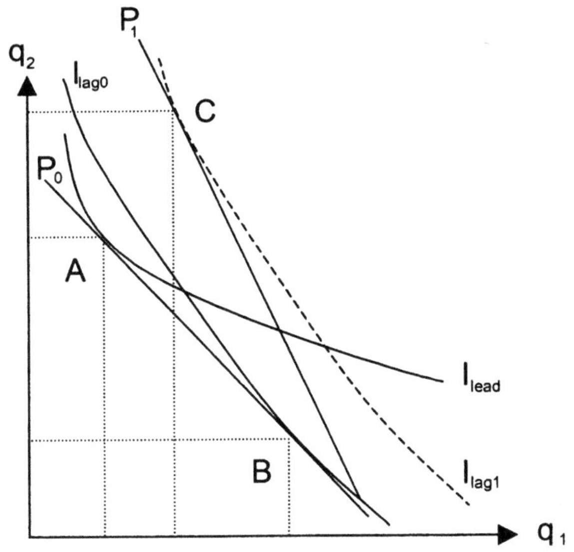

lag market, however, do not change their preferences as Levitt's phrasing implies. They just substitute goods along the indifference curve.[70]

From the graphic presentation in Figure 3-2 that a high substitution elasticity of the two goods in the lag market make the switch and the abandonment of the previously preferred good by the lag market users more conducive. It seems that users in the lag market are more price sensitive (a high cross-price or substitution elasticity indicated by the lower curvature of the indifference curve of the lag market) and more indifferent toward the two goods than users in the lead market who clearly prefer good q_2.

A different price reduction potential can be expected for the traditional case in which an innovation competes against the established good. In our standard example, the mature fixed-line technology cannot achieve the same cost reductions as the digital technology of cellular mobile phones after its introduction and adoption in the first market. In the case of competing innovation designs, different price-reductions are possible as well because different technologies could make different economies of scale possible. For instance, digital technology has a larger cost reduction potential than analog technology because digitally integrated electronic

[70] During the substitution process the indifference curve is switched (from I_{lag0} to I_{lag1}), because of an income effect that accompanies the substitution effect. The income effect means that the nominal decrease of the price of one good increases total utility, see Deaton, Muelbauser (1980, p. 35-36).

components have larger economies-of-scale than analog components (see Chapter 4). Incidentally, the lead market is the market that initially favours a technology or product that has the highest price reduction potential.

An example of the price reduction effect over time is depicted in Figure 3-3. Although technology or design A is more expensive than technology or design B and as a result has a lower demand in most countries, it has a larger cost reduction potential after adoption in a lead market. While the price of design B decreases only slightly over time, price reduction of design A is substantial. This leaves A less expensive after some time. As a result, the lag markets start to switch to design A. The time of the switch depends on the share of the users already using B, the switching costs of users in the lag markets and the product life time of B. These factors have to be included in a full model of the international diffusion of an innovation design based on the price-reduction effect.

Figure 3-3: Price paths of the price reduction effect

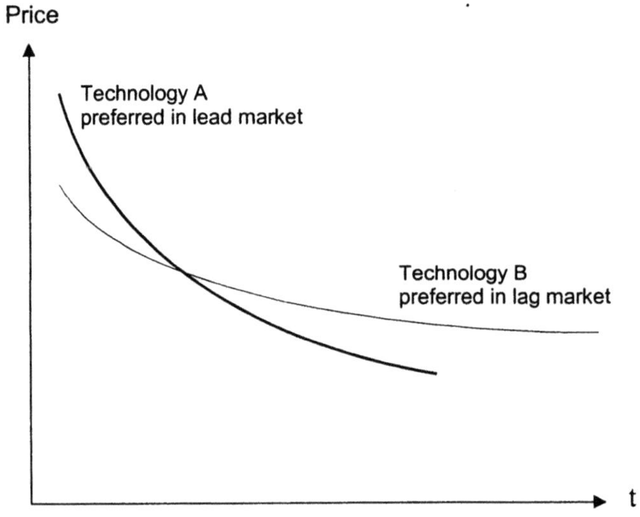

3.1.3 The price-lead effect

In the second case, prices for the two goods are initially different in the two countries but preferences are the same in both countries. Internationally varying relative prices lead to internationally different consumption patterns. Prices can differ from country to country, for instance, because of varying factor costs, high transportation costs, taxes and other governmental regulations or different degrees of competition in country markets. Price changes can differ from country to country as well. In the price-anticipation type of lead markets, price changes occur first in the lead market: the lead market anticipates or foreshadows international relative price changes of goods prevailing in the worldwide. A country can be more advanced in global price trends when domestic competition is more intense than in other countries. Fierce competition pressures firms to lower the price immediately when their factor prices decrease and it pressures them to seek cost reductions wherever possible. If a relative price change over time for one good first occurs in one country then this country will shift consumption earlier than other countries, in which the price changes occur later. Figure 3-4 shows indifference curves that are equal in both countries. Prices for the two goods differ in both countries, which results in the lag country preferring good q_1 and the lead country preferring q_2. Over time the price of good q_2 becomes relatively cheaper in the lag country as well and converge to the price prevailing in the lead market. This price convergence can occur when market restrictions are lowered. This increases the degree of internal competition, when trade is liberalised through the reduction of trade restrictions, when transportation becomes cheaper or when nation-specific governmental regulations are revoked. For instance, trade in services is facilitated by communication technologies such as online services.

In the price-lead mechanism case the lead market is the country where relative price changes occur before they occur in other countries. Figure 3-5 depicts an example of the paths of the relative prices of q_2 in the lag market and the lead market. Over time the relative prices in the lag market converge to the relative prices in the lead market. This results in the same consumption pattern of the lag market that already prevails in the lead market. The figure shows that price trends can even be reversed in the two countries. For instance, the relative price of the

Figure 3-4: Price trend anticipation effect

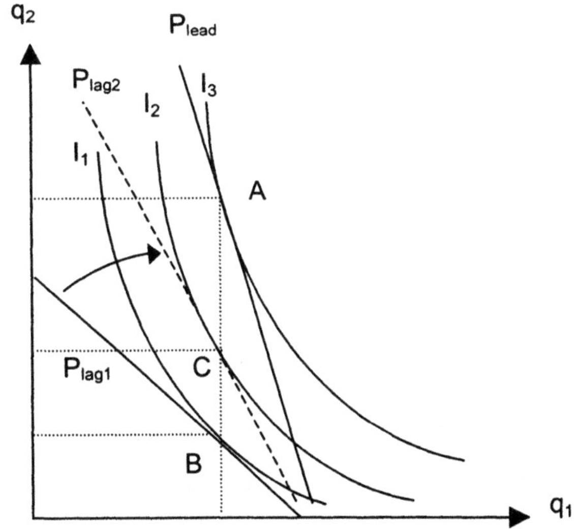

Figure 3-5: Example for national price paths of the price-lead effect

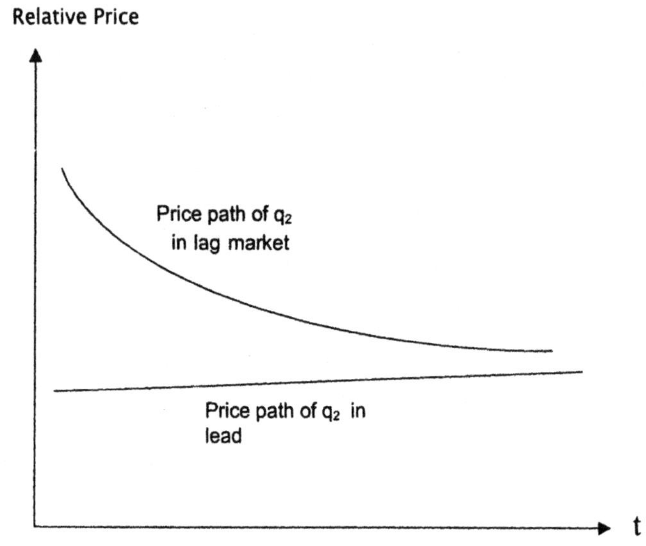

dominant good in the lead market increases slightly while its relative price decreases in the lag market.

3.1.4 The demand-lead effect

In the third case of the time-lead effect, users in the lead market have a higher benefit of q_2 than other countries because of differences in social habits, taste, culture, ecological conditions, political structure or other circumstances. The utility function for q_1 and q_2 can be written as

$$u_{it} = v(q_{1i}, \epsilon_{it}, q_{2i}) \tag{3.4}$$

where ϵ_{it} denotes the international differences of the market context that influence the benefit of specific innovation designs such as the environment or the socio-political system. The index i denotes the country and t indicates that the national context changes over time. If conditions in the lead market emerge in the lag market after a time period as well, so that $\epsilon_{lag,t1} = \epsilon_{lead,t0}$, the benefit pattern of q_1 and q_2 that prevails in the lead market appears in the lag market with a time lag. Then the lead market foreshadows or anticipates the benefit of the innovation in other countries in the future. The increase of benefit of a design in the lag markets can be caused by changes in the lag market environment or post invention improvements. A global trend, for which the lead market is most advanced, causes the benefit of an innovation to emerge in the lead market before it emerges in the lag markets. For instance, if the mobility of consumers increases the utility of mobile communication, the lead market is the market in which the global trend of enhanced mobility is most advanced, i.e. where consumers are most mobile.[71]

Preferences change when the relative benefit of a good changes. Post-invention improvements are common in R&D intensive products and can lead to an increased benefit for users in the lag market. Relative benefit increases of the design preferred in the lead market compared to the design preferred in the lag market lead lag market users to switch from their previously preferred design to the lead market design. In addition, preferences in the lag market can be influenced by the consumer choices of users in the lead market or producers through marketing activities. In this case $\epsilon_{lag,t}$ is a function of the consumption pattern of q_2 and q_1 in the lead market. Economies of adoption that spill over to other countries are global externalities that increase the benefit of an innovation adopted in the lead market for users in lag markets.

Other reasons for the alignment of preferences are global cultural shifts such as westernisation. This is the observed adoption of consumer preferences common in western countries by the younger generations in developing countries that occurs instead of the transmission of local lifestyles from generation to generation. Furthermore, mobile users such as travellers and multinational firms can bring their own preferences across countries. Multinational firms attempt to transfer home market preferences abroad through marketing activities. In addition, literature has been argued that the decision of a user depends not on the utility of an good but on the perceived utility. The perceived utility is influences by observations of other users experience. Often, potential users form their expectations on the usability of an innovation design by communicating with other users.

In these case, a lead market is a country that has the ability to change preferences in other markets. In the mobile communication example, a country that is often imitated could have initiated the mobile telephony boom. It just became "hip" in countries with a dense fixed line telephone net to use mobile phones instead, despite its doubtful additional real benefit. Real benefit of goods and therefore preferences, however, can change with working conditions and lifestyle. Increasing mobility, environmental pollution, and female work participation are global trends that change the preferences of consumers as well as industrial users.

Figure 3-6 depicts this mechanism of relative benefit increases. Preferences in the two countries are initially different because the benefit of the two designs is initially different in the two national environments. Figure 3-6 shows two representative indifference curves for the lead market and the lag market at time t_0. The

71 A trend is the internationalisation mechanism of a nationally preferred innovation. A lead market can also become the lead market when it just happens to have a high benefit from an innovation design because of the special context; e.g. a low density of population makes it more profitable to adopt mobile telephones instead of fixed line telephones.

Figure 3-6: Lead market through utility anticipation

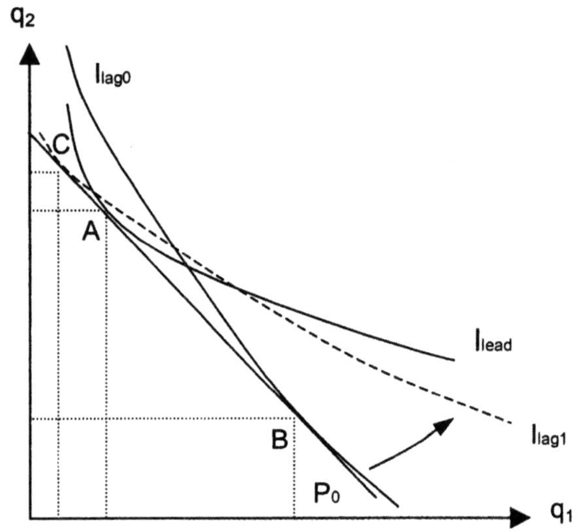

lead market favours product q_2 because of circumstances initially unique to the lead market. In the lag market product q_1 is preferred, q_2 is consumed at a much lower share than in the lead market. Again the lead market is the largest market for product q_2, thus setting the pace for the development and refinement of the product. By $\epsilon_{lag,t}$ converging to $\epsilon_{lead,0}$ over time, the indifference curves of the lag market bend more and more towards the indifference curve system of the lead market at time t=0. Demand for q_2 increases in the lag market from point B to point C, thus reversing the previously prevailing large market share of good q_1 in favour of good q_2. Users in the lead market therefore anticipated the benefit of q_2 for users in other countries. In Figure 3-6 the indifference curve of the lag market bends to the right, meaning that the benefit of good q_1 decreased; the benefit of good q_2 increased only relatively to good q_1. Indeed, a trend can lower the benefit of a design, thus raising the relative benefit of another design. In our example, the increasing mobility of consumers lowers the benefit of a fixed line telephone (q_1), making the mobile phone (q_2) more important as a mean of communication.

3.1.5 The dynamic patterns of the demand-lead effect

Shifting indifference curves to fit the consumption pattern at each time is itself not very persuasive and is apt to become a tautology. It has been argued that a shift of an indifference curve at one tail reflects a change in the relative utility of the good or technological design initially preferred in the lead country for users in the lag market. Changes in the relative benefits of the two goods are followed by adjustments of the consumption of both goods in the markets. If one good increases its utility for users relative to the other good, then users in the market substitute the good that became more beneficial for the other good that became relatively less beneficial. If the good preferred in the lead market continuously increases the relative utility for users in the lag market, it will increase its market share to the point where it finally squeezes out the good initially preferred in the lag market. The relative increase of utility of the lead market good can be caused by several factors that are already mentioned above. In addition there are different patterns of utility increases of the two designs in the lag market that lead to the replacement of the lag market design by the lead market design.

The relative increase of utility in the two period static model can be visualised in a diagram that shows the utility of both goods for users in the lag market over time (Figure 3-7). This model presents three scenarios in which a design preferred by the lead market becomes more beneficial for users in the lag markets than the design initially preferred in the lag market. First, the lead market design increases its utility over time and exceeds that of the lag market design. Second, the lead market design already incorporates features that enhance its utility in the lag market so that the lead market design is almost as beneficial in the lag market as the domestic design of the lag market. And third, users in the lead market find a design by trial that is even better for users in the lag market than the domestic design in the lag market. This can happen when preferences are not perfectly known and more alternatives are offered, tested and evaluated in the lead market because of fierce local competition. The lead market then has a higher probability of finding the most overall beneficial technological design. In the third scenario the initial adoption of innovation designs is actually a supply effect. The designs preferred initially in the lag markets result from the unavailability of better alternatives offered only in the lead market.

The curves I to III in Figure 3-7 denote different utility functions of the lead market designs over time. Curve IV represents the benefit of the technological design that is initially preferred in the lag market. Curve I denotes a design that increases its utility over time for the user in the lag market and exceeds the benefit of the domestic design. In section 3.2 I will divide this effect into the effect of a trend that increases the benefit of a design relative to other designs (demand advantage) and the benefit growth that results from global externalities of the adoption of a design and the transfer of preferences abroad (transfer advantage). Curve II presents the case that the lead market design is initially developed to be beneficial for users in the lag market as well so that the utility is almost as high as the domestic design of the lag market (IV). The difference between II and IV at the time of introduction (A) represents a remainder of the home market advantage of innovations designed for the lag market. The lead market design needs only a little improvement over time to exceed the benefit of the lag market design. The initial offset of utility of the lead market design can be achieved by producers of the lead market through the incorporation of features that make it more beneficial in the lag market. This utility can be described as an export advantage.

Figure 3-7: The three types of a demand-lead effect

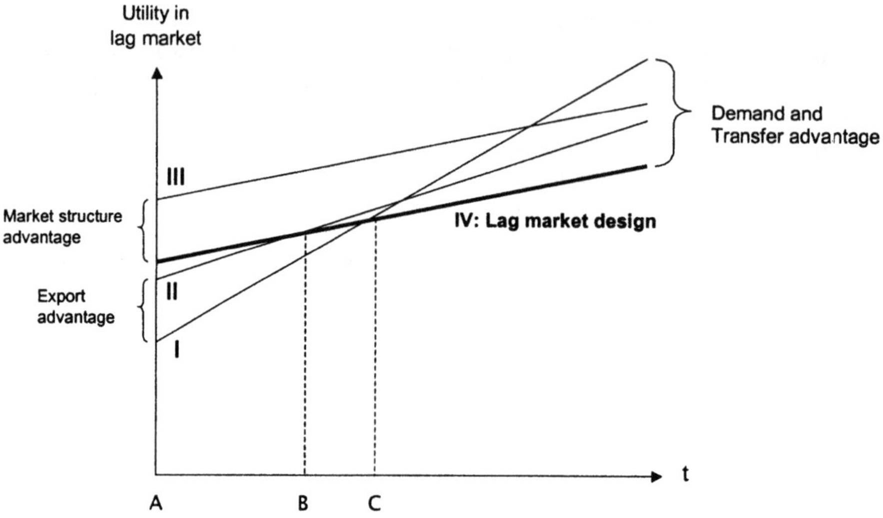

In the first two scenarios the lag market design at time A is more beneficial to users in the lag market, but loses this home market advantage at times B and C respectively. At these points in time, the utility of the lead market design exceeds the utility of the domestic design in the lag market and starts to substitute the domestic design in the lag market.[72] The third scenario is different from the first and second ones and it differs from the demand effect in the static two-period model. But its importance becomes clear in the dynamic model. In contrast to the static model, I now assume that the producers are not perfectly aware of preferences in the markets and that all designs are not equally available in both markets. Users in the lead market and lag market select different technological designs offered in the markets. Each market selects the best design available. In the lead market the design represented by curve III that is even initially more beneficial in both the lead market and lag market than the design selected in the lag market is offered and selected. The reason that this design is offered only in the lead market is either that producers in the lead market have more information on user preferences, are more willing to follow user preferences or competition is higher, so that a larger variety of alternatives compete in the market. The users select the most beneficial one in a market learning process. This supply effect can be called a market structure advantage of the lead market. The technological design IV was initially pre-

---

72 In the comparative static model the substitution process is continuous because it assumes the continuous combination of the two goods and a falling rate of substitution. This can also be interpreted as the heterogeneity of users in the lag market. The utility in the dynamic illustration can then be interpreted as the mean over all users in the lag market.

ferred in the lag market because this was the most beneficial design available in the lag market. If the lead market design had initially been introduced in the lag market as well it would have been adopted and the lag market design would not have been materialised.

3.1.6 The similarity effect

The simple model has demonstrated so far that the phenomenon of lead markets can be explained theoretically by three basic mechanisms: a global growth of income, asymmetric price reductions and asymmetric increases of benefits of competing innovation designs. There is a fourth possible lead market explanation that is central to the traditional market expansion strategy of firms. According to the process theory of internationalisation (Johanson, Vahlne 1977) after innovations have been successfully introduced in the home market they are first introduced in foreign markets that are most similar to the home market in terms of preferences and per-capita-income. The similarity of two countries enhances their mutual intra-industry trade (see section 2.3.3). This trade emerges because of user heterogeneity. This means that a minority of users initially prefers foreign designs to domestic designs.

At first glance, similarity is not an autonomous lead market mechanism, because it is symmetric: none of two similar countries would have an advantage to set a globally dominant design; trade would be balanced within the industry (intra-industry trade). But the international expansion of an innovation design into similar markets can start and reinforce a lead market mechanism described above: a price reduction as a result of economies-of-scale through exports or benefit increases due to global economies-of-adoption. The argument given in this section is therefore a sub-case of both the price-reduction and the demand-lead effect. Together with these reinforcing mechanisms a country can gain an international advantage from similarity to other countries if the degree of similarity is not equal between all countries.

A country that has a market context that is very different from other countries' contexts adopts product designs that are rarely demanded in other countries. There is little foreign demand because products that fit a different context are of little benefit in other environments. These designs often have features that make them more expensive but are of little benefit in foreign environments, e.g. a motor vehicle with air conditioning in a country with a year-round mild climate. Products designed to fit the extreme conditions of a market have a low benefit-price relation in other markets and therefore cannot be easily exported. Export performance can be expected as related to the similarity of the market of origin and the export markets. The more similar the context of a country is to other countries, the more it can export and reap economies of scale and adoption. Markets whose conditions are the average of the conditions of all other country markets are thus expected to have the best export performance. The lead market is the market where preferences are most similar to all other countries. Although it is the same internationalisation mechanism, the character of this lead market type is different in that it is not an extreme country, e.g. most advanced in a global trend, but instead the most average market. What is maximised is not the single characteristic of a market but the degree of similarity of all characteristics relevant for the innovation-environment relationship to all other markets. If the similarity argument holds, the extreme countries are the idiosyncratic country markets prone to lock-in to idiosyncratic innovation designs.

To model the similarity argument I use the consumer model by Lancaster (1981). Lancaster uses product characteristics to model product variety. Product design can be described by a specific set of product characteristics or attributes. Each design can be classified by specific amounts of each attribute. In the international context, we assume that users in different countries prefer a different mix of attributes and therefore different innovation designs. If countries differ in their context of the use of an innovation, there are countries with extreme preferences and countries that lie in the middle between these extremes. Figure 3-8 shows the case of two characteristics z_1 and z_2 of a product and three countries with different preferences described by the indifference curves I_1, I_2 and I_3. The markets of the countries are of equal size. The countries with the indifference curves I_1 and I_3 prefer products C and B respectively with a set of characteristics that are most dissimilar. Trade between these two countries would be low. The country with the indifference curve I_2 prefers product A with the set of characteristics that are more similar to the other two countries' preferred designs. The country that prefers A would be able to export its preferred design to both countries and therefore more in sum than the other two countries. The country that prefers design A would therefore be able to reap more economies of scale and adoption than both other countries. When these economies can compensate the differences between A and B and A and C, the extreme countries switch consumption from their initially preferred set of characteristics to the characteristics of A. Design A is therefore more likely to become the global dominant design than designs B and C. With *n* characteristics the distance of a country's preferred design to the average design could be quantified, for instance, by the Euclidean distance. The lead market is the country with the minimal distance d_i, i.e.

$$\min d_i = \sqrt{\sum_n (z_i - \bar{z})^2} \tag{3.5}$$

In the dynamic model of section 0, the similarity effect is an export advantage because the similarity of context between two countries narrows the gap between the utility of the two national specific designs (II and IV).

Figure 3-8: The lead market as the average market

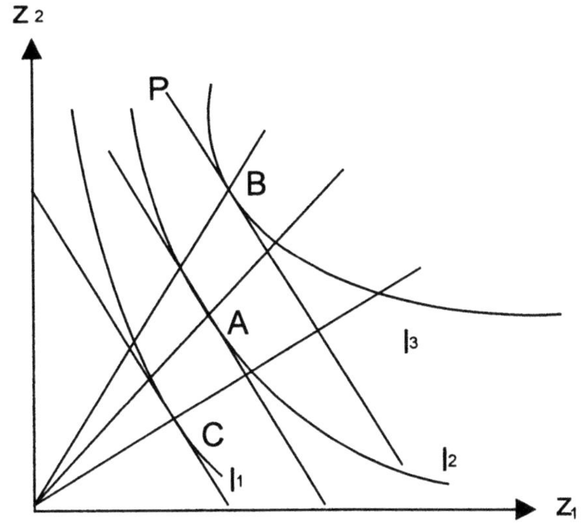

3.1.7 Discussion

The advantage of the theoretical model presented here is that several basically different lead effects can be demonstrated: an income, a price and a demand lead effect. The demand lead effect can be further subdivided into a demand advantage, a transfer advantage and an export advantage plus a market structure advantage, that can be included after the perfect information assumptions of the static model is relaxed. Yet the model presented simply demonstrates different lead market *mechanisms*. It is the aim of the next chapter to present and illustrate the basic country specific characteristics that are behind the lead role of international changes in prices and preferences. The model itself, however, has several shortcomings as well. A problem to be considered here is that preferences for an innovation are probably not given before the full benefit of the innovation is known to potential users. In our example, it can be argued that preferences for mobile phones did not exist in countries where no mobile communications network had been built up. It can be argued that preferences are thus only revealed preferences in the sense of observable purchases of an innovation. Users must be aware of an innovation. After an assessment of its benefits through observation of its usage or test-driving they can form preferences for a new good. Users in foreign countries thus follow a country that first adopts an innovation that proved to be of considerable benefit. This leads to the characterisation of lead countries as country markets that are the first to become aware of the benefit of a new product. The anticipation of the utility of a product would not result from the preferences for that particular innovation but would rather be the result of early awareness of the utility of a new product. These types of lead markets would be markets where a variety of innovations are tested frequently and are compared by innovative domestic users and they are markets that are watched by users in many other countries. Regional incentives for innovations increase with demanding users, competition among users and among producers and other cultural factors such as risk-seeking. These factors have been identified by literature as supporting the "innovativeness" of country markets.

The second problem is that individual users not countries make their choices on the basis of their individual budgets. I use the budget constraint of a country, although there is no single budget of a country. It is assumed that all users in the country have the same budget. In cases of a mass-market product (for which the lead market concept is most interesting) per-capita-income seems to be a sufficient variable for the budget constraint. If income varies within a country, it is useful to interpret the budget constraint as the size-weighted per-capita-income of the potential user group. The distribution of income within a country, however, can be relevant as a lead market factor, too. Some countries have a low per-capita-income but a small fraction of the very rich (e.g. Indonesia) and some have a very evenly distributed income with few consumers who have very large budgets (e.g. Sweden). The relationship between income distribution and lead market function is not clear. On the one hand, a high-income segment in the population induces early demand for superior new goods, allowing firms to introduce the good early and get on the learning curve to lower cost of production over time. On the other hand, the rate of within-diffusion is slower if income is more heterogeneous. This is certainly a point of further research beyond this thesis.

3.2 Lead Market Factors

The purpose of this section is to organise the theoretical lead market mechanisms elaborated on in the first section of this chapter into a practical system of lead factors. Second, this section shall illustrate the factors that are nation-specific and product-specific and that support these international diffusion mechanisms. These factors must be nation-specific and product-specific to explain that a particular country leads the adoption of innovations in a particular product domain. The international cost-benefit patterns underlying the lead effects are formulated as nation-specific characteristics. The nation-specific attributes are identified and finally assigned to five groups of lead market advantages. This assignment has been made according to the theoretical dynamic model as discussed in section 0. This section presents five main groups of nation-specific characteristics, which I call lead market factors, as the determinants of an international diffusion of a domestically preferred innovation design:

1. *Price advantage*. Conditions that result either in relative price decreases of a nationally preferred innovation design compared to designs preferred in foreign markets or in anticipation of international factor price changes.
2. *Demand advantage*. Conditions that result in the anticipation of the benefit of an innovation designs emerging at a global level.
3. *Transfer advantage*. Conditions that increase the perceived benefit of a nationally preferred innovation design for foreign countries or by which national demand conditions are actively transferred abroad.
4. *Export advantage*. Conditions that support the inclusion of foreign demand preferences in nationally preferred innovation designs.
5. *Market structure advantage*. Conditions that increase the level of competition between domestic firms and facilitate low market entry barriers for new firms.

Each group is not necessarily uni-dimensional because each collects a multitude of sub-factors that could be unrelated or even contrasting. These sub-factors are detailed in the following section. The section shows that the lead factors of national markets depend on the economic, social, political, cultural and ecological systems of a nation. In section 3.3.3. I briefly address the influence of a nation's systems on its lead market role. Figure 3-9 depicts the determinants of the complete lead market system. Like the determinants in Porter's diamond, the lead factors interact with each other and with other factors. The relationships between the lead market factors are discussed in section 3.3.1.

Figure 3-9: Overview of lead market factors and related factors of national competitiveness

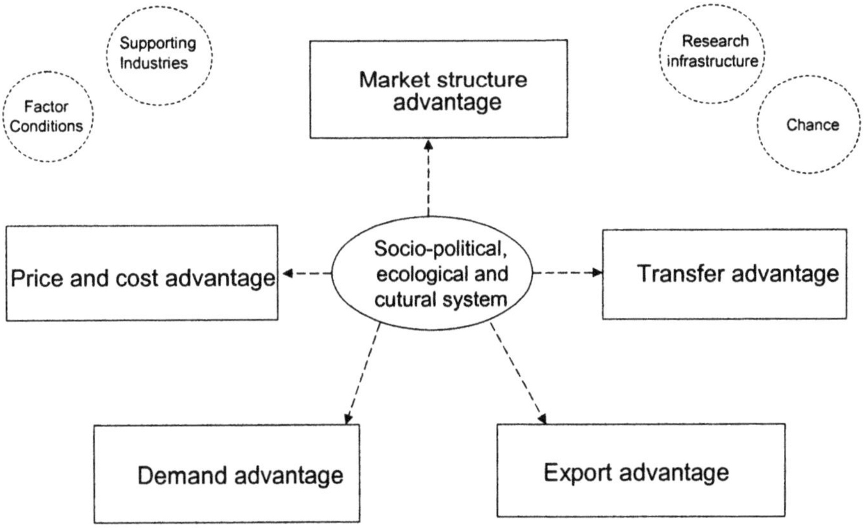

Figure 3-9 includes some of the other factors[73] that are not lead markets factors, but either support the lead market factors or they are the result of the lead market role of a market. For instance, supporting and related industries that are internationally competitive can support the export advantage and therefore the lead market role of a country in an industry. Factor endowments such as physical resources and availability of capital can influence the lead market factors such as the factor price advantage. The availability of financial resources, sources of technical and market knowledge, can support the lead market factors, but they are mainly considered a result of the early adoption of an innovation by a market. In section 3.3 in particular I address the question of how national technical superiority is related to the lead market role of countries. Finally, chance is a determinant of many processes in the economy. As mentioned above (2.4), in models of technical choice under externalities historical accidents are considered mainly responsible for the outcome. Chance controls a basic invention based on serendipity (inventions-by-chance) and oil price shocks, war and political shifts. It can be expected that chance may play a role in the lead market processes as well. The lead market system is therefore not a deterministic theory. However, this thesis is predominantly about nation-specific attributes or "national success factors" that support the lead market function of a country as well. In this chapter I will describe these nation-specific lead factors.

3.2.1 Price advantage

The most powerful means to overcome international demand differences is price. Countries can gain a price advantage if the relative price of the nationally preferred innovation design decreases so that differences in demand preference to foreign countries can be compensated. Price reductions are mainly due to cost reductions based on static and dynamic economies-of-scale. Nation-specific factors of economies-of-scale are market size and market growth. Another price advantage results from price changes of factors complementary to the innovation design that anticipate factor price changes in the lag markets.

Size of demand

The size of the home market provides the economies-of-scale in production and early amortisation of large R&D investments. For instance, the large Japanese market for facsimile machines made it easier for Japanese producers to exploit static and dynamic economies-of-scale (Scherer 1992, p. 101). The cost of machines dropped thirtyfold from 1980 until 1992 (Coopersmith 1993, p. 48). A sufficiently large domestic market enables innovations to be profitable at all for specialised high-tech products with few applications (Kravis, Lipsey 1971). The

---

[73] Porter (1990) suggests these factors as determinants of national competitiveness besides demand conditions. He shows that all factors are interrelated.

size of a market is the volume of sales. For consumer goods the scale of the population and per-capita-income mainly determine it (Kotabe, Helsen 1998, p. 192).[74] For capital goods, market size is the scale of domestic industry that uses the product. The lead market is not always the largest country. First, the customer industry can be large in a small country, e.g. the watch industry in Switzerland. The size of the segment of the population for which the good is designed can vary internationally. Innovations are not initially designed for the mass market but rather to fit a niche market, which can be large in a small country as well. Second, for consumer goods, size of market is determined by the willingness to purchase a new product for a particular price (demand function). Third, the mass market that offers large cost advantages can emerge in a small country. A mass market in a small country can exceed the niche market in a large country, for instance the mobile telephony market in Finland in 1980 was one of the largest in the world.

The price reduction of an innovation design can also result from the falling prices of complementary goods. A lead market can be the country where the complementary good is initially cheaper and falls in the price in other countries as a result of the adoption of an innovation in the lead market. The price of the complementary good can fall internationally when economies-of-scale in the production of the complementary good can be exploited as the result of the adoption in the lead market. Adoption of an innovation in a large market encourages additional investments to produce the complementary good or input factor are only made when the innovation is adopted. For instance, the widespread adoption of fuel-efficient vehicles in one country would increase the incentives for a raw material supplier to exploit new deposits of very light raw materials such as magnesium. As a result, the innovation design that has a higher cost reduction potential of complementary goods garners an international price advantage. In sum, a larger market can be expected to induce a larger cost reduction potential of the innovation or the complementary goods.

Growth of market

The growth of market has been suggested to be a decisively pushing demand for innovations since Schmookler's (1966) hypothesis that growth of demand is an incentive for firms to turn out more innovations. When demand grows, many new adopters, who are not inhibited from adopting an innovation by brand loyalty and switching costs, can be attracted for the newest of products. Growth therefore raises the incentives for adoption of innovations in a product domain with high

74 Market potential is likely to be influenced by several other structural indicators of a regional market as well. Demand for a particular good can be closely related to a set of demographic, socio-economic, and cultural variables that can be used to estimate the country market potential, see Kotabe, Helsen (1998, pp. 166-172).

switching costs.[75] The growth of demand has a direct cost effect: The cost of a new technology is higher for the potential adopter if existing production techniques have to be replaced than if new capacity has to be deployed. In addition, faster growth will lower the risk of producers making full use of new investments (Porter 1990, p. 94).[76] A weak positive effect of market growth on diffusion rate has been found for new steel making processes (Poznanski 1983, p. 319).

A high diffusion rate at the time of the market introduction of an innovation gives a country market a lead in cost reduction because these markets are at the same time likely to be among the largest markets during the introduction phase regardless of the size of the country. Among innovation designs that are initially adopted in different countries at the same time, the design preferred in the country with a high diffusion rate could gain a cost advantage over designs preferred in markets with lower diffusion rates unless the economies-of-scale gained in large countries do not compensate for their slower diffusion. The innovation design preferred locally in a fast growing country market gets a head start in moving down the learning curve. The relationship between lead markets and the rate of diffusion, however, is ambiguous. Literature does not present general evidence that the countries that adopted an internationally successful innovation design were attributed with the highest diffusion rates among the group of countries that adopted nation-specific designs. In contrast, the national learning hypothesis mentioned in 2.5.1 suggests that the rate of diffusion increases with the time lag of national diffusion, meaning that the lead market generally has a lower diffusion rate. Yet this international learning hypothesis is neither convincingly empirically confirmed.[77] Cross-border diffusion studies testing determinants of the diffusion rate (see 2.5.1) find some significant positive effects of general nation-specific attrib-

---

[75] Ohmae (1985) warns, however, that higher growth of demand is not enough on its own, but instead has to be accompanied by a sufficient size of demand since developing nations often have high growth rates but much smaller market sizes.

[76] There is an opposite argument noted by Maddala and Knight (1967). Falling growth can spur the introduction of innovations "shelved" by producers to attract new buyers. In marketing this is known as a relaunch of stagnating products. The automobile industry is an example for this argument. It refers, however, more to the growth of demand for a specific brand and not for the total industry.

[77] Diffusion studies by Ganesh et al. (1997), Putsis et al. (1997) and Takada and Jain (1991) support the hypothesis of a learning effect or experience effect among lag countries (Dekimpe et al. 1998c). A lag market should have higher rates of diffusion because users in lag markets have more information on a new product and thus more confidence in the benefit of a new product because it was already tested in the lead market. Other authors found that the diffusion rate decreases the higher the diffusion lag (e.g., Poznanski 1983; Antonelli 1986). Benvignati (1982) explains this with the positive effect of proximity between R&D and users on the diffusion rate: domestic innovations are more suitable to domestic user needs and therefore diffuse faster domestically. The slower diffusion rate emerges when a country adopts a foreign design. Then the learning argument is neutralised as a lead market effect in the presence of national varying contexts.

utes on innovation diffusion rates such as cosmopolitanism, mobility and per-capita income (see Ihde 1996, Kumar et al. 1998 for reviews). Deaton and Muellbauer (1980) suggest that the higher the equality of income within a country the higher the rate of diffusion within this country. These nation-specific attributes of innovativeness, however, are not very useful for explaining the lead market role of certain countries for particular innovations.

Anticipatory factor costs

The second price advantage is the price lead effect: prices of innovation designs converge to the price pattern initially prevailing in the lead market. The most important reason for the price lead advantages is a time lag in global changes of factor prices for input factors of production of a technological design or for the use of a good such as the fuel to power a vehicle (different degrees of domestic competition can cause internationally varying prices as well, but shall be discussed in section 3.2.5). When these global changes in factor prices initially occur in a country (the country "anticipates" global prices trends) it can adjust to the new factor cost earlier than other countries. According to the induced innovation theory, these adjustments consists of the development of new products and processes that economise the factor that became relatively more expensive or used more of the factor that became relatively cheaper. Anticipatory factor price changes induce innovation designs that are initially country-specific but fit to global market needs when factor prices in foreign markets reach the level that induced the innovation in the lead market. Then foreign demand shifts from domestic designs to the foreign design that already had a head start. The price changes can be exogenous, such as a global trend towards scarcity of a good, or they can be endogenous (caused by the lead market itself) resulting from the adoption of an innovation design in a country itself. The latter is equal with the price reduction potential of a complementary good, as mentioned above.

The anticipatory factor price theory seems to be important for new process technologies and capital goods. A country where labour costs are at such high levels that machinery firms concentrate their innovation efforts on automating machinery will then be a lead market if other countries follow the trend of raising labour costs relatively to the cost of other factors. Price differences from country to country are frequent in non-tradable goods, such as labour and business services, because transport costs, duties and the access to raw materials play a waning role in the national price of factor costs. Price differences often result from political decisions such as the level of taxes. For instance, a country where the use of the environment becomes more expensive, e.g. because pollution is highly taxed, will be a lead market for environmental conserving technology if other countries follow the front-runner in valuing the environment as highly. The role of policies to create a lead market role will be discussed in Chapter 7.

3.2.2 Demand advantage

A national demand advantage results from local conditions that facilitate the anticipation of the benefit of nationally preferred innovation designs in foreign markets. Central to this internationalisation-of-design-mechanism is a global trend in which specific innovations become increasingly beneficial or preferable in most countries. Lead markets are at the forefront of the international trend. Users of a country are at the forefront of a trend either because they have the highest income or the national context foreshadows global environmental changes or the accumulation of complementary assets, such as infrastructure, are most advanced in this country. The demand advantage is rather exogenous, meaning that the global trend occurs independent from the adoption decision of the lead market. The case in which firms of one country transfer domestic needs or influences decisions of foreign countries (adoption, creation of infrastructure) will be discussed as *transfer advantage* below.

Income

The income-lead effect is the basic internationalisation mechanism of Vernon's international product-life-cycle described in section 2.6.1 and falls within the demand advantage: Innovations are demanded first in countries in which the personal income is highest.[78] High per-capita-income reflects a greater willingness to pay for new products and a lead in economic living-standards that foreshadows the future global demand. Since other countries will catch up in per-capita-income the demand is likely to emerge there but with a time lag. This mechanism, however, is limited to innovations that are highly superior goods. For instance, as income increases the preference for convenience innovations increases because the marginal benefit of other goods is smaller than the marginal benefit of convenience. The share of consumption of such innovations increases with income. The lead market is the country with the highest income within the potential user group.

Although the convergence between the many industrialised countries has left very small differences in per-capita-income, the income of certain user groups can still considerably vary between countries. For example, the disposable income of young persons, the elderly, the unemployed, the wealthy, women and chronically ill persons can vary between countries more than the per-capita-income of coun-

[78] The international product-life-cycle suggested that many commercially successful innovations were developed in the United States in the first half of the twentieth century because the per-capita-income in the United States was the highest in the world (Vernon 1971). As other countries caught up and reached the level of per- capita-income that the United States had at the time the innovation was demanded in the United States, the same demand for the new product emerged in these markets as well. In general, the wealth of a nation has frequently been empirically proven to have a positive effect on the rate and time of adoption (see the literature review by Dekimpe et al. 1998c).

tries. These specific international income differences depend on varying national socio-economic systems such as the social security systems, gender roles and the share of employment of women.[79]

Anticipatory needs

Demand preferences change over time and are caused by changes in the environment, in the economy or in culture. Changes in the demand context result in new needs and this induces innovations. This is the classical *demand-pull* hypothesis of technical change (cf., Thirtle, Ruttan 1987, p. 8). If these environmental changes are a global trend, the demand for innovations responding to the change will emerge first in those countries where the change occurred initially or where the trend is most advanced. I call the demand of the country where the changes first occur anticipatory demand, without assuming awareness in the country that their needs are at the forefront of a global trend. In general, anticipatory needs of domestic buyers are needs that will subsequently emerge (automatically) in other countries as well and prevail worldwide.

Global trends can occur in technological, economical, social and environmental contexts. For instance, population growth or the increase of population density in cities are global trends and affect some cities earlier more than others. Population density problems occur in highly populated regions early and foreshadow a global problem. Demand for innovations that ease problems caused by high population density, such as traffic congestion and the high cost of real estate is greatest in highly populated regions. Other global trends that occur in certain countries first are the cost of environmental pollution, an increase in life expectancy and thus in the number of elderly people, individual mobility, and information needs and the number of diseases caused by civilisation. Global trends can be consumer trends or mere fads as well. For instance, there are global trends towards fat-free food, high quality pet food or plant extracts in shampoos.

When problems occur in other countries as well, firms that have responded to the demand in the country where the problem occurred first have garnered a competitive advantage over other firms. They have collected rich experiences in the functionality and production of the innovation and it is likely that they have already refined the innovation design into a reliable product. Static and dynamic economies-of-scale are pioneer advantages. According to the home market advantage, domestic firms are more suited to respond to new local needs. As a result, firms in

[79] In addition, the internationalisation mechanism demonstrates, that innovations that target a low income user group in fast growing countries such as the newly industrialised countries in Southeast Asia are likely to get superseded by product designs that were developed in response to demand from high income users (as happened in Europe after the world war with the 'Ersatz'-products, when income rose continuously). Therefore firms in developing countries do not gain a competitive advantage if they develop innovations for the present income level in their countries.

the lead market gain an international advantage. Imitations of firms in the countries where the need occurs later can be pre-empted by the pioneer firms with direct investments in these countries (Vernon 1966).

Anticipatory availability of complementary goods

The availability of complementary goods increases the benefit of an innovation (see 2.4.2). The benefit of an innovation design is highest in the country that offers the largest stock of complementary goods. The innovation is therefore more likely to be adopted in the country with the largest collateral asset stock. If other countries increase their stock of complementary goods over time to the same level, the innovation becomes adopted more widely there as well. Complementary goods can be innovation-design-specific. When a collateral asset is created it increases the benefit of certain designs more than other designs. For instance, a dense network of highways increases the utility of a street vehicle, as well as a dense distribution network of gas stations. A new design, for example an electric vehicle or a car powered by hydrogen, requires a network of recharge stations. As these networks are created the benefit of the new vehicle design increases. The availability of complementary goods has the same benefit- increasing effect of new innovation designs. Easy access to and the variety of videocassettes for VCRs together with new applications such as at-home aerobics were responsible for the high diffusion of VCRs in the United States (Rosenbloom, Cusamano 1987). As videocassettes became available in other countries through the creation of a retail infrastructure, the benefit of VCRs increased there, too.

The creation of complementary assets is not always a direct response to the introduction of innovations. Complementary assets that have been designed for other applications can nevertheless facilitate the adoption of innovation designs not directly related to them. Complementary goods can include information and telecommunication infrastructure, retail networks and other types of infrastructure. New innovations use these general assets. For instance, purchases via the internet were facilitated by the use of credit cards. Countries in which credit cards are more common have a lead in the adoption of e-commerce services over other countries in which credit cards are slowly taking off (Economist 1998).

Complementary goods can come in the form of general or specific education and experiences. Education of users and employees can improve the ability of consumers and firms to use an innovation. For instance, a more computer literate population, resulting from the deployment of computers at work, is more apt to adopt computer based services within its private consumption. User know-how can increase the utility of a good. Past experiences with similar products have increased knowledge on how to use a product efficiently. Users in other countries with less experience have to learn more about the efficient use of an innovation design than more experienced countries. Learning effects among succeeding generations of an innovation lead to the persistence of lead markets (3.4.2).

Again, for all complementary goods to induce internationally successful innovation designs a global trend is needed to internationalise the preferences of certain countries abroad. On the other hand, idiosyncratic complementary goods can lead to the adoption of idiosyncratic innovation designs. A country that has created an infrastructure and other complementary goods that are not part of a global trend are prone to prefer and lock in to idiosyncratic designs.

3.2.3 Transfer advantage

The demand advantage emerges from an exogenous global trend independent of the actual adoption of innovations in the lead market. But country markets for innovations do not always develop independently. The adoption of one innovation design in one country can influence the adoption decisions of users in other countries because the perceived benefit of an adopted design increases for users in other countries. The perceived benefit increases when information on the usability of the innovation design is made available. Information on the innovation not only enhances the awareness of the innovation design but also reduces the uncertainty surrounding new products and processes. The reputation and sophistication of a user can be a signal for the quality of an innovation design. International externalities, such as increasing-returns of adoption, increase the core benefit of an innovation design. In addition, the preference for a design can be actively transferred abroad. A country can have a transfer advantage if its market context supports increases in the perceived benefit of a nationally preferred innovation design for users in foreign countries.

The international demonstration effect

The adoption of an innovation design in one country increases awareness and generates information on the benefit of the innovation design. If several countries adopt different innovation designs at the same time, a higher international observability of a country's adoption is an advantage for that country, because the likelihood that other countries adopt the same design is higher than that of other countries' designs. Diffusion theory suggests that the international diffusion of durable goods depends on the intensity of communication between two countries (Takada, Jain 1991). The lead market could therefore be the country that has the strongest communication ties with other countries, the country that sits in the centre of a star-shaped communication network. Lead countries are those that are generally watched by many other countries, for instance, countries that are intensively covered by mass media or those life styles are often present in television series and motion pictures. In the international diffusion of innovation context, the "demonstration effect" (Mansfield 1968) becomes an international "lead effect" (Kalish et al. 1995). Potential adopters in a second country would observe the success of the innovation in the first market earlier than the success of innovations adopted in other, not so keenly watched countries.

Putsis et al. (1997) show that the number of cross-border communication ties are not equally distributed among nations and are not symmetrical. A case study included in Nabseth and Ray (1974, p. 115) demonstrates that users get information on new innovations of a product domain from preferred countries. In the case study on special presses for the paper industry information flowed from the United States to Sweden, from Sweden to Germany and from Germany to Austria, resulting in a similar international rank of adoption.

An analogy of the phenomenon of a country as a source of information on innovations for many other countries can be drawn from the theory of opinion leadership. Opinion leaders are individuals or firms whose input is commonly sought by others during the selection decision because of their knowledge or expertise (Rogers 1995). Opinion leaders can influence others' opinions about the innovations. Nations, regional markets or dominant users in a country could become international opinion leaders who are sought by users in other countries because of their high experience and reputation. Often a leading role in terms of technology or adoption in the main or preceding technology constitutes a reputation for the succeeding technology. The United States was the undisputed lead market for mainframe computers for a long time when it became the lead market for personal computers. In consideration of a still uncertain future of the coming PC standard, users around the world were prone to choose a US design, notably when the most reputed computer firm, IBM, offered its own line of PCs. By introducing its own design, IBM endorsed the PC as a viable commercial product (Freiberger, Swaine 1984).

In addition, peer pressure can lead countries to adopt a new technology or build the infrastructure necessary for it in order to belong to a club of countries. For instance, an innovation design such as a high-speed-train or a mobile cellular network can become "a must have" even for less developed countries. Influencing other nations' demands means "bending" other local demand preferences in favour of its own features. Another example is taste. Cultures vary in their tastes, but US food companies such as McDonald's, Dunkin'Donuts and Coca-Cola managed to change their different tastes into one global taste, sometimes by marginally adjusting the product into the global standard.[80]

Uncertainty reduction

The adoption of an innovation is associated with uncertainty about the usefulness of the innovation and a risk of failure. An adoption demonstrates the reliability of

[80] Ohmae (1985) gives one example for this. The cinnamon content in donuts sold in Japan was continually increased to the levels common in the United States to make Japanese customers accustomed to it (Ohmae 1985, p. 124). Yet local nuances in the taste of almost all "global" products still exist while the overall core of the product is still global (Keegan, Green 1997, p. 5). Marketing at least still has to adapt products for regional markets, which is expressed in the famous phrase "think globally and act locally".

the innovation design. The adoption of an innovation design by users of a country can reduce the uncertainty about the risk of failure for users in other countries adopting the same design. The reduction of uncertainty increases the likelihood of additional adoptions if potential adopters can observe the success of an innovation design. The reduction of uncertainty about the benefit of a new technology was identified in section 2.3.1 as a factor leading to a dominant design. This risk reduction mechanism can be a driver of a global dominant design as well. The failure of innovations can even result in personal injuries. Uncertainty and risk is lowered the more users adopt the innovation and prove its benefit and reliability. The choice of the proved foreign technology would be rational even if the foreign design does not fit domestic context and if domestic design were theoretically better except for the price of higher risk of failure. Risk reduction can compensate unsuitability up to a point. The risk reduction behaviour of lag countries is especially relevant when the risk and complexity of a new technology is high.

Although the demonstration effect alone does not explain the choice of a country to switch from one design to the global dominant design, because a user has full information of the benefit of an innovation design after adopting an innovation, uncertainty reduction effects can. In the model (see 2.4.2) uncertainty is reduced after each adoption. If the use of innovation is associated with high failure risk and large learning effects, the relative uncertainty of a design adopted more widely decreases and it therefore becomes more attractive than another designs. Taking the same example as presented in section 2.4.2 the light-water nuclear reactor prevailed in many countries despite the fact that other more unreliable designs were tested there as well. Reliability of a design can compensate for initial international differences in preferences. A tested design becomes preferred against an untested design that better suits the local context, i.e. has a higher real benefit, but for which the benefit is uncertain.

A bandwagon market is one characteristic of the lead market because it reduces the uncertainty of the benefits of the technology employed and signals other markets that it is valuable and standardised, and cured of teething troubles. International differences in the product liability law[81] and governmental safety regulation, too, play a role in the international allocation of risk. A strict national safety regulation signals a lower risk of the nationally preferred design to foreign countries.

---

[81] Product liability is the risk for the producing firm involved in the introduction of an innovation to the market. Product liability jurisdiction varies from country to country but it is still disputed which jurisdiction lowers the innovativeness of countries. In the United States precedents show an ever-increasing risk for the producer of goods if personal injuries are possible even if the goods pass governmental safety tests. This means that producers are more reluctant to offer an unproved innovation, but follow another country quickly when it has proved the reliability of a particular design or the firm can use the foreign records to exculpate itself. The car airbag is one example for this behaviour. It was adopted in the United States after it showed its general reliability in Europe.

The US Food and Drugs Agency (FDA) sets the standards for clinical testing procedures and approval for other countries and acts as a global trendsetter (Jungmittag et al. 2000, p. 184). An additional factor is the international reputation of a country. Reputation and experience can signal a lower risk of adoption of the same design to firms in other countries.

Uncertainty reduction mechanisms can also apply between large and small firms. Larger firms are supposed to adopt a new technique earlier than small firms because the risk associated with the adoption of a new technique is relatively smaller for a larger firm than for a smaller firm (Edquist, Jacobsson 1988, p. 10). In this model smaller firms follow larger firms after larger firms have evaluated the merits of the new technique. A country with a large share of large firms would thus have a lead advantage over countries with a large share of smaller firms.

Global and local externalities

As discussed in section 2.4 externalities increase the benefit of an innovation's design during the diffusion process. The benefit of many innovation designs increase with the number of adopters. For instance, as computers of a particular operation system are adopted more software becomes available for this standard. Global externalities are benefit enhancements beneficial for all potential users worldwide. Local externalities increase the benefit of a design with the number of adopters within a specific user group only, such as friends, colleagues and relatives. In section 2.4.3 I argued that externalities generated by the adoption process of an innovation design are normally strong within countries and that externalities are often not effective enough to cross national borders. For instance, the adoption of the facsimile machine in Japan did not increase the benefit of a facsimile machine for a potential adopter in Europe but rather only for Japanese users. These national-local externalities often lead to nation-specific standards and the lock-in of a country to an idiosyncratic innovation design. A national transfer advantage is gained when the diffusion process in a country generates global externalities or local externalities that can cross borders. Global externalities are generated if the product improvements are not concentrated on specific features of the design that are only preferred by domestic users but are of interest for all users. To repeat the example given before, perfection of the air conditioning system in a motor vehicle is of little interest for most users in Europe and Japan, while enhancing the reliability of a vehicle is of general interest. Second, global increasing returns of adoption are generated by international compatibility. Innovation designs are not always internationally compatible even when they are introduced in several countries. International incompatibility inhibits global externalities. A country that prefers a design that offers international compatibility could increase global externalities. For instance, digital technology is more compatible in general. Local externalities can cross borders when international communication ties are strong. A country would have a lead advantage if it were the centre of an international communications network, which is the same success factor of the demonstration effect.

When there are large economies of adoption, a potential user of a new technology who is able to choose among domestic and foreign designs, can be expected to choose strategically. Large economies-of-scale and increasing returns of adoption would lead a potential adopter to expect the emergence of an internationally dominant design. The common strategy for a firm is either a wait-and-see position or the selection of the design that is most likely to become the dominant design even if this design is not the technically superior one (Tirole 1988, p. 405). In a situation with large economies-of-scale firms form expectations that the national design become dominant worldwide. The expectations can be influenced by all factors discussed previously as the lead market factors, such as size of market, availability of complementary goods and reputation.[82] Thus, the strategic behaviour of firms in the adoption of technology would self-reinforce some national lead market factors.

Structure and sophistication of demand

Porter (1990) already points out that it is not only the quantity, but also the *quality* of the home demand that determines the international competitive advantage of a nation. Therefore, even a small country with a small market size can achieve a competitive advantage in certain segments. The quality of home demand can be interpreted as information from users on the specification of an innovation based on users' competence, know-how and former experience with related products or processes.[83] Porter mentions three attributes of the quality of demand that give local countries an international competitive advantage: segment structure, sophistication and anticipation. In the context of the global diffusion of innovations, anticipation has been described in this thesis as a demand advantage. I suggest that the structure and sophistication of demand is a transfer advantage because the main internationalisation mechanism of both demand attributes is the increase of the perceived benefit of a domestic design for users in other countries.

The segment structure of a country market shapes the attention and priorities of a nation's firms. Demand segments look more profitable for firms in countries in which these segments have a larger share of domestic demand than in other countries and thus receive higher priority in allocating resources for innovations. For instance, the nation's best engineers are working on new solutions in these segments. A higher consumption share of a good in a country means a higher prefer-

---

82 If all firms form the same expectations about the lead markets and the future global dominant design, the lead market can indeed become a self-fulfilling prophecy.

83 User competence and former experience are also regarded as the main determinants of "innovativeness" of users, i.e. the degree to which users adopt an innovation earlier than other potential users, see Hirschman (1980) and Link (1997).

ence for the good. It can be expected that consumers who spend a higher share of their income on a specific good are more sensitive towards the quality of the product, more willing to buy innovations and that they have a higher product comprehension and are more competent in evaluating innovations.[84] The competence and knowledge of users can be defined as sophistication.

Sophistication of demand means that users are competent in using innovations of a specific domain. If domestic buyers are more sophisticated and demanding than buyers in other countries, then they "pressure domestic producers to meet high standards in quality, features and service" (Porter 1990, p. 89). Producers also perceive new needs in their domestic markets earlier than in other countries. Experience and knowledge about products of a domain help manufacturers to develop a better design. Competence leads to a faster new product evaluation by the market. User knowledge increases the benefit of an innovation. Users accumulate know-how about the use of goods and give the producer feedback on how to improve them. Faster learning processes by producers through learning-by-doing and learning-by-using lead to cost advantages and quality enhancement through refinement in a user-producer interaction as outlined by Lundvall (1988). Lag markets, in contrast, are often inhibited by close links of producers with non-innovative customers that could weaken the competence of producers (Dosi 1988, p. 356). Internationally, sophistication of demand of a country lowers the uncertainty of innovation designs preferred there, signals quality and is an attribute of national reputation. Other markets follow because the attributes of the country are taken as a proxy of quality and benefit.[85]

It has been suggested that innovators as well as demanding users are more willing to pay for an innovation. Gerybadze et al. (1997, p. 209) suggest that a low price-elasticity of demand is a lead market attribute. Yet the willingness to pay a high price could make the innovation too expensive for users in other countries. If the quality demanded by the average customer in one country exceeds the quality demanded in all other markets, products from the high-quality country might not fit the world demand. Products that meet the local high-quality standard could be too expensive, i.e. they could exceed the price-quality ratio of the marginal customer at the point of market share in most foreign markets that is sufficient to dominate competitors' products. German products, for instance, are often described as "over-engineered" and fitting only minor applications in markets with a

---

84 In pricing theory it is commonly assumed that the willingness to seek information on the quality of a product compared to alternatives increases with the share of income the product cost, see Nagle, Holden (1995, p. 103).

85 One example is given by Kotabe, Helsen (1998, pp. 228-9). Procter and Gamble developed a substitute for phosphate to match the German customer demand concerned with the pollution of rivers and they developed a surfactant to remove grease effectively in tepid water that the Japanese use to wash their clothes. Despite the local responsiveness origin of these innovations, Procter and Gamble was able to market these innovations worldwide.

lower-than-average willingness to pay for quality.[86] The German high-speed train, ICE, which had to meet extensive quality targets imposed by the state-owned railway company, proved to be too costly for the world market. Ohmae (1985, p. 119) describes Japanese customers as among the most demanding and that sometimes this demand is highly idiosyncratic, as is the case in their demand for food products or cosmetics.

An additional argument against the low price elasticity attribute of lead markets is that the competence of users increases the price sensitivity.[87] Link (1997) argues that there might be different types of early adopters of innovations. Competent users have a high price awareness and are not biased towards the quality signalling effect of price. On the contrary, the first adopters (innovators) are often almost obsessed with adopting an innovation (Rogers 1995, p. 248) and are more willing to pay for innovation. They are price-blind and take the price as a proxy for quality, which results in a snob effect: demand increases when prices increase. The competent user not only knows more about what constitutes an innovation design but he knows the fair price as well because former experiences with similar products form reference prices. A lead market is characterised by the competent users, whereas the obsessed innovators are more like the first user of an idiosyncratic market, demanding overly engineered innovations.[88]

The price-lowering effect of user competence is an argument that shows that Levitt's (1983) low-price argument, incorporated in the price advantage as a lead market factor, is not basically opposed to the sophistication of demand argument.[89] Levitt's low-price argument, however, seems more applicable to products

---

86 See e.g. press reports in Chemical Week (1996) and Economist (1996). Christensen (1997) describes this as performance oversupply: technologies exceeded the performance demanded by most of the users who subsequently switched to a cheaper and simpler technology that remained inferior to the first technology but, over time, reached the performance demanded by most of the market. He calls the second technology disruptive. It is first adopted by a newly emerging application and later spreads to other traditional applications.

87 As has been mentioned before (Fn. 84) the share of income a product cost increases the information a consumer is willing to gather information on the quality of the innovation and its alternatives. This increases price sensitivity (Gabor, Granger 1966).

88 Douglas and Wind (1987) point to empirical evidence that shows that product quality is an important market success factor even in developing countries. In addition, it is much easier for a producer to downgrade a sophisticated product to lower quality levels for foreign markets that are more price sensitive (Hill, Still 1984) than it is to upgrade a low-quality product to fit sophisticated demand in foreign countries. In addition, the loss of reputation is hard to recover.

89 Low price-elasticity of demand as a feature of lead-market demand is therefore ambiguous. In addition, although a low price-elasticity raises the incentives for product innovations,because new products can be introduced in the market at higher prices, incentives for process innovations, on the other hand, decrease with the price elasticity. Furthermore, low price elasticity can lower the product quality because by reducing the

with a general high price-elasticity of demand and for which quality either plays a minor role for customers or does not vary much. If quality is an important attribute or if the worldwide customer base is oriented more externally, the most demanding market is a lead market. Quality is maximised by customers if the risk of non-performance is high and involves humans at risk and in defence systems (see e.g. Cvar 1986). Cvar (1986) presents other examples of an internationally successful high-quality strategy. Medical equipment was tailored to the most demanding countries, but nevertheless sold as globally standardised products, although the standards were more stringent than was necessary for most other markets. The company was able to educate other markets, i.e. doctors and nurses in developing countries, to accept more sophisticated items and thus maintained a consistent high-quality image worldwide with a medical customer base that had become more cosmopolitan and homogeneous worldwide.

Proprietary technologies

Proprietary innovation designs are often disadvantaged in the international diffusion against non-proprietary designs. First of all, non-proprietary standards can be imitated by other firms and therefore disseminated broader (Anderson, Tushman 1990). Second, proprietary standards are expected to improve less over time than non-proprietary or open designs. Users are often very creative in improving an innovation design after market introduction. Open designs can be more easily improved by many other producers and users, not only by the firm that owns the property rights of a design. Third, the willingness to adopt a foreign design often decreases with an increasing degree of property of technology. Nations are often reluctant to adopt a standard that is seen as the property of foreign firms. National property is signalled by high governmental subsidies and the adoption of an innovation design by state-owned firms. Public subsidies shall favour domestic firms and are often interpreted as international rent-shifting behaviour of governments (Brander, Spencer 1985). For instance, for a long time the Franco-German relationship was marked by the choice of different national standards (colour television systems, high speed trains) because of a mutual reluctance to choose the standards of the other country. A country has a transfer advantage if it prefers a design that is more non-proprietary in character or that is not labelled by governmental influence. Non-proprietary technologies, however, often require governmental regulation that in turn intensify the national label of a technology. For instance, a national standardisation body that formulates a non-proprietary standard is at the same time labelling the standard as national. Designs that are selected by the domestic market rather than by the government are more non-

quality, a monopolist, which innovators frequently are, can save on costs without losing as much revenue as with more price-elastic demand. For a discussion, see Tirole (1988, p. 100).

national in character. Countries that adopt designs that are standardised by international standardisation bodies can gain a transfer advantage.

Multinational firms and mobile users

I mentioned in Chapter 2 that multinational firms often transfer products and technologies abroad through massive worldwide marketing investments and internal technology transfers. They are regarded as *cross-cultural change agents* (Fayerweather 1969, p. 216). Investments by multinational firms abroad could thus change foreign preferences in favour of preferences in the home market of the firm. Large marketing investments often have the purpose of changing local attitudes in order to establish a standardised product in foreign countries.[90] Others have pointed to the limited power of marketing activities to change local preferences (Kotler 1978, p. 286). A greater effect can be expected from multinational firms' worldwide employment of the same components and other input factors within the group of affiliates. Multinational firms can exploit economies-of-scale by using the same input factors and processes worldwide. For instance, using the same software is necessary for an internal communication network and the exchange of standardised corporate information. Foreign affiliates of multinational firms transfer home preferences abroad. In addition, multinational firms train local managers to represent a coherent firm philosophy (Kumar 1982, p. 162; Kreutzer 1989, p. 47) often reflecting the home market preference context (e.g., a preference for quality, reliability, high-tech). Multinational firms can also play a role in harmonising regulation of countries in that they pressure governments to introduce a common regulatory framework in order to secure the standardisation of its products (Bennett 1991, p. 228). This issue of policy convergence is addressed in the next section. A country has therefore a transfer advantage if it is the home country of many multinational firms. On the contrary, a country is disadvantaged if it is a host country of multinational firms.

Mobile users, too, transfer preferences abroad. Mobile buyers who travel extensively to other countries, such as businessmen, tourists and military personnel, can transfer their home-specific demand to foreign countries and initiate the adoption by domestic users.[91] The other direction is that foreign buyers, who travel, study or work in a foreign market, take foreign markets' domestic consumer habits back to their home market (e.g., espresso cafe, liquor, fashion).

---

90 For instance, Procter & Gamble, a large American producer of household products, was accused of trying to make consumers in less developed countries feel guilty if they did not use new cleansers (Swasy 1993).

91 See Porter (1990), Douglas, Wind (1987). Craig and Douglas (2000) note that product markets can be linked by mobile customers. "There are highly mobile customers who travel extensively and look for the same brands and services wherever they are. This includes products such as cigarettes, toothpaste, or pain relievers, as well as services such as car hire, hotel chains and telephone service." (Craig, Douglas 2000, p. 134).

The United States is often regarded as the kind of country that has the ability to transfer its preferences abroad. The use of new innovations in the United States is highly visible in mass media such as television and motion pictures around the world. Mobile consumers and US multinational firms transfer US consumption patterns to foreign countries. The United States is indeed a lead market for many innovations in consumer goods. There are nations, however, such as the Nordic countries, which are not watched by the global community and are not considered to be global trend-setters, but nevertheless they have been the first to adopt innovations that went on to become global standards (examples of this will be presented in the next chapter). The United States is also not immune to idiosyncratic local demand. For instance, some food brands and sporting activities that hold a strong market share in the United States are not demanded in foreign countries. Examples for this are other soft drinks that were invented in the south of the United States, such as Root Beer, Dr. Pepper and Welch's Grape Soda (Cvar 1986, p. 495) and could not imitate the global market success of Coca-Cola. The idiosyncratic demand for wide-screen television sets in the United States isolated US manufactures from most other country markets (Porter 1986, p. 28). Communication ties can certainly spur the global diffusion between countries, but its weight within the system of lead market factors could be limited to goods for which adoption depends on global status and international life-style trends.

Cross-national policy convergence[92]

Policy convergence as discussed in the field of policy science, is the frequently observed convergence of policy instruments or policy content, i.e. the institutional tools available for administering policy (Bennett 1991, p. 218) across administrative borders. One process of policy convergence is the cross-national diffusion of policies, the pattern of successive adoptions of a policy innovation by imitation. A new policy can be called a policy innovation and the adoption of a specific policy by most countries worldwide an international diffusion of policy innovations (Bennett 1991, Kern et al. 2000). Cross-national policy diffusion can explain the international diffusion of technical innovation designs as well. New regulations of national government can induce innovations for instance if they require the adoption of new technologies, change relative factors costs or in general change the relative benefits of different designs. If one country introduces a new regulation that induces innovations or spurs the adoption of a specific innovation design, this innovation design will be adopted by users in other countries as well, when other countries introduce this same regulation. The international diffusion of policies in a broad range of fields has already been studied such as bureaucratic accountability (Bennett 1997), administrative reform (Peters 1997) and most notably in environmental regulation (see Kern et al. 2000, Jänicke 2000). Kern et al. (2000, p. 509) observe the same phenomenon that was to be seen in the international diffu-

---

[92] I owe this topic to Prof. Jänicke who studies international policy diffusion.

sion of innovations: Despite the fact that countries differ in conditions such as environmental problems, requiring different policy instruments, these countries often adopt the same regulations, even down to the wording used by an other country (Bennett 1991, p. 222). Some countries "sacrifice...autonomy to avoid unnecessary cross-national divergence" (Bennett 1991, p. 227). Therefore a country has an international transfer advantage if it is more likely that policy makers follow this country than other countries.

In reviewing the literature of cross-border policy convergence Bennett (1991) and Dolowitz, Marsh (1996) describe policy internationalisation mechanisms that are analogous to the transfer mechanisms constituting the diffusion of technical innovations. First of all, social problems and policy instruments intended to ease these problems are surrounded by uncertainty. The introduction of regulation offers a test of effectiveness and reduces uncertainty (lesson drawing).[93] Obviously, countries adopt foreign policies that proved to be effective in one country without harming that country's economy.[94] For instance, deregulation in the telecommunications industry in the United States drove down the price of telephone calls. This led governments of many other countries to deregulation of the telecom sector as well.[95]

Policy communities as well as international organisations such as the OECD, the WTO and transnational professional organisations (e.g. aviation, telecommunication, etc.) share experience and have an incentive to harmonise policies among countries, most notably if countries' policies are interdependent, and taking so-called *best practises* as a guidance. In keeping with the transfer effect of multinational firms, international organisations such as NGOs (Non-governmental organisations) can pressure (or convince) governments worldwide to adopt a specific policy. For instance Greenpeace has transferred the policy of chlorine-free paper worldwide (Sonnenfeld 2000). In addition, it has been argued that governments of large countries can force other governments to introduce a specific regulation, for example this international transfer process is suggested to had have happened to in the case of anti-cartel laws in Europe (Majorne 1991), deregulation of telecommunication (Hill 1986) or by the regulatory requirements of the IMF for the granting of loans (Dolowitz, Marsh 1996, p. 348).

---

93 "Uncertainty about the cause of problems, the effects of previous decisions or the future causes actors to search for policies they can borrow" (Dolowitz, Marsh 1996, p. 347).

94 Effective regulation in turn can lead to the fear of political actors in other countries of falling behind its competitors triggering the adoption of the same policies (Dolowitz, Marsh 1996, p. 349). However, foreign policies not only 'draw lessons' but also legitimate conclusions already reached domestically and are taken to put pressure on the domestic legislation process (Bennett 1991, p. 223).

95 A detailed but rather disapproving assessment of the international adoption of telecom deregulation policies initiated by the United States is suggested by Hills (1986).

It has been observed that some countries' policies are more likely to be copied that others, for instance the United States and Germany (Dolowitz, Marsh 1996, p. 352). Yet, political science literature offers little nation-specific characteristics of these regulatory leaders.[96] However, the theoretical incentives behind adopting a similar regulation are already mentioned earlier in this chapter: risk reduction, global externalities and other incentives of multinational organisations to harmonise international conditions and the international reputation and attention a country receives. It follows that a country is more likely to be followed in the adoption of specific policy instruments if that country lowers risk most visibly, draws most international attention, spreads political ideas internationally, has more power in international organisations and has a good reputation on a political rather than technical level. As well, and in line with the argument of the next section, the more ideological and institutional similarities to other countries a country has, the more support the international transfer of domestic policies receives (Dolowitz, Marsh 1996, p. 353).

3.2.4 Export advantage

Firms in a country have an advantage over foreign competitors of other countries if their innovations can be exported more easily. Innovations can be exported more easily if (1) the environment and market conditions of foreign countries are similar to the market the innovation was designed for and (2) features are included in an innovation design that make the design suitable for a diversity of environments. A country can constitute a lead market if the market context pressures domestic firms to develop innovation designs that are exportable. One can derive three factors of a national export advantage: domestic demand that is sensitive to the problems and needs of foreign countries, long-time export experience of domestic firms and the similarity of local market conditions to foreign market conditions.

Sensitivity to global problems and needs

Even if the domestic environment is not at the front of a global trend, domestic users can be more sensitive to global problems and needs than potential adopters in countries where the problem is more advanced. This sensitivity of demand can push domestic firms into a global perspective and increase its ability to meet global problems before firms in other countries. For instance, consumers in a country can be sensitive to the effects of worldwide climatic change even if their domestic environment is not affected as much compared to other countries. Other examples are wildlife protection, wood cutting in the tropics and pollution of raw material extraction. In Germany, consumers (as well as politicians of all political

[96] Rather, the characteristics of political instruments that are more transferable internationally are offered for example by Rose (1993).

parties) were most eager to support a boycott of Shell petrol stations after the company's UK affiliate announced that it would sink an oil platform in the North Sea that threatened to pollute a part of the North Sea far away from the German shore. The public in Britain was less interested or even supportive. However, the German protest – Shell petrol stations in Germany experienced a 30 to 70 % decline of sales (Scherler 1996, p. 264) – was mainly responsible for a more environmental-friendly course of Shell UK (Hecker 1997, p. 118). The German market acted as an international leader of demand for environment protection.

Market orientation of domestic firms

Firms can increase their ability to export new products to foreign countries with different environments if they deliberately anticipate as many foreign demand specifics in the innovation as possible. Firms that attach importance to introducing their own innovations in foreign markets are sensitive to matching the demand specifics of large foreign markets and implement global requirements already in the prototype. With the innovation fitting a mixture of different environments, scale economies could balance cost disadvantages against each simpler national specific innovation. With these "dual-use" or "robust" innovation designs[97] a firm can catch up with foreign firms' innovations in their home markets at an early stage to pre-empt the international competition of nation-specific technologies. Conditions that support the inclusion of foreign demand preferences in nationally preferred innovation designs constitute a national export advantage. The national environment can support the export orientation of domestic firms (1) by providing information on foreign demand preferences, (2) by market participants who demand innovations that can be exported and (3) by tradition.

Accessibility to information on requirements of innovation designs in foreign markets, such as technical norms, governmental regulation and property rights, help domestic firms to raise the exportability of their innovations. Information on foreign requirements can be embodied in trained personal and documentation can be supplied by institutions and related industries. Foreign demand preferences can also be a content of the domestic demand preferences if residents of foreign descent that add foreign demand preferences to the demand preferences of native cultures form a significant share of domestic population. For instance, they are many consumers of Chinese and Indian origin living in Malaysia and Singapore, that provided local firms with information on consumer patterns of the Indian and Chinese market (see section 7.2).

---

97 The term "dual-use" is often used for products that are designed for the military but can be used in civil applications as well. Robust design is a term suggested by Urban and Hauser (1993, p. 350) for design concepts that can be used for a variety of potential uses and under a variety of conditions. For instance, baking powder mix is a product that can be used under a variety of national environmental conditions (climate, oven temperatures, altitude).

The pressure for export can come from local users, suppliers, financial sources and other national institutions. Some customers pressure producers to develop globally successful and not idiosyncratic solutions if they can expect lower prices of an innovation that can be exported, even if the idiosyncratic version would technically fit their own environment better. Pressure can come from multinational firms that demand technical solutions that can be used in their foreign affiliates or headquarters as well taking advantage of intra-firm economies of adoption.

Suppliers of components, too, can profit from the export orientation of product manufacturers. Suppliers thus have an incentive to push the customers to export their innovations. On the other hand, exporting customers demand components that are viable for export and they are likely to know the requirements for components for global products. Kreutzer (1989, p. 248) reports that the disk drive manufacturer Tandon expanded to a globally leading company in a 'piggy-back' fashion by supplying disk drives to computer firms in Silicon Valley. The extensive export activity of the computer firms substituted the lack of knowledge about world market intelligence and helped to set a globally dominant design for disk drives in step with the computer designs.

Although the size of a local market has been denoted as necessary for the lead function of a market (Ohmae 1995), a strong world-market orientation of firms often results from the small home market which does not suffice in amortising the investment in R&D and is therefore more export oriented (Walsh 1988). This is the case, for instance, for Swiss, Dutch and Swedish firms. For instance, Sweden's Ericsson developed a public-telephone switch for the home market but included features that made it easier to subsequently adapt it to other markets (Bartlett, Ghoshal 1989, p. 25; Pehrsson 1996, pp. 104-130). Another explanation is that it could simply reflect the traditional export commitment of local firms, as is the case in Germany.

The argument of export orientation is similar to what Ohmae (1995) calls a port of entry: a region state that is shaped by the demands of the global economy and characterised by large export shares. A strong export orientation of local firms shapes the political, social and cultural system of a nation, the education of its engineers and managers, export competence of employment and its supporting institutions (governmental agencies). This facilitates the ability of firms to develop innovations that are beneficial for users in foreign countries as well as for local users. These regions are also centres of a communications network between several large economies because firms that serve foreign markets "develop a high-level intelligence gathering capability in order to identify world trends in output, demand, market potential and scientific and technological constraints" (Walsh 1988, p. 53). The latter reverses the former argument – that other countries would subsequently adapt to the local demand preferences – and understands the lead market as a regional information centre of a global market's preferences.

Similarity of local demand to foreign market conditions

Similarity between countries has been suggested as accelerating the cross-border adoption of innovation. Similarity includes the physical similarity and the socio-political and cultural proximity of countries and Rogers' complementary criteria of diffusion. The reduction of a variety of nation-specific designs is faster because it is easier for a country to retreat to a foreign design if the loss of benefit is small. Dekimpe et al. (1998b) support the hypothesis already suggested by Vernon (1979) that the higher the similarity of cultural, social and economic factors between two countries, the greater the likelihood that an innovation design adopted by one of two countries will be adopted by the other country as well. First of all, similar countries have similar needs and preferences; the international diffusion of an innovation design is not as inhibited between more dissimilar countries. Second, socio-political and cultural proximity increases the communication and interaction between countries, the influence and peer pressure on each other. As a result, a country is more apt to follow the adoption of innovation designs from similar countries than the designs from less similar countries. Another argument is that the more cultural similar a foreign country is, the more knowledge firms have about the foreign market context making it therefore easier for firms to include requirements into the innovation. This conclusion results from the studies on psychic distance (see footnote 41).

A lead market is a country whose specifics are not too different from all other national demand specifics, i.e. it is the one that lies in the middle of the variety of national demand specifics or it is the one whose sum of distances to other countries' demand preferences is minimal. Its national favourite, the technology that has the highest benefit for local users also has the highest average benefit for all users in foreign markets.

Examples for the advantage of similarity can be found in the motor vehicle industry. With the laws for environmental protection much more restrictive and the storage technologies heavily improved, electric cars are expected to supersede the combustion motor. Nevertheless, the dominant design of the future is completely unclear. Toyota of Japan invented a hybrid car, powered by both a conventional petrol-driven engine for normal and higher speed and an electric engine for lower speed. As is usual for a Japanese firm, Toyota designed the car for the Japanese market and introduced it there first, hoping to reap the lead-advantage of the demanding Japanese market through cost advantages from economies-of-scale and learning in the market for such a new design. Yet every design has its advantages and disadvantages. Though the *Prius*, as the car is called, fits the Japanese conditions well and has low switching costs on the side of the user (with the combustion motor the battery does not need to be recharged externally), it does not fit the huge US market quite so well. This is because cars in the US are driven at speeds that are, on average, much faster than in Japan and also because the driving conditions are different from the driving conditions in Japan. The hybrid motor is efficient for

Japanese driving conditions, however, where much of the driving takes place in congested cities. In the American environment the hybrid motor is not much more fuel-efficient than conventional cars are, thus lowering the incentive for an American consumer to switch to the new design (Pollack 1998). Designs by US auto firms for electric-only powered cars will be aimed towards the American market (Economist 1999b) with the focus on improved batteries and in particular to meet the future Californian requirement for zero-emission vehicles. The crucial question is how similar the other large markets in Europe and Asia will be to the Japanese and US markets (or whether other countries adopt the Californian regulation). This could decide which design will be adopted there and could finally be called the global design.

3.2.5 Market structure advantage

A lead market is not purely determined by demand factors. The degree of competition in the domestic market is also a lead market factor. Competition has already been identified as a promoter of technical progress (Nelson 1990; Mowery 1995). Entrepreneurial effort is one of the main determinants of international patterns of innovations for Posner (1961), Lindbeck (1981) and Dosi et al. (1990). A lead market is a competitive market. First of all, buyers tend to be more demanding when they face competition than when they are tightly regulated or hold a monopoly (Porter 1990). Second, competing firms are more strongly pressured to follow those who have already adopted a new technology (Mansfield 1968, p. 144). And third, maybe most importantly, more innovation designs are tested in a competitive market. As a result, a competitive market is more apt to find a design that is not only the best within the domestic environment but also the best across all national environments.

Competition facilitates a market's anticipatory capacity. Fierce competition between firms active in the local market reveals information on buyers' needs earlier than less competitive markets. Competitive markets are more likely to discover latent needs and select globally successful products that fit those needs the most. Competitive markets are able to generate information on a buyer's needs because more alternatives can be tested and experience can be collected on a variety of product types. In a competitive market, a firm can turn any technological advantage into a market share taken from less creative rivals (Metcalfe 1995, p. 488). The absence of barriers to entry (the contestablility of markets, i.e. firms can enter and exit a market, see Baumol, Panzar, Willig, 1982) is essential for lead markets because new products and technologies are frequently brought about by new firms (see, e.g., Audretsch 1995). Because of this openness new firms can enter the market and test the reception of new designs by users. This makes the process of finding the best product, i.e. the product that is most profitable for the users and thus the dominant design, by means of search and selection more efficient. Since the dominant design of a competitive market has to prevail against other designs, it has an advantage in the world market over other national designs that were selected by monopolists or monopolistic users. In the supply side case lead markets are not characterised by demand advantages but by the market context of competition. Lead markets emerge in a world of varying degrees of competition through *lead competition*.

Again, the example given involves the telecommunications industry. Since at least the 1930s, this industry has been characterised by state-owned network providers that are either vertically integrated or purchase their equipment from domestic firms that are not exposed to international competition. When the German public telecommunication network operator opened the procurement of public switches to competitive bids in the early 1980s and included foreign suppliers of network electronics, it attracted foreign multinational R&D activities into Germany. It also facilitated the development of two public digital switches in Germany that subsequently became highly successful worldwide. Fierce competition between different suppliers constituted a lead market.[98]

Porter (1990) finds additional reasons why competitive markets support the competitive advantage of nations. The high number of independent buyers, together with an early saturation of a market, urges a reduction of prices and an improvement in product performance. This gives buyers an incentive to replace an old product with the new version. Competition drives costs down and makes a new technology more competitive in replacing the old technologies. The liberalisation of the communication equipment market initiated intense competition among Japanese companies and caused the cost of fax machines to decrease (Coopersmith 1993). The United States leads innovations in express package transportation because it led the deregulation of a heavily regulated transport sector. Deregulation of air cargo and interstate trucking in 1980 led to new carriers, increased competition and lower prices and US express carriers dominated the market in share and technology employed (Council on Competitiveness 1998, p. 116).

Taking competition into consideration also makes the example of the soft drink industry, mentioned above, more comprehensible. Carbonated beverages existed long before the soft drink industry was established in America and the technology was refined in many places within Europe and the United States. Yet as Riley (1958) notes, the variety of flavours added made it a typical American industry. In the South of the United States a strong increasing demand initiated fierce competition, which spurred the search and market test of new flavours by local bottlers. A very large variety of flavoured carbonated beverages was tested on the local market. Many of these were rejected or demanded by a few locals only. As noted above, many soft drinks that are popular in the South or in the whole United States did not became popular in foreign markets. But as a result of the intensive search process by competitors, the Cola flavour was invented and finally found to be a globally preferred taste. That means that local demand in the South of the United

98 For details see the case study by Beise (1999).

States anticipated a global taste only because they were the first in the position to test that unique design.

3.3 The System of Lead Market Factors

The lead market's factors are part of a lead market system. This section addresses the systemic nature of the lead market theory. First, what is the relationship between the five lead market factors? The lead market factors influence each other and they are influenced by other factors. Are they consistent with each other or are there conflicting relationships? Second, what is the role of the technological knowledge of inventors and producers for the ability of a country to lead the adoption of innovations? As noted in the literature review, technological leads are often considered a main determinant of national competitiveness. This thesis argues the ability to lead can result in a technological lead of the firms of a country. Third, one may ask what socio-political, cultural and economic system supports the lead market role of a country. Are there institutional conditions that facilitate the lead effect of a market? The third section briefly discusses the origins of the lead market factors in the socio-economic and political system of a country.

3.3.1 The dynamics of lead market advantage

The five factors that constitute a lead market are interrelated. They form a system such as the factors in Porter's diamond of national competitive advantage. Most of the relationships between the factors are mutually reinforcing. In practise this means that often no single factor constitutes a lead market alone but rather a mixture of interdependent lead market factors. In this section I will discuss the relationships between the five lead factor advantages.

The *price advantage* is supported by the other lead market factors because the adoption of a domestic design abroad can increase economies-of-scale. A transfer advantage lowers prices through low information, transfer costs and costs caused by risk. A transfer advantage means that information on the technological design of the lead market is more available than information on any other design. Risk can be associated with additional cost, e.g. additional investments to secure a possible failure. The use of the design in the lead market reduces the uncertainty and this lowers the cost of the lead market design for users in other markets relative to unimproved technological design. An export advantage means lower adaptation cost of the lead market design in the lag market context. Another strong positive impact on the price advantage is expected to emanate from the market structure advantage. Competition and low entry barriers drive prices down. Price reductions should discourage potential new entrants. This strategy is known as predatory pricing (Tirole 1988, p. 373). In addition, competition is necessary to ensure that decreasing costs of production result in decreasing prices. Otherwise, a monopolist could maintain prices even if costs can be lowered.

It has already been discussed that demanding customers could push prices up because they demand higher quality, which makes a design over-engineered for other markets. Yet it has been argued that customers in the lead market are at the same time the most competent and price-aware users. Link (1997) suggests that first users are less willing to pay for a new product than the users immediately following the first users. This means that fast follower markets will adopt an innovation design in the lead market even if the price of the design cannot be reduced. Only foreign markets that are resistant to adopting an innovation (laggards) or that have to switch from one domestic design previously adopted to the lead market design have to be attracted with lower prices. It can be said, however, that normally lead markets are likely to be accompanied by a price advantage.

A *demand advantage* is basically a special local context that is independent of foreign contexts and does not seem to be influenced much by other factors. At least a large total market size can reinforce the demand advantage because a large market is likely to host some high-income users and users that are at the front of a trend able to justify R&D investments even if its market context is not the trend leader as a whole. A large country offers more incentives for making complementary goods available. Competition in a demanding market increases the responsiveness of local firms. International attention could make local users more demanding and risk taking could increase their willingness to adopt untested innovations. They may feel obliged to be the first adopter if they are watched by the world that is willing to follow them. In addition, this willingness of foreign nations to follow their own country's choice promises exports for local firms in exchange for the higher risk.

The *export advantage* is strengthened by the market structure advantage but is weakened by the demand and transfer advantage. If a country has a transfer or demand advantage it is unlikely that at the same time it has an export advantage. Countries at the front of a trend and countries that are mostly followed by other countries are less apt to gather information on foreign market preferences (the US is an example). In addition, demanding users in the market are likely to attract all the attention of domestic firms and away from foreign users. One could argue, however, that in the long run a demand and transfer advantage could lead to an export orientation of the domestic firms as well. Large exports to foreign countries that followed the lead market make a firm more aware of the importance of foreign markets (many US companies are indeed export oriented).

The market structure advantage clearly reinforces the export advantage because fierce competition in the home market lowers profit margins and allows local firms to look for more profitable (lag) markets abroad. The relation of the export advantage to the cost advantage is ambiguous. It has been argued that small countries in particular are more eager to export and are more export oriented. Companies located in large markets tend to have less knowledge about foreign markets and are more likely to ignore foreign demand preferences because they could rely solely on their large home markets. On the other hand, large countries lead to an economies-of-scale advantage over small countries. Price advantage and demand advantage are therefore initially not consistent. An export advantage, however, can compensate the price disadvantage of the small home market size by supplying foreign markets. International usability of a design results in economies-of-scale and economies-of-adoption. Firms with dual-use innovations finally gain a cost advantage over firms focused on their idiosyncratic home markets. In the long run, the international competitiveness of a country with an export advantage can be reinforced by a price advantage.

A *transfer advantage* seems to be reinforced by all other advantages. The reputation of the country results in international attention and lowers risk associated with local innovations, i. e. a transfer advantage. Reputation is built up by local demanding users (demand advantage), high competition or low governmental influence (market structure advantage) and the large size of the market (price advantage). Export advantage results in international contacts and international firms, both reinforcing a transfer advantage. Transfer advantage includes increases in the benefit of the diffusion process that are beneficial for foreign users. The size of home market demand does not only lower prices but could also enhance technological advances that increase the benefit. Competition has a benefit increasing effect as well.

Like the transfer advantage a *market structure advantage* is expected to be reinforced by all other factors. A large market size offers opportunities for more firms and lowers entry barriers.[99] High income and demanding users set incentives for foreign firms to enter the market, thus increasing local competition. Export and transfer advantage attributes expose local firms to the international market by losing the constraint of the home market and giving more local firms market opportunities independent of domestic market size.

Overall, the discussion leads to the conclusion that the system of lead market factors is mainly consistent. Most lead market factors reinforce each other with certain exceptions.

3.3.2 Technological advantages

One common explanation for export success that I have ignored in this chapter is that an innovation becomes dominant in the world market as a result of the technological lead of the home country. Where does this technological advantage of regions or countries come from? Technology gap theories suggest that technological progress is derived mainly from entrepreneurial effort, R&D activities of firms and scientific progress (science-push). In this hypothesis, it is assumed that tech-

---

[99] Tilton (1971) showed that the demand for the first specialised semiconductors were mostly matched by new firms that thereafter became large multinational firms. In general, first adopters are often in niche markets that are unattractive for large firms, e.g. Christensen (1997).

nological opportunities, technological capabilities and the stock of technological knowledge can vary from country to country because new technological knowledge diffuses only slowly in space. A small geographical distance between the research-performing institution and the knowledge-using firm (regional knowledge spillovers) facilitates the access to knowledge. Countries with the largest scientific output would gain a technological lead over other countries. A competitive country, restated in the science-push view, is a country in which the national science system pushes the scientific progress in a direction, which is most successful for technological progress and which the world will follow, regardless of local market conditions. This means that technological applications built on scientific findings generated in the lead country become globally dominant.[100] This assumption leads to the technology-sourcing hypothesis of direct investment theory[101]: firms seeking access to technical knowledge invest in countries that hold a scientific knowledge lead (see Chapter 5).

In this thesis, I argue that in many industries there is no technological gap between advanced countries. If there is a technology gap, it is often the result of a lead market advantage. The adoption lead can cause a technological gap that reinforces the competitive advantages. First of all, some determinants of a technology gap are also part of the lead market factors. Entrepreneurial effort is part of a market structure advantage and at the same time supports the generation of inventions. Yet, to be successful, an innovation has to be adopted by domestic users. Examples show that the first adoption of an invention by an entrepreneur is not always in the country-of-origin. The R&D activities of firms are normally allocated by the domestic demand preferences. Demanding and sophisticated users, export orientation, competitive markets and growth of demand raise the incentives of firms to invest in R&D. Demand-pull theories since Schmookler's (1966) empirical work suggest that shifts in demand in the home market were the main explanation for the firms' growth of inventions.

Compared to factors on the demand and cost side that induce innovations, there is only weak empirical evidence for a pure science-push explanation of technical change (Thirtle, Ruttan 1987, p. 10). It has been argued instead that science is rather endogenous, resulting more from technological progress. Funds for scientific work are induced by commercial success of a related industry (Stephan

---

[100] Dosi (1982) suggested that technical progress follows technological trajectories because R&D activities built on accumulated knowledge and commercial problems and scientific questions are normally tackled within a technological paradigm.

[101] In this hypothesis, technology is not transferred along the flow of direct investments as the traditional theory suggests but rather against the flow of direct investment, see for instance Neven, Siotis (1996); Lichtenberg, van Pottelsberghe de la Potterie (1996); Shan, Song (1997).

1994). The adoption of innovation spurred the investment in science and technology in these countries and not vice versa.[102]

It would be wrong to explain technical progress with demand alone. Early estimates of future markets have been widely inaccurate (Freeman, Soete 1997, p. 249). But demand always plays a role in technological progress. As a result, the view of the interrelated science and demand factors of technical change has been widely shared in the literature since the 1980s (see Dosi 1988; Freeman, Soete 1997; Kline, Rosenberg 1986). The hypothesis of lead markets neither disputes science-push theories of technical change nor is it a pure demand-pull theory itself. It argues that technical push is not the origin of *national* competitive advantage in many product domains. A (weaker type of) lead market exists even if technical progress overall is mainly based on scientific advance. This is because local markets can be more or less reluctant to adopt a technology that will prevail on the world market later because of its technical advantage. This technical advantage is transparent to sensitive adopters at the time of introduction or it gains a benefit through learning-by-doing or through learning-by-using afterwards. If producers are not (perfectly) informed about demand preferences, but innovate instead on the basis of scientific findings alone, demand does not induce technical change directly but rather it *selects* the technology within a variety of innovations during the diffusion process.[103] Users will select the variant that fits its purposes best – or is "the lesser of the various evils on offer" (Grupp, Maital 1998, p. 74). If demand and environmental conditions vary, the benefit of technology alternatives may differ from country to country and different alternatives might fit local conditions best. As a result, users in one country will select a different technology than users in other countries. If demand conditions in one country are highly idiosyncratic compared to other countries, it is likely that demand would at least 'bend' the technological progress of local firms towards an idiosyncratic direction, if not in the invention phase then in the diffusion phase. This scenario leads back to the question of why one local demand picks the "right" technology, i.e. the prevailing technical trajectory and another backs the "wrong" horse, i.e. the dead end trajectory.

The argument against the technology-gap-as-origin-of-competitiveness theory is as follows. When applied to the location decision of multinational firms, it is not so much the question of whether *the* technical change can be explained by de-

---

[102] Historically, science-push explanations of technical change came up after the Second World War, when the United States had built up a sophisticated public and private science system and at the same time succeeded on the world market. As has been noted above there is evidence that the United States did not command scientific knowledge over Europe, see Vernon (1971), Schmookler (1966), Franko (1976), Hufbauer (1966).

[103] This is the search-and-selection model introduced by evolutionary theories of technical change, see Nelson and Winter (1982): firms innovate on the basis of technological opportunities and the users select a variant that proved to yield the highest benefit for them.

mand-pull or science-push factors but how much regional proximity is important for access to knowledge about demand preferences and scientific findings. Whereas scientific findings are widely exchanged within the worldwide scientific community, there is no such established trade of knowledge about foreign market preferences.[104] When introducing the product life-cycle theory, Vernon (1971) presents two reasons that the science system was not the decisive advantage of US firms in the post-World War period. The United States had gained a lead in scientific advance after World War II and government related and mainly defence oriented research programs are made responsible for the lead in electronics and aviation. Scientific results, however, are freely available to any prospective user, foreign or domestic, if he is advanced enough to adopt these scientific findings, which European firms certainly were. Even more important, it is not the scientific results that induce the lead, but the "promise of new markets which the [research] programs have offered to the U.S. enterprises".

Examples such as the fax machine, the personal computer and cellular telephony also suggest that even in science-related industries local demand specifics are often essential for successful global innovations, which subsequently leads to the technological lead of a firm or a country. A previously held technological lead in the same or related technologies does not always provide the basis of the technological advantage in the final global product. According to Peterson (1995), technological knowledge in fax technology was equally distributed among the United States, Japan and Germany in the 1980s and early products from these countries were equally advanced. Peterson even observes additional similarities between Japan and the United States: "Both the US and Japanese telephone systems accommodated fax machines and offered low line charges. Both countries also had a large potential market" (Peterson 1995, p. 481). It would therefore be reasonable to expect a mass market to develop simultaneously in both markets. Yet the mass market started in Japan and demand took off later in other countries, but only with varying time delays. The lead of the Japanese market has been attributed to differences in the societal, cultural and political structures of different countries. In the fax example, the salient national difference makes it appear as if it were the pictorial character of the Japanese language that has made fax more useful than telex in Japan. From the European market perspective, betting on telex seemed reasonable since telex was cheaper, more reliable and technologically mature. The Japanese language, however, with its vast variety and pictorial nature of characters, made facsimile communication advantageous. Mass application in Japan refined the fax machine so that it began to dominate the world market in the area of text communication. In the 1990s, Japanese firms became the world market leaders in fax

104 Regional knowledge spillovers from scientific activities are unambiguously empirically confirmed. The most referred studies about regional scientific spillover are Jaffe (1989); Acs, Audretsch, Feldman (1992) and Jaffe et al. (1993). On the other hand, the empirical evidence for a firm's better perception of local demand preferences is weak as well, see Cornish (1997).

machines and Japan was certainly the lead country as far as fax was concerned. This resulted in a diversified and initially heterogeneous world market containing several competing alternative technologies that differed according to local environments. In spite of the commonly held belief the first personal computer was not invented in the United States but in France. The Boston computer museum officially declared the *Micral* the first microprocessor-based personal computer invented by the Vietnamese-born André Thi Truong in 1973 using a US processor chip, the Intel 8008 processor. The first PC of US origin, the *Altair*, was developed only two years later. Yet, the US-designs became an instant success with hobbyists and mass market users, attracting new firms to built mass-produced, consumer-friendly models. In the next chapter, the long-held technological lead of the United States in cellular mobile telephony will be described in detail. The next section will discuss these socio-economic characteristics of lead markets.

When demand preferences, the market context and other factors of the propensity to adopt innovations do not vary considerably, however, and technical solutions are mainly based on scientific findings, e.g. in biotechnological pharmaceuticals, one can argue that the effectiveness of the science and technology transfer system of a country would be the dominant lead characteristic of a country. Only in this extreme setting is the main lead effect the scientific advantage of a country.

3.3.3 Economic, social, political, cultural and environmental systems

The factors that have been identified as constituting a lead market are influenced by a country's economic, socio-political, ecological and cultural systems (Figure 3-9). First of all, the national industry structure clearly influences the lead function of a market. Porter (1990), in particular, stresses industry structure as a determinant of national competitive advantage. Industries are interconnected by supplier-user and complementary-goods relationships. Related industries cluster around the peculiar technology. The main industry structure effect is that if the customers are internationally competitive, local suppliers can gain an international advantage as well. Lead market advantages can be transmitted along the value chain and within the technical cluster as well. If one product domain is characterised by demanding and sophisticated users, cost advantages or export oriented firms, it affects related industries and is likely to contaminate related product domains all over with its demand for quality. If the domestic market is a lead market for the customer industry, then the firms of the customer industry are likely to be demanding toward their supplier. As a result, if a country has lead market advantages in one product domain, this strengthens lead market advantages in related industries. For instance, lead markets of end-user products can spread the value chain back to special machinery producers or material and intermediate suppliers. For instance, computer manufacturers benefited from the demand for graphic visualisation of computer animated movies (Dertouzos et al. 1989), inducing demand for fast graphic processing microchips.

Diffusion studies have in fact focused on the effect of cultural factors on the rate of diffusion and have consistently found that social heterogeneity has a negative effect on diffusion (Dekimpe et al. 1998c). General innovativeness of a country is certainly necessary for a lead market. Demand for innovations can be a characteristic of the lead market, in that a country may try many innovations and may be the first to discover the most useful innovation (market structure advantage). Other attributes of the social system can be important for the lead role of a country. For instance, the demand advantage is influenced by the income distribution of a country, its factor price setting mechanisms, the level of its general educational system and its public infrastructure. Market structure is determined by the political framework, such as the degree of freedom of business, other barriers to entry, attitude against foreign companies' investments, governmental ownership of companies, state sanctioned monopolies and the effectiveness of jurisdiction, governmental bureaucracy and anti-trust prevention. Transfer advantages are a characteristic of a culture of risk taking, reputation and trend setting, the ability to lead and be followed by others and mobile and cosmopolitan people. Price changes are also influenced by political and cultural factors, such as governmental regulation, the tax system, the distribution of income and the price elasticity of demand. Export orientation of a country and the sensitivity to global problems are based in part on its cultural tradition of outward orientation and cosmopolitanism – to use a main cultural characteristic introduced by Hofstede (1980) – in contrast to isolationist and inward looking attitudes. The similarity of the local context to other countries is determined by the degree of similarity of the political and ecological and cultural systems to the systems of other countries. The similarity of these systems in turn could reflect a country's willingness to follow other countries.

Lead markets anticipate the global adoption of innovations. What are the anticipating factors of cultural environments? According to Porter (1990, p. 91), anticipatory needs arise when a nation's political or social values reveal global needs before they emerge in other countries. It remains unclear, though, what sociopolitical system facilitates this anticipation. I have argued that a society that is open to the diversity of needs worldwide can incorporate in their innovations the compatibility to diverse environments, i.e. it is export oriented. A society anticipates needs if it is responsive to problems when they are still small and not perceived or not regarded as pressing by the general public. Social values amplify weak signals of imminent problems. For instance, some nations are more sensitive to environmental pollution, while others are concerned that food is free of chemicals and hygienically packaged. The political system certainly has an influence on the responsiveness of the government and legislation to problems before they amount to real struggles. When problems amount in other countries as well, the hypersensitive market could be called a lead market; if not, it would be called an idiosyncratic market. Here, lead and idiosyncratic demand are close and anticipation is not a general attribute of local demand, but rather an outcome of global environmental changes. Not everything turns out to be a global trend.

If there is no global trend, it is hard to draw a line *ex ante* between idiosyncratic and lead demand. There is, however, an important asymmetry between markets with demanding and hypersensitive users and other markets. Products appropriate for the most demanding market can be introduced in other markets too. In contrast, products designed for less demanding markets are likely to fail on more demanding markets. Overall, a country is more likely to generate internationally successful innovations that in turn generates more innovations than other countries. On average, even if a global trend is taken as a question of chance, the demanding markets export more than non-demanding markets. This reasoning does not really help, however, if a firm asks for the potential lead market for a specific innovation idea (see Chapter 5).

3.4 Related Aspects of Lead Markets

There are several additional issues concerning lead markets that shall be discussed in this section. It is obvious that not only the term but also the reasoning of lead markets is related to Eric von Hippel's lead user theory. In this section I will discuss the important differences between lead users and lead markets. Second, I will address the relationship between pioneer advantages and lead markets. Third, there is the question of the persistence of lead markets. Does the lead market role shift from country to country over time and why? Hitherto I have discussed lead markets as countries. One could ask, whether regions within countries or transnational regions can be lead markets as well.

3.4.1 Lead users and lead markets

It is obvious that one may ask how lead markets relate to the lead user and whether lead markets can be constituted by the presence of lead users in a country. Lead users have two characteristics. Lead users first perceive a need for innovative products within their own production processes, which is not idiosyncratic but foreshadows a general future need. Second, the benefit from an innovation is distributed unequally among all potential adopters and lead users have the greatest benefits from the innovation. As the users of an innovation who profit most from an adoption of the innovation, lead users have the highest incentive to adopt it and, if the producers have no benefit from the innovation, would innovate individually.

On the international level, lead users concentrated in a particular country could be the users that anticipate a global demand. Lead users could constitute the anticipatory demand advantage of a country as described above. The country would then become a lead market because lead users happen to be concentrated in the country. Yet lead users can be quite different from lead markets and they can be located outside the lead market. While lead users are basically inventors who use their inventions themselves, lead markets, on the other hand, are defined predominantly as the first adopters of a new technology. In their most recent work, Hippel,

Tomke and Sonnack (1999) stress again that lead users are a useful source of new technical concepts for manufacturers but not necessarily their customers. In their examples, a manufacturer of surgical drapes finds ideas for new product lines at veterinary hospitals and from makeup artists. In contrast, a lead market need not be the country of the inventor. Lead users can even be located in a different country from the lead markets. For instance, the Formula I racing teams are sometimes considered as lead users. The engineering firms, such as McLaren, that develop the technology necessary to match the high demand on racing performance are mainly clustered in south-east England (Economist 2000a, p. 109). Yet the UK in general is no lead market for high performance cars. There is no high quality demand there like there is in Germany where users of this segment of the automobile market are highly demanding (Porter 1990, p. 91; Johansson 2000, p. 108).[105] Another example is automated guided vehicle technology for the use of public highways, which was first adopted by the largest ports in Rotterdam and Singapore within their premises (Beise, Cleff 2000). In accordance with the lead user model, these two ports were deeply involved in the development of the technology. Yet neither the Netherlands nor Singapore are the lead markets for automated guided vehicles in general. As a study by Beise and Cleff (2000) suggests, the lead market function depends on the public acceptance of automated guided vehicles within public areas. This study will be reviewed in Chapter 6.

The second difference between lead users and lead markets is that the existence of lead users are only explained by a trend. Lead markets can be constituted by other mechanisms as well for instance a high degree of domestic competition.

3.4.2 Lead markets and pioneer advantage

Pioneers are described as the technical leaders of an industry and they have an advantage because they have the most sophisticated knowledge of, skills in and experience with new technology (e.g., Robinson, Fornell 1985; Urban et al. 1986). If pioneers do not respond to lead markets, however, but rather to idiosyncratic or other lag markets, they cannot leverage their advantages and often fail.[106] If a firm does not focus innovation design on the lead market conditions, it gains little from

[105] Consequently and in accordance with the lead user concept, DaimlerChrysler AG of Germany holds a minority stake in and co-operates greatly with McLaren, one of the most successful racing car specialists, outside their Formula I relationship.

[106] Often, innovations are introduced in lag markets and fail. This discourages local firms from improving the innovation and causes them to abandon the innovation. Once the innovation has been adapted to the lead market context it becomes a success. Golder and Tellis (1993) interpret the pattern of successful technical followers as rejecting the pioneer advantage hypothesis. Their empirical study includes the facsimile machine, the video recorder, the personal computer and soft drinks, all of which exhibit a lead market pattern. Controlling for lead-lag attributes of home markets is likely to reverse the results. It can be expected that pioneers in the lead market are more successful than fast followers in the lead market in confirming a pioneer advantage.

a technically pioneering role. Once competitors have adopted the technological knowledge generated by the pioneer and have adapted it to the lead market preferences, they can overtake the technical leader. The diffusion of an innovation generates the technological knowledge of post-invention improvements and market knowledge. The technology lead results from the dynamic learning effects in production and use.

But firms in the lead market need not be the technical leaders to gain a competitive advantage. Lead market firms have advantages in producing and selling the *innovation design* preferred in the domestic market and adopted by the world market. The home market hypothesis presented in section 2.3.1 suggests that firms located in the country benefit more from the local demand for innovations than foreign firms because of efficient preference perception and feedback from the market. The early adoption of a globally dominant innovation design in their home markets gives them pioneer advantages that are not based on superior core technological knowledge but that are generated during the diffusion of an innovation. Pioneer advantages include advantages in access to supplies, costs, product quality, distribution, long term market share and information. Market knowledge on demand preferences seems to be especially important for the competitive advantage of firms in lead markets. The country with the highest penetration rates offers information on preferences of late adopters. A high penetration rate means that late adopters started to use the innovations. And these late adopters, for instance elderly people, have different preferences and demand additional features. In addition, a high penetration rate itself can require improvements in the innovations. For instance, a high penetration rate of motor vehicles requires new traffic and parking concepts. A high penetration rate of Internet users requires faster data transmission and offers new opportunities for e-commerce.

Firms in the lead market have the right *timing* with innovations. The local success spurs firms in the lead market to refine the innovation and build up production capabilities. When demand for the product emerges in foreign countries as well, the lead market firms can enter the markets with a proven, standardised product, for which the lead market firms have additionally gained a cost advantage over foreign firms that have just started to develop and produce the innovation. For instance, the facsimile machine was a failure in Europe and the United States and many firms abandoned the product in favour of the telex system. After the fax was a success in Japan, Japanese firms had a large market experience and cost advantage over their competitors (Scherer 1992, p. 101).

Vernon (1966) has already shown that firms first respond to the demand for a home market product from foreign countries with exports but subsequently with local production to deter imitators in the foreign countries. If there are cost advantages in foreign countries the lead market firms can maintain their knowledge lead or ownership advantage by shifting production to these countries. This pattern of lead market firms becoming multinational firms in serving foreign markets with local production can still be observed frequently. For instance, Tilton (1971) observed that the new US semiconductor firms built up production capabilities in Europe when demand emerged there as well. Yet multinational firms are often capable of selecting the location for the production of innovations worldwide. Volkswagen's New Beetle was designed in the United States, the technology was developed in Germany and it is produced in Mexico. Therefore, the question whether the innovation will ever be manufactured in the lead market depends on the independence of the production from the development activities.[107]

3.4.3 Persistence and international shifts of the lead market role

International diffusion patterns of many innovations resemble the pattern depicted in Figure 1-1. One country leads penetration rates over a long time. The lead in penetration of a specific innovation rarely changes between the point of take-off and the time of saturation. Persistence of the leading role of a country is the characteristic of the lead market. A national lead can even be observed for succeeding generations of a product or related products of a product domain, for instance the United States' lead penetration of mainframe computers and personal computers. The learning processes in the diffusion process seem to reinforce the lead of a country. The lead market is the market that is confronted with higher penetration rates first and can learn in this situation. Firms that are oriented on the lead market always have a learning lead over firms that are oriented on lag markets until the learning economies in the technical domain of the innovation abate. Other firms cannot leapfrog the lead market firms with market information derived from lag countries.[108] But it is still unclear whether a lag country can take the *lead* in the adoption of an innovation from a lead country after it has managed to catch up or even leapfrog. Does a country keep the lead function once it has achieved that role?

---

[107] The relationship between lead markets and trade depends on many other factors that cannot be discussed in this thesis. A simple model of trade in an international lead lag market context, however, would result in no exports of an innovation from idiosyncratic countries (e.g., German 'Ersatz'-coffee) and limited intra-industry trade between countries when internationalisation mechanisms are not large enough to compensate international differences, e.g., the trade between the US and Europe of motor vehicles. A further result involves large exports and high export shares of lead markets until lag countries with factor-relation advantages can close the (adoption-induced) technology gap and overcome the economies-of-scale advantage of the production in the lead market, e.g. personal computers.

[108] Growth theory suggests that a less developed country can grow faster than an advanced country and therefore can catch up. A similar catching-up process can sometimes be observed in the international diffusion pattern of an innovation. The learning-hypothesis of international diffusion mentioned above suggests that diffusion rates of lag countries are higher than those of the lead country. Besides the weak empirical evidence for this pattern, learning alone cannot result in a lag country exceeding penetration rates.

There are several empirical observations and theoretical arguments that the lead function can shift over time from one market to another. First of all, there are historic cases that a leading role of a country has shifted. For instance, Germany was the leading market for pharmaceuticals before World War II because the social security system enabled a mass health market. But it lost that function to the United States after the War when the US pharmaceutical market overtook those in Europe. The United States had a lead in automation until labour costs in Europe exceeded those prevailing in the US. The lead market for semiconductors usually follows the lead market for its special applications. Langloise and Steinmüller (1999) note that the leadership in semiconductors shifted from the United States to Japan when the most demanding application shifted from computers to calculators and back to the United States when personal computer became the main driver of chip technology. The electronic industry became more differentiated as well. While the United States is still the lead market for computer processor chips, Europe has become the lead market for mobile telecommunications electronics, France is the lead market for smart card chips and Germany is the lead market for automotive electronics. The UK led deregulation in telecommunication services and was the most dynamic market for telecommunication equipment. After the Europe-wide deregulation of fixed lines, Germany grabbed the lead function not only because it is the largest market in Europe but also because of the unexpected fierce competition between network operators and service providers that took off with deregulation. Market entry, however, was stimulated by the size of the market now open to other service providers. From the lead market theory presented in this thesis one could conclude that, if the attributes of a market that constituted the lead market role change, a market might lose the lead function to other more dynamic markets. For instance, local competition can abate because of consolidation and monopolisation. Entrepreneurial effort dwindles and surges over time, per-capita-income falls in some advanced countries, demanding users can become satisfied and cumbersome. A country can change from being a predominant host country of multinational companies to a predominant home country, which happened to Germany in the early 1980s (Beise, Belitz 1998). Factor price differences can change internationally as a result of taxation, e.g. fuels, or subsidies, e.g. sustainable energies. The success of a country in one industry can weaken the competitiveness of a country in another industry, because resources are reallocated towards the more attractive industry. Yet overall, these structural changes should not occur frequently but exceptionally. The lead market role should therefore be a persistent phenomenon.

There are, however, other theoretical reasons for shifts in the lead role of markets that will be discussed in this section. Diffusion theory, the theory of industrial organisation and an endogenous-growth theory offer some hypotheses of international lead shifts. In the innovation diffusion theory users adopt innovations for a particular period. Once a new technology has been adopted, it has to be utilised at least for as long as the investment amortises. During this time new and better technologies become available. An early adopter, however, will not always adopt the latest versions. The dependency of probability of the adoption of a new innovation on the time which has passed since the last adoption and on the current investment stock is known as the vintage and stock adjustment models respectively (Thirtle, Ruttan 1987, p. 99). These models aim to explain the delay in the adoption of new technologies.[109] Users could decide not to adopt a generation adopted by users in the lead market. Instead they may leapfrog the current generation and adopt the next generation of the innovation immediately after it is available.[110] Local externalities would bring into line the individual choices within a country because it pressures users of a country to choose the same generation of technology. The lead could then *alternate* over time between countries after each generation of a product. This effect increases the higher the relation between payback time and product-life-cycle. This relation is highest in technology infrastructure that requires large investments. The effect of alternating country leads can also be drawn from industrial organisation models that describe incentives to innovate. For example, a monopolist, a sole user of an innovation protected by patent rights, has a lower incentive to innovate since this "replaces himself" than the competitive firm, which can become a monopoly through innovation (see e.g., Tirole 1988, p. 392; Arrow, 1962a). In industries that are characterised by temporary monopolies (e.g. software, steel) periods of less and more innovative market contexts could alternate in all countries. This results in continuos shifts of the lead market role if the most innovative market constitutes the lead market.

An example for these arguments is the telecommunications industry. For investments in a public switch infrastructure to exceed billions of $US, a switch technology is employed by a service provider for decades. In addition, the installation of a new switch generation takes up to a decade itself. Germany used an electromechanical switch from 1950 to 1980 and started digitalisation of the public net in 1983. It is still building up the largest ISDN-Network while a new generation of data communication technology (ATM) is already being used by national service providers from other countries that leapfrog ISDN but do not compete with the German Telekom. In semiconductors, magnetic cards diffused rapidly and are used in a vast variety of applications. Since vendors and firms invested heavily in magnetic card readers, they are not willing to invest in the next generation of card technology, the so-called smart card. In Europe, where magnetic cards lagged behind the US market, the market is more attracted to the adoption of smart card technology.[111]

These examples are less persuasive in the case of lead markets because a monopolist's adoption decision constitutes what technology a country employs. Unlike a competing company, a monopolist can wait until the revenues have justified

---

[109] There are not many empirical studies of these models. Weak and contradicting evidence for this hypothesis is presented in Nabseth and Ray (1974).

[110] Empirical studies confirm this pattern of leapfrogging by users, see Gierl (1997).

[111] Both examples are from the Reger et al. (1999) study, presented in section 5.3.5.

the investment. First of all, countries with monopolistic market structures are less likely to be lead markets. Second, infrastructure becomes less monopolistic due to worldwide deregulation and technological progress. In the mobile telecommunications industry deregulation has opened the competition between separate networks. In fixed-line telephony there are already competing backbone networks and "the last mile" to the customer can already be connected through wireless transmission. Competition keeps firms investing in the newest technology because they can lose the market to a new entrant who invests in state of the art technology. As a result, an incumbent will push its suppliers to develop technology that can frequently be upgraded in order to keep up with technological progress. A shift of the lead market is therefore not automatically given in industries with high infrastructure investments, but is more likely when competition intensity in one country exceeds the one in the lead market.

Another aspect of international shifts in national leadership has been proposed by growth theory. Brezis et al. (1993) model the situation that the leadership role of countries change. Assuming external localised learning they assert that a new, untried technology may initially be assessed inferior by firms of the leading nation compared to older technologies with which these firms have extensive experience and of which they have tacit knowledge. Lagging nations use the old technology not at all or with a lower productivity than the lead nation because they did not accumulate as much knowledge through learning-by-doing. The relative benefit of the old technology compared to the new one is therefore lower and the propensity to adopt the new technology is higher for the lagging firms than for the firms in the leading nation.[112] Brezis et al. (1993) conclude that the probability of a shift in leadership of a nation is higher (a) the higher the lag of the lag countries in wage costs , (b) the lower the usefulness of experience in the old technology for the new technology and (c) the lower the *initial* productivity of the new (untried) technology compared to the refined old technology. But the probability of a shift in leadership of a nation is also higher (d) the higher the productivity advantage of the refined new technology over the old one. Condition (a) contradicts the result that a high per-capita income is an important attribute of a lead country,[113] but the other three conditions indicate a likely shift in the lead role when technological progress is not incremental but *discontinuous*. Together with the other restrictive assumptions of the model it rather suggests that lead market are more likely to persist over a long time.

---

112 Even if firms know the superiority of a refined new technology, they would not adopt the new technology, because Brezis et al. (1993) assume learning-by-doing externalities on the national level and autonomous adoption decision by firms. If firms in the lead country act collectively, the adoption of the new technology would be rational through its anticipation of the future productivity increase of the refined new technology. This points to the technology policy of keeping the lead role, see Chapter 5.

113 The theoretical model assumes that lower wages cause higher productivity.

3.4.4 Regional dimension of lead markets

Hitherto, I have referred to lead markets as countries without formal reasoning. The question arises whether lead markets can be other regional extensions. Ohmae (1985) advocates the diminishing importance of nations in the world economy and speaks instead of triad regions as key markets, looking for instance at European countries as a whole. Regional trading blocks such as the EU, NAFTA, and Asean are said to constitute the main regional markets in the world. On the other hand, Ohmae (1995) also indicates the growing importance of subnational regions. The heterogeneity within countries can be large. Industrial agglomerations of high dynamics could become more attractive as locations than countries as a whole. Regions within countries can vary substantially in their climatic, physical and social environments. Regions such as Silicon Valley, Metropolitan Boston and other agglomerations have other market contexts (e.g., entrepreneurial effort, firm formation, competition, see Saxenian 1994) than other parts of the United States. Singapore and parts of Malaysia and Indonesia constitute the modern regional state. In Europe, subnational regions are said to compete rather than nations.[114]

The evaluation of the regional dimension of lead markets depends on the availability of data of adoption preferences. Until now, I have only gathered national data on penetration rates. A few empirical studies have analysed the adoption at the US state level, such as Griliches (1957), Redmond (1994) and Chen, Takada (1994). These studies and anecdotal evidence suggest that adoption rates can vary considerably within countries. As noted above, soft drinks were predominantly adopted in the late 19th century in the southeastern United States, because of the extreme climatic circumstances and local attitudes. Different adoption rates are expected when the environmental context and factor prices differ. Lead market factors can vary within regions as well. Per-capita income varies in advanced countries. Some regions within countries allow regional governments to set different taxes and implement different local policies. California, for instance, introduced a law requiring motor vehicle producers to sell no-emission cars by 2010 because of the extreme local pollution. Competition is most fierce in industry agglomerations such as Silicon Valley compared to other regions in the United States. On the other hand, trade blocks such as the European Union have standardised many regulations suggesting that the market contexts are converging quickly.

There are, however, still a lot more similarities within countries than among them. On average, demand is more homogenous within a country than within a trade block. Europe is still a collection of nationally specific consumers, although many institutional differences have been levelled out. As a result, the examples of lead markets in Europe (motor vehicles in Germany, smart cards in France, mobile

---

[114] In the global-regions-concept, regions compete against each other, not firms; see e.g., Amin, Thrift (1994), Huggins (1997), Storper (1993).

telephony in the Nordic countries) are mostly single European countries and not Europe as a whole. In sum, lead markets can indeed be single regions within countries or they may include a group of countries. Some countries are more heterogeneous, such as the United States and some are more integrated in a trading block, such as the Scandinavian countries. It promises to have a closer look when these countries are observed as the lead markets.

3.5 Conditions of Lead Markets Existence

The significance of a lead market is that innovation designs adopted in one market will later be adopted by other markets as well. Until now, I have outlined the definitions of the theoretical mechanisms of the internationalisation of innovations and the market-specific characteristics that facilitate these mechanisms. The lead market theory does not suggest that lead markets exist for all internationally successful innovations. In reviewing the arguments presented in this chapter, I will summarise conditions that make it more possible for a lead market phenomenon of an innovation to emerge.

The existence of lead markets requires that the stimuli of adoption of innovations vary internationally. In the theoretical consumption model the stimuli included the preferences, the prices of different designs and the income. The likelihood of a lead market existing therefore increases with the international variety of demand preferences and market conditions. If the stimuli of adoption vary internationally, *countries* prefer different innovation designs. If the stimuli were equal from country to country, there would be a globally interspersed pattern of adoption of innovations; no regional market would actually lead the international adoption of an innovation.

The internationalisation mechanisms described in this thesis can compensate for the different adoption preferences. The larger the international differences, the larger the internationalisation mechanisms must be. If countries vary so much that standardisation advantages are unlikely to compensate these differences, lead markets cannot occur.[115] Instead, there would be the persistent adoption of region-specific innovation designs. The stylised relationship between international variety and the likelihood of a country leading the adoption path of new technology is depicted in Figure 3-10. The result is an inverted u-function between variety and lead market probability.

---

[115] For instance, the government regulation for trucks and the driving behaviour of the lorry drivers differ so much between Europe and North America that truck designs preferred in both regions are totally different. Since it is unlikely that the conditions will converge, there will be no dominant design for long. Personal communication with DaimlerChrysler AG.

Figure 3-10: Relationship between lead market probability and heterogeneity of market conditions

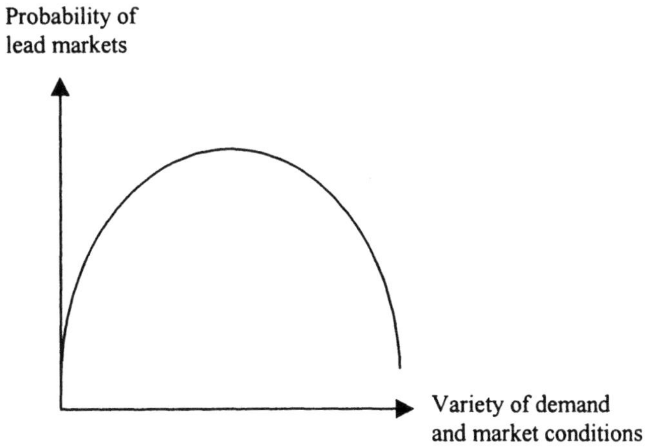

Regional adoption stimuli vary more,

- the higher the environmental specificity of technology (i.e. the higher the variance of benefit of a technology from environment to environment),
- the higher the divergence of national economic regulations in the product domain,
- the less multinational companies or mobile persons dominate as customers,
- the more the application context varies internationally,
- the higher the average income differences of the user group and
- the higher the technical variety of possible innovation designs.

The probability of the emergence of a lead market is higher, the larger the internationalisation mechanisms are that pressure towards a convergence of internationally varying designs. The larger the international standardisation advantages, the more international differences can be compensated. From the discussion of the lead market factors above, it can be concluded that the internationalisation mechanisms are larger,

- the larger the static and dynamic economies-of-scale (Price),
- the higher the price elasticity of demand in lag markets (Price),
- the larger the changes of market context (Demand),
- the larger the increasing returns-of-adoption (Transfer),
- the higher the risk and the lower the triability of the innovation (Transfer),
- the more steeply the benefits increase with learning-by-using (Transfer),

- the higher the substitutability of nationally preferred innovation designs (Export),
- the higher the R&D and capital investments for the innovation (Export)
- the higher the degree of competition (Market structure)
- the more they are still in the phase of deregulation, liberalisation and privatisation (Market structure) and
- the lower the barriers to entry (Market structure).

If the internationalisation mechanisms are large enough to compensate international differences, the innovation design becomes globally dominant whose relative advantages compared to other designs is largest. For instance, one innovation design has an advantage to become the global dominant design if it has a relatively higher cost reduction potential, higher global increasing returns-of-adoption and so on.

Finally, lead markets are more prominent in markets with more technical opportunities. It was suggested that the industry life cycle, as outlined above (2.4), does not exist for industries if there are no rich opportunities for innovations (see Tether and Storey 1998, p. 949 for a review). In industries with low technical opportunities the main problem for a firm is how to generate innovations. There are not that many innovations and innovation designs competing.

This thesis will proceed with a case study on the cellular mobile telephone industry. The case study is intended to further assess the applicability of the system of lead market factors derived in this chapter. Chapter 5 will address the question of how multinational firms can use the lead market concept to generate global innovations.

4 The Case of Cellular Mobile Telephony

God sent Mobiles...
GEORG SCHMITT, PRESIDENT D2 MANNESMANN, GERMANY

Although the final decision was not made until February 1987, a digital [mobile] system was what we were all working towards for quite a few years.
THOMAS HAUG, TELEKOM SWEDEN

Since their invention in the 1920s, mobile telephone services have evolved only gradually over time as a niche market unnoticed by most businesses and consumers. Yet, mobile telephony has revolutionised telecommunications in the 1990s. The international diffusion of mobile telephony took off in the 1990s when new digital technology was introduced and prices fell so that more and more private consumers could afford it. From an industry ridiculed as "Mom and Pop"-operator business in the United States (Calhoun 1988), the mobile telephone business emerged as one of the industries most valued by stock markets around the world. The International Telecommunications Union (ITU) now admits that against all former predictions mobile telephony is on its way to substituting fixed-line telephony. Mobile data communications is rapidly evolving as a totally new form of communications, transforming the daily life of most people in almost all countries.[116] Among several technical concepts, digital cellular mobile systems have become the global dominant design of mobile telephony. This case study will examine whether a country or a region adopted the dominant design earlier than others and, if this is the case, why it did so and what this has meant for the international competitiveness of companies in these countries. At first glance, there are two surprising outcomes of the world-wide mobile telephone industry: first, despite their technological knowledge advantage in radio technology, the United States have not become the market with the highest penetration rates that led the

[116] See for instance ITU (1999), OECD (1999), Economist (1999c).

world into a new area of telecommunications. Second, Japanese manufacturers do not dominate the mobile telecommunications equipment market despite their advantage in electronics, miniaturisation of electronic devices, and their dominance in other telecommunications equipment sectors such as facsimile machines, consumer electronics and cameras. In contrast to the prediction derived from technological gap and comparative advantage theory, the Nordic countries, as I will call Norway, Sweden, Finland and Denmark, happened to be the markets where cellular mobile telephony was first widely adopted; these countries' companies dominate the world mobile telephone equipment industry.

In this case study, four hypotheses shall be supported. First, that mobile telephony is a lead market phenomenon. Second, that the lead market can be differentiated by the lead market factors derived in the first chapter. Third, that the firms located or having their headquarters in the lead market became internationally competitive. Fourth, that the lead market could have been identified before the mobile telephony industry emerged as a mass market in the early 1990s.

4.1 Methodology

The methodology followed here is based on the lead market concept elaborated on earlier. The study is an international comparison of lead market factors for the case of mobile telephony. It is examined whether the rank of adoption of the dominant design in mobile telephony is correlated with the degree of markedness of the lead market factors. For some lead market factors quantitative indicators could be found, for other factors the international comparison has to be qualitative. In addition, the roles of supply factors for the international diffusion of mobile telephony, such as technological knowledge leads and suppliers, are discussed.

This case study was prepared on the basis of the existing literature on the mobile cellular telephony industry complemented by extensive non-structured interviews with key-officials from telecom equipment producers and telecom operators. The cellular mobile telephone industry has attracted many researchers since it became successful internationally. There are two strands of literature. First, there are econometric estimations of diffusion models.[117] These formal diffusion studies were enabled (or induced) by the availability of time series data on the number of subscribers for almost all countries published by the International Telecommunication Union (ITU). They focus on the diffusion pattern of mobile phones within countries, while the lag between the diffusion in countries was not explained and the different cellular standards not taken into account. The second strand of literature contains rich case studies on the success factors of cellular telephony and the GSM standard in particular.[118] Among the existing studies reviewed, the most

[117] Ihde (1996), Dekimpe et al. (1998a), Frank (1992), Gruber, Verboven (1999).

[118] Cattaneo (1994), Mölleryd (1997), Calhoun (1988), Paetsch (1993).

insightful were the detailed study of Calhoun (1988) concerning what he calls the "disaster" of the US analog cellular mobile telephone industry and the analysis of the Swedish mobile industry by Mölleryd (1997). The shortcoming of these studies is that the theoretical model is not clear. Furthermore, most studies are limited to the mobile telephony industry in one country. The factors of the international diffusion of digital mobile telephony have scarcely been discussed as yet.

The interview partners have been carefully selected for their knowledge surrounding the historical background of the mobile telephone industry. Most of them were actively involved in the development of cellular mobile telephone systems. The questions discussed concentrated on the success factors of the cellular mobile telephony and the GSM standard in particular. The findings of the interviews and the literature were then assigned to the lead market and supply factors. The interview partners were Dr. Werner Irler (Lucent), Markku Sari (Nokia), Karl Kammerlander (Siemens), Hans-Jürgen von der Neyen (Siemens), Heinz Blanckenfeld (Siemens), Friedhelm Hillebrand (Deutsche Bundespost, MoU GSM, ETSI) and Dr. Manfred Böhm (SEL Alcatel). In addition to literature and interview sources, I have collected data on indicators of the lead market factors discussed from a range of sources such as telecom operators, public and private market research data bases and journals. This data, however, does not allow an econometric analysis. First, most of the data is difficult to obtain on a multi-country level. Second, I am interested in lags in the adoption of mobile telephony among the highly industrialised countries that are similar in general stimuli of adoption such as per-capita income, infrastructure and technological capabilities. The study is therefore mostly confined to the United States, Japan, and the European countries.

I start by describing the technical concept of radio telephony and history of mobile telephony. Before turning to the international comparison of lead market factors, cellular telephony is presented as a lead market phenomenon. In this first section, three characteristics of cellular telephony as a lead market phenomenon will be described. First, that countries initially preferred different designs of mobile telephony due to their market context and environment. Second, that there is a considerable adoption lag of cellular telephony between the most advanced countries. Third, that cellular telephony prevailed on the world market and other competing designs that were initially favoured by a few countries failed. The main body of the case study is the discussion of the lead market factors. The last section discusses how the companies of lead markets benefited from their home market advantage becoming the internationally leading producers of mobile telephony equipment. I conclude with the question of whether firms could have anticipated the success of cellular telephony and could have set the right strategy at the right time to participate in the lead market advantage and the success of a new technology.

4.2 Cellular Mobile Telephony as a Dominant Design

4.2.1 Technical concept

To understand the economics of mobile telephony, one has to familiarise oneself with some technical details. Mobile telephony is defined as radio communication between a land station and mobile phones within a specific regional zone. In contrast with private mobile radio systems that offer only mobile-to-mobile connections, such as CB radio, a mobile telephone system connects mobile units with the public fixed-line telephone system. Radio communication uses a frequency band for sending and, in the case of simultaneous two way communication (duplex), another one for receiving speech. The band, which is divided into channels, is part of the frequency spectrum. The spectrum is the range of frequencies of electromagnetic waves which transmit information through space. The frequency of a wave is measured by the inverse of the time of one oscillation; a continuous oscillation of one second has a frequency of 1 Hz. The spectrum is allocated by national agencies to broadcasting stations, TV channels and various public and private mobile telephone services. Although the spectrum is infinite, physical properties of the propagation of radio waves limit the spectrum suitable for land-mobile communication to the range between 30 MHz and 3 GHz (Paetsch 1993, p. 55). The amount of information of a telephone call transmitted through radio waves requires typically two channels with a bandwidth of about 20 kHz. Therefore the spectrum is a scarce good, as only a limited number of mobile units can use the spectrum allocated to mobile telephony at any one time.

A mobile telephone system generally consists of base stations and one or more mobile switching centres (MSC). Each base station contains the antenna, radio transmitter and receiver and maintains the two-way radio links to and from the mobile units that are moving within the zone around the base station. The mobile switching centre connects the mobile calls to the communication partner in the fixed-line network. A MSC is similar to a conventional fixed-line switching centre. Base stations are connected to mobile switching centres through cables or microwave radio transmission. In adjacent zones different frequencies are used for transmitting calls so that the radio waves of calls cannot interfere (Lee 1989, p. 47).

The first mobile telephony systems were „pre-cellular" services. The base station was hosted by a powerful broadcast tower, which was normally located in the centre of a metropolitan area covering a wide area of 60-80 km radius (Paetsch 1993, p. 23). Subscribers could not move from one of these areas to another during calls and the caller had to know in which area the person he or she wanted to call was circulating. The difference between cellular and pre-cellular mobile telephony is that in a cellular system, a user can move from one zone to another zone during a call without reinitiating the call. This is possible because a cellular system has a hand-over or a handoff capability. A handoff is "a process of automatically changing frequencies as the mobile unit moves into a different frequency zone so that the conversation can be continued in a new frequency zone without redialing" (Lee 1989, p. 2). During the handoff process, the base station in the zone that the user is leaving transfers the handling of the call to the base station in the zone the caller is entering. Handoffs are especially important for calls made from moving motor vehicles and trains, which are likely to exit one zone and enter another one during a call. In cellular technology a zone is called a cell. Because of the handoff capability, many smaller and lower-powered broadcast towers, each covering a cell of between 2 and 20 km radius, can be employed than in pre-cellular telephony, in which large towers each cover a whole metropolitan area. A cellular system covers a country like a fine patchwork.

An additional service of cellular telephony is known as "roaming": a user can operate a mobile phone in a cellular system which he is not subscribed to. When a user enters a system of a different operator, he is registered as a visitor and gains access to the network. The two network operators must have an agreement in order to provide the roaming service. Roaming is possible only between networks of the same standard. A cellular standard is predominantly a technical specification of the interface between mobile units, base stations and switching centers, in essence how the voice is converted into electromagnetic signals (Warnecke, Jung 1998, p. 4-123). Besides these features, another main reason for the development of cellular telephony is its increased frequency efficiency. A cellular system uses frequencies more economically than pre-cellular systems and therefore provides more capacity (Lee 1989, p. 2). The smaller the cells, the more subscribers can make calls at the same time because a frequency used in a cell can be *reused* in other cells. Furthermore, when traffic density reaches the limit of a cell, the cell can be divided to increase the capacity of a cellular system at "hot spots" such as densely populated cities (Lee 1989, p. 61).

The first cellular systems were analog systems. In an analog system the call is transmitted between the mobile phone and the land base station as an analog signal, a continuous function of the waveform of the voice (Lee 1989, p. 401). In a digital system, the voice is transmitted through the air as a digital (discrete) signal and transformed into an analog signal in the mobile unit and vice versa. Digital systems offer a much higher frequency efficiency due to lower signal-to-noise ratios that enable large penetration rates of mobile telephony. Although a digital signal needs more bandwidth than an analog signal, in a digital system a frequency can be used by several subscribers at the same time in the same cell by time division (TDMA) or code division (CDMA) techniques. Digital systems were already used in the 1980s in defense-related mobile communication systems since they can use encrypted signals and are better suited for rough media and to counteract enemy jamming (Lee 1989, p. 402, Calhoun 1988, p. 344). However, because voice quality of digital mobile systems in terms of fidelity was initially lower than the quality of analog systems, digital systems were not used for civil mobile telephony until microelectronic devices allowed better quality. The cellular systems of the second generation that were introduced in the 1990s were digital systems.

Cellular telephony is only one type of mobile telephony and it itself has a large variety of possible technical specifications. The cell size, modulation, coding, required power level, bit rate, quality, error code, multiplexing have each to be selected from a variety of possible modes. There are several trade-offs between speech quality, amount of investment as well as cost of service, frequency efficiency, capacity in rural and densely populated areas, size of terminals (phones) and data transmission capacity. There is no unique "best" standard; the benefit of a cellular system varies from country to country depending on user demands, geography, vegetation and population density. As a result, countries would select different systems and a variety of incompatible systems would be employed. At the end of the 1990s a global dominant design emerged within this variety: digital cellular telephony prevailed against other mobile systems and among the several standards, the GSM dominates internationally. This international success implies that the disadvantage of international standardisation must have been overcompensated by standardisation advantages. Therefore, mobile cellular telephony has the *technical characteristic* of a lead market technology. The next question is whether there are countries that favoured cellular telephony and GSM early and facilitated the international diffusion of that particular mode of mobile communication and of that standard. In this section, the international adoption gap of cellular telephony in general and the GSM standard in particular is reviewed. Next, I demonstrate that the cellular design and the GSM standard prevailed internationally against other mobile services and other cellular standards. After this, I discuss whether the international adoption gap of cellular telephony was due to a technology gap or a demand gap. For the latter, I apply the concept of lead market factors to the case of mobile cellular telephony to test whether lead markets as defined above were the source of the global diffusion pattern. It will be argued in this thesis that the evolution of the mobile telephone industry towards a global dominant design, the digital cellular mobile system, was mainly a market-driven international diffusion of an innovation that started in the lead market of the Nordic countries.

4.2.2 The history of mobile telephony

The pattern of the international diffusion of cellular mobile telephony between 1980 and 1998 shows that some countries, in this case the Nordic countries, have a continuing lead in its adoption (Figure 4-1). During the whole period the penetration rates of cellular telephony were continually highest in Sweden and Finland. This observation is consistent with the lead market phenomenon. Second, it can be suggested that the global evolution of cellular telephony was shaped by the systems and standards adopted in the leading countries. Cellular mobile telephony is embedded in the history of mobile telephony that reaches back to the 1940s. Cellular mobile telephony was introduced in the 1970s and adopted in the 1980s. Mobile telephone services are developing from national industries towards a

Figure 4-1: Diffusion of cellular telephony in several countries 1980-2000

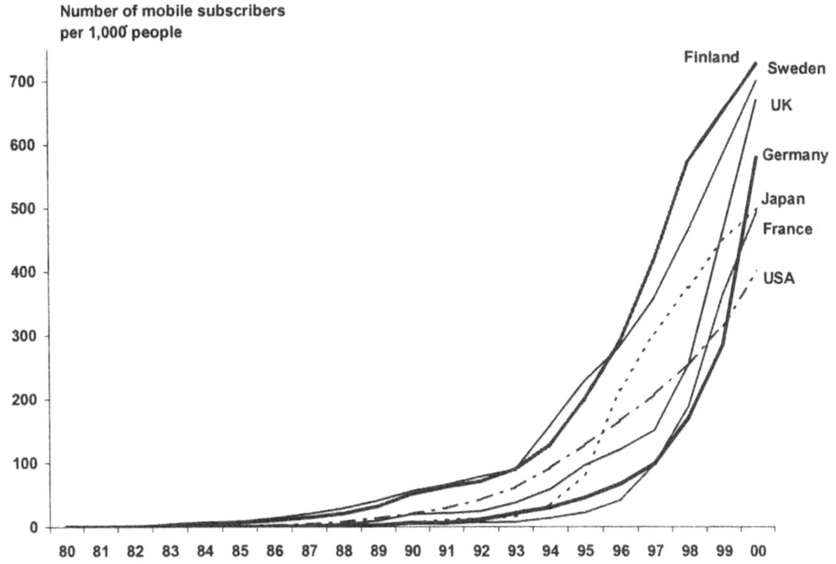

Source: ITU, own calculations.

global industry and from national standards to a globally dominating standard. Figure 4-2 gives an overview of the evolution of the main pre-cellular and cellular mobile telephony standards. The horizontal axis shows the geographic dimension, the vertical axis the time. The diagram visualises a trend from national standards to regional standards towards world standards that started in the Nordic countries (from right to left). The Nordic countries first anticipated the trend in adopting a transnational cellular standard. At present, the third cellular generation is expected to become a globally dominant standard (WCDMA).

Before I elaborate on the lead market factors that were responsible for the successful international diffusion, I shall briefly review the history of mobile telephony. Three distinct periods in which the usage of mobile communication fundamentally changed can be identified: the period of pre-cellular telephony, of analog cellular and of digital cellular mobile telephony.

The era of pre-cellular mobile telephony

Mobile radio communication started in the 1920s in the United States as a one-way service to police cars. In 1946, a mobile telephone service for private users, the Mobile telephony system (MTS), was introduced in the US market by AT&T (Calhoun 1988). This service was later operated by several private operators, the radio common carriers (RCC). In the 1950s mobile telephony started in Europe.

Figure 4-2: Evolution of mobile standards

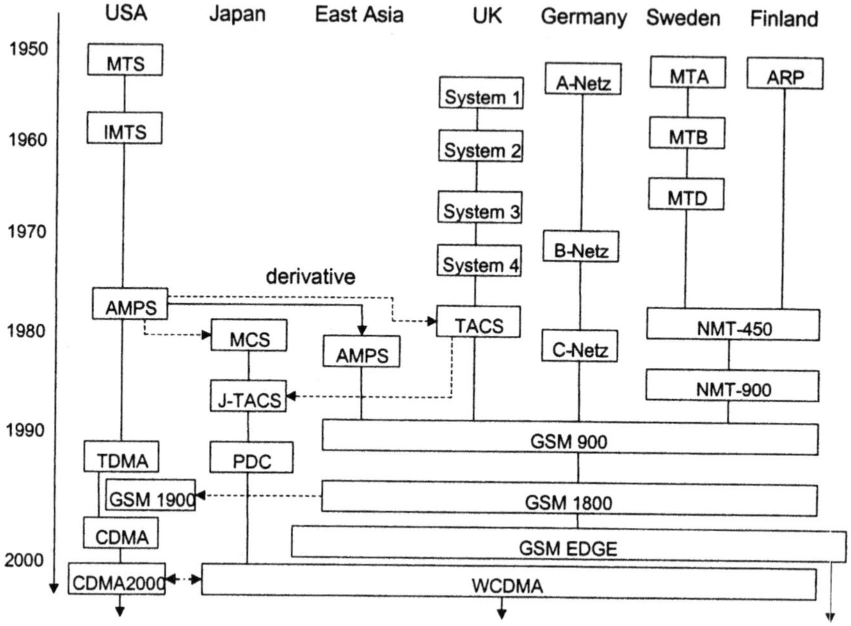

Source: Author on the basis of Scheele (1992).

Swedish Telecom was the first to operate an automatic mobile telephone system (MTA) in 1956. The development of the MTA system started at the end of the 1940s (Hultén, Mölleryd 1995). Germany introduced its first mobile service in 1958, the so-called A-Netz[119].

These first pre-cellular mobile systems had a small capacity and were confined to a small group of subscribers who used mobile telephony predominantly for their jobs, such as doctors and taxi drivers. For instance, the German A-Netz had a capacity of 1,000 subscribers and its successor, the B-Netz, which started in 1970, could handle 10,000 subscribers. In New York City, only 12 users among the 543 subscribers could make calls at the same time (1976); 2,400 customers were on a waiting list to subscribe to the service (Lee 1989, p. 2). In other countries, too, there was much more demand for mobile telephony than could be offered by the telephone operator. In the 1970s the first networks were substituted with gradually improved systems like the B-Netz in Germany, the MTC and a manual interim system MTD in Scandinavia, and the IMTS (Improved Mobile telephony system)

[119] The A-Netz was basically the interconnection of previously existing special mobile services such as maritime and emergency radio services (Stolcke 1991, Jung, Warnecke 1998, p. 3-57).

in the US. However, subscriber numbers remained low compared to existing demand (see e.g. Calhoun 1988, p. 12).

The transition to cellular mobile telephony

At the end of the 1970s, cellular mobile telephony was first realised in the US. It was an improvement on pre-cellular mobile telephony. After the Federal Communications commission (FCC), the national regulator, allocated significant spectrum in the UHF band to mobile telephony in 1970, Bell labs, the research laboratory of AT&T, immediately started to develop a cellular mobile system (Millman 1984, p. 232). At the same time, technological progress such as large-scale integrated chips (VLSI) paved the way for advanced mobile systems (Lee 1989, p. 4). The new technology also lowered the size and the cost of mobile transceivers. In the 1970s, AT&T developed the cellular mobile standard AMPS (Advanced Mobile Phone Service). In 1978, developmental cellular systems were tested in Chicago (Young 1979). Public cellular services started in the US in 1983, after a decade-long delay of granting licenses for the 800 MHz band by the FCC. Nation-wide operation of cellular telephony was again heavily delayed. As a result of the deregulation process in telephony in the early 1980s, licenses for mobile communication services started to be granted for 306 metropolitan areas (MSA) from 1982 on, and for 428 rural service areas (RSA) from 1988 on (Paetsch 1993, p. 154). About 1500 licences were finally granted, with two licences in each of the metropolitan or rural areas, one to a Bell-system operator, the other by a lottery to new wireless competitors. Most metropolitan areas commenced operation between 1984 and 1987, while many rural areas remained without cellular services for a few more years.

In the meantime, the first cellular mobile systems had been introduced in the Tokyo area of Japan in 1979, in Sweden in 1981 and in Finland in 1982. All Nordic countries used the same standard, the NMT system (Nordic Mobile Telephony) while in Japan a national standard was developed. In contrast to Japan, where no pre-cellular service had been available for private users before that time (Pemple 1978), pre-cellular mobile service was already a big market success in Sweden and Finland. The Japanese system commenced service within metropolitan areas[120], while in the Nordic countries rural areas were included early in the coverage.

Other countries followed in the mid-1980s. In the UK, two operators were given mobile licenses and operated a mobile network from early 1985 and 1987 respectively. A committee specified a variant of the AMPS system, called TACS (Total access cellular system), adapted to the special conditions in the UK, (Garrett 1984, Scheele 1992, p. 74). In Germany, the first cellular net, the C-450 developed by Siemens, was commercially launched at the end of 1985. Like their predecessors,

[120] In 1985 about three quarters of the subscribers lived in the metropolitan Tokyo area, 25 % of the inhabitable area was covered (Lee 1989, p. 29).

these mobile services were considered as services to and from automobiles. The phones were therefore large, heavy, vehicle-mounted phones. In the mid-1980s the first "mobile" phones were introduced, but they were still as large as a briefcase. In 1987 the first handheld phones for the US, the Japanese, the British and the Scandinavian mobile systems became available. It took a few more years before handheld phones became available for latecomer systems like the C-Net in Germany, as well. Cellular phones were predominantly used for business. The consumer mass market for mobile telephony finally emerged in the 1990s in the Nordic countries. In the year 1990, the penetration rate in the US was about 2 %, compared to more than 5 % in the Nordic countries. A consumer market was not established in the United States and in other parts of the world until the mid-1990s (Paetsch 1993, p. 165). In these countries, the mass market came with the transition from analog to digital technology.

Digital cellular systems and the emergence of the mobile mass-market

Digital technology was introduced into the fixed-line telephone networks in the 1970s in the United States and in the 1980s it became clear that digital switching would prevail in fixed-line telephony worldwide. As a result, digital cellular mobile telephony was also discussed in the 1980s as an alternative to analog systems, but it was unclear whether it would prevail in mobile communications as well due to inferior speech quality. Digital technology required large R&D investments before complex problems could be solved and a digital service could be offered to demanding users.[121] Digital technology was chosen, first in Europe and later in Japan and the US, because it offered several advantages. The most important advantages are among others (see Calhoun 1988, pp. 187-195, Lee 1989, pp. 402, 431, Paetsch 1993):

- enhanced spectrum capacity due to reduced signal-to-noise ratios and multiplexing techniques enables large subscriber numbers,
- VLSI chips makes large cost reductions possible,
- handheld phones could be smaller, lighter in weight and have a lower power consumption than analog phones,
- additional services such as data transmission can be offered (intelligent network),
- it could be improved over time without needing to redesign the entire system (Paetsch 1993, p. 69, p. 288).

[121] Estimates for the GSM standard are difficult to achieve, but telecom operators in countries such as Germany, Sweden and France are estimated to have spent about $150 million each for the standard specification phase only, see e.g. Päch (1994, p. 88), Hultén, Mölleryd (1995).

Figure 4-3: Number of subscribers world-wide of several digital standards 1991-1999

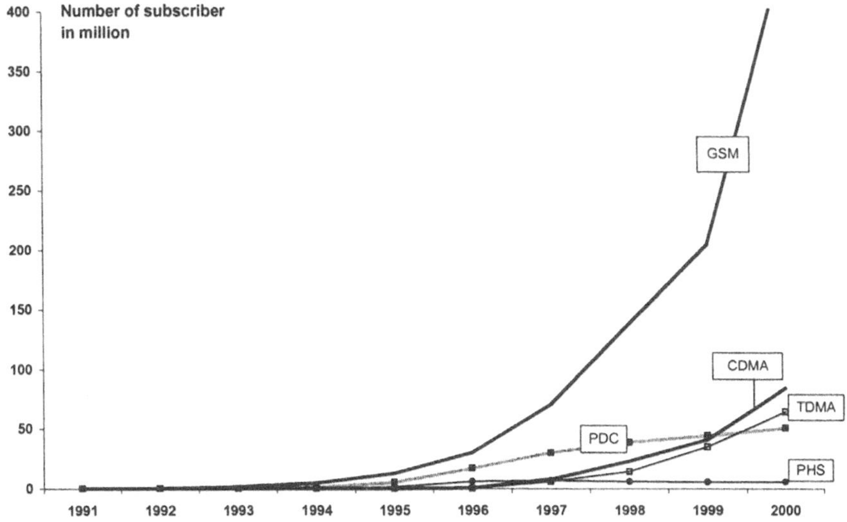

Source: ITU, CDMA Development Group, EMC, TCA, GSM MoU.

Rather unexpectedly, digital technology actually enabled a mass market. With the introduction of digital service, capacity constraints ceased and penetration rates soared to unexpected heights throughout the 1990s (Figure 4-1). No market forecasting study predicted that success. First considered as an additional service for people who had to be mobile due to their job, new users became constantly younger, less prosperous and less educated. In 1997 mobile penetration exceeded fixed line-penetration in Finland (Äckermark 1999). Cellular telephony is beginning to substitute subscriber fixed-line telephony. At the end of the 1990s mobile telephony operators such as NTT DoCoMo and Deutsche Telekom were incorporated and listed on the stock market and became one of the most valued public traded companies.

Among several proposals of communications equipment firms and operators, four main standards for digital cellular mobile systems competed at the end of the 1980s. These standards, the pan-European standard GSM, the Japanese standard PDC and two American standards D-AMPS and CDMA, compete on the world market. Over time the European standard GSM got to dominate digital cellular mobile telephony (Figure 4-3).

The international success of GSM

The GSM standard setting process was coordinated in the GSM group (Groupe Spécial Mobile) in which the European public post administrations (PTT) and manufacturers of telecommunications equipment participated. The idea of a common European cellular standard was originally initiated in 1980 by the Dutch and Scandinavian PTTs within the CEPT, the union of 26 European public telecom administrations (Cattaneo 1994, p. 62). CEPT established a working group in 1982 that had the task of evaluating the possibility of a pan-European standard for the next decade. Although CEPT working groups had before had limited impact, this one would emerge as most important for the mobile telecommunication industry in the 1990s. Two years later, France and Germany's political administrations took the initiative to promote a Franco-German digital standard as the nucleus of a European standard, after attempts for a joint Franco-British and Franco-German analog cellular system (C900) failed (Päch 1994, p. 82). This bilateral agreement was then joined by Italy and the UK and merged with the European CEPT group GSM, which set up its permanent headquarters in Paris in June 1986.

The Groupe Spécial Mobile (GSM) specified the new pan-European standard, the Global System for Mobile Communication between 1986 and 1990. Between November 1986 and January 1987, the new standard was at a cross-roads when the GSM group tested eight technical proposals of PTTs and equipment manufacturers from France, Germany, Sweden and Norway. Although the Franco-German initiative revitalised the European standardisation effort, the politically sponsored Franco-German wideband technology was rejected by all other participants at a technical meeting in Madeira in February 1987. The group decided in favour of the Scandinavian favourite of digital narrowband TDMA which finally became the GSM standard. The decisive factors for the choice were economic criteria and mass market suitability of high frequency efficiency, flexibility and phone portability, economical deployment in rural areas and low investments (Böhm 1987). Politicians in Bonn and Paris were outraged but after mere cosmetic changes in the specification a compromise was pretended at Ministerial level in May in Bonn. At a conference in Brussels in June 1987, all participants agreed unanimously on the proposed system. And in September of the same year, 13 countries signed a memorandum of understanding (MoU) to introduce GSM services in the 1990s. In February 1988 all participating PTTs issued invitations-to-tender.

The MoU initially called for a launch of the first GSM service by July 1st 1991, but the commercial launch of GSM was delayed because the agreement on the final specification between all the participants came too late to develop test equipment needed to develop GSM base stations and handsets. As a result, handsets were not yet available when the first operators switched on their networks in 1992. The cellular boom started in Europe in 1994.[122] In the same year the first

122 The European network operators decided in the mid-1980s to jointly develop a digital standard for the 1990s, the GSM standard. However, during the mid-1980s the growth of subscribers for mobile cellular telephony was so high in many European countries that additional analog networks had to be installed before the digital standard was available. These networks were called interim systems and were mostly TACS and

country outside Europe adopted GSM. Australia's PTT chose the European standard as its digital system because it was the only digital system already online (Kennedy 1999). Other countries in Asia followed. Although the European analog cellular standard NMT was already successful in the 1980s in Asia and the Middle East, several countries had previously adopted a non-European standard but switched to GSM. Australia operated an AMPS mobile system in the 1980s. The same transition from the US to the European standard took place in Pakistan, Singapore, Hong Kong and the Philippines. Only two countries adopted a Japanese system built by Matsushita, namely Egypt and Qatar; both countries switched to GSM in the 1990s. In contrast to this, however, there are no countries that switched from a European to a US and Japanese analog standard. Although Europeans have a record of export successes, GSM was even more successful than the European analog systems and began to dominate the world-wide subscriber numbers even with respect to the large home market of the US standards.

At the end of the 1980s a new concept of mobile communications was discussed, the personal communication network (PCN). Not the automobile but the individual was seen as the holder of a mobile terminal. Although PCN was not a technical but a market concept, it was at that time expected that capacity and the size, weight and price could not been matched by existing cellular networks (Paetsch 1993, p. 325). Yet, the ongoing technical progress induced by the tremendous success of the first GSM services enabled GSM to become the PCN concept with light handheld phones and the personal services envisioned. In 1989 the UK Department of Trade and Industry published its support for PCN mainly to increase competition in the local loop, the fixed-line connection between the backbone telephone network and the individual homes, which is in most countries monopolised by the incumbent PTT. PCN was anticipated as the future mass market mobile communication system using even newer technology than GSM. To overcome the capacity constraints already visible in the 900 MHz band, PCN should use the 1800 MHz band. As a result of the rapid growth in subscribers to cellular services, the British government acted quickly and awarded three PCN licenses in December 1989. The British, however, were pressured into letting the newly founded European standardisation institution (ETSI) determine the technical specification.

NMT systems. France is the only country that introduced a separate new analog system, Radiocom2000 developed by the French company Matra (Scheele 1992, p. 71). These interim networks eased the pressure from demand until GSM networks could start. In Germany, no interim network was built up because there were still doubts concerning the prospects of cellular telephony and the belief that other systems like pagers and cordless telephony would attract more subscribers (Scheele 1992, p. 59). This led to the situation that GSM was so highly needed at the beginning of the 1990s that German licensees pressed harder than anyone else for an early launch of GSM. The first GSM service started in 1992 in Finland and Germany and shortly after in most other European countries. Germany, however, did not "leap-frog" other countries in the adoption of cellular services as penetration rates in GSM service remained far behind the penetration rates of most other European countries throughout the 1990s.

After reviewing the merit of cordless and cellular technology in Europe, ETSI decided to use the cellular GSM specification for the 1800 MHz band, first named DCS1800 and later GSM1800 (Paetsch 1993, p. 329). Most European countries adopted the new GSM standard as well.

The failure of the other digital cellular standards

In the United States the process towards digital cellular standards was quite different from that in Europe. US cellular operators contemplated introducing a digital cellular system at the end of the 1980s due to capacity shortages of the analog system in some metropolitan areas. In contrast to Europe, no particular digital standard was governmentally sponsored. A variety of potential digital standards were proposed: TDMA on the basis of the GSM standard, CDMA, a spread spectrum technique developed by Qualcomm, Inc. for defense-related communication, E-TDMA proposed by Hughes, and even a new analog standard, N-AMPS, proposed by Motorola using narrower band channels. The cellular operators association CTIA finally endorsed TDMA as the digital standard in 1991 (Mason 1991). While the GSM network is incompatible with the analog networks, the shift from analog to digital service in the USA went off incrementally through a dual-use phase with dual cellular infrastructure and dual-mode phones. While the standard was specified at the same time as GSM, the commercial launch of TDMA was delayed. The delay was caused by technical problems, and the low market prospect of heavier and bulkier dual-mode handheld phones (Paetsch 1993, p. 183). But even when the first TDMA service was launched in 1993, suspicions about its technical inferiority (Mason 1993) and uncertainty about its chance of becoming the dominant digital standard in the US (Anthony 1994) prevented total TDMA coverage in the 1990s. Operators decided on an individual basis when and what standard to deploy – in contrast to the previously mandatory adoption of the AMPS system. A dispute between CDMA and TDMA remained heated and some operators backed off from the TMDA decision and announced they were to adopt CDMA instead (Anthony 1993). The new PCS frequency spectrum on the 1900 MHz band made available by the FCC in the 1990s was another uncertainty. The FCC followed a "let the best standard win" strategy and auctioned frequency bands letting the operator decide what standard to use. Although the CDMA standard gained support as a superior digital standard, technical problems delayed the commercial CDMA service until 1996. Korean firms supported the development for CDMA equipment and launched a service in 1996. While the transition from AMPS to TDMA dragged on for years, CDMA could initially gain a small lead in subscriber numbers. The two standards are, however, incompatible, dividing the US market once again into fragmented regional markets without total coverage.

Timing was the big problem of the US digital standards: TDMA was offered later than GSM and a CDMA system was not available in the first half of the 1990s. GSM emerged as the digital frontrunner and gained a lead in subscriber base which the US standards could never make up (Figure 4-3). The US standards

CDMA and TDMA were refined to the Americas and Korea. Outside the US, GSM and US standards competed directly only in Hong Kong in the 1990s and GSM attracted most of the subscribers. Within the digital cellular services the GSM standards keep a world-wide market share of two thirds against 18 % PDC, 7 % TDMA and 9 % CDMA (as of end of 1998, all market share data from EMC world cellular database). GSM even made inroads into the US market. In 1995, when the PCS licenses on the 1900 MHz band were granted in the US, the first commercial GSM service was launched in the United States. A GSM variant was adapted to the 1900 MHz band and introduced in the US, first as DSM1900 but swiftly renamed to GSM1900. Over time, 18 network operators acquired licences for PCS and joined in a GSM alliance (O'Keefe 1997). By 1999, handheld phones which could operate on all three GSM bands (tri-band) were offered by the industry. Although GSM services achieved only the status of a minor player, with a digital cellular market share of 18 % at the end of the 1990s against the TDMA (45%) and CDMA (36%), subsequently launched by the large US-public telephone operators like Airtouch and Sprint as PCS service in 1987, the establishment of GSM in the US was a most unexpected success. At first glance, political sponsorship seems to be an important factor in the success and failure of standards. Yet a closer analysis shows that the pressure from the markets in Europe pushed new technology development. On the other side of the coin, market uncertainty about mobile markets and the right technology (cellular vs. satellites) in the United States inhibited new technology employment much more than political indecisiveness. Below, the lead market factors guiding and channelling the political administration's effort will be discussed in detail.

In Japan, digital service was based on a national standard, JDC renamed to PDC, and commenced operation in 1994. Despite export promotion it was not adopted outside Japan. Another Japanese mobile standard, PHS, fared even worse. Two years after its introduction, PHS started to lose subscribers to cellular services. PHS is not a cellular but a cordless standard and its failure is described in the next section. Several alternative systems for mobile telephony have been developed and adopted in countries where the benefit of these systems were high, but which never became widely adopted world-wide. In contrast to cellular technology, other technologies such as the cordless and hybrid system, which were suggested and tested on the market as PCNs, could not gain acceptance. Although these alternative mobile systems were initially successful in several countries, they were – even there – swiftly squeezed out by cellular systems. The next section reviews these alternative systems.

4.2.3 The competition from other mobile communication systems

Cellular mobile telephony is only one means of mobile communications; there are other technologies such as satellites, cordless telephones and pagers which competed against cellular telephony. In contrast to the commercially successful mobile cellular telephony, these other systems of personal mobile communications failed in the market, or have been successful in a few countries only and were rejected by the market of most other countries. While cellular telephony generated high profits, these other services were often financial losses – fiascos even. This is a remaining principal characteristic of a lead market phenomenon of cellular telephony. The failure of three systems will be briefly discussed: pagers, cordless telephony and satellite-based personal communication. Pagers, a word derived from the meaning of a page calling for someone (Stolcke 1991), are used to send messages to people on the move. The most common usage is to notify a person that he or she should contact a previously known number. Pagers are passive receivers of messages. Pager services are either tone-only, notifying the subscriber by an audible tone, numeric, transmitting a number on a pager's display, or alphanumeric, transmitting a text message (Paetsch 1993, p. 32). Simple pager services were introduced in the United States from 1950 and later in other countries. Pagers were most successful in the United States, Singapore and Hong Kong and to a lesser extent in other countries. When cellular telephony emerged, penetration rates of pagers declined in most countries. Since digital cellular telephony offers the same functionality as pagers most subscribers of pagers switched to cellular in the 1990s. Figure 4-4 depicts the penetration rates of pagers and cellular in Hong Kong, Finland and Japan from 1980 on. When penetration rates of cellular services took off, those of pagers declined rapidly. In Finland, where cellular telephony was adopted by more people than anywhere else in the early 1980s, pagers were never adopted widely. It seems that Finland followed an adoption path early on which later prevailed world-wide. Other countries, notably the Asian city states and Japan, followed a technology adoption path which they later abandoned in order to switch to a different one.

The same pattern can be observed in public cordless telephony. Cordless telephony or public access mobile cordless telephony is another variant of mobile telephony. Cordless telephones first replaced subscriber-line telephones within buildings using a low-power radio link to a fixed-line station located in the building (Paetsch 1993, p. 32). In the 1980s public cordless telephone systems were developed that extended the reach to several hundred meters around a base station. These base stations are located at places with high public traffic, for instance at gas stations, while most other areas are not covered. The advantage of cordless telephony was that cordless phones were initially smaller, lighter and cheaper than cellular phones due to the low power consumption and reduced functionality. However, public cordless telephones could not receive calls. Several standards for cordless telephony were proposed in Europe, e.g. DECT, CT2 (Turtlebee 1996), and Japan (PHS) (Wakabayashi 1994).

Figure 4-4: Number of subscribers to pager and cellular services in Finland, Hong Kong and Japan 1980-1999

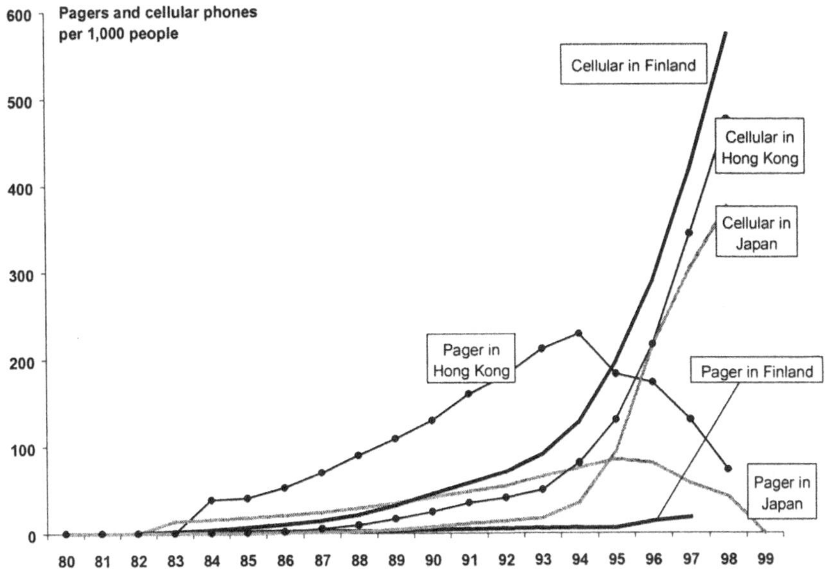

Source: ITU

Public cordless telephony was initiated in the UK and tested in several countries in Europe and Asia since the end of the 1980s under the name telepoint. It was expected that the telepoint service would be able to complement the communication pattern of pagers, meaning that cordless services would be accepted in countries with high pager penetration. Yet telepoint failed in Europe, a "telepoint graveyard" (Montefiore 1996), and was never introduced in the US, where pagers are used widely. However, it grew rapidly in metropolitan areas of Asian countries. Between 1993 and 1994 the number of Asian subscribers grew from 196,000 to 290,000 (Montefiore 1996, p. 60). Despite their initial success in South-East Asia and in particular in the city states Hong Kong and Singapore, "where operators could establish rapid coverage in key business and residential districts with minimum infrastructure investments" (Montefiore 1996, p. 66), they were quickly squeezed out of the market by local cellular services and in particular the GSM system in the mid-1990s. After local cellular operators reduced prices and introduced new marketing promotions offering subsidised handsets, telepoint subscribers migrated to cellular services. Telepoint services were then closed in most countries and the remaining subscribers transferred to cellular networks.[123]

[123] Unfortunately, no data on telepoint subscribers by country and year is available.

A similar concept was introduced by Japanese telephone operators in 1994. The Personal Handy Phone System (PHS) is a mobile telephone that can be used in micro cells of 300 meter radius. A handover of a call from cell to cell is not possible but PHS avoided the main disadvantage of telepoint in that calls could be made as well as received (Fransman 1995, p. 418). The rational for PHS was a much cheaper monthly charge than the cellular telephone, because handsets and base stations were technically much simpler than those of other cellular standards. While a cellular telephone set cost about $100 a month to lease, PHS could be subscribed for a monthly rate of $16 and $0.24 for three minutes (Fransman 1995, p. 418). PHS was expected to reap a large market share besides cellular and satellite services (Wakabayashi 1994). After 1994, however, three factors drove down prices of cellular phones in Japan. First, NTT eliminated the ¥100,000 ($840) guarantee it charged (Ayu 1999); second, cell phones could be bought in stores (previously, subscribers had to rent phones from the telephone operators) and thirdly, cell phone rates were totally deregulated (previously, rate changes had to be approved by the regulator) (Wakabayashi 1994). With the prices of cellular telephones constantly falling, the success of PHS was short-lived. Subscriber rates started to decline from as early as 1998 (Figure 4-3).

The most costly failure in mobile telephony has become satellite personal communication. Satellite-based personal mobile communication is a radio link between a mobile unit and a land-based station via a satellite (Jung, Warnecke 1998, pp. 4-148). The first public satellite service was introduced by Inmarsat Ltd. in 1982 for ships and is now used by journalists, businessmen and diplomats around the world. This service uses geostationary satellites. In the late 1980s new satellite systems using medium-earth- and low-orbit satellites were proposed. The advantage of low-orbit satellite systems is the low transmitting power of the user phone, facilitating small phones without the satellite dishes required by geostationary satellites. In the 1990s several public satellite systems were planned to offer mobile services for those who are not covered by cellular services and who demand true global roaming.[124] Finally, three ventures began launching satellites: ICO, Iridium and Globalstar. ICO, founded by the satellite pioneer Inmarsat, invested $4.8 billion before filing for bankruptcy in 1999 due to a lack of customers. Iridium was initiated by the US communications equipment company Motorola and entered the market in November 1998, but demand did not materialise for them either. In 1999 Iridium had about 20,000 subscribers – a lot short of the 1 million customers expected and needed to make the investments in the 66 satellites profitable. Motorola, the main participant at Iridium, aimed at the global market, not US customers alone. After spending $5 billion to create a network of 66 low-orbit satellites and 9 months after starting the service, Iridium LLC, the operator, filed

[124] For the motivation for and a short history of the satellite-based personal communication services, see Sweeney (1993), Dwyre (1998), Jung, Warnecke (1998, pp. 4-148). About the failed Iridium venture see Feder (2000), Grimes (2000).

for bankruptcy. The remaining venture, Globalstar, owned mainly by the US satellite company Loral, invested $2.8 billion and started its commercial service in 27 countries in March 2000. It plans to introduce services in 80 countries and focuses on servicing the markets that are not covered by cellular services. However, these regional holes in cellular coverage are continuously shrinking, squeezing the satellite service areas. According to the FCC, regional coverage of cellular service in the US reached 90 % at the end of the 1990s. In the year 2000 it became certain that satellite mobile communication would be a small niche market.

Satellite-based mobile communications service seems to be a real global business with no regional bias, because it is offered to customers around the world. Yet this innovation is strongly regionally induced. The benefits of satellite-based personal communication was already discussed in the United States many years ago (see e.g. Millman 1984, pp. 224-232). The US regulator, operators and manufacturers of mobile equipment alike seemed to favour satellite communication as a valuable public mobile telephony system, because it seemed unlikely that cellular telephony could adequately or profitably cover the vast rural area of the United States. In addition, seamless roaming within the US was complicated enough, let alone global roaming. This made a satellite system for mobile phones an attractive service for customers in the US who travel within and outside the USA. The higher price of satellite service would be compensated by the much higher benefit compared to cellular service. In Europe, however, the situation of cellular service was very different from that in the USA. In the Nordic countries, total geographic coverage even of less populated areas was achieved by cellular technology in the 1980s.[125] NMT showed that seamless international roaming is a question of international standard-setting. A pan-European standard was therefore expected to leave very few areas within Europe uncovered. A satellite system would not have been advantageous and even less useful since calls can only be made outdoors and not within buildings and subways.

US communication equipment manufacturers therefore put more effort into developing satellite systems than European firms. National regulators were biased towards domestically-preferred technologies as well. At the WARC conference in 1992 the US and Europe disagreed as to how spectrum should be allocated in the 1-3 GHz band. The US regulator favoured allocation for satellite-based systems while Europe successfully lobbied for the assignment of 230 MHz for the 3rd generation (3G) land mobile system (Paetsch 1993, p. 112). Overall, like Singapore and Hong Kong, the United States market was a *lag market* in mobile telephony, because of its extreme geographic structure, which initially induced a technology which could not prevail world-wide.

---

[125] In 1990 Sweden had a geographic coverage of analog cellular mobile telephony of 90 %, Finland and Norway 96 % and Denmark 95 % (BIS Mackintosh LTD. cited in Götzke 1991, p. 32), these were above average in Europe.

4.3 Technological Gaps, Suppliers and Spectrum Availability

Conventional wisdom would expect countries which hold a technological knowledge gap to be the first to adopt a new technology. Another theory suggests that the closeness to leading suppliers supports a technological lead. In this section the role of international technology gaps and related suppliers for the international success of cellular telephony and of the GSM standard are discussed. First, different technological capabilities and early breakthroughs in radio telephone technology achieved by a country's private and public R&D activities may lead to the early introduction of cellular telephony in these countries and the international export success of firms in these countries. Second, related suppliers of electronic devices enabled a mass-market in mobile radio telephony through spectrum efficient technologies. A third supply factor, which is specific to the mobile telephony industry, may be important as well. Countries in which spectrum was available for mobile telephony early facilitated the introduction of mobile services. In countries in which spectrum was made available for mobile telephony, the supply of mobile telecommunications was offered to a larger number of users. As a result, mobile telephony was adopted earlier, domestic companies were able to build up a lead in technological knowledge and in production cost by learning-by-doing and learning-by-using. These hypotheses are challenging the lead market hypothesis, that mobile cellular services are driven by regional markets and not that the mass-market emerged in countries with the best technology, the best suppliers and the highest spectrum availability. In the next section, it will be argued, however, that the supply advantages are rather the result of national specific demand and lead market conditions and not the basis for early adoption of mobile telephony.

The main arguments against the technology and spectrum-driven hypotheses are, first, that technological knowledge of radio telephony originated from the US and that European firms used this US knowledge in the 1980s. Second, the first suppliers of electronic components vital for spectrum efficient mobile telephony were US firms. Third, national allocation of spectrum to various radio media (broadcasting, television, mobile telephony, private radio telecommunication and satellite radio services) reflects the domestic preferences of demand for specific radio services. Regulators respond to local demand and do not shape them. If demand for a specific radio service increases *relative* to other radio services, then the regulator will make spectrum available for the service in greater demand relatively. Nowhere is this more obvious than in the United States.

4.3.1 Technological knowledge

Technological progress and utilisation of new technologies can be pushed by scientific advances, to which local producers and users could gain access first. The technology gap theory suggests that a country gains international competitiveness in R&D intensive industries if its companies hold a technological lead. A technological lead of European firms over their US and Japanese competitors could explain the success of the European mobile standard. To evaluate this hypothesis, two questions are discussed: first, what is the role of scientific progress for the rate and direction of innovation in the mobile telephony industry? Second, what differences in technological capabilities within the triad can be observed? According to the experts interviewed and related literature, there has either never been a technological gap between the US, Japan and Europe in mobile telephony, or US firms held a lead until the 1980s. Both assertions contradict the first supply hypothesis.

First, scientific advances indeed enabled the mass market potential of mobile telephony in the 1980s (Lee 1989, p. 431). The growth of mobile communication was supported by technological innovations and breakthroughs. Notably large-scale integrated circuits (LSI), which reduces size and speeds up speech processing (Gibson 1987, p. 9), made light handheld mobile phones possible. In the 1980s, breakthroughs in digitalisation technology were necessary for fast digital-analog conversion in phones. These technological advances were necessary for the mobile mass market, because it raised spectrum efficiency and lowered the price of phones and calls appropriate for a mobile mass-market.[126]

However, these technological advances have been made neither in countries with the highest penetration rates nor where penetration rates rose later on, rather in countries which continuously lagged penetration rates, in particular the United States. The United States has often been suggested as holding a technological lead in many – especially defense-related – high technologies (see 2.1). In mobile radio technology, however, scientific findings were mainly available to all firms in the triad in the 1980s. Even if there was an initial technological lead by the US, at the end of the 1970s that technological gap was already closed (Pemple 1978, p. 317). European firms that experienced strong demand for mobile telephony used the technology available for the development of their own cellular systems. European companies relied on technical advances made by the Bell Laboratories and military applications of mobile telephony technology in the United States in developing both analog and digital systems. In particular, the most successful Nordic telecommunications equipment firms Ericsson and Nokia, which have been domi-

[126] However, the question of whether cellular mobile telephony is rather a technology-push or demand-pull phenomenon is in general not forestalled by the lead market hypothesis. On the one hand, a technology push model would be suggested by the fact that the cellular concept was developed in the 1940s but adopted only in the 1980s. In other words, technology was ready but the market was not, because people did not perceive a need for the service or because spectrum was not made available. On the other hand it is reported that "the growth in demand continued to outstrip the technological ability to cope with increasing congestion" (Nadel et al. 1978, p. 67). That would mean that there was always a strong demand for mobile services which "pulled" technological advances. In this perspective, a mass market for mobile communication could only become real when digital technology enabled high spectrum efficiency to serve the existing mass demand.

nating the market of mobile infrastructure since the 1990s, lagged mobile teleph-ony know-how compared to the US industry and even other European and Japanese firms in the 1980s and acquired external technological expertise to build up in-house technical competence.

The concept of cellular mobile telephony that was to become the blueprint of the globally dominating mobile telephone system was invented in the United States by the Bell laboratories in 1947 (Millman 1984, p. 235, Young 1979, p. 7). Although this first work was not published, Bell laboratories traditionally follows a policy of publication of their findings and widespread licensing.[127] The first article entitled "Multi-Area Mobile Telephone System", introducing the adjoining hexagonal cell mobile system, was published in 1960 by Bell Lab scientists. Other publications of fundamental technical problems of radio communication to mobile units followed (Millman 1984, p. 235). A range of special journals, such as *IRE Transactions on Vehicle Communication*, *IEEE Transactions on Vehicular Technology* and *Bell Systems Technical Journal*, ensured that the science community world-wide could monitor the scientific activities at Bell labs. The first system, the AMPS standard, was developed by Bell in the 1970s and was tested in Chicago in 1978 (Young 1979, p. 7), but commercial operation of AMPS did not begin until late 1983. Other cellular mobile systems were commercially introduced earlier but were technically based on the US specification. The first cellular mobile system, the Japanese system developed by NEC, was "virtually identical to that proposed by AT&T" (Pemple 1978, p. 325). The first European system, the Nordic mobile telephone system (NMT), was developed after the AMPS system but started commercial service two years before. Hultén and Mölleryd (1995) note that although the engineering groups led by Swedish telecom's radio laboratory worked independently from AT&T's Bell Labs, they knew the AMPS system and followed the development at the Bell labs. It can be assumed that the developers of the NMT system emulated technical concepts of the AMPS system. The market concept, however, was different. Mölleryd (1997) quotes the head of the Swedish laboratory, that while technology advance was "equal", the Americans followed a concept of a geographically delimited system. The Nordic countries followed a concept of full coverage and high subscriber capacity.

In the 1970s the US company Motorola, manufacturer of mobile telephones and pagers, developed a similar cellular mobile telephone system. While disadvantaged in infrastructure equipment making, Motorola succeeded in mobile telephone sets. Motorola invented the first prototyped portable mobile phone in 1973, called Dyna-Tac, and became a leading manufacturer in portable cellular phones in the 1980s (corporate information from Motorola). Yet the first commercial cellular phones were developed by the Japanese Oki Corporation for the Japanese

[127] See e.g. Tilton (1971) for the licensing policy of Bell labs in their pioneering semiconductor research.

cellular system in Tokyo, which commenced operation in 1979, and supplied AT&T with AMPS phones (Calhoun 1988, p. 52).

The former US lead in radio technology is mainly attributable to demand from military customers. According to industry officials interviewed, the first generation of cellular telephony was developed without much help from public research, but with a decisive technology transfer from military applications of mobile telephony. Based on the largest military budget, the Americans hold a knowledge lead in military technology. Even in this field, other countries participated. For instance, the C-450 developer group at Siemens were drawn from the company's defense-communications department. The defense-related technology lead of US firms applies even more to digital mobile telephony. In civil telephony, AT&T of the US was the first to develop and deploy digital transmission of voice in 1962 (Calhoun 1988, p. 147), digital switching in 1965 (Fransman 1995, p. 46) and digital mobile radio communications. Besides early technology adoption in fixed-line telephony, the US technological lead in mobile radio technology derives from military applications. Radio – and in particular digital radio technology – largely derived from military applications which were pushed forward by the large US military budget. Digital radio was developed for military communications. The TDMA modulation used for GSM was a military "spin-off" (Böhm). The most advanced digital telecommunication technique, the spread spectrum broadband technology, was developed in secrecy. Although the key patents held by ITT were suppressed from publication until 1978 (Calhoun 1988, p. 341), technological advances could subsequently be utilised by European firms for civil applications.[128] Even in digital wireless data communications, which Europe introduced much earlier in private mobile telephony, the ITU concludes that Europe used US-technology: "although a great deal of wireless data technology is developed in the United States, the fact is that Europeans are the true early movers in adopting the technology, where mobile phones usage is much more a part of daily life" (ITU 1999, p. 26).

The development of the GMS likewise built on US technology and on concepts from German and French telecommunications equipment firms, but to a lesser extent from Scandinavian firms. The time division multiplexing method (TDMA) used for GSM was first proposed by P.S. Henry, a scientist at Bell labs, and published in 1981 (Millman 1984, p. 237). The speech coding[129] used for GSM was

[128] Multinational firms played a vital role in the international technology transfer. ITT SEL, a German affiliate of the US telecommunications equipment firm ITT, developed the digital spread spectrum broadband system CD900, which was defeated at the CEPT conference in 1987 by the narrowband concept that finally became the GSM standard. The project team came from the defense-communications department and used the ITT in-house knowledge base, in particular knowledge on the radio system used in AWACS surveillance planes.

[129] The speech coding is one of the most crucial factors of digital mobile radio technology. Engineers face a tradeoff between speech quality and spectrum efficiency in mass mar-

also developed by the Bell labs. Several other GSM concepts were derived from the German analog C-450 system, e.g. the SIM card (Jung, Warnecke 1998, pp. 3-58). The US equipment company Motorola held key patents of the GSM technology (Cataneo 1994, Päch 1993, p. 93). In contrast to their influence in supporting the development of standardised cellular systems, the contribution of the Nordic firms to technical advancements were much more limited, according to industry officials.

Publicly funded research programmes for advances in digital technology may also have played a role in the success of digital telephony. Once again, these subsidies do not explain the regional pattern of adoption of digital mobile technology. For instance, the German Ministry for Research and Technology supported research in digital technology at public institutions and firms from the early 1980s. The Ministry sponsored a research project of the German subsidiary of ITT on digital telephony used in motor vehicles (Böhm 1980). The European Esprit program sponsored chip technologies essential for mobile telephony (Cattaneo 1994). Yet the necessity of public research for GSM next to the R&D activities of the government-owned PTTs is not clear. The assertions of the experts interviewed are inconclusive. Public research is difficult to evaluate in retrospect. However, the public research funds for these programmes are very small compared to military budgets and the investments made by the PTTs and private firms to develop GSM. What can therefore be assumed is that these research programmes were not decisive in the decision to adopt digital technology by mobile operators in Europe as the next cellular mobile standard, though they contributed to their technical superiority compared to analog systems.

4.3.2 Related suppliers

The supplier-manufacturer interaction is often stated as an important determinant of the competitive advantage of nations (Porter 1990, pp. 100-107). In line with this user-supplier interaction hypothesis, Hagenauer (1998) suggests that the European semiconductor industry was important for the success of the European

---

ket mobile telephony (Paetsch 1993, p. 72). The bandwidth occupied by a call is equivalent to the number of bits that need to be transmitted. This bit steam has to be minimised, while maintaining "telephone voice quality" (Calhoun 1988, p. 318). The lower the bit rate, the less the bandwidth required and the more subscribers can be served. Since the invention of the first talking machines in the 1930s, the Bell labs searched for bandwidth conserving-methods of speech transmission (Millman 1984, p. 102, p. 114). In the 1960s, Bishnu Atal, a director at Bell labs, pioneered work on linear predictive coding (LPC) and refined this technique in the 1970s and 1980s. He invented the code-exited linear prediction coding (CELP) that he presented in 1982 at an international conference in Paris (Atal, Remde 1982) and that has been adopted as standard for digital transmission of voice in most cellular radio systems including GSM (AT&T information). In the GSM standardisation process, PKI of Germany and IBM France adapted the coding method for the GSM system (interview sources).

standard in supplying integrated chips. Yet all company experts interviewed for this study denied that proposition straightforwardly. European companies certainly started with a disadvantage in the components industry, suggesting the international competitive advantage of European firms in the telecommunications components industry is a result of the dynamic market for mobile phones. Funk (1997) reports that in the 1980s, most people expected the dominance of the US and Japanese firms in the mobile telecommunications technology. "Even Ericsson was pessimistic about them succeeding in digital phones due to the strength of Japanese chip technology." (Funk 1997, p. 148)

According to the technicians involved in the development of the European cellular mobile industry, mobile equipment manufacturers relied on US chip suppliers until the mobile mass market let European electronic firms produce large quantities of integrated components. Basic electronic components enabling cellular mobile telephony came from US suppliers. According to industry statistics published by the trade magazine *Electronic Buyers' News*, the largest producers of IC's for cellular telephony were Motorola and AT&T. In the mid-1980s digitalisation became feasible for civil applications because of technical progress in A/D conversion processors.[130] For fast digital-analog conversion digital signal processors (DSP) were crucial. These specialised processors were streamlined for the task of processing the voice data in real time and much faster than the general purpose processors used in computers and digital switches (nowadays, Asics are fast enough). DSPs were made available in the mid 1980s and were first offered by AT&T and Motorola.[131] DSPs were immediately available for all manufacturers of telephone systems. According to the interviews of industry sources, there was no better access to these DSI's by US-firms against European or Japanese firms. The market success of GSM could have weakened the American digital telephony technology which was to be adopted later. According to Forward Concept (1999), a market research firm, "most DSP chip suppliers have chosen to address the GSM market and ignore the slow-growing North American market". For the American CDMA standard for digital mobile telephony only few DSP's were available in mid-1996, when CDMA service was introduced into the US market.

[130] For military purposes digital systems were implemented in the past because voice transmission quality was not important rather that signals could be encrypted, which can be achieved securely with digital signals.

[131] According to *Electronic Buyers' News*, four US-semiconductor firms dominate the DSP world market. In 1998 Texas Instruments held a 50 % market share of general-purpose DSP's, followed by Lucent Technologies (formerly AT&T) with 28 %, Motorola with 12 % and Analog Devices Inc. with 10 %. Texas Instruments even enjoys a market share of 60 % of the DSP market for wireless handsets.

4.3.3 Spectrum availability

In the history of mobile telephony the scarcity of spectrum is a supply-restricting factor curbing large demand. The low capacity of pre-cellular mobile telephony systems was due to the scarcity of spectrum capacity. Since the spectrum is used by ships, aeroplanes to communicate with base stations, and to a great extent for military purposes as well as for radio and television transmission, only a small frequency band can be made available for private mobile communication. As a result only few could use the frequency spectrum available. Technical improvements such as bandwidth reduction and truncation focussed on increasing frequency efficiency. But the slow development of wireless telephony (Levinthal 1998, p. 237) was often interpreted as a symbol that mobile telephony could never become a mass communication medium and will ever be refined to niche markets and special users.[132]

The government has a large influence on mobile communications because the spectrum is tightly regulated. International agreements are implemented by the international telecommunications union (ITU) to harmonise the usage of frequency internationally. However, despite these international recommendations not all countries allocate the frequency band the same. Most frequency bands are idiosyncratically allocated to different users groups. There is normally no free spectrum available. When a new technology is made available and applies for market entry, each national regulator has to reassign spectrum to new radio communication media and to the operators of radio communications. Mobile telephony could not have become a mass service if the necessary spectrum capacity had not been assigned to it.

Spectrum availability is certainly one of the main obstacles for new mobile technology to be tested on the market, because a new technological design needs some free spectrum and this means that it normally needs the regulator to allocate spectrum to it. It was therefore argued that the development of mobile telephony is mainly driven by the supply factor spectrum availability (Paetsch 1993, p. 8) and that the mass market in mobile telephony emerged where the national regulator allocated the necessary spectrum for new mobile technologies first. Paetsch (1993), for instance, sees the reluctance of the FCC to allocate spectrum to mobile cellular technology as the main reason for the market delay. Gruber and Verboven (2001) suggest that the introduction of capacity was the main effect for mass market penetration in mobile telephony. Capacity enhancement through digitalisation

[132] There were, however, some "visionaries" who believed that technology, especially digital technology, could be improved so that capacity could be increased to offer the spectrum capacity sufficient for a mass market. These visionaries, like Böhm (1980), Stenekamp, who founded Comvic of Sweden, were often even ridiculed by their profession according to industry officials witnessing their proposals in the early 1980s. The mainstream belief was that cellular telephony was not only needed by a few people but could not be realised as a mass consumer service.

accelerated the diffusion of mobile communications as this increased supply with no additional marginal cost (only investments in infrastructure). This is expected to induce even monopolists to cut prices to attract more users. Gruber and Verboven (2001) estimate the effects of the capacity enhancing introduction of digital technology and competition on the speed of diffusion. They find a positive effect of both variables. Gruber and Verboven (2001) essentially explain the market growth and timing of a mass market in mobile telephony with a technological push. They fail to explain why some countries introduced digital technology first, and why the Nordic countries command a lead in mobile phones over a long time, before and after the Nordic countries employed digital mobile technology.

There are several arguments which suggest that spectrum availability is not the constituting factor of early adoption of new mobile services. In contrast, spectrum availability and spectrum efficiency is a result of the strong local demand for mobile services. First, regulators rather react to demand pressures in allocating spectrum and do not normally follow a policy of promoting a special technology. This argument will be discussed in detail below. Second, scarcity of spectrum was only a problem in densely populated areas, not in small cities and rural areas (Calhoun 1988, p. 10). Therefore penetration rates of mobile telephony in large parts of the countries are not supply restricted, but are set by market forces alone. And thirdly, spectrum efficiency of a cellular mobile system is a result of the R&D investments of PTTs and manufacturers. The R&D effort of firms is responding to the expected demand and profitability of enhanced mobile services (evidence for this is seen by market studies mobile operators continuously carried out in the 1980s). Digital technology is the most spectrum efficient technology. It was deployed early in Europe because scarcity and demand pressure were most hurting and mobile telephony most profitable there. In contrast to the Nordic countries, where the coming mass market was preceded by high penetration rates, in the US there were doubts about the profitability of digital mobile telephony throughout the 1980s (Calhoun 1988).

Spectrum was made available for a variety of alternative mobile communications and broadcasting systems. Some of them were demanded more than others and others were a total failure on the market. Demand pressured regulators to release more and more spectrum for the commercially successful technologies. A review of governmental spectrum management shows that public administration reacts to market forces by reallocating spectrum from less successful or maturing technologies to emerging mass-market technologies. However, spectrum availability at an early stage of the market development could play a role in constituting the early adoption of a successful technology. Early spectrum availability enables the testing of new technologies and makes a latent demand for mobile services transparent. The question is to what extent the early availability of spectrum is caused by technological opportunity on the one hand and signals from demand and the sensitivity to early demand on the other. The first would support the technological lead hypothesis, the latter the lead market hypothesis. In reviewing the spectrum allocation by countries, there is little evidence for the first argument and much supporting the latter.

Frequency spectrum is a scarce resource. With the increase in demand for mobile telephony, the economic value of spectrum increases. As a result, availability of spectrum for private mobile services was subject to political discussions and regulatory efforts. The strong demand for and high profitability of mobile services pressured regulators into making more frequencies available for land mobile services since mobile telephony was invented. Until the beginning of the 1980s, however, little spectrum was available for mobile services, leading to the conclusion that mobile services would not be suitable as a mass service. Over time, demand for mobile services grew steadily, led by the Nordic markets. As a result, national regulators allocated more and more spectrum to land mobile services. Traditional users of the newly reallocated frequency bands, e.g. defense-related agencies or private telephone operators, had to retreat from the frequencies they were occupying. At the WARC conference in 1992, the dominance of cellular mobile services over fixed radio services was finally made possible. Member countries agreed to allocate the 1-3 GHz band to the 3rd generation cellular mobile telephony. Operators of microwave relay systems like utilities, railroad companies and long-distance carriers had to retreat from the band and either upgrade to frequencies above 10 GHz or replace their radio links through fiber-optic networks (Paetsch 1993, p. 113).

In the US, the FCC had more problems to find spectrum band for cellular mobile telephony than regulators in other countries (Lee 1989, p. 5). Cahoun (1988) explains why: strong demand for broadcast service had continuously weakened the position of cellular telephony to get more spectrum.

"In the late 1940s and 1950s the nation [the US] was tuning in to the Television Age, and the visionaries of that new and profitable technology were not to be denied. TV needs large amounts of spectrum – a picture is worth a thousand words, and images need much more bandwidth in transmission than voice. Each TV channel utilises 6 MHz of spectrum, enough for more than 100 mobile telephone channels. [...] On the other hand, each TV channel provided service to millions of people, while a mobile telephone circuit benefited only an elite few. Measured by the utilitarian yardstick of 'the greatest good to the greatest number', TV was viewed as a superior service. For the next two decades, the spectrum allocation policies of the FCC would be strongly skewed to the broadcasters." (Calhoun 1988, p. 46)

The pressure on the regulator to make spectrum available was successful when industry lobbyists persuaded the government that mobile telephony was unfairly suppressed by the broadcasting interests. Finally, the 800 MHz band – originally allocated for television services – was opened up and allocated to mobile radio in the 1970s. The regulator normally reacted to the industrial-political interests.[133] "Regulation tended to follow, not lead the process. In the early and mid-1970s, the FCC was more a mirror of industry politics than an activist agency working through its own agenda." (Calhoun 1988, p. 50). The FCC was, however, not responsible for the delay that occurred between the time when spectrum was allocated to cellular mobile telephony and the start of cellular service.[134] According to Hardman (1982, as cited in Calhoun 1988) the delay was caused by a complicated litigation process initiated by the traditional mobile operators, the RCCs, and Motorola against AT&T which would hurt competition in the mobile telephony industry when it would be allowed to operate its own cellular system. It took the FCC until the year 1982 to decide on the licensing process. The same delay happened in 1989 when the legislation proposed to shift an additional 200 MHz spectrum used by federal agencies, notably the Department of Defense, from the federal spectrum usage, which is regulated by the National Telecommunications and Information Administration (NTIA), to the public sector, which is regulated by the Federal Communications Commission (FCC) (Paetsch 1993, p. 137). These initiatives cannot be explained purely by the emergence of new mobile telecommunications technologies. Instead, political initiatives are induced by strong demand for new mobile services, which mobilises industry lobbyists lured by profits. The FCC's reluctance to assign spectrum to mobile services certainly was an obstacle for new cellular technology. Yet, taking the strong influence of industry lobbyist and legislation into account, it seems unlikely that the FCC would have been as reluctant as it has been, if mobile telephony had played a similar role as it did in the Nordic countries during the 1980s.

In other countries, too, regulators responded to demand expectations of operators and industry. In Germany, the expectation of demand for cellular mobile telephony was particularly low. At the beginning of the 1980s the German PTT expected a lower subscriber base than was already using pre-cellular services in the Nordic countries. Little spectrum was therefore assigned to mobile services in Germany. The C-450 net had to economise a smaller frequency band than networks in other countries. When demand exceeded expectations rapidly, the frequency band was extended two times by about 1.3 MHz (Jung, Warnecke 1998, pp. 4-124).

The conclusion is that spectrum availability is part of the market context, because spectrum availability is merely the reaction to demand articulation. Lead markets can be characterised by the willingness to test new technology in the market. This

---

133 The history of pressures from broadcasters and mobile radio operators and manufacturers on the FCC and its reaction is discussed in Nadel et al. (1978), see also Calhoun (1988).

134 According to Calhoun (1988), the "ten-year-delay" until 1983 of cellular telephony in the US caused a decisive competitive disadvantage of the US cellular telephony industry. The further impact was the delay of digital cellular technology. The industry underwent tremendous changes in the regulatory and technical context.

willingness increases with demand for services enabled by new technologies. In that spectrum allocation is a trade-off between several new technologies, such as satellite, cellular, cordless communications, market signals from the market are vital for the allocation process. One could finally formulate that a lead market can be constituted by the responsiveness of the political system to weak market signals in reducing the barriers to new technology. I shall now assess the lead market according to the five lead market factors.

4.4 The Lead Market Factors

The hypothesis suggested is that cellular mobile telephony is a lead market phenomenon. This means that the adoption of cellular telephony in the Nordic countries and the subsequent international success is mainly attributable to the nation-specific market factors and not to technological superiority. After this review of the history of cellular mobile telephony, the significance of the lead market factors elaborated on earlier for the international success of cellular technology shall now be validated. Wherever possible, quantitative country data is presented to test the significance of the lead market factors. For some factors, only qualitative data is available.

4.4.1 Demand advantage

Mobile telephony was invented in the 1940s. It grew continuously but only slowly over time, so that most observers were not aware of a "trend" towards mobile telephony. Only when cellular mobile telephony was introduced and the market success became visible in the second half of the 1980s, did an international trend in mobile telephony become obvious to all. Yet, there was a trend in mobile telephony before then, and the Nordic countries were at the front of that trend. The mass market of mobile telephony was retained by high prices and spectrum shortages but penetration rates in the Nordic countries was a sign that there existed a larger market than had been anticipated by many telecom operators. Table 4-1 offers a closer look at the mobile subscriber numbers at the beginning of the 1980s. In the Nordic countries, pre-cellular mobile telephony was used to a greater extent than in any other countries. During the 1970s and 1980s the Nordic countries had larger penetration rates of pre-cellular telephony than any other country. Not only were the penetration rates already highest in the Nordic countries, but the absolute network size also. Until the mid-1980s the biggest single mobile systems in terms of number of subscribers were operating in Finland, Sweden and Denmark. In 1981 more than 28,000 subscribers were registered to the ARP net. In Sweden the number exceeded 20,000 and in Denmark the figure was 15,000, compared to 15,000 subscribers in Germany. In contrast, in the United States each RCC-network was much smaller, serving around a hundred subscribers. All US-networks together handled only around 60,000 subscribers.

Most operators in other countries did not take notice of the situation in the Nordic countries but forecast domestic market demand by counting would-be users who "really need" a mobile phone. In 1980 the German national operator estimated 50,000 potential users, a penetration rate of less than 0.01 %. In this respect, Finland already had a penetration rate of more than 0.5 %.

Table 4-1: Mobile telephony subscribers in the 1980s

	Pre-cellular subscribers	Cellular subscribers			Pre-cellular penetration rate in %	Cellular penetration rate in %
	1981	1982	1984	1985	1981	1985
Japan	1)	19,804	40,394	61,800	-	0.05
United Kingdom	?	0	0	50,000	-	0.09
Germany	17,490	0	0	1,080	0.03	0.02
Denmark	15,000	7,200	35,000	49,650	0.3	1.0
Finland	28,278	2,648	17,865	32,301	0.6	0.7[2)]
Sweden	>20,000	27,236	58,588	73,000	>0.2	0.9
Norway	?	11,059	39,050	63,075	-	1.5
United States	140,000[3)]	0	91,600	340,123	0.05	0.1

1 Experimental system used for emergency.

2 The figure doubles if pre-cellular subscribers are included.

3 Independent regional radio networks, 1978.

Source: OECD, Germany: Regulierungsbehörde für Telekommunikation und Post, USA: Young (1979), Finland: Ministry of Transport and Communications Finland, Denmark/Sweden: Scheele (1992), own calculations.

What was the reason for the demand in the Nordic countries? The early adoption of mobile telephony in a country may result from higher demand for mobile communications than in other countries. If demand for mobile communications increases world-wide, the diffusion of mobile telephony would internationalise. Yet, this case study has not found a significant demand advantage on the part of the Nordic countries. It has been argued – also by the experts interviewed – that the large demand for communication in the Nordic countries results from the low density of population in these countries (ITU 1999, Echikson 1994). The popularity of weekend cottages should have spurred mobile telephony (see e.g. citations in Stolcke 1991, p. 72). This argument leads to an expectation that cellular mobile telephony be a substitute for fixed lines not only in the Nordic countries, but generally in countries with low fixed-line infrastructure, where investments in fixed-lines per subscriber exceeds investments in a mobile infrastructure. However, these arguments are not in accord with the general observation. There are two counter arguments. First, in the Nordic countries and in Sweden in particular, mainline penetration is among the highest in the world (see Figure 4-5). Even if

Helsinki and Stockholm are excluded (to estimate rural area penetration), Sweden (647 per 1,000) and Finland (509 per 1,000) still have higher or the same fixed-line penetration rates than Germany including metropolitan areas (513 per 1,000), suggesting that mobile telephony is not generally used to compensate the lack of fixed-lines. In general, a regression across countries shows that the penetrations of mobile and fixed-line telephony are positively correlated.[135] Second, even in the Nordic countries, the urban areas were first equipped with mobile infrastructure. Dekimpe et al. (1998b) find that the timing of adoption of mobile telephony by a country is highly correlated with the number of major population centres. This was even the "most important driver of the countries' speed of adoption" (Dekimpe et al. 1998b, p. 18).

Figure 4-5: Fixed-line telephone penetration 1960-1997

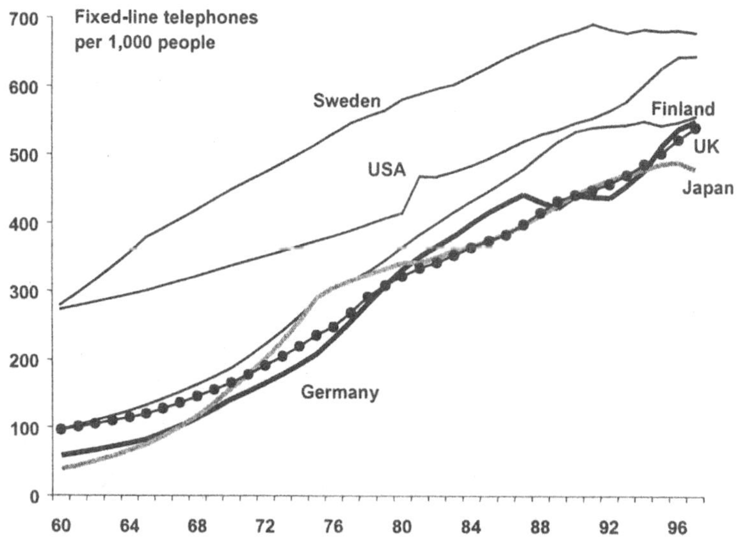

Source: ITU, own calculations.

Other demand advantages are also not persuasive. Businessmen were the first adopters of mobile telephony (ITU 1999), but there is no evidence that they are unequally distributed across industrialised countries. There are few differences in per-capita income between the Nordic countries and Germany, the two extreme poles of market penetration with mobile telephony in Europe. Cultural factors are

135 Although Gruber and Verboven (1999) find a significant negative correlation between mainline penetration and *speed* of diffusion of mobile telephone in Europe, the penetration rates with mobile and fixed-line telephones correlate within the OECD with a correlation coefficient of r^2=0.55 between 1987 and 1995.

sometimes proposed.[136] The acceptance of mobile phones could be culturally related. For some countries mobile phones could be a status symbol; for others a common device. Yet, according to one Nokia official, mobile phone users in Finland were attributed with the same pretentious image in the 1980s as occurred years later in other countries. The population in Finland and in other Nordic countries simply had more time to get used to cellular phone users in public than other countries and over time, with growing penetration rates, the 'geek factor' vanished before cellular mobile telephony was introduced in other countries. What remains is simply that nations which had both the most experience with mobile telephony before cellular telephony and also introduced cellular telephony early discovered the mass market earlier than other countries. These early-adopter countries discovered more and more market sectors, more applications for mobile phones during work and private life and accepted mobile telephony as a means of telecommunications. The within-country diffusion of an innovation takes time and Scandinavia merely had the ideal combination of early experience and low prices so that within-diffusion could take off. Since the prices were anticipatory, other countries followed that diffusion path.

4.4.2 Price advantage

In the case of mobile cellular telephony the lead price effect is the most obvious lead market effect. The charges for mobile cellular telephone calls differ greatly from country to country. Price differences even between neighbouring European countries are possible because every country granted mobile service licences to domestic operators and a customer in one country cannot make domestic calls through foreign operators. A comparison of national average prices and national penetrations shows that prices had indeed a dominating effect on the width of adoption within a country. Figure 4-6 shows that for the year 1996, call charges and national penetration rates of mobile telephony in the OECD countries correlate to a high degree.[137]

---

[136] Some claim that the Scandinavians are "traditionally more interested" in new technology (see e.g. Stolcke 1991, p. 72). Indeed, the penetration rates of internet host and computers are higher in Scandinavia, too. However, observing the prices shows that these penetration rates are correlated with internet access charges (OECD 1999): Finland has among the lowest charges and Japan, with a low internet usage, the highest.

[137] Price comparisons between countries and operators are difficult to obtain because the total price of a mobile telephone for a subscriber is a mixture of connections fees, monthly fees, call charges at peak-hour and at non-peak-hours, and the cost of the mobile phone. The OECD (1997a, p. 129) published a price basket of mobile telephone tariffs which was used in the figure. Yet, there is also a strong correlation between penetration rate and charges per min at peak-hour time. Ihde (1998) and Frank (1992), who used prices as a determinant for the penetration rate of cellular telephony, find a strong positive effect of prices on penetration.

Figure 4-6: Mobile tariffs and penetration rates for OECD countries 1996

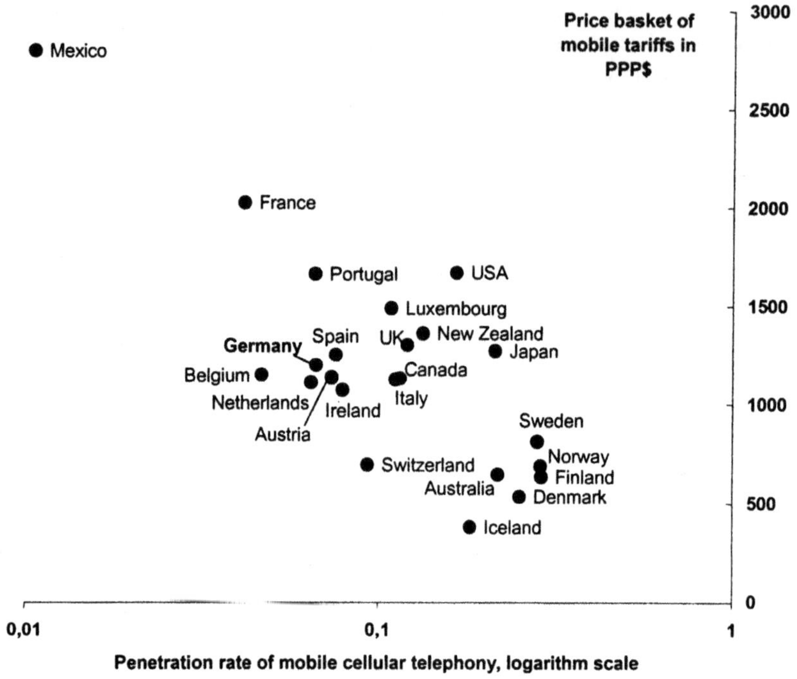

The price basket includes monthly rates and 679 calls at different times of analog mobile service in the year 1995.

Source: OECD (prices); ITU (pentration rates).

A simple linear regression for 23 OECD countries confirms a negative logarithm correlation between prices and the penetration rate:

$$\ln(subscribers_i \,/\, population_i) = \underset{(3.54)}{-0.91} - \underset{(5.63)}{0.0011}\, price_i \qquad R^2 = 0.58$$

with country *i* and the price basket as *price* (t values in brackets). Most of the variation of the penetration rate across countries can thus be explained by the price variation leaving little explanatory power to cultural and other factors described by diffusion studies such as DeKimpe et al. (1998a) and Gruber, Verboven (2001).[138] The strong demand for mobile service in the Nordic countries since the early 1980s can therefore be explained by low prices.

138 However, if Mexico is excluded, the R^2 decreases to 0.34 and there is no difference between linear and logarithm regression of the penetration rate.

Comparable national price information on mobile telephony for the 1980s is not available from a single source. Exemplary data[139], however, derived from varying sources for Germany, the US, Sweden and Finland, gives some further evidence for the price dynamics since 1981. The main components of the price basket of mobile telephony are the monthly subscription rate, call charges and the price of the mobile phone. Figure 4-7 depicts a price basket of monthly rates plus 200 min call charges for Germany, the UK, Sweden, Finland and the US between 1981 and 1993. From as early as the 1980s, the lowest prices were offered in the Nordic countries. Charges remained stable in contrast to the other countries, where prices decreased in the early 1990s when digital technology and competition was introduced in mobile telephony (ITU 1999, p. 73).

As a result of these price reductions, in particular in Germany, penetration grew rapidly (Jung, Warnecke 1998, pp. 5-65). Data on mobile phone retail prices could be reconstructed for countries in which phones could be bought by consumers. Figure 4-8 shows the price trends of mobile phones from 1980 to the early 1990s in the US, Sweden, the UK and Germany.[140] In Japan, phones could only be rented until 1994. Phone prices generally decreased rapidly in all countries from the mid-1980s. National prices started at different levels and converged to prices below $1,000 around 1993. In Sweden and Finland, NMT phones started with a price of $3,000 in the early 1980s, while in the UK and Germany the first price tag for phones was much higher. In the US, phones started at prices comparable to prices in the Nordic countries but price decreased even more rapidly. The downward trend of call charges in most countries in the 1990s means that the Nordic countries had *anticipatory prices* in the 1980s, constituting a lead market through price advantage.

---

[139] The number of operators and price packages offered complicates the estimation of national prices. Price information on the US is particularly vague. First, prices vary considerably from region to region. Some operators offer very low monthly charges and higher call charges (Calhoun 1988, p. 87). The OECD (1997a) used the price offered in New York by Nynex, a rather high price region, so that the US penetration rate is higher than the price would lead one to expect (Figure 4-6). The data presented here are average prices of the largest operator and the most common package. Second, subscribers in the US have to pay for the incoming calls as well (Funk 1997, p. 153), which is not the case in most of the other countries.

[140] Prices in Finland are expected to be the same as in Sweden because of the same standard employed. For France no time series could be reconstructed, but a McKinsey study put the price of a mobile phone of the French system Radiocom at $3,300 at the end of 1991, 50 % more expensive than in Germany (McKinsey 1997, telecom case, p. 6). In the UK, phones were even cheaper as a result of the unique service provider market, in which operators subsidised phones to attract more subscribers (see below and Cave, Williamson 1996).

Figure 4-7: Monthly mobile call charges[1] in Germany, Finland[2], Sweden, the UK and the US 1980-1995

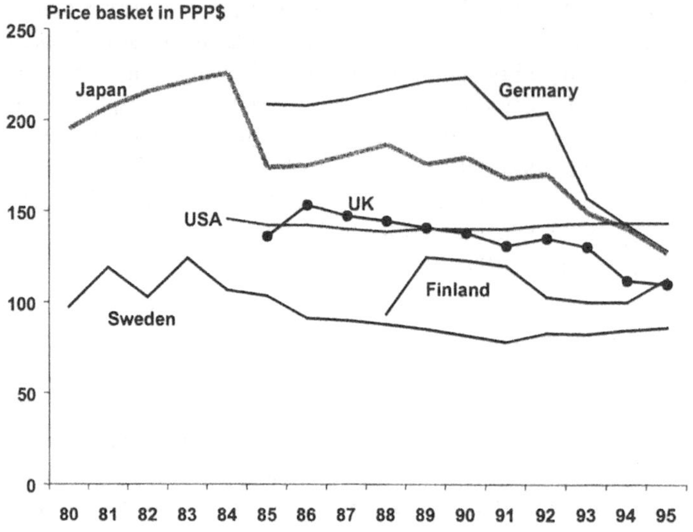

[1] The Price Basket includes the monthly charge and 200 minutes calling charges.
[2] No data available for Finland before 1988.

Source: OECD, Sweden: Hultén, Mölleryd (1995), Germany: RegB, USA: Paetsch (1993), Finland: Ministry of Telecommunication Finland, Japan: Telecommunications Carrier Association, UK: Valetti, Cave (1998), own estimates.

Figure 4-8: Mobile phone prices in Germany, Sweden, the UK and the US 1981-1993

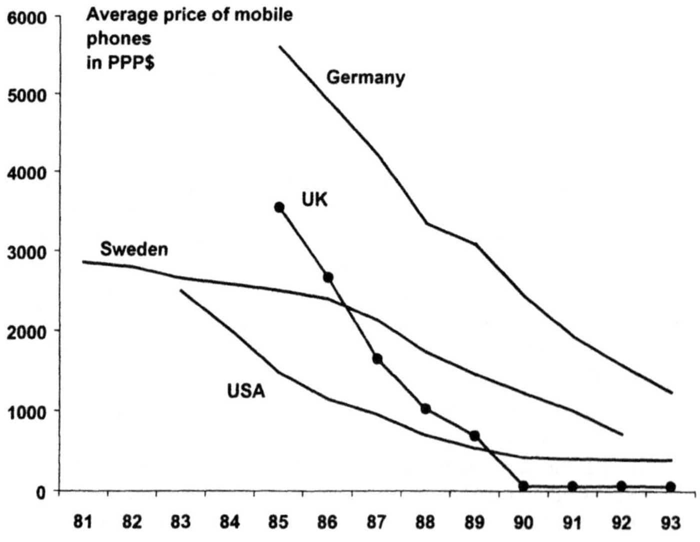

Source: Stolcke (1991), Hultén, Mölleryd (1995), Paetsch (1993), own estimates.

There is a second price effect that explains the lead market role of the Nordic countries: a *relative price-reduction potential* of technology preferred in the lead market. Relative prices of cellular mobile phones decreased compared to other mobile communication designs. Although all prices of electronic components and phones decreased continuously, the price reduction of cellular phones was the steepest compared to pagers, cordless phones and other communications equipment. Other systems of mobile communications were squeezed out of the market when cellular telephony became dramatically cheaper. The usage of public access telephony like telepoint, which were adopted widely in city-states like Hong Kong and Singapore, plummeted when cellular telephony became affordable for middle-class users of the telepoint service (Montefiore 1996). The substitution process of telepoint with cellular services was quick because the telepoint niche was highly price sensitive. Pager services likewise decreased in popularity, because GSM, too, allowed text messages through the built-in short-message-service.

Therefore, the price-lead effect of lead markets is clearly supported in the case of cellular mobile telephony as the mechanism of international diffusion and prevalence. National price differences in mobile telephony can be the result of national differences in

1) the planned capacity of the mobile system,
2) the international subscriber base of a mobile standard
3) prices of fixed-line telephone services,
4) the existence of a retail market for mobile phones,
5) the degree of competition between operators.

1. The price of mobile telephony is based on the planned capacity of a mobile network. Countries differ in price because of the different capacity of the mobile network. The planned capacity of a network can be the result of the expected demand, how much spectrum is allocated to mobile telephony in a country and how economically the allocated frequency band is used. The capacity of a mobile system has to be set before the system is implemented and can only be extended to a limited degree. Marginal cost of network extensions is increasing, meaning that supply is highly inelastic in the short and medium term. Unused capacity allowed operators to lower prices in order to follow the price demand curve downwards, but capacity enhancements are expensive as new base stations have to be purchased. In metropolitan areas operators have to lease additional real estate for new base stations. Investment per subscriber for one system thus follows a u-curve (Paetsch 1993, p. 167): Once the subscriber level is reached in which the incremental investment exceeds the value of an additional subscriber, the operator has no incentive to lower the service charges. This limits the decrease in prices and the increase in subscriber base in systems which have reached their previously planned subscriber limit. When the public interest for mobile telephony unexpectedly grew, capacity prices were kept high or even raised (Böhm 1980).

The capacity in countries differed because of different expectations of the market demand, mainly as a result of different market segments targeted by the operator. In Germany the C-450 system was aimed at businessmen and wealthy consumers. Price elasticity of demand from business is low but quality elasticity high (Jung, Warnecke 1998, pp. 3-58). As a result, the initial capacity of the C-450 net was only 100 thousand subscribers, and call charges and voice quality of the mobile system high. In Japan, NTT did not expect a large market either and installed a low capacity and set users fees at high levels (Funk 1997, p. 152). In the Nordic countries more initial capacity was offered because the targeted market segment was wider (Nordic PTT, too, still underestimated real growth of cellular mobile telephony, see Mölleryd 1997, p. 10). The availability of spectrum and spectrum efficiency is a supply factor. In section 4.3.3 the role of spectrum allocation is discussed in detail. It was argued that spectrum allocation is – like the planned capacity – a reaction to the expected demand relative to other spectrum-using services. Spectrum efficiency is likewise a function of R&D investment for mobile system development. Spectrum efficiency increased rapidly when demand increased to levels which justified large R&D investments.

2. Scale economies are a clear price determinant. The larger the networks and the more countries that chose a mobile standard, the lower the equipment cost of a standard will be. Equipment cost decreases with growing international subscriber base, because the large initial fix R&D cost has a large share of the total cost of a system. Mobile standards with a large home market like US-system AMPS or which were exported to other countries such as the NMT system gained an international advantage through economies of scale. NMT was adopted by 40 countries and held a market world share of 44% of subscriber base in 1985 and still 12 % in 1993 (Hultén, Mölleryd 1995, p. 16). Other national systems besides the systems employed in the US and the UK were limited to a much smaller subscriber base. The international diffusion of NMT lowered prices of its components and mobile phones (Hultén, Mölleryd 1995, p. 26). Domestic systems which were not adopted by other countries, like the German C-450 or the French Radiocom, offered less economies of scale and phones were sold at a considerably higher price.

In the largest market, the United States, call prices were not the lowest. Charges were higher absolutely, because the division of the large US market into the 734 regional markets (306 metropolitan and 428 rural areas) lowered some of the scale advantages of the US market. As a result, a single cellular market licence was smaller than the market in Denmark. The lottery process of granting licences led to a "highly fragmented, structurally unsound non-wireline market" (Paetsch 1993, p. 154); about 500 operators were known in 1990. In effect, no operator could build up a nation-wide cellular system easily. Furthermore, the licensed regional areas were "drawn according to the conventional telephone network and sometimes made no sense in the cellular business" (Brerresford 1989, p. 728). Buying out the lottery winner to build up larger regional services areas pushed the call rates higher (Berresford 1989, p. 730). In addition, since the AMPS system was developed by AT&T as a large operator system,[141] it was not cost efficient for small regional operators, who were finally granted licenses for metropolitan areas. These small operators had to charge higher call charges, in order to be profitable, than those in countries with nation-wide licenses. High costs raised call charges, lowering penetration rates, which in turn lowered investment returns which delayed investments. High call charges, not phone prices, were made responsible for the fact that a consumer market could not emerge in the United States in the 1980s (Calhoun 1988, p. 90).

3. A mobile operator has to take the price of fixed-line calls into consideration because the two means of communications are substitutes. In order to attract the same number of mobile subscribers, mobile call charges have to be lower in countries where fixed-call charges are lower than in other countries. In the Nordic countries, fixed-line call charges are generally lower than in other countries and this ensued lower mobile charges. However, if mobile call charges cannot be reduced, low fixed-line charges reduce demand for mobile services. In the US, mobile call charges were high relative to fixed-line calls.[142] The liberalisation of long-distance telephony worsened the relative price disadvantage of mobile services. While the charges for mobile calls remained almost the same throughout the 1980s, charges for fixed-line calls decreased. Local calls were often offered free of charge, only the monthly subscription fee was charged.[143] Since fixed-line telephony in other countries was still monopolised, prices for fixed-line calls did not fall in Europe until the liberalisation in 1998. Low cost of fixed-line calls in the US raised price-competitiveness of fixed-line against mobile telephony. As a result, US customers did not substitute fixed-line calls with mobile calls as much as consumers in countries with high fixed-line call charges, such as Japan and Germany.

4. and 5. In addition to economies of scale, the large differences in phone prices reflect the price policy of operators and the different degree of competition in the retail of mobile phones. Geroski et al (1989, p. 95) show that the price of mobile phones decrease with an increasing number of phone suppliers. In Germany, the market of mobile telephony was viewed as business executives only (McKinsey 1997). Since the capacity was restricted to large income users, the prices could therefore be set much higher than they would have been in a consumer market,

---

[141] When the AMPS system was developed, AT&T assumed that it would be allowed to build up a nation-wide network. As a result, a system was designed with high overhead costs and high investments with a long pay-back period. Capacity extension requires high initial costs and the mandatory low blocking probability required a high capacity-subscriber relationship (Calhoun 1988, pp. 74-91). For small markets, AMPS was less economical than other analog systems.

[142] Competition in long-distance calls was introduced in the 1970s in the US. However, before the divestiture of AT&T in 1984, profits from long-distance calls subsidized local calls (Green, Teece 1998, p. 625). The separation of long-distance and local telephony ended these cross-subsidies and drove long-distance prices down.

[143] I owe this argument to Jane Katz. See also ITU (1999, p. 78).

which emerged in the Nordic countries.[144] Third, operators in Germany and France were free to set their own prices because they had a retail monopoly for phones. In the Nordic countries, as well as in the UK, retail of phones was open to independent retailers and several phones manufacturers sold phones directly to customers (see below in the section on competition). In the United States, retail prices dropped sharply in the mid-1980s due to an initial oversupply of phones (Calhoun 1988, p. 69). In the UK, service providers started to subsidise phones with the bonus incentives that service providers receive from the network operators as a bounty for each new customer rather than selling cheaper airtime to the customers (Geroski et al. 1989, p. 97). Therefore, call charges there remained higher than in Scandinavia. This practice (low phone prices and high call charges) became common in other countries as well when competition between operators was introduced. National penetration rates, however, reflect the total cost of mobile telephony much better than phone costs alone.

Despite the introduction of competition in fixed-line and mobile telephony in 1985 in Japan and the subsequent reductions in charges, prices there remained higher for mobile and fixed-line calls than in the US or UK. Since price setting was regulated, long-distance charges were higher than in other countries. NTT was forced to cross-subsidise local calls with long-distance calls, because it was not allowed to raise charges sufficiently for local calls (Fransman 1997, p. 368). The diffusion of mobile telephony was additionally limited by a large deposit of ¥100,000 ($840) which a subscriber had to pay before he could make calls with the mobile phone. Mobile phones could only be rented from operators at a high monthly charge.[145]

It is apparent that the most important factor for low prices in mobile telephony is competition. Competition is a main factor for the price policy of operators. It will be discussed in greater detail in the section concerning the market structure advantage.

4.4.3 Export advantage

According to the lead market hypothesis, a country has an export advantage if the context of a country's market facilitates innovation designs that match demand in other countries. The export advantage can derive from the effort of domestic market participants (users, producers, government) to develop innovations for the world market. This would include deliberate deviation from the best domestic solution towards a design which is more suitable for foreign environments. Simi-

144 The German phone could have been more expensive because of the higher functionality (Jung, Warnecke 1998, pp. 5-65). An official from a manufacturing company, however, remembered that the German operator procured the phones at a much lower wholesale price of about a third the retail price charged.

145 Price data for mobile phones are not available for the 1980s. Fransman (1997, p. 418) mentions a monthly rental price of about $100 for a cellular phone in Japan.

larity of the market context to the context of other countries is another export advantage. In the case of mobile telephony three export advantages of the Nordic countries can be identified that facilitated the success of GSM: the traditional export orientation of the Nordic countries, an average population density in rural areas and the multinational environment in Europe.

The Nordic countries have a traditionally export-oriented industry. Since the home markets are rather small, exports in industries requiring larger R&D and capital investments are necessary to justify the large investments. For instance, Ericsson developed a digital telecommunication switch for the world market to avoid dependence on telecom operators in Sweden (Bartlett, Goshal 1989, p. 25, Pehrsson 1996, p. 104). Ericsson was such export-oriented a firm that it developed AMPS and later TDMA systems for export although the Nordic countries did not adopt these standards. Nokia had an even greater interest in exporting. Its growth strategy focussed on foreign markets (Kennedy 1992). In 1998 both companies show export shares of about 95 %. The export orientation of the firms were supported by other domestic institutions. In the 1970s the Swedish PTT was convinced that a cellular mobile system had to be exported in order to justify the R&D investments required. First, the Nordic countries were won for a joint standard (Hultén, Mölleryd 1995, p. 4). In order to get manufacturers interested, this Nordic Mobile Telephone system had to expand outside the Scandinavian countries. The Nordic operators developed the NMT system in cooperation with Saudi Arabia and Spain who adopted the standard together with Sweden in 1981 (Mölleryd 1997, p. 32). Institutions in Sweden supported exporting activity as well. According to Mölleryd (1997), the Swedish Investment Bank financed the supplement of an AMPS system to a small private US operator in 1983 and secured the deal. The additional export effort led to 29 nations adopting the NMT system mainly in Western and Eastern Europe, but also the Middle East, Asia (Malaysia, Thailand) and Africa (Morocco, Tunisia) (Information from Ericsson). Figure 4-9 shows the number of world-wide subscribers of analog cellular mobile standards that were adopted outside their home countries. Although the AMPS standard is used by the largest number of subscribers, it was used outside the United States by less subscribers than NMT until 1992. In 1993 NMT had an "export share", indicated by the relation of subscribers outside the Nordic countries to total, of more than 50 %. For the UK's TACS, the respective figure is 31 % and for AMPS 22 %. The German C-450 standard had a foreign subscriber base of 8 %. Other national standards like Italy's RMTS, France's RC2000 and the Japanese standards were not adopted outside their home countries at all.

Judging by the number and share of subscribers outside the "home" country, NMT is the most successful analog mobile system. The high export orientation of the Nordic countries had an positive effect on the price advantage factor, because the international diffusion of the NMT system lowered prices for telephone sets and system components (Hultén, Mölleryd 1995, p. 26). It strengthened the transfer advantage because it demonstrated the reliability of the NMT system in different

Figure 4-9: Subscribers of analog cellular mobile telephony standards 1980-1993

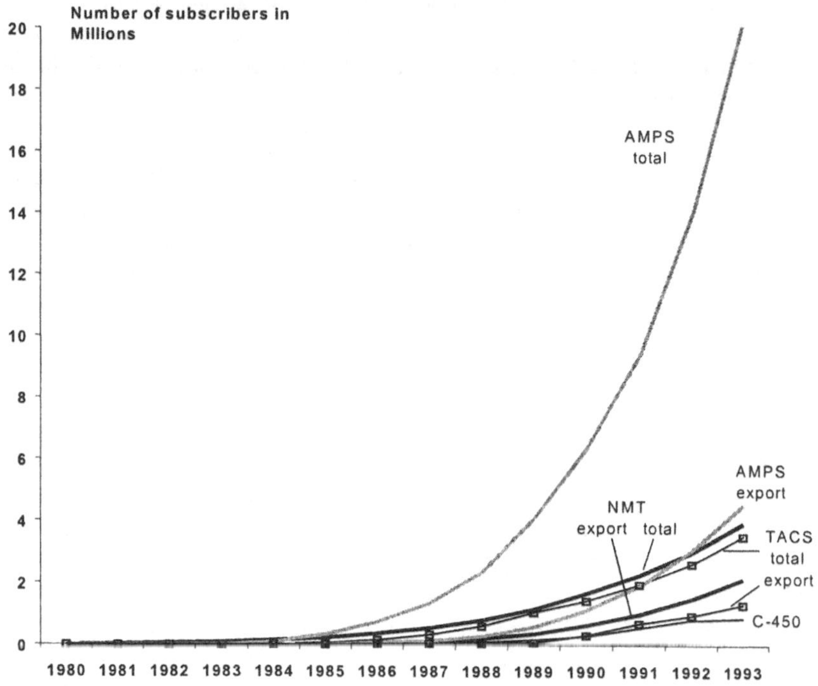

Source: Own calculations and estimations on the basis of national numbers of subscribers and standards adopted by each country.

country markets. In contrast, the German and the Japanese context was not export-oriented. Although the German standard C-450 is considered to be technically superior, it was only adopted by two countries other than Germany: Portugal and South Africa.

The export failure of the German mobile system is put down to the fact that it was too customised to the German PTT, and its late market entry. The PTT's main interest was that the system fit as good as possible to Germany's idiosyncratic telecommunication network. Quality requirements were higher compared to other standards.[146] Over time, additional requirements were even added by the German

146 For instance, Siemens required a signal-to-noise ratio of 60 dB, which was much higher than the internationally successful standards achieved. The exact distance measurement of the C-450 system, which is an important feature for the handoff from cell to cell, was only useful in densely populated cities with high numbers of users but not in most other countries. The extremely demanding equipment specifications of the German PTT are also a result of a political mission of high quality service and support of technological advance (McKinsey 1997). This pressure on the national PTTs to support industrial policy is reported for France as well (Cattaneo 1994, p. 65).

PTT. Although Siemens started developing the cellular system in 1979, it could not turn on the system until late 1985, whereas the Nordic system NMT-450 had already demonstrated its reliability in several countries 3 to 4 years back. Lack of domestic competition and a governmental agency ethic of the German PTT pushed C-450 towards being the best technical but not the best economical system. Although high quality requirements by the PTT made the Siemens system more technologically sophisticated than the other cellular systems, it also made the German system too expensive for other countries. The quality standards required by German telecom were not appreciated by other operators, they were not willing to pay a premium for extra quality which they did not need.

The Japanese manufacturers faced a similar problem, although they did not enter the market late. In the late 1970s, NEC developed a mobile cellular system, a variant of the US-AMPS system, for the Japanese PTT, Nippon Telegraph & Telephone (NTT). In the early 1990s a digital cellular system was designed and introduced in Japan, operating since 1994, by NTT and private carriers. A simpler system, PHS, was introduced in 1996 by NTT and IDO, the largest private Japanese carrier. All these Japanese systems were only employed in Japan and complete export failures. The Japanese cellular telephony industry is an example showing that being first is not sufficient for being a lead market. First, Japan had no experience with pre-cellular mobile telephony. It started with a totally new means of communication, compared to the Nordic countries, where pre-cellular telephony was a success and many were used to making mobile calls. Second, Japanese manufacturers seemed to have the same export disadvantage that curbed exports in the digital central office switching industry. NTT procured equipment mainly from four Japanese suppliers: NEC, Fujitsu, Oki and Hitachi. NTT designed equipment in its own laboratories in cooperation with the supplier and programmed the software itself (Grupp 1990). In his extensive study about the telecommunication switching industry, Fransman (1995, p. 76) notes that "NTT's prime concern was the requirements of its own network. In designing the switches little attention had been paid to the requirements of potential export markets". In another paper, he calls this fixation on national requirements a 'national myopia' which intrudes all large countries but stresses that Sweden was a notable exception (Fransman 1992, p. 275). The documentation of the digital system, which literally stressed its domestic character by its initial name Japanese digital cellular (JDC), was mostly in Japanese (Gabraith 1993). NTT's procurement practice was made responsible for Japanese failure to dominate the telecommunications market. In this sector they could not use the Japanese home market as a 'learning springboard' (Fransman 1992), which is considered as the success factor of Japan's domination in consumer electronics, cameras and small motor vehicles.[147] It re-

[147] This criticism is discussed in detail in Fransman (1992). He elaborates that the Japanese failure on the telecommunications world market cannot be explained by lower technological capabilities of Japanese manufacturers.

Table 4-2: "Export"-shares in telecom equipment

	Exports of telecommunications equipment in \$[1] per 1,000 \$[1] domestic telecom investments	
	1981	1993
Sweden	86.5	211.4
Netherlands	44.5	39.2
Finland	16.8	164.2
UK	15.7	50.5
Germany	9.4	20.5
Japan	7.8	29.9
USA	4.4	25.4

[1] In purchasing power parity-\$

Source: OECD, own calculations

veals that Japanese manufacturers dominate those parts of the telecommunications equipment sector that they developed independently from NTT, notably the facsimile machine, and failed in products that were developed through the NTT system of cooperative research (Fransman 1992, p. 261). Without elaborating in detail, the low export orientation of the dominating customer (NTT) is likely to be responsible for the surprising failure of Japanese firms in the mobile telephony equipment industry as well.

Export orientation of countries can be indicated by export shares. In the telecommunication equipment sector, the relation of exports of equipment and investments of domestic network operators should approximate the export share since most of the equipment in the industrialised countries under consideration are procured from domestic manufacturers (Doz 1986, p. 89). In Table 4-2 this indicator for national "export share" of telecommunications equipment is compiled for 1981 and 1993. Among the countries studied, Sweden always had the highest export compared to domestic investments, while Finland rose only in the mid-1980s above the respective figure of other industrialised countries. Both countries improved their export performances over time as a result of the world-wide mobile telephony boom. The US has the lowest export orientation with Germany and the UK lying between these two extremes.

The second export advantage results from the average environmental conditions in the Nordic countries. These conditions induced a design that is useful for other countries' environments as well. The cellular mobile telephony faces a variety of technical problems: fading, multiple-path interference, depending on environmental conditions like the geography, building sizes and materials, trees and the speed of moving mobile units (see e.g. Calhoun 1988, Lee 1989). The cell size depends on the environmental context as well as the population density, the density of buildings and so on (Paetsch 1993, pp. 80-82). Therefore, the environmental context determines a particular system specification that is optimal for this environment. A mobile system designed for the US with large less populated regions would be different from a system designed for a metropolitan area like New York or Singapore with their extreme population densities. Systems of mobile communications failed internationally when they were designed to fit idiosyncratic contexts of countries. These countries lie quasi on the extreme poles of a continuum of diversity. The small densely populated urban areas of Hong Kong and Singapore and cities like Tokyo are an ideal environment for small cell structure, low power, low handoff-performance offered by cordless telephony technology. Induced by high population densities, the Japanese digital cellular standard had a larger spectrum efficiency than GSM and small-cell systems, e.g. PHS, telepoint, were initially widely adopted in city states, and the Japanese Ministry of Post and Telecommunication expected that countries with high-population density would adopt these systems as well (Funk 1997, p. 155).

On the other extreme, in vast unpopulated areas in the United states, cellular services could not economically be offered in the 1980s. A satellite service is the only means of mobile communication service in the United States with complete geographical coverage. For US-oriented firms it seemed clear that a satellite system has many advantages and the potential to become the future dominant design for mobile communication. Yet, in other places of the industrialised world, coverage with cellular service was just right and there was no need for satellite services which were, in addition, offered at a much higher price. Cellular telephony was ultimately sufficient for the United States metropolitan areas as it compensated for smaller coverage with lower prices.

To test the hypothesis of similarity, data on population density are compiled for several countries. Table 4-3 shows two variables of population density for several countries. Countries can be characterised by the overall population density, the density of metropolitan areas and the density of rural areas. However, data is only available for the overall and the rural area population density. In Japan, both metropolitan areas as well as rural areas are more populated than in most other countries; the United States is characterised by densely populated metropolitan areas and very small populated rural regions. In Europe there are differences between countries, but most of them lay between the extreme population pattern of the US and Australia on the one hand and Hong Kong and Japan on the other. Europe's context offers an environment that lays the 'center' of a cross-national continuum of environmental diversity for mobile communication. Taking the average of the two indicators, density and rural density, of high-income countries as 'middle', Table 4-3 presents the Euclidian distance of each country to the 'middle'. Without over-interpreting these findings, the closest countries to the 'centre' are Finland, Sweden and France. This offers the impression that having the average environment of all countries can indeed be an advantage when a variety of technological designs converge into a dominant design. These 'average' countries prefer a cellular mobile system design which could be transferred to other countries better than designs preferred by countries with more idiosyncratic environments. The GSM cellular could be more easily adapted to other environments than the system developed for the extreme environments. In including the concept of micro-cells, the spectrum efficiency of GSM could be increased in areas of cities with high population density such as Hong Kong (Funk 1997, footnote 9).

On the other side of the coin, coverage with cellular telephony in less developed areas increased as it became profitable to deploy cellular services there as well. In

Table 4-3: Indicators of population density

	Density people per sq km	Density in rural areas[1] people per sq km	Deviation from average of High Income countries[2]
Hong Kong	6375	5084	7998
Japan	334	693	566
Netherlands	457	191	427
United Kingdom	243	103	240
Germany	235	92	239
France	106	80	155
Finland	17	76	139
Sweden	21	53	162
United States	29	36	179
Australia	2	5	212
Average of high income countries	30	215	0

[1] Arable land only

[2] Euclidian distance to total density and density in rural areas

Source: FAO, UNCHS, World Bank, own calculations

the US, the coverage of cellular telephony is almost complete at the end of the 1990s. In conclusion, the similarity argument of lead markets outlined theoretically above seems to apply to the mobile communications industry: it was not systems that fitted extreme environments which became adopted globally, rather systems designed for an "average" environment.

The GSM standard had an additional export advantage compared to the US and Japanese standards. The joint development of a pan-European standard led to the inclusion of a multitude of features which different countries required due to their preferences. The GSM standard became therefore a multi-environment standard. For instance, Germany required the inclusion of the SIM card for security reasons, Britain and the Nordic countries required technical features that made small handsets possible. Britain wanted data communication abilities. These different national requirements mirrored their own good experiences with their first cellular generations. Although this led to nerve-breaking discussions in the standardisation committees, GSM became an amalgamation of the best features of what different environments made transparent.

4.4.4 Transfer advantage

Telephony has been a rather national business; nationally and mostly governmentally owned PTTs operated more or less idiosyncratic networks supplied by national equipment manufactures. International calls were transformed from one national to another national standard at international switching centres. In cellular mobile telephony, too, most large nations employed their own standards. Standards were exported to smaller countries that were not large enough to justify the development of their own system.[148] Three transfer advantages of the successful

[148] With the deregulation in telecommunications, trade in equipment intensified because the new private network operators preferred not to be supplied by the same equipment firm which had close ties to the traditional PTT.

mobile standards can be observed: the maturity of a standard reduces the risk of adoption, the internationalisation of demand for a specific mobile service (roaming) and degree of property of a standard.

A mobile telephone network is a complex system. Until the 1980s neither the technical feasibility nor the market profitability of cellular systems were clear. Large networks are not easy to manage and require extensive test driving and learning-by-doing to be reliable and available under extremely demanding conditions. A considerable risk is involved in the decision for a cellular system. At the same time, a mobile system requires large investments. Reliability is one of the main competitive advantages of a mobile standard. Since new cellular networks are rather unstable and have many teething problems, the first networks installed gain an advantage over their competing standards launched later. NMT was already launched in 1981. GSM had a head start against the US and the Japanese digital mobile systems. While the GSM service was already commercially available in 1992 and GSM accepted by a rapidly growing subscriber base, the US-standard TDMA was deployed amid suspicions regarding its technical inferiority and because of the dual-use phase in the US rather quietly (Buhrmann 1997), and CDMA was not available commercially until 1996. The success of the GSM networks in Europe was highly visible in other countries, too. Telecom operators in these countries then realised the huge market potential in their own countries as well. Two factors made the telecom operators outside Europe adopt the GSM standard. First, it was notably the GSM standard which demonstrated that a large portion of the population is willing to pay for mobile services and not only a small segment which the large investments of a GSM network would not pay off for. Second, when the telecom operators decided to build up a new cellular network, GSM was a more advanced system than the analog ones. GSM was the only available digital system which would offer additional services in the future and that already proved to be reliable. All of this lowered the risks in the telecom operators investing in a GSM system. The choice for a GSM system outside Europe by the Australian PTT was reported to be mainly guided by these considerations (Kennedy 1999).

The second transfer advantage of the GSM standard is its international roaming ability, i.e. the ability to make and receive calls in other countries which adopted the GSM standard. NMT offered international roaming albeit only within the Nordic countries. International roaming was one of the main reasons for the development of a pan-European standard and one of its essential features. Because international roaming causes so many technical challenges, no US or Japanese standard offered an easy-to-use international roaming capability like GSM. Even within the US, roaming was not seamless; a user had to know the access number which he first had to dial before using the network of a different operator. For the European telecom operators, roaming within Europe was important because the first generation cellular service showed that the demand for international roaming of users travelling within Europe was strong. With the integration of the European

Union, nowhere else was it so easy to cross borders with one's own car – and Europeans frequently did so. This trend of cross-border demand for mobile telephony had, again, already been anticipated in the Nordic countries, which was one reason why local operators adopted a common Nordic standard, the NMT.

In the US and in Japan, rather isolated countries where cross-border traffic is much lower, the benefit of international roaming was small. Even worse, roaming was a problem within the US. The inferior roaming performance is the most important disadvantage of AMPS-based mobile services (Mason 1993). Two factors caused this disadvantage: the system design and the fragmentation of the US market. The AMPS system was designed to be operated by only one operator, AT&T (Paetsch 1993, p. 352), therefore roaming between different operators was not considered as a technical feature to put much engineering effort into. Months after the market introduction of cellular mobile service, AT&T was divested and the market fragmented into 1,600 regional licences. The lottery process made it difficult for operators to build up a nation-wide or even regionally integrated networks. This first prevented handoffs between different operator areas; driving in or out of a metropolitan area during a call meant that a call had to be redialed (Calhoun 1988, p. 385). Second, the large number of 500 network operators complicated roaming agreements and fraud prevention. Even with a roaming agreement, a subscriber had to know the access number of the operator he did not subscribe to. This was expected to lower demand (Mason 1993). Nation-wide seamless roaming, i.e. without access numbers, was only achieved in the mid-1990s. International roaming was never offered by operators using AMPS. The international roaming capability facilitated the transfer of a specific demand for GSM services abroad. Businessmen and later tourists from European countries attracted telecom operators in several countries with lower per-capita incomes (e.g. Turkey) to choose the GSM standard because these customers are willing to pay more than the domestic subscribers. International roaming is a global network effect: the more countries adopt GSM the higher the benefit for users in all other countries, for they can use their mobile phones in all countries that offer a GSM services.

The third transfer advantage of NMT and GSM is their non-proprietary status. Although GSM equipment manufacturers had to pay license fees[149], GSM is less proprietary than other standards, which could have played a role in the decision of non-European countries to adopt GSM against the proprietary and clear "nation labelled" US and Japanese standards. Non-proprietary standards secured that several telecommunications equipment producers would offer GSM equipment competitively. Operators would not have to rely on one supplier only. It became common within the GSM-services for network operators to procure their infrastructure

[149] GSM was first planned by the PTTs as a totally open standard that could be used without paying any license fees. After Motorola demanded license fees for its patents, which are vital parts of the GSM standard, cross-license agreements between the manufacturing firms were negotiated (Cattaneo 1994, pp. 92-94).

from two manufacturers. Since GSM is not only an air interface standard but also specifies all interconnections between base stations and network systems, smaller companies could participate in the GSM market with components (Paetsch 1993, p. 287). And finally, competition would drive prices down. The transfer advantage has thus reinforced the competition and price advantages of GSM.

4.4.5 Market structure advantage

Competition played a vital role in the success of mobile cellular systems and the GSM standard. The introduction of competition created lead market effects: 1) it drove prices of calls and phones down from the time of market entry; 2) through the entrepreneurial effort new services and applications for mobile telephony were discovered; 3) competing firms promoted cellular services through marketing activities and attracted new consumer segments, and 4) competition supported the mass-market suitability of cellular telephony with lower quality for lower prices.

Public telephone services are traditionally operated as a state-owned or accepted monopoly in order to deliver universal access to telephone services for all consumers in a country.[150] However, in the early 1980s competition was seen by the US and the UK government as an important welfare enhancing mechanism and these countries started to introduce competition in telecommunications (Armstrong 1997, Newbery 1997, Laffont, Tirole 2000). Deregulation coincided with the start of cellular mobile telephony. Over time, other governments followed with the introduction of competition in mobile telephony. As network investments are high and spectrum scarce, only two mobile licenses were usually granted, creating duopolies. Yet, real competition in mobile cellular telephony was not achieved first in the Anglo-Saxon countries but in the Nordic countries as will be shown.

An international comparison shows that the introduction of cellular telephony and the introduction of competition varies internationally (Table 4-4). Most European countries only granted licenses to private operators in the 1990s, when the digital systems became available and after the EU commission recommended competition (Paetsch 1993).[151] Although the time of introduction of cellular telephony is seen in this thesis as endogenous, the time of introduction of competition can explain some deviations from the correlation between start of cellular service and market penetration. For instance, although cellular telephony was introduced in Japan first in 1979, the penetration rate in 1995 was much lower than in other

---

150 Competing private firms were expected to concentrate their network investments on profitable connections and leave other less populated regions uncovered (Flichy 1991, p. 96).

151 Cross-border studies on the impact of competition on the diffusion of mobile telephony are scarce. Only Gruber and Verboven (1999) included an indicator for competition in their diffusion estimation. They found a significantly positive but small effect of the introduction competition (mostly duopolies) in digital mobile communication service on the speed of diffusion in the 1990s.

Table 4-4: Introduction of competition in telephony services

	Start of cellular telephony	Competition in Mobile telephony	Mobile telephony penetration rate 1995 (%)
Sweden	1981	1981(1965[1])	22.7
Finland	1982	1991(1982[2])	19.9
USA	1983	1984(1950[1])	12.8
UK	1985	1987	9.7
Japan	1979	1988	8.1
Germany	1986	1992	5.6
Netherlands	1985	1995	3.0
France	1986	1989	2.2

[1] Competition in pre-cellular mobile telephony

[2] Different mobile and fixed-line operator competing on the regional level

Source: Paetsch (1993), OECD (1997)

countries. The late start of competition explains the lag. First, the Japanese PTT monopolist did not expect a strong demand for mobile service within Japan; it set prices at high levels. As a result, there was indeed no great demand. Yet, Wakabayashi (1994, p. 31) stresses that the real problem in Japan was not that the potential demand was not detected early by the PTT, but that "the main reason for the slower development of a mobile phone market in Japan was unquestionably the lack of government policy promoting competition", which supports the discovery of tacit demand. The first private mobile operator was allowed only in 1988. However, cellular telephony was still regulated and prices remained higher than in other countries. A mass market in the mobile telephony industry did not start until 1994, when telecommunications were totally deregulated and cell phones could also be purchased in stores (Wakabayashi 1994).

In Finland, competition existed between the mobile operator and the regional fixed-line operators, which explains the high penetration rates (see below). Because competition played an important role in the development of the cellular telephone industry, the market structure in Sweden, Finland, the US and the UK is now discussed in more detail.

Competition in the Nordic countries

The study by Mölleryd (1997) concerning the first cellular industry of Sweden recounts the market context in the early 1980s. At the end of the 1970s, a Swedish entrepreneur, Jan Stenbeck, expected mobile telephony to become a big success in the future. He began operations in the USA, Sweden and the UK. The US was expected to deregulate mobile telephony early, supposedly because of its deregulation policy. But the allocation of frequencies by the federal regulation agency (FCC) was delayed and the US project of Stenbeck was a market failure. In the UK, however, his project resulted in the mobile operator Racal-Vodafone, which successfully acquired a mobile licence in 1984 and later became a successful multinational operator. Yet, the trend towards competition and marketing started in Sweden. Private Swedish firms had already been operating pre-cellular mobile networks since 1965. In 1980, Stenbeck acquired a telephone company which held licences for a number of frequency bands. He renamed it Comvic and decided to build a new automatic mobile system. Yet, Swedish telecom denied Comvic the operation of an automatic system connected to the public fixed-line network on the basis of the existing law that gave the Swedish PTT a monopoly on public telephony service. Comvic appealed to the Swedish government on the basis of the existing mobile licence. In order to increase competition, the Swedish government gave Comvic an exemption that it could legally operate its network from 1981 onwards. Comvic operated a mobile telephony service supplied by the American firm E.F Johnson and offered phones built by Technophone, a UK firm founded by a Swedish engineer, which would innovate the first handheld phones in the mid-1980s. Although Comvic remained a small mobile operator compared to Telecom Sweden, its marketing activities were strong and innovative. Comvic was granted additional licences in 1985 under the exemption rule and was also among the first to operate a GSM network in September 1992. Again, Comvic is "marketing [the GSM service] aggressively" (Hultén, Mölleryd 1995, p. 20). From the Start, three licences for GSM service were granted in Sweden, while all other European countries started with one or two licences. All three Swedish operators competed fiercely in order to attract the number of subscribers necessary to cover investments. Hultén and Mölleryd (1995) conclude that early competition between operators was the most important factor for the development of the mobile industry in Sweden, while the study of Mölleryd (1997) further reveals that the entrepreneurial effort in particular was the main success factor for the emergence of the mobile cellular telephone industry in Sweden.

Although only the PTT offers mobile telephone service, competition emerged in Finland between fixed-line and mobile operators.[152] McClelland (1991) calls the Finish telecommunications market "the most competitive communications regimes in the Western world". In fixed-line telephony, Finland has had a multi-operator environment since the beginning. About 52 regional private, communal or public telecommunication operators provide telephone service for their concession area. Often, these local operators were established as non-profit-making co-operatives in order to finance the investment needed. Profits are used to reduce call charges (McClelland 1991). As a result, call charges were low and this in turn raised penetration rates to high levels. In the mid-1980s regional firms entered the long-distance telephone market. In cellular mobile telephone service, Telecom Finland, the Finnish PTT, was granted a monopoly. However, since Telecom Finland did not have a monopoly for fixed-line telephony, it priced mobile calls competitive to fixed-line calls. In order to be successful and to attract fixed-line subscribers to switch to mobile telephony, mobile tariffs had to be low. According

[152] Åkermarck (1999), ITU (1999, p. 4) and interviews with experts.

to officials interviewed, mobile services were priced higher and as an additional service not supposed to substitute fixed-line calls in countries where the national carrier had the monopoly for both fixed-line and mobile telephony.[153] This low price strategy of Telecom Finland was supported by low prices of mobile phones, for the international successful NMT standard allowed Finish manufacturers like Nokia to reap economies of scale in production.

The situation in the United States

Although the US-regulator was most eager to implement competition in mobile telephony in the 1980s, contemplation about the best way towards competition caused a delay that made the US a lag market. The United States has a long tradition of private mobile radio services. Private-carriers licensees (RCC) operating since the 1940s were typically local businesses with a few hundred subscribers and less than ten employees (Calhoun 1988, p. 35). Although the US regulator (FCC) intended first to grant the national PTT, AT&T, a monopoly for cellular mobile telephony, regulation policy changed at the beginning of the 1980s as a result of the new administration and strong pressure from the other pre-cellular operators (RCCs), which demanded access to cellular licences (Paetsch 1993, p. 151). The FCC's main aim now was to implement a competitive environment in the cellular service. However, the process of license assignment delayed a competitive market in the cellular industry and caused call charges to remain higher than in Sweden during the 1980s.[154] Since cellular telephony has the character of a natural monopoly, the FCC concluded that in the cellular mobile telephony industry competition can be sustained if no national licence would be granted, rather regional licenses to two – but not more than two – operators in each area. Therefore, two licences were granted for each of 732 regional markets, of which 306 were metropolitan areas (MSA) and the rest rural areas (RSA). AT&T would be granted one of these licences and a new operator the other. At the same time, AT&T was forced to divest into a long distance service operator and regional bell operators, who inherited one licence for each regional market.

At first glance, the US therefore implemented a competitive market in cellular telephone services at the beginning of the 1980s. Yet, the licensing process did not facilitate a market as competitive as the Nordic countries. First, the sheer number of licences to be granted delayed the introduction of cellular telephony. Licenses for the 600 areas were granted in blocks, starting with the 30 largest cities in 1983.

---

[153] The US Department of Justice pointed as early as 1974 to the competition between fixed-line and wireless services, when it argued against the FCC allowing the telephone companies in the United States to operate their own cellular networks because the "telephone companies, wanting to protect their position in the basic local telephone business would stunt the growth of cellular service and thus prevent it from ever reaching the high capacity and low price where it would compete with their established service" (Berresford 1989, p. 726).

[154] The following description of the licensing process is based on Calhoun (1988).

A total of 200 proposals were received for the first 30 city licences. The FCC started with comparative hearings for the selection of operators but the time it took showed that a simpler selection mechanism had to be found. Starting with the 91st market a lottery process was conducted to grant licenses. Even the lottery process[155] with its pre-screening to exclude unqualified proposals was time-consuming. It took until 1986 for the 5000 applications for markets 91 to 120 to be screened and granted. For the 306 MSA licenses, more than 15,000 applications were received. In 1990, licenses for the last two rural areas were licensed; in only 50 % of all RSAs cellular service was offered (Mason 1991).

Second, the national market was fragmented into a large number of regional carriers with low financial resources and some with no experience in the mobile industry. When the lottery process was adopted, the most experienced mobile operators began to exit the cellular mobile market because there technical advantage was no longer relevant to be granted a license. Instead, housewives, truck-drivers and businessmen were among the licensees, who applied only to resell the licence thereafter (Calhoun 1988, p. 134). More than 90 % of the lottery's winners sold their licenses (Mason 1991). Operators decided on an individual basis when to introduce cellular telephony and in the 1990s how fast the transition from analog to digital technology would go (Paetsch 1993, p. 353). An overview of the 90 metropolitan areas for which licences were first granted[156] shows that in 1984, the launch of cellular service in the US, only in seven areas were both operators online. In 1985, another 14 areas had a competitive market and in mid-1986, 22 areas were added. The introduction of real competition as well as cellular telephony itself was delayed even in metropolitan areas until the second half of the 1980s. Rural areas for which licences were subsequently granted again by a lottery remained uncovered by cellular services for the rest of the 1980s because investment was not profitable for a single operator with no service in metropolitan areas. The following years were marked by a consolidation process, the regional expansion of cellular operators by mergers and acquisitions (Mason 1991).

It can be concluded that the assignment process of licences delayed cellular telephony and additionally did not create a real competitive environment suitable for cellular telephony as has been constituted in the Nordic countries, until the 1990s.[157] The delay in nation-wide cellular service resulted in the delay in the adoption of the next cellular generation, the digital standard. Although the US standard for a digital cellular system was agreed on at the same time as when the

---

155 At that time, the FCC was not allowed to auction off spectrum to the highest bidder by the courts (Calhoun 1988, p. 124). In the 1990s spectrum auctions became the prevailing process of granting licenses in the USA. At the end of the 1990s, mobile licenses for the third cellular generation began to be auctioned off in Europe as well.

156 The status of the first 90 cities is published in Lee (1989, pp. 42-46).

157 In fixed-line telephony as well, competition in the US was inhibited by legal problems and theoretical discussions. As a result, regulation remained rampant during the 1980s, see Crandall (1988).

European operators adopted the GSM standard, digital mobile service started about five years earlier in Europe, while most US mobile operators had little incentive to switch to the digital standard unless they did not manage to break even with their analog system.

Competition and collusion

Competition in mobile telecommunications can be at work in four relationships: competition between mobile network operators, between mobile and fixed-line operators, between equipment manufacturers and in the retail market for phones and services. The retail service market in cellular mobile telephony was introduced in the UK in 1985 as a third-tier market. Network operators were not allowed to sell to private customers directly until 1993. Instead, independent service providers buy air time from the network operators on a wholesale basis and package this time with a handset for sale to private customers (Cave, Williamson 1996, p. 116). Yet, prices for calls remained stable between 1987 and 1992. The retail market had no additional price lowering effect on the call charges, but only on mobile phones, which were subsidised by service providers with the bonuses they received from network operators for airtime and new subscribers (Geroski et al. 1989). Low mobile phone costs and marketing activities should have promoted the demand for mobile telephony in the UK, albeit only in the second half of the 1980s. Valletti, Cave (1998) make the low capacity of the networks, restricting supply, responsible for the price stability in the UK. Yet, the strong growth in demand for mobile service was hard to predict (Geroski et al. 1989). In many countries with two mobile operators, prices remained stable. This suggests that duoplistic collusion may have occurred (Parler, Röller 1997). This argument is supported by the fact that when new operators were allowed in the UK in 1993, real competition between operators emerged and penetration rates exploded (Cave, Williamson 1996, p. 118). The duopoly policy should generally encourage the two operators to make the large investments in networks without facing additional competition from subsequent entrants (Cave, Williamson 1996, p. 102). In Sweden, however, a duopoly led to low prices. An explanation could be that in countries which introduced cellular mobile service late and where penetration rates of pre-cellular telephony were previously low, subscriber growth rates were so high that both operators had no incentive to lower the prices since they could hardly manage the subscriber growth which emerged in spite of high call charges. According to an official interviewed, this was especially the case in Germany, where prices were higher than in all other countries throughout the 1990s. This, together with the collusion problem of duopolies, might explain the weak positive effect of competition on the penetration rate in Gruber and Verboven's (2001) study. The first market segments of mobile telephony are high income users willing to pay high charges. The effects of competition in Sweden and Finland were quite different. New segments of users in the population were attracted to mobile telephony. In both countries the operators had to attract new consumer segments, for whom price elasticity is much higher than for the early users of mobile telephony. Real competition therefore supports mass-market suitability of cellular telephony. In a competitive market, firms set quality and prices according to the marginal customer (the additional market segments), the monopolist according to the average customer, who is more willing to pay for quality and is less price sensitive than mass-market consumers.[158]

Competition in the supplier market and marketing

Another question of competition intensity is the number of and competition between suppliers. Again, the Nordic countries differ from other European countries, the US and Japan. In the Nordic countries, PTTs did not automatically choose a national champion as supplier but instead let suppliers compete for orders. For the first NMT system, eight manufacturing companies competed. Although Ericsson has been chosen by Swedish Telecom as the main supplier after "stiff competition", radio base stations were supplied by Japan's Mitsubishi and Finland's Nokia (Hultén, Mölleryd, 1995, p. 5). According to a Nokia executive, there was always competition between Nokia and Ericsson in each home country, which motivated both companies to innovate. In addition, Sweden opened the market for mobile phones as early as 1971 and the telephone sets connected to the fixed network in 1985 – much earlier than in other European countries. In the US the national telephony company was at the same time the sole manufacturer of switching equipment, although mobile equipment was procured from independent suppliers such as Motorola. In Japan the national PTT (NTT) designs, develops and operates its network equipment, which is supplied by four main manufacturers, who compete against each other (Fransman 1995). In both countries competition between different mobile systems was limited to the production of the national standard by the in-house research of the national carrier.

Competition in the 1980s had the additional effect of competing firms promoting cellular mobile telephony with marketing activities in order to gain market share and attract new user segments such as private consumers and young persons in particular, who used mobile phones for fun. The private Swedish operator is said to have used "aggressive ways of marketing" to attract private users (Mölleryd 1997, p. 29). PTTs and monopolistic PTTs in particular did not promote cellular telephony in the 1980s at least, because they swiftly reached capacity constraints and enhancements were expensive. Comvic on the other hand always had free capacity. The private operator in Sweden had to heavily promote its service because of its technical and image disadvantage against the public operator. In addition, PTTs often considered themselves as governmental agencies, which provide

[158] For a theoretical discussion of quality and price setting, see e.g. Tirole (1988, pp. 100-101). It has been mentioned before (4.4.3) that some monopolistic countries, such as Germany, set quality levels of cellular services and prices too high for the average customers, thus inhibiting domestic mass markets as well as exports of the cellular system.

a public mobile service to users who really need it and not as profit maximisers, which had to persuade users to use a new service. Hultén and Mölleryd (1995, p. 12) particularly stress the additional promotion effect in Sweden of competing mobile phone sales companies (the market for phones has been liberalised since 1971). Mölleryd (1997) points to the effect entrepreneurs in the retail market had on promoting mobile telephony. Independent retail chains offered leasing contracts in order to attract customer segments with low income. These shops have been responsible for a large share of new subscribers to NMT since the mid-1980s. Deregulation of telephones sets and competition between manufacturers seemed be an important factor for the success of mobile services since the high price of handsets limited subscriber numbers dramatically.

To summarise, the factor of competition on lead markets is therefore much more complex than simply a question of the *number* of operators. The market structure advantage in the case of mobile telephony derived from a competitive environment. The Nordic countries, the UK and the US had introduced competition in cellular telephony at an early stage. Yet, only the Nordic countries happened to constitute a dynamic mobile market and could gain a lead market advantage from domestic competition. The regulatory implementation of competition in the US delayed cellular telephony, added uncertainty and kept mobile operators too small compared to the large investments which were necessary.

Political influence

Since the PTTs in Europe were all state-owned, the GSM initiative was sometimes misinterpreted as being politically motivated and a vehicle of industrial policy. Although the political level tried to influence GSM decisions, it becomes clear that the GSM group decided in the *economic* interest of the PTTs. Even for private PTTs, it would have been economically sound to agree on one standard in order to gain economies of scale and facilitate international roaming. In this sense, GSM was a "user"-driven standard. Even the French and German PTTs unofficially did not back the politically supported Franco-German proposal (according to a key official). Instead, there was an overwhelming consensus among the PTTs for the need for economic soundness of a digital system. Political backing was certainly helpful in pushing a pan-European standard. GSM, however, stands in the tradition of the Nordic standards, pursuing high frequency economy for as many customers as possible and high cost-performance ratio, and not in the tradition of Franco-German industrial policy of technology-oriented, proprietary standard-setting. In Cattaneo's (1994, p. 66) view, the compromise in the GSM specification of 1987 was a mixture of two cultures, the French and German philosophy of technological superiority and the market orientation of the Nordic countries. Yet, the latter finally became rampant. Cattaneo (1994, p. 65) explains that the successful NMT standard in particular convinced other European PTTs that a pan-European standard would enable a "sharing of risks and costs of development of a new technology and establishing an open standardised technology, it allowed freedom from national supplier, sensibly reducing the price of equipment". Consequently, Telekom Sweden's Thomas Haug, who served as secretary and chairman of the NMT working group (Gerdes 1991), became chairman of the CEPT working group in 1982 and of the GSM MoU.

In reviewing the success of the GSM standard, pan-European standardisation seems to be an important success factor for GSM (Cattaneo 1994). Theoretically, the impact of standardisation on market success is ambiguous (Tirole 1994, p. 406). International standardisation has its advantages. Standardisation increases the number of suppliers. In the presence of network externalities, an operator must anticipate which standard will be widely adopted by other operators. If there is uncertainty about the next dominant standard, operators wait to adopt a standard until this uncertainty is reduced. This was the situation in the US in the 1990s, when the deployment of a digital standard was delayed because US operators were unsure about the merit of two competing standards (TDMA and CDMA). In Europe, the commitment of all European PTTs to adopt the GSM standard lowered the risk of adoption. On the other hand, premature standardisation could lead to the adoption of an inferior technology, because they lock out other technological designs to compete. Indeed, CDMA, which was dismissed initially by the US cellular industry, later seemed to be the superior technology as it has been chosen as the 3rd generation cellular technology. Competition between the standards in the US revealed their merits. An additional argument against standardisation was put forward by Calhoun (1988). He argues that early standardisation limits innovation in the United States because US manufacturers get most of their innovation incentives from the prospect of setting a proprietary standard. Since they anticipate a disadvantage in the production of a system of a non-proprietary standard against Japanese competitors, a mandatory non-proprietary standard reduces their R&D efforts. While premature standardisation is a disadvantage in rapidly changing technologies, GSM, however, was certainly not an inferior technology when it was developed in the 1980s.

The circumstances surrounding the specification of GSM was certainly the basis for its success. Yet, specification of a pan-European standard itself could not have been a main international success factor of GSM. European standards which were not adopted outside Europe are legion. GSM made a difference because it was shaped by the demand and market context of the lead market. The controversy of the Nordic vs. the Franco-German proposal for the GSM specification within the GSM group makes this distinction clear. First, NMT and Tacs were already internationally successful, the German and the French standards were not. The latter countries pushed for a pan-European standard they did not want to be excluded from the world market again. The same happened at the end of the 1990s, when Japan lobbied to be included in the 3rd generation standard. Second, GSM was not a standard set by the national governments but a user standard shaped by PTTs' anticipation of the market demand. The Franco-German proposal was more intended to support technology in Europe.

Table 4-5: Summary of lead market factors

Country	Demand advantage	Price advantage	Export advantage	Transfer advantage	Market structure advantage
Sweden	● Trend: High pre-cellular penetration	● Anticipatory prices: low prices of call charges ● Favouring cellular and digital techno-logy with high price reduction potential	● High export orientation of firms, PTTs, and institutions ● Average population density	● Early cellular systems re-duced risk for other countries ● Roaming standards ● Non-proprietary standards	● Competition in pre-cellular service, two operators of cellular service since 1981
Finland	● Trend: High pre-cellular penetration	● Anticipatory prices: low prices of call charges ● Favouring cellular and digital techno-logy with high price reduction potential	● High export orientation of firms, PTTs, and institutions ● Average population density	● Roaming orientation ● Non-proprietary standards	● Monopolistic mobile operator, but competition between mobile and fixed-line operators in pre-cellular and cellular services
USA	❍ Low pene-tration of pre-cellular teleph-ony	● Low prices of cellular service ● Large market offering high economies of scale	❍ Low export orientation of domestic indus-try ❍ Low density in rural areas favouring satel-lite communica-tion	❍ No roaming	● Competition in pre-cellular and cellular service 1983
UK	❍ Low pene-tration of pre-cellular teleph-ony, late start of cellular service	●❍ Average prices of mobile service			● Competition in cellular service
Ger-many	❍ Low pene-tration of pre-cellular teleph-ony, late start of cellular service	❍ High call charges, high phone prices	❍ PTT requir-ing idiosyncratic standard	❍ Proprietary standards	❍ No competi-tion in cellular service until 1992
Japan	❍ Low pene-tration of pre-cellular teleph-ony ● Early start of cellular service	❍ High deposit, high monthly charge	❍ PTT requiring idiosyncratic standard ❍ High popula-tion density favouring cord-less technology	❍ Japanese proprietary standards ❍ No roaming	❍ No competi-tion in cellular service until 1988

● advantage

❍ disadvantage

Third, there are no network externalities between countries but only within countries – except the capability of international roaming. The roaming ability, however, was described as a transfer advantage. Fourthly, not standardisation itself increases the number of possible suppliers but how proprietary the standard is. France and Germany proposed a more proprietary standard for GSM, but the GSM group was committed to a non-proprietary standard. In the US, in contrast, proprietary standards competed in the market and "cultivated monopolistically oriented pricing" (Paetsch 1993, p. 348) among suppliers.

4.4.6 Summary

In this study, it is argued that the lead market factors of the Nordic countries are success factors of cellular telephony and the GSM standard. The case study shows that lead markets were constituted by market conditions that made latent demand transparent for manufacturers and service providers. A competitive and entrepreneurial market tests new technology at an early stage, pressures regulators into opening up restrictions to new technology, drives prices down and demonstrates that there is a considerable demand for new products and services. There are, of course, other success factors as well, which should not be neglected. The GSM standard was built on the successful pan-European cooperation, combined resources, the personal efforts and visions of many of the participants and the political support they received.

The success of the GSM standard can only be explained fully by taking all historical accidents into account. However, it is argued that the particular nation-specific market contexts of the European markets guided the European PTTs and the manufacturers towards a pan-European standard, spurred their effort and shaped its outcome. The successful features of GSM and the digital technology employed were the consequences of the emergence of a mass market in Northern Europe and not historical accidents.

A summary of the lead market factors (Table 4-5) for selected countries recapitulates that the Nordic countries have advantages in all five factors, while other countries have advantages in one or two categories only. Laggards among the large industrialised countries like Germany and Japan have mostly disadvantages in the lead market factors. At this point no single factor can be called decisive, instead the interaction of the five lead market factors is important. In each factor, the theoretical model of a lead market factor can be applied but one model alone seems inappropriate. It is the sum of the lead market factors that gives a country a lead in the adoption of a subsequently internationally successful technological design. This is an important conclusion for the question of whether a lead market can be identified ex-ante. Before this question shall be discussed, the home market advantage of firms in the lead market is examined for the case of mobile telephony in the next section.

4.5 The Competitive Advantage of Equipment Firms

4.5.1 The market success of Nordic telecommunications equipment firms

The home market hypothesis suggests that firms that have their headquarters in or at least are committed in the lead market gain a competitive advantage over competitors. In the case of mobile telephone equipment, a comparison between the competitiveness of Nordic firms and their competitors supports this hypothesis. Nokia of Finland and Ericsson of Sweden are the biggest mobile equipment manufacturers in the world (ITU 1999), together with the US company Motorola. In 1998 Ericsson held 30 % of the world market for wireless infrastructure, Motorola 16 % and Nokia 11 %. Nokia held a market share in mobile handheld phones of about 23 %, Motorola 20 % and Ericsson 15 % (Ericsson corporate information).

In contrast to Motorola, the Nordic firms' success was not based on long-standing competencies in radio technology. Ericsson and, in particular, Nokia increased its market share in mobile telephony continuously over the 1980s and 1990s. Until the 1980s Ericsson was mainly a switch company similar to Siemens' telecommunications division. Mölleryd (1997) reports that it was at first reluctant to get involved in mobile telephony. In the beginning of the cellular telephony industry, Ericsson still intended to focus on the switch and assigned the radio technology development to another Swedish company, SRA, which was founded as a joint venture with the radio pioneer, the UK's Marconi. The technology used mainly came from Marconi. Yet, orders from its Scandinavian home market proved the market potential for mobile telephony (Mölleryd 1997) and in 1983 Ericsson fully acquired SRA but still ran the radio division separately from the main company. When the home market grew steadily, Ericsson augmented the radio business by several acquisitions of other Swedish radio companies. It purchased Sonab (1978), the leader in mobile telephones in the Scandinavian countries, Magnetic (1983), which built the radio base stations for the MTD and the NMT system, and Radiosystems (1988), which was founded by an employee of Magnetic and manufactured mobile equipment as a sub-contractor. Ericsson gathered almost all technological knowledge in radio technology through acquisitions. In 1993 the radio division generated more revenue than the public telecommunications division.

Ericsson's success was not merely a by-product of the success of the GSM standard. Ericsson's early sensitivity to the prospects of mobile telephony made it interested in radio equipment in general. Ericsson was among the first to deliver mobile switching equipment for the AMPS standard. Since NMT was similar to AMPS, experience with NMT gave Ericsson an advantage in supplying AMPS systems to US operators (Pehrsson 1996, p. 136). Ericsson's international approach motivated it to simultaneously develop mobile infrastructure and phones for the digital US (TDMA, CDMA) and the Japanese standard (PDC) (Pehrsson 1996, p. 132). It has more than 50 % of the TDMA infrastructure market, the digital version of AMPS and it is a supplier to the Japanese operators.

Nokia was a long-standing chemical and paper processing firm located near the river Nokia in Finland with little technological competence in telecommunications equipment. From the 1970s on, it diversified into consumer electronics, computers and telecommunications through acquisitions. According to Kennedy (1992), the market entry in mobile telephony equipment is owed to the former chief executive "who spotted the potential in the radiotelephony business and decided to exploit it by acquiring a series of electronic firms" (Kennedy 1992, p. 24). Besides television set and computer manufacturers, Nokia acquired the radio-telephony part of Salora, a Finnish television firm, and the production facility of the US firm Tandy in Korea, where phones were manufactured for the US market. In 1981 it started making NMT mobile phones (Echikson 1994). Although there is no clear evidence to support it, it can be assumed that the early demand in mobile telephony in Finland led the firm to shift its resources more and more towards telecommunications equipment and away from computers and television sets. Over time it built up experience and competence in the development and production of mobile terminals. A further milestone was in 1991 the acquisition of the British company Technophone Ltd, which pioneered hand-held mobile telephones as well as digital handsets (Kennedy 1992). In the 1990s, Nokia concentrated on cellular handsets and exited the cordless phone market when they realised that cellular would be more demanded than cordless telephones (McClelland 1991). Nokia developed the whole range of GSM infrastructure equipment and became the world's prime supplier for GSM1800 infrastructure. Since Finland was a small country, Nokia was traditionally eager to export its technology and serve foreign markets. It built up a world-wide network of large-scale production facilities. According to a company official, Nokia was chosen as a partner for GSM development in the late 1980s by Alcatel mostly because of its export experience and knowledge on foreign markets and not because of technological superiority. Nokia's success is based far more on the GSM standard, in particular GSM1800, than Ericsson's, but Nokia's rise to the number 1 mobile phone manufacturer in the world is more spectacular and unexpected.

Besides these two large multinational Nordic firms there are several smaller firms which became successful. Benefon of Finland produces and exports handheld phones, as well as Storno of Denmark, Salora, AP, Handic, and Spectronic of Sweden. These firms competed for the smallest and cheapest handheld phones (Mölleryd 1997, p. 36). Although Denmark does not host multinational firms, it has a very successful mobile telecommunications equipment industry. Over time, most of these smaller companies were acquired by foreign multinational firms in order to acquire their competence in GSM and radio technology. In 1985, Motorola acquired Storno. In the mid-1990s, Bosch of Germany, which supplied radio systems in the GSM consortium with Siemens and PKI, acquired the Danish company Dancall, which successfully marketed a portfolio of GSM handsets.

Communications equipment firms from other countries fared less well or even failed on the world market. In contrast to Nokia and Ericsson, they either remained concentrated on fixed-line telephony equipment instead of radically shifting resources to mobile infrastructure, or they did not venture the high R&D investment necessary for developing GSM equipment. Even firms with competence in radio communications did not succeed. Although radio equipment firms such as the French Matra, UK's Marconi, Bosch and Telefunken from Germany entered the cellular telephony market, they remained focussed on private radio equipment or developed only the radio part of cellular systems. Japanese electronic firms could not repeat their international success in consumer electronics.

4.5.2 Advantages of firms in the lead market

The Nordic countries as a lead market became a source of information on the technological *design* that prevails in the world market and *timing* of the development of technology. There are several indications supporting the hypothesis that the increasing competitiveness of the Nordic firms in mobile telephone equipment emanated from a home market advantage: the early sensing of the demand for mobile telephony in Nordic markets, and which were mainly ignored by foreign companies; the tacit knowledge of technical standards together with the preferential selection of domestic suppliers by operators. The Nordic countries were, over a long period of time, a need-forecasting laboratory. Firms can sense new opportunities and experience needs in an environment where a new technology is used more widely than in other countries. High penetration rates mean that the technology is already used by market segments such as the younger generation or the elderly, who in other countries adopt the technology much later. Domestic firms in the lead market get feedback from these segments which can be very different from the feedback of early users. For instance, the Nordic firms were already oriented to the importance of portable and handheld phones (Cattaneo 1994, p. 65), which are less important for car-mounted phones used by businessmen, the early adopters of mobile telephones. When the younger generation in the Nordic countries started to use mobile phones, firms realised that a modern design is very important for this segment. In 1998 the penetration of mobile telephony exceeded the penetration of fixed-lines. This suggests that mobile telephony is likely to substitute fixed-line telephony. Domestic firms realised that first and began to concentrate their line of business on mobile radio technology. Furthermore, they get early feedback from a changing environment. They can experience what needs and applications occur when people shift their communication from fixed to mobile lines. With the penetration rate so high that almost anybody has a mobile phone, mobile telephony can be used in other contexts, e.g. as a credit card or payment for automated soft drink dispenser. Phone ringers have to sound different, in order to identify one's personal phone when together with others. All these are features of phones pioneered by Nordic firms. In accordance with the lead market theory, the ITU posits in its World Telecommunication Development Report 1999 that "contact with end users in the highly evolved consumer markets in the Nordic region has allowed Nokia and Ericsson to receive feedback directly and respond quickly by offering cellular phones with user-friendly features and attractive designs." (ITU 1999, p. 8). Hultén and Mölleryd (1995) come to the same conclusion. The strong home market demand for mobile telephony pushed Ericsson into becoming totally committed to mobile communications equipment. A technological knowledge lead was the result of a commitment to mobile telephony and not the origin of the commitment to mobile technology.

Not only companies that have their headquarters in the lead markets benefit from lead market proximity. Firms which are active in the lead market can achieve a competitive advantage. Firms which have considerable marketing activities in the lead market and consider it important to hold a large market share in the country fare much better than firms which are not present in the market. An example is Motorola, which was present in the European market and participated in the GSM standardisation process.[159] Market information is often not easily acquired by foreign firms. The GSM standardisation is an example of tacit knowledge which gave the firms which participated in the GSM standardisation a knowledge lead and a competitive advantage in the production of GSM equipment. Outsiders of the standardisation process found it hard to develop and produce GSM equipment as fast and at the same cost as European firms. According to company officials interviewed, even the detailed GSM specification, physically a multi-volume paperwork of about 6000 pages, includes some tacit knowledge. First, the specification of GSM uses a technical language that was perfectly familiar to the people who participated in the technical committees but not for other technicians of other companies, especially in non-English speaking countries such as Japan. Second, all measurements specified were metric and not used by US competitors. Third, the GSM specification does not specify every part of the equipment unambiguously. There is some leeway in the specification, which could easily be filled by technical personnel who participated in the standardisation proceedings. Outsiders had to find out some details themselves.

Finally, domestic firms have better access to market information, because users often prefer local suppliers over foreign ones. Local users want the supplier to be close to them for efficient interaction, especially when new products are going to

[159] Besides the Nordic and other European manufacturers, the only industry leader outside Europe for mobile equipment is the US firm Motorola. Motorola attained a dominant market position in mobile equipment in the United States and on foreign markets after AT&T ceased to produce mobile equipment as a result of the Consent Decree of 1956, one of the first antitrust rules against AT&T (Paetsch 1993, p. 120). Motorola was, in contrast to its US rival AT&T, an international firm with large market share in Europe as well as in Japan (Keegan, Green 1989, p. 99, Dörrenbächer 1999, p. 90). As a result, it got involved in the European mobile telephony initiatives and closely monitored the GSM development. This continual close contact to the lead markets in Europe and its long-standing technical competence in handheld phones can explain why Motorola was able to maintain its competitive position at least in the handheld phone segment. It was, however, less successful with its GSM base stations, which was attributed by company officials to its lesser knowledge of European fixed-line infrastructure.

be adopted which need maintenance, such as telecommunications networks. Teething problems and continuous refinement require the commitment of the supplier and users might expect a local firm to show a higher commitment towards local customers. Long-standing relationships between telecom operators and manufacturers exist and the inherent risks of adopters of innovations are reduced by the trust that has been built over time. In the telecom industry, political reasons for choosing domestic suppliers are also apparent. PTTs are often government-owned and therefore prefer domestic suppliers as part of the national industry policy (Dörrenbächer 1999, European Commission 1997a). In Finland and in Sweden, too, the local manufacturers were the indisputable suppliers of the local telecom operators. In most countries, however, political discrimination between domestically owned and foreign owned firms with production and R&D capacity are scarce. Therefore international telecom equipment producers such as ITT built up manufacturing and developing affiliates in foreign countries to supply the local telecom operator (Beise 1999).

Lead market timing

Firms in the lead market did not only gain an advantage in choosing the technological design that prevailed on the world market. In addition, they could offer the technology in the world market at the right time. The main disadvantage of the several systems of each of the cellular telephony generations obviously resulted from delays in market entry and not from technical inferiority. These delays occurred because the profitability of the industry was less sure than in other countries. Market signals indicating a mass-market demand varied from country to country. In the United States cellular telephony was invented but market entry of the first as well as the second generation was seriously delayed, so that the US systems had a considerable competitive disadvantage on the world market against Nordic and pan-European systems. The delay was due to the lack of pressure from local demand and the geographical structure of the US leading to the expectation that a satellite system would be more beneficial. Because of the late start of the cellular telephony, the second generation, the digital systems, were delayed in the US as well. The transition from AMPS to TDMA was still not completed in the 1990s and CDMA was commercially launched in 1996, although the standards were specified in the late 1980s. Manufacturing firms obviously did not have enough incentives to spur the development of the respective systems. In Germany, the first generation system was technically superior to other systems but market entry was delayed by the German PTT. The US waited too long to introduce AMPS and this delayed the second generation of cellular telephony as well. The Nordic standard and European system GSM was introduced just at the right time. Its development was spurred by high demand in Europe and especially by the apparent emerging mass-market that was signalled by the success of mobile telephony in the Nordic countries.

4.5.3 Disadvantages of firms in lag markets

Firms located in lag markets have distinct disadvantages, even if they are willing to innovate and enter new technologies. The biggest problem for firms in lag markets is that they are regularly discouraged by their home markets to invest in a new technology. Second, lag markets are often idiosyncratic markets; innovations are demanded that users in other countries will not adopt. A study by Funk (1997) supports the finding of this hypothesis. Funk (1997) finds that the international adoption of different cellular standards and the export success of firms from countries of origin of the standard are positively correlated. He observes that despite their world-wide operations, firms have "ignored the standards that have been created outside of their own region." (Funk 1997, p. 138). Funk (1997) offers several explanations for this: firms are disadvantaged in developing equipment of a foreign standard because of their late market entry, patent problems, a lack of design engineers with skills in the non-domestic standard, and poor access to the chips and components of these standards. He stresses that these disadvantages *compensated* the technological advantage of Japanese firms.

The most surprising outcome of the 1990 mobile telephony market is that Japanese firms hold a low market share and have even fallen behind since the early 1980s. The ITU (1999, p. 32) study states: "[...] Japanese companies have generally not done well abroad for wireless equipment." Although Japan was the first country to operate a cellular mobile telephony system and Japanese firms like Oki won contracts to equip AT&T's Chicago trial system in 1983 (Calhoun 1988, p. 52), Japanese equipment companies are neither internationally successful suppliers of mobile infrastructure equipment nor handheld phones. The Japanese digital system, which was renamed Personal Digital Cellular (PDC) to enhance its export chances, was not even adopted with governmental funding by Asian markets traditionally penetrated by Japanese firms (Galbraith 1993). In mobile phones, Japanese "equipment manufacturers have not been able to keep up with their European competitors in global cellular sales" (ITU 1999, p.20). The failure in handheld phones comes as more of a surprise since Japanese manufacturers are expected to be competitive in sectors of miniaturised electronics (Economist 1995, p. 60). Since the end of the 1970s there were even fears in the United States that Japanese firms would take over the market for mobile equipment (Pemple 1978, p. 331). Japanese manufacturers, such as Oki and Matsushita through its Panasonic brand, did indeed design phones for non-Japanese mobile systems early but they were eventually overtaken by European manufacturers and US' Motorola, which designed smaller and more attractive phones. In the mid-1980s Japanese firms held 45 % of the US mobile phones market (Calhoun 1988, p. 70). Yet, the market share of Japanese manufacturers in the world cellular phone market slipped from 23 % in 1992 to nearly 10 % at the end of the 1990s (Dataquest, as cited in the Economist 1995). Despite strong demand for mobile phones in Japan, Panasonic had only 8 % of the world-wide mobile phone market in 1998 (ITU 1999, p. 30).

Since Japanese electronic producers were successful in other product ranges (e.g. games consoles), a general weakness in the development of software, which is a vital part of a cellular phone, is an unconvincing explanation. The most persuasive explanation for this market failure is the lack of a home market advantage. Japanese firms were not as close to the markets in Europe that set the trends of mobile telephony as the domestic manufacturers were. As a result of proprietary Japanese standards, which were not adopted outside Japan for the reasons elaborated on previously, Japanese equipment firms did not concentrate equipment development on cellular standards that became internationally successful. In focussing on domestic Japanese demand – and probably the US market that was seen as the most important market – Japanese producers could not devote their research and marketing efforts to the demand preferences in Europe and European mobile standards. On account of regulation and the restricting marketing policy of NTT, the Japanese market did not offer the feedback which could guide domestic companies towards the future world market. By contrast, the Nordic companies sensed the demand for small and trendy handheld phones early and concentrated on improving these phone characteristics. In addition, Japanese manufacturers were not as close to the standard-setting of GSM as were their European competitors, which could develop GSM equipment faster and more cost-efficiently. As outsiders they were not offered the same conditions for cross-license agreements as their European competitors (Cataneo 1994).

Even other European firms were not as successful as Nordic firms. It is most insightful to compare Ericsson to Siemens of Germany. Both were internationally competitive in the communications switch industry and reluctant to take up niche telecommunication markets. It was even said that Telecom of Sweden had to push Ericsson to play a part in the mobile industry beyond delivering the mere switch (Mölleryd 1997). Ericsson first objected to the NMT system and was not the most active participant in the GSM standardisation. Siemens responded to German telecom's plans to develop an analog cellular system for a limited number of subscribers but with high quality standards. Despite its technological superiority, the German system was a failure on the world market. This failure prevented Siemens from investing in the development of a full GSM system family. Expecting small market opportunities, Siemens decided to focus on switch technology and the radio part in a consortium with PKI of Philips and Bosch, a strategy which Ericsson had previously also preferred. However, Ericsson realised the great prospects of cellular telephony much earlier than Siemens, which only developed a GSM base station itself in 1994.[160]

[160] In addition, Ericsson's approach of outsourcing and organising the radio division in a separated firm with profit responsibility turned out to be an advantage. The traditional switch division resisted the idea of substituting fixed lines with mobile telephony. The radio division saw it as a chance and eagerly pursued the early market entry. Through its independence it was more free to market its business. The cellular business within Siemens fared less free, the switch division had more power and hindered market entry.

4.5.4 Lead market strategy in the cellular mobile telephony industry

While the success of firms in the lead market was no coincidence, at what time could the lead market have been identified by firms? The tremendous success of cellular telephony as a mass market industry beginning to substitute subscriber fixed-line service, was totally unexpected. Even when GSM service was introduced in 1992, it was not expected to become that successful. In retrospect, it is unreasonable to claim that the success of cellular telephony could have been predicted, because it was never clear how many consumers would use a cellular mobile phone and how frequently they would use it.[161] The lead market concept does not make the claim of directly forecasting the success of a technology. However, the lead market concept would at least suggest a conditioned hypothesis: if mobile telephony has a broad appeal to consumers in the long run, the mass market would first emerge in a country or region that has the biggest lead market advantage. This country could have been used as a technology forecasting laboratory in the 1980s: it is the country that either makes an international latent demand for mobile telephony transparent and points at an early stage to the technological design which will prevail on the world market. The lead market either anticipates the advantageous technological design or it has the power to push a particular preferred technology and squeeze technological designs preferred by other countries out of the world market. The success of cellular mobile telephony is interrelated with the failure of other mobile concepts in which billions of dollars were invested and lost.

If the Nordic countries could have been identified as a lead market for mobile telephony in the early 1980s, two strategic conclusions could have been made for network operators and telecommunications equipment manufacturers after closely analysing the Nordic markets. First, cellular mobile telephony is likely to prevail against other mobile communications concepts such as pagers, cordless telephony and satellite telephony. Second, international roaming is a key feature of a system requiring a multinational standard and considerable export efforts. Third, portabil-

---

[161] Quantitative market analysis was unable to predict demand for cellular mobile telephony, although in the 1970s a large demand for mobile service at lower prices was expected (Young 1979, p. 5). Market prognoses documented in literature underestimated cellular subscribers but overestimated demand for alternative mobile systems like telepoint. Likewise, a company marketing director interviewed stated that *every* market prognosis he saw since 1980 underestimated the following market growth. Even in Scandinavia, where mobile telephony was used far more than anywhere else, few had imagined that it would be one of the most successful business stories in the 1990s (Mölleryd 1997). The problem was predicting the market segments attracted by cellular telephony especially when prices continuously decrease. For instance, in the mid-1990s, 60 % of all schoolchildren in Sweden had cellular phones; in Japan, cellular phones became a trend for teenagers to use at home (Ayu 1999). In addition, the sigmoid curves of a within-diffusion cannot be econometrically estimated before the point of inflection is reached.

ity of mobile phones is an important success factor. Fourthly, a digital system is required to achieve the spectrum efficiency necessary to accommodate a mass-market in mobile telephony. A firm that would have concentrated its R&D activities on these features of mobile systems would have been optimally positioned in the mobile market in the 1990s.

Could the Nordic countries have been identified as lead markets in the 1980s? In comparing and benchmarking the lead market factors of European countries, Japan and the United States in the early 1980s, clear hints could have been discovered showing that several countries in Europe, in particular the Scandinavian countries and the UK, had the potential to set the pace in mobile telephony and prefer the prevailing mobile concept in the 1990s. Some facts were already known in the 1980s, facts which could have been used to identify the Nordic countries as a possible lead market: telephone prices, degree of competition, export orientation of domestic economy, efforts to realise international roaming and, in particular, the high penetration rates in the Nordic countries for pre-cellular and cellular telephony. Although the United States looked most likely in the late 1970s to lead the world in the adoption of mobile telephony, the delays from the allocation of spectrum to cellular mobile telephony and the commercial operation of cellular telephony in 1983, the small penetration and the initially low market growth, the higher prices of cellular calls and the idiosyncratic US environment context could have been warnings for the firms ready to develop a mobile standard not to focus on the United States market.

The Nordic firms were the first to realise the potential of mobile telephony and reacted earlier than their competitors. The most important market information from the Nordic countries was that cellular mobile telephony is a potential mass market. A multinational company outside Scandinavia could have made use of the Nordic countries by closely monitoring what was demanded in these countries and it could have reacted much earlier than its competitors in turning to the right technology. First, the Nordic countries proved that cellular telephony is capable of covering less populated areas, making satellite systems unnecessary. Second, the number of potential users of mobile telephony would exceed the number that could be accommodated by analog systems. Through the awareness of the market situation in the Nordic countries, a mass market for mobile telephony was already envisioned in 1980 with the success of mobile telephony. Those who believed in the mass market worked towards a digital system from the beginning (Haug, cited in Kennedy 1999, Böhm 1980, Mölleryd 1997, p. 43). Early visionaries like Böhm (1980) published as early as 1980 the conclusion that if a large segment of consumers were to use mobile telephone services, a digital mobile system would be necessary to deliver these services. Depending on the stage of home market in the mobile telephony trajectory, these visionaries were not taken seriously. In Germany, the United States and Japan they were not, because mobile telephony was seen as a small market for a limited market segment. In the Nordic countries, however, penetration rates already indicated in the mid-1980s that much more

Figure 4-10: Stylised trend of spectrum efficiency of mobile telephony 1940-2000

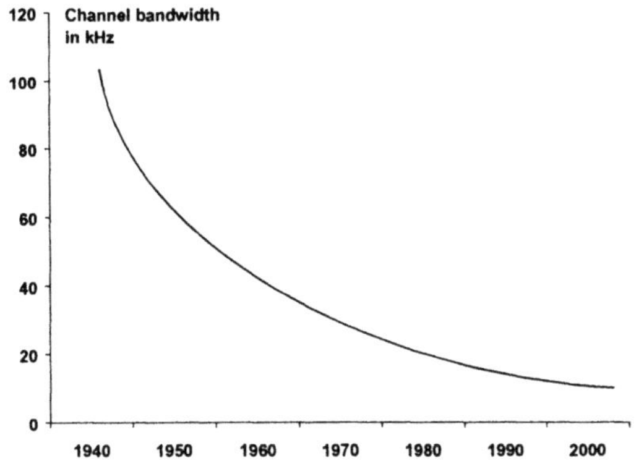

Source: Own estimations based on Calhoun (1988)

subscribers could be attracted than previously thought. In the Nordic countries it became clear in the first half of the 1980s that digital technology would be the only technology which could enable the spectrum efficiency necessary for a mass market.

Technical breakthroughs were still necessary but, again, many facts were already known in the early 1980s. The spectrum efficiency had to be increased considerably to enable a large segment of consumers to make mobile calls. Figure 4-10 shows the reduction of channel bandwidth, the frequency width occupied by a caller, since the introduction of pre-cellular mobile telephony in the 1940s. This spectrum efficiency was considerably reduced before as well as after the introduction of cellular systems. Second, mobile telephony was mostly seen as a telephone for automobiles, because of the heavy weight and the high price of the mobile unit. Yet, handheld phones were envisioned from as early as the 1970s.[162] Miniaturisation could be achieved through large integrated circuits and a small cell structure. Frey and Lee (1978, p. 64) conclude at the end of the 1970s: "A cellular system offering portable telephone service, enabling a subscriber to have an instrument with him at all times if desired, is clearly possible". Prices of phones could be expected to drop by economies of scale in production and advances in integrated circuits. A price of $1,000 per phone was already expected (Legace, Pastan, 1976, cited in Pemple 1978, p. 325).

At the end of the 1980s, at the latest in applying the lead market criteria US and Japanese firms could have sensed that a pan-European cellular standard would be a promising candidate for a dominant design in the 1990s, because of its

- large cost reduction potential of digital technology,
- the ability of international roaming,
- the export orientation of the European communications equipment industry,
- the introduction of competition in most European countries.

162 In 1973, Martin Cooper, a project manager at Motorola, presented a working handheld radio phone, the Dyna-Tac, to the public (Motorola corporate information). Pimple (1978) reports that Japanese NTT had developed a prototype for a handheld phone in the late 1970s and expected to introduce it in the 1980s. The Wall Street Journal reported on Sep. 25, 1980, the headline "Mobile Phones Fit for Pocket, May be Near".

The lead market concept would have given all telecommunications equipment manufacturers additional information for strategic planning. It would have pointed to the digital technology and the GSM system in particular developed in Europe. Participation in the GSM standardisation was not impossible for foreign companies. Other strategic options were the acquisition of European firms involved in the development and manufacturing of GSM components, and a strategic alliance or a joint venture with them. Many companies decided on such measures in the 1990s. The Bell labs, renamed Lucent following independence from AT&T, bought PKI of Germany; Japanese firms like Sony and NEC established R&D centres in Europe to develop GSM handheld phones, and Motorola develops GSM systems in France.

Outlook

The third generation of mobile telephony will provide enhanced data communication for multimedia services like internet browsing and real-time video transmission. However, the US on the one side and European and Japanese actors on the other side could not agree on one standard for the third generation of cellular mobile telephony. US officials are accusing Europeans of an industrial trade policy to support European exporters; European firms, on the other hand, do not want to expose their advantage based on the already-installed world-wide GSM infrastructure. In contrast, the Japanese PTT joined the European standardisation process towards the 3rd generation cellular system and ensured that Japanese firms are no longer excluded from the European standard (Drexel 1999). In 1999 the European and Japanese operators and manufacturers agreed on a joint third generation standard (WCDMA) which uses parts of the existing GSM infrastructure. Most US-operators will instead implement their own new standard, CDMA2000, which is based on the existing narrowband CDMA standard, to leverage their existing infrastructure. Yet, these two new network standards do not only compete against each other but also with the existing GSM standard. GSM will be continuously improved with soft- and hardware upgrades introducing new voice coding software to increase frequency efficiency and package switching for data transmission at a much higher speed (GPRS). Even the future dominant standard of mobile telephony is therefore less than certain. Despite international standard-setting bodies, there will still be competition between different cellular standards. A market process leads towards global dominant standards. And some countries will still first adopt the coming global dominant standard, as occurred with GSM. Unsurprisingly, Finland was the first country to grant UMTS licenses in March 1999. And in the United States, there another feeling of déja-vu, when the spectrum allocated to the 3rd generation was found to be already occupied by television stations, that have to be coaxed to give up frequencies before mobile services can be started (Economist 2000b, p. 61).

5 Harnessing Lead Markets for Global Innovations

Tap your subsidiaries for global reach!
CHRISTOPHER A. BARTLETT & SUMANTRA GHOSHAL

In this chapter I will outline how international firms can use lead markets. One of the main goals of a multinational firm is to develop innovations that can be introduced around the world. Global innovations offer standardisation advantages that are at the core of the competitive advantage of multinational firms. A lead market concept of innovation can help a multinational firm to generate global products and to avoid getting locked-in to idiosyncratic national market environments. I will begin this chapter by reviewing the traditional responsiveness-standardisation problem of multinational firms. On the one hand multinational firms seek to develop globally standardised innovations, several factors make globally standardised products advantageous or even necessary. On the other hand, responsiveness of firms to local markets is an success factor for innovations as well. When confronted with conflicting demand preferences from country to country, multinational firms with strong commitments to serving all large markets are prone to respond with highly differentiated product variants each fitting nation-specific demand characteristics. Applying the lead market concept I come to the following conclusions for a firm's innovation strategy. A firm can develop global innovations by being responding to the lead market and ignorant to other markets' needs. By locating resources in lead markets, companies can increase the probability of global market success of standardised innovations. In the last section of this chapter I embark on developing a method of identifying lead markets ex ante.

5.1 The Search for Global Products

Industries are becoming more and more global. A global industry is an industry, in which a firm's competitive position in each country is increasingly interdependent (Porter 1986). Multinational firms are increasingly pressured to develop global products. Growing R&D investments for new product development and increasing minimum efficient scale of production plants foil customised solutions for single regions. Most innovations are no longer profitable when introduced solely to one local market.[163] Rapidly increasing R&D investment in industries such as pharmaceuticals, telecommunications equipment, medical devices and factory automation force firms to commercialised innovations worldwide in order to attain global volumes (Ohmae 1985, p. 25). The minimum efficient scale of an auto assembly plant more than tripled between 1960 and 1975 (Porter 1986). The new development of a car costs more than a billion US-$ and the development of a new public telephone switch costs the same amount; a new pharmaceutical product takes 15 years from initial research to market entry and costs several billion US-$, quadrupling in 15 years. This puts additional pressure on multinational firms to generate global products. Second, even if a country-centred strategy is feasible in terms of costs of regionally differentiated products multinational firms that choose this strategy risk facing competition from firms with globally integrated strategies, which in turn reaps the cost advantages from global integration and international transfers (Porter 1986).

The globalisation of markets, indicated by the convergence of per-capita-income, enables firms to subsequently introduce innovations that are designed for sophisticated markets into many other markets without much adaptation. A global product is defined as a product that has standardised physical attributes (Takeuchi, Porter 1986). Global products employ the same basic design and technology to produce them and allow only relatively minor modifications to adapt to local environments. Besides the previously mentioned global shakcout of product variants, globally standardised products have many intrinsic advantages. They can provide economies of scale in production, economies of adoption and they enable consistency in worldwide advertising (Buzzell 1968), international mobility of customers (e.g. multinational firms) and technological content (Paliwoda 1993). Takeuchi and Porter (1986) conclude that the ability of a firm to successfully sell a standardised product worldwide is significant to competitive advantage.

Keegan (1969) distinguishes three basic strategies for global product policy: Extension, Adaptation and Invention. The traditional approach of the multinational firm has been to ignore the opportunities provided by foreign environments, to innovate at its headquarters and extend its homegrown products to foreign markets. Foreign markets, however, are likely to be different because of international varying per capita income, level of education, legal and technical requirements, and consumer tastes and climates that require product modifications or prevent market entry totally (Paliwoda 1993, p. 211). These adaptations to local market conditions are frequently completed at foreign subsidiaries' R&D facilities. The third strategy aims to design products from scratch with global scope.

---

163 For an excellent balanced review of globalisation forces see Bartlett and Ghoshal (1995, pp. 112-124). They emphasis that globalisation is merely a stage of the long-term process of business transformation based on economies of scale and scope observed by Chandler (1990).

Livingstone (1989) sees three product policies for globally standardised products without market modifications. First, he sees a policy of designing a *universal* product that focuses on the commonality of all markets or "greatest common denominator" and employs attributes demanded worldwide (Takeuchi, Nonaka 1986). A firm can achieve this by collecting information about all features that must be included in the product to fit different markets or by identifying a common market segment such as high-income consumers or sophisticated business users (Takeuchi, Porter 1986). In the tradition of this 'centre-for-global' innovation approach the search for global products is the search for local segments with global equivalents (Levitt, 1983). Taking a local perception bias into account, this commonality approach is prone to mean the selection of innovation projects derived from local innovation incentives with the criterion, that it is possible to commercialise the innovation internationally.

The second policy for global product innovations that Livingstone (1989) mentions is the introduction of the product into a market without adapting to local preferences if this is possible and cheaper than modifications. This policy of ignorance is congruent with Levitt's (1983) argument that foreign markets may be persuaded to accept products that are not obviously designed for them, but are cheaper than products that the local market would prefer. This policy is likely to lead to small foreign market share until foreign demand preferences can be changed, e.g. through intensive advertising campaigns (Keegan, Green 1997; Cvar 1986; Takeuchi, Porter 1986). Third, Livingstone proposes a policy of phasing out the product and transferring the production to foreign markets when demand in the first market declines. Here, again, the low price of the product once designed for the first market may persuade foreign customers to favour it. This policy is a version of the life cycle theory that is confined, however, to the relationship between developed and developing countries as a result of the time period between first and secondary market introduction. Livingstone (1989) stresses the advantages of the last two policies, for they do not require market research and test marketing in the secondary markets.

Lead markets certainly facilitate the feasibility of globally standardised innovations. The lead market phenomenon has been described as a conglomeration of various diffusion mechanisms. Thus, all three policies correspond to specific lead market factors. The price, demand and transfer advantage corresponds to the policy of ignorance, a global trend can be such slow that is comes close to the product-life-cycle type of market entry. The search for global segments is the appropriate policy for firms in countries where the export advantage prevails. Therefore the policy of a firm towards the generation of global innovations depend on the characteristic of the lead market phenomenon. A firm can derive the right product policy according to the international diffusion mechanism. In the lead market concept, the product policy is a result of the underlying process of globalisation of a market. Most lead market factors suggest a traditional innovation policy of ignorance. A firm can develop global innovations by being responsive to the demand in the lead market and ignorant of other countries' needs. Only if the factors included in the export advantage are the main driver of the international diffusion, a firm must include other countries' preferences in the product development and apply the global segment strategy of innovation generation.

5.2 Responsiveness Versus Technology Convergence

Responsiveness to customers and local needs is a success factor of innovations. Most firms, including foreign affiliates of multinational firms, are indeed sensing this opportunity and respond to regional demand for innovations. As a result, foreign affiliates are inclined to invest R&D to develop innovations that respond to local needs. These local-for-local innovations have been an important determinant for the increase of R&D share of multinational firms (Ronstadt 1977; Behrman and Fisher 1980; Bartlett and Ghoshal 1990, see section 5.3.2). Responsiveness to local needs on the other hand is prone to result in idiosyncratic solutions suitable only to local conditions. Companies that have started to penetrate foreign countries and have become highly internationalised through local responsiveness often overemphasise the time persistence of international demand differences and innovate local-for-local in many foreign countries to match local tastes and requirements. This has created multinational firms with a polycentric organisation, in which foreign affiliates – at least in large foreign markets – develop their own products independently from their company headquarters. While many multinational enterprises are highly successful concerning the traditional local-for-local innovation strategies, in many industries the traditional approaches become inefficient, especially in those with high R&D intensity.

Contrasting to the local responsiveness approach, the multinational corporation aims to allocate its worldwide resources in order to maximise its overall competitiveness and create global products. This is the main strategic dilemma that multinational firms have faced over time and still face today. Authors have called this dilemma "standardisation vs. adaptation" (Buzzell 1966), "uniformity vs. fragmentation" (Fayerweather 1969), "globalisation vs. localisation", "responsiveness versus integration" (Prahalad, Doz 1987), and "scale vs. sensitivity" (Sorell 1995 as cited by Kotabe, Helsen 1998, p. ix). Several authors disagree with the view that globalisation diminishes cultural divergence (Ohmae 1985; Levitt 1983) and stress that this dilemma will remain unchanged for years to come (Bartlett, Ghoshal 1992; Douglas, Wind 1987; Kotabe, Helsen 1998). The responsiveness versus integration dilemma of multinational firms escalates when growing R&D investments for new product development and increasing minimum efficient scale of production plants foil customised solutions for single regions and global economies of adoption are threatening domestic products.

Increasing returns of adoption and strongly competing technologies are likely to lead to a global shakeout of technological variants. With competing technologies, although each is often successful and dominant in one region, one finally emerges as a globally dominant design. The trend towards globally dominant designs is not only a chance, but also a threat to home-market-oriented firms because the dominant design squeezes previously favourable domestic designs out of the home market as well, as did the fax machine with telex in Europe. Multinational firms that aim to penetrate the world market in those industries where globally dominant designs are emerging amongst competing technologies, cannot stay oriented towards the home-market alone.

The responsiveness vs. standardisation dilemma has attracted considerable research. Scholars suggest that as a consequence a successful firm has to be informed about all technologies favoured by key regional markets – markets where the coming global technological trend is likely to start. As Bartlett and Ghoshal (1990 p. 216) point out: "Companies must be sensitive to market or technological trends no matter where they occur, be creatively responsive to the opportunities and threats they perceive worldwide, and be able to exploit their new ideas and products globally in a rapid and efficient manner". At the same time, multinational firms are still faced with different local needs and attempt to adapt existing products or develop innovations locally, but at a cost. The risk of globalisation is that many countries or regions now look just equally attractive for high-tech innovations. A multinational firm that is engaged in R&D in many countries, runs the risk of ending up with either one innovation – albeit developed for the world market but tacitly oriented towards a local idiosyncratic environment-, or with several local-for-local innovations. If innovations derived from foreign R&D activities should be commercialised on an international basis, the lead features of local demand conditions are vital.

Prahalad and Doz (1987) have introduced a grid to visualise the pressures for global co-ordination and integration on the one side and local responsiveness on the other. One can analyse industries by using several criteria for evaluating the pressures for integration and responsiveness. In addition, Prahalad and Doz demonstrate that the need for integration and responsiveness can indeed change over time in both directions. For some industries the need for integration increased during the 1980s while the need for responsiveness decreased, which led to the development of true global businesses. Other industries, on the other hand, moved to locally responsive businesses during the same time with the need for local responsiveness increasing and the need for global integration decreasing. One reason that the need for local responsiveness has decreased over time is that the local preferences have changed and shifted towards a globally homogenous demand. National markets whose demand preferences converge towards the preferences of other national markets are lag markets. Although initially necessary to gain a large share of the local market it would be inefficient for a multinational firm to respond to the lag market's initially different demand conditions. On the other hand, markets that remain idiosyncratic can only be accessed by being responsive to the diverse local demand depending on their size or other factors that make up their attractiveness for a multinational firm. This means that markets within an industry can vary in their need for integration and responsiveness.

Figure 5-1: Lead, lag and idiosyncratic markets in the Integration-Responsiveness Grid

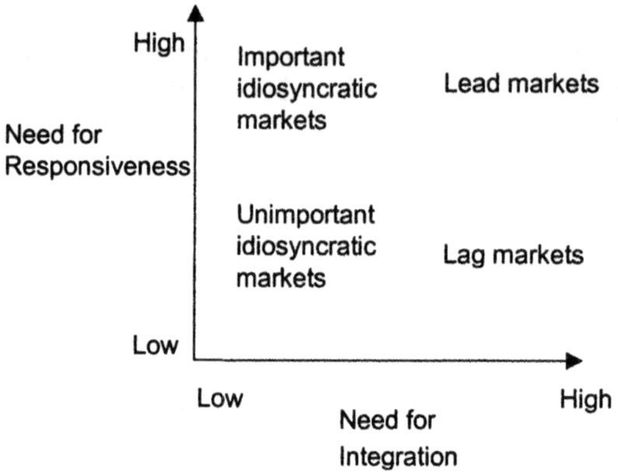

Using the IR-Grid suggested by Prahalad and Doz (1987) I now assign lead markets, lag markets and idiosyncratic markets to the need for integration and responsiveness while taking time lags between the markets' demand conditions into account (Figure 5-1). From the lead market theory is follows that a firm must be responsive to lead markets and at the same time must integrate the lead market into its worldwide activity in order to transfer lead market innovations to all lag markets. Accordingly lag markets must be globally integrated in order to adapt to the lead market innovations. Responsiveness to the local market is not necessary and leads to innovations suitable only for a short transition period. Permanent idiosyncratic markets need local responsiveness to be accessed by a foreign firm. Yet the attractiveness of an idiosyncratic national market and the degree of adaptation necessary determines whether a firm can make a profit in an idiosyncratic market. The attraction of a market normally depends on its size, but other reasons can make it reasonable for a firm to access an idiosyncratic market as well. Prahalad and Doz (1987) emphasise the need to access the home markets of global competitors where they make the profit necessary to finance price competition in globally attractive large markets.

Ohmae (1985) requests a firm to become an insider in the key markets in order to understand local markets and create global products, which amalgamate market information. But to be an insider in the key market requires responsiveness. The lead market concept requires a firm to be an insider in the lead market. In the next section I will argue that the utmost amount of closeness to the lead market is achieved by doing R&D in the lead market.

5.3 R&D in the Lead Market

If the lead market concept can be applied to a planned innovation, that is if lead markets exist in the product line, firms must be responsive to the lead market. The lead market is the reference market for the development of prototypes. I will now turn to the question of how firms can be responsive to the lead market. I will argue in this chapter that the most efficient reaction to the emergence of lead markets is the localisation of R&D tasks in the lead market. In the next section I will present some alternative strategy options for companies that are not able to locate R&D resources abroad.

5.3.1 Learning in the Lead Market

The most important location advantage of the lead market is that a firm can learn in the lead market. The lead market theory suggests that in lead markets firms can learn about what particular technological design is prevailing on the world market. Lead markets are not necessarily a source of core technological and scientific knowledge. Instead, the transformation of new technologies and scientific findings into new products require user learning and induce behaviour changes; the evolution of technology is characterised by the discovery of new uses, the reduction of prices, the growth of infrastructure and the entry of competition (Urban et al. 1996). The close interaction between producers and customers in the lead market thus helps to find the real preferences of users, to define the best design and the optimal specification of an innovation, and to find new applications. These specifications can then be transferred to the less demanding customers in lag markets (Johansson, Roehl 1994). Firms in the lead market get access to the information generated in the user-producer interaction process that leads the global evolution of technology. The lead market pools all the relevant information of new product concepts. Lead markets reveal information on usefulness of new technology gradually and first to insiders in the lead market.[164]

In the lead market a firm can also learn what technological design to *avoid* despite demand for it from users in lag countries. Idiosyncratic countries initially prefer innovation design that they either continuously adopt exclusively or abandon later to switch to the prevailing design. The argument of the lead market concept is exactly the same as the lead-user concept: to avoid over-customisation and investment in innovations to fit idiosyncratic needs. Instead it is necessary to concentrate the development of innovations on users or environments which are able to impose their design on all other customers and leave idiosyncratic customers to adapt to the standard (or pay for customisation). The lead market is used in v. Hippel's words as a "need-forecasting laboratory" for a particular technology or product line.[165] A producer can perceive future needs of the average user which

---

[164] This is an analogy of the concept that the market as a whole and no single agent embodies all the knowledge of preferences and expectations. In financial markets the price setting mechanism reveals this aggregated knowledge in prices of stock prices and option prices (Miller 1991, p. 131).

[165] Learning in the lead market is not forecasting and thus does not require forecasting methods. Learning in the lead market means technology evaluation in the lead market instead of technology forecasting. Technology forecasting comprises methods of forecasting the evolution of the scientific and technological paths in the future that have not been realised yet (Gerybadze 1996). Technological forecasting methods can neverthe-

the producer could hardly identify through extensive market analysis, because users with idiosyncratic needs and (lag-)users, who tend to be satisfied with the present products, often blur the resulting technological trends and needs which lie in the future for most of the users. When concentrating on customers in the lead market, a firm can focus on a narrow range of feedback, avoiding the temptation for other foreign affiliates to adapt the product prematurely to their local demand.

This thesis suggests further that the learning process is most efficient when firms' R&D activities are located in the lead market. The reasons are that (1) firms whose main R&D functions are located in the lead market have better access to vital information about market and technological trends than foreign firms, (2) that the interaction process during the development and testing of new products and processes are supported by proximity and (3) that firms that are not conducting R&D in the lead market risk being excluded from the technology sharing of lead market firms. It has been argued throughout this thesis that innovation designs are induced or at least biased by the local environment and the local market condition. The R&D department is the main organisational locus of innovations and technological learning within firms. R&D is not an isolated function of laboratories but is instead embedded in the whole innovation process. Innovation is an interaction process in which researchers and engineers interact with customers and their environment.[166] Participating in the lead market is not only important to learn about user preferences. A firm risks being excluded from the design preferred in the lead market and in turn risks being excluded from the world market. As the case study in Chapter 4 indicated, firms that are insiders in the lead market are prone to cooperate and exclude outsider firms from international competition by excluding them from joint-research programmes, standardisation processes, alliances and cross-license agreements.

Literature has previously indicated advantages of R&D in the lead markets. Johansson and Roehl (1994) emphasise the traditional home market advantage of companies headquartered in lead markets, but propose that foreign companies can learn in lead markets and build up competitive capabilities, "invisible assets" in their vocabulary, with which follower (lag) markets can be attacked. Bartlett and Ghoshal (1990) suggest that a multinational firm can reap the highest benefits from lead markets if it is able to shift its R&D activities to lead markets, thus generating successful products and processes for the global market place. Vernon

---

less support lead market learning. For instance, trend extrapolation of technical parameters that can be lead market factors such as growth of benefit and decreases of production costs of particular designs are valuable information about the leverage factor of a nationally preferred design. Another option of a firm to use lead markets could be to concentrate technology-forecasting activities in the lead market. The application of these methods depends, however, on how one assesses the appropriateness of technology forecasting methods in general.

166 See Hauschildt (1993, p. 133-145), Brockhoff (1992, p. 28-33), Katz (1988) and the literature reviewed in section 2.5.

(1971) already observes that during the 1960s US firms gained the ability to respond to innovation opportunities in foreign markets. When firms developed global organisations they became able to "match product innovations with market opportunities almost immediately wherever they [might have occurred]" (Harrigan 1984, p. 53) with subsidiaries developing their own innovations. This ability was supported by the accumulation of R&D activities of US multinational firms in Europe and in other countries, which helped the firms to adapt and generate innovations for foreign markets (see section 5.3.2).[167] Based on extensive case studies Gerybadze et al. (1997, p. 13) state that the lead function of the local market, along with local conditions for high-tech production and the sophistication of the national science system, are *already* among the dominant factors of location-specific advantages for the R&D of multinational companies.

It has been suggested that even if core competencies are concentrated at the headquarters or in foreign units other than in the lead market, the firm could locate a small unit with a "scanning function" to gather information on technical trends in the lead-market (Yip 1992, p. 124). Locating marketing functions in the lead market and focusing market research on the lead market demand is helpful, too. It is not always sufficient or it is inefficient, however, compared to locating R&D in the lead market. Based on a detailed case study, Workman (1993) concludes that in many high-tech firms marketing has little direct control over new product development decisions. Instead, engineers and technical considerations guide the technological path that a firm follows. Engineers complete vital marketing activities such as gathering information on the needs of users, interacting with customers and monitoring the products of competitors. The impact of market research information from the lead market for R&D units in lag or idiosyncratic markets could therefore be limited. As I noted in section 2.2 regional differences lead to different innovations. An additional interpretation of the induced innovation theory is that creativity of R&D personnel is locally biased. The perception and social interaction of R&D personnel is highly prejudiced by the employees' own environments. R&D personnel as well as all employees are biased by their own experiences and their daily lives. And innovations of particular R&D sites are likely to bring about innovations shaped by their local factors. Therefore it can be expected

[167] Leroy (1976) provides an empirical add-on study of Vernon's (1971) hint that US corporations acquired a global scanning function to utilise foreign environments for global innovations. While not merely focussed on international R&D but on the process of international diffusion of innovations within the multinational corporation, he shows through cased studies of 52 product innovations of four US MNCs and one Canadian, that foreign affiliates not only respond in the 1970s to innovation opportunities on foreign markets, but are able to introduce their new products in markets outside their host country. Among the 52 product innovations studied 15 were developed in foreign affiliates and only 2 of these were not introduced in other markets than the host country. Foreign innovations, which could be successfully introduced in the US are mainly derived from foreign markets, which are more sophisticated or advanced than the US market and where competition is strongest (Leroy 1976, p. 5).

that the R&D in the lead market is the most efficient way of linking up new product and process development with the environment of the lead market.

The concept of R&D in the lead market follows from the following chain of arguments. Market interaction potential is a success factor for the development and introduction of innovations.[168] The market orientation of firms requires the proximity between R&D and markets because first, information about user needs are required from the first phase of the R&D process. Second, researchers and engineers often neglect marketing information and are biased by their environment, social interaction and contacts to customers and competitors. Third, proximity between R&D and the reference market is important for efficient communication and interaction.[169] The last argument was already given in section 2.5 and refers to Linder's home market thesis.

Together with these two hypotheses the thesis suggests that if lead markets exist, it is reasonable for a multinational company to do the research and development for innovation in the lead market. R&D in the lead market is the organisational realisation of "staying close to right customers" (Johansson, Roehl 1994). I will now turn to the actual R&D allocation abroad by multinational firms. I will argue that the proximity to markets has always and still plays the dominating role as the determinant of foreign R&D suggesting that interaction of R&D and markets is still more efficient in close proximity.

5.3.2 The international allocation of R&D by multinational firms

Traditionally, most of the R&D is done at the headquarters.[170] Therefore in the product life cycle model, a multinational firm not headquartered in the lead market is at a disadvantage compared to competitors headquartered in the lead market. Many multinational firms, however, have already built up an extensive worldwide network of R&D laboratories. Aside from the firms' active shift of R&D abroad, mergers and acquisitions also lead to regionally dispersed R&D activities of mul-

[168] This hypothesis was extensively confirmed by innovation studies, see for instance the review of literature in Hauschildt (1993, p. 139-141).

[169] The second condition, based on early studies by Linder (1961) and Vernon (1966), is challenged by the ascendance of the Internet, which is suggested to revolutionise marketing, diminish the importance of distance and be spurring globalisation of markets. Though the commercialisation of the Internet is still in its beginning stages, what is true is that the Internet enables instant world market access and that it facilitates customer-producer interaction over a long distance. Yet the Internet is unlikely to equalise the perception of customer needs and simulate the local environment of the lead market. To use an analogy, one can sell new books instantly and worldwide over the Internet but books are still being written while embedded in a local environment and culture. R&D is about writing books.

[170] Aside from growing shares of R&D in foreign affiliates, many multinationals keep core technologies and strategic projects at the headquarters out of fear of leaking knowledge from not so well controlled foreign affiliates to competitors, see Patel, Pavitt (1992).

tinational firms. The share of foreign R&D to total R&D varies from around 2 % for Japanese firms, 10 % for US firms, 15 % for German firms and more than 50 % for Swiss firms (OECD 1998). Literature, reviewed in the next section, conveys three main location specific factors for R&D: Knowledge spillovers from local markets and local R&D and the co-location of R&D and production activities.[171]

(1) *Local markets*: Most studies find local markets to be the main incentive for foreign R&D. [172] When markets vary in their preferences and conditions, multinational firms respond by adapting existing products to local conditions. This adaptation process is often carried out in the foreign affiliate. Proximity between R&D and customers is important for making use of the efficiency of close interaction with local users in order to adapt to local conditions and gain a larger market share in the host country. Local R&D is also necessary to respond to indigenous innovation opportunities that call for new product development. "By developing a new product in the vicinity of the targeted markets, it is possible to incorporate local market flavours and uniqueness into the new product" (Ogbuehi, Bellas 1992, p. 61). Multinational firms often follow their customers abroad, who require that their suppliers locate R&D close to their R&D facilities that support better interaction between both R&D organisations, especially in high technology industries and systems (Gerpott 1990).

---

[171] Other factors such as the appropriability condition in the country, i.e. the effectiveness of patent protection, public R&D policy (Soete 1991), tax incentives (Hines 1994) or the national level of R&D cost are rarely discussed in literature anymore. Patent protection is a critical factor only for a few developing countries such as China or Thailand, where patent rights are still not ubiquitously secured (Lerner 2000, Ginarte, Park 1997). Labour cost in R&D as a factor for location decisions for R&D activities was rejected by most of the earlier studies (Mansfield et al. 1979, Böhmer 1996). The reason for the low influence of labour cost does lie in the nature of innovation because the innovation process can be modelled as a race for patent rights (Scherer, Ross 1990, p. 630). In this model, it is not sufficient for a firm to maximise the efficiency of the innovation process (the cost-benefit relation). The reaction of other companies must be taken into account. In the outcome, the quality of R&D has to be maximised. Only when R&D personnel becomes a scarce factor, which is sometimes the case in small countries such as Switzerland, Sweden and Finland, strongly increasing labour cost, which reflects the scarcity, will drive R&D out of the home country (Cordell 1973, p. 26; Granstrand, Håkanson, Sjölander 1993, p. 414). Teece (1977) starts with the idea that foreign R&D and technology transfer are alternatives and explains how foreign R&D serves the foreign market if it is more effective than technology transfer from the home country. This model led to the studies by Hines (1994), who discusses whether the taxation of licence payments determines the propensity of foreign R&D.

[172] In case studies on foreign R&D activities of multinational firms the technology transfer function and the local market orientation of foreign R&D units are the most frequently found characteristics of foreign R&D. See Ronstadt (1977), Cordell (1973), Pearce (1989), Håkanson, Nobel (1993), Pausenberger (1982), Behrman, Fisher (1980), Mansfield et al. (1979). For reviews of these studies see Cheng, Bolon (1993) and Granstrand et al. (1993).

(2) *Local knowledge endowments*: The technology-sourcing hypothesis suggests that firms are more able to assess new technologies through R&D activities in regions where these technologies are most advanced.[173] In locating research activities, multinational firms intend to exploit regional knowledge spillovers from private and public R&D and the local scientific community.[174] Technological knowledge spillovers occur through close collaboration, hiring experienced scientists and engineers and informal knowledge trading. These transfer mechanisms seemed to be facilitated by proximity (see e.g. Feldman, 1994, Katz, 1994). Kümmerle (1996) emphasises the importance of proximity to universities in order to receive knowledge spillover in contrast to other R&D performing firms because of the lower volatility of the externalities from universities than from firms. Another probably more compelling argument for the proximity of R&D sites to elite universities is better access to top graduates. Especially foreign companies can hardly attract the scientific elite from American universities like Stanford or Harvard to work at their base R&D site in the home country. Knowledge spillovers from research has been made responsible for high-tech agglomerations (Feldman 1994, Harhoff 2000). Multinational pharmaceutical firms are often observed trying to get access to local knowledge spillovers by establishing their own R&D laboratories in regional research agglomerations like Silicon Valley or Boston (Teece 1992b, Florida 1996). Research collaboration with local research organisations has grown as well; the most spectacular German example is Hoechst AG, which invested in a research centre at the Massachusetts General Hospital (Kümmerle 1996, p. 143).

(3) *Local production activities* of the firm: This is what I like to call the by-product hypothesis. If the R&D activities are an appendix of production, the R&D location is a mere by-product of the selection of production because the location decision for R&D is closely related to the prior location decision for production. The location choice for production facilities often does not take subsequent R&D into consideration.[175] The degree of the extent to which R&D and production can be separated determines how precisely a location of R&D is selected. In many

---

[173] This hypothesis assumes that markets are global and technological knowledge is locally bounded, e.g., Anand, Kogut (1997), Perrino, Tipping (1990). The technology-sourcing hypothesis is discussed as a determinant of direct investments as well, see e.g. Neven, Siotis (1996) and Shan, Song (1997). A suggestion is that contrary to traditional direct investment theory (i.e. investments and technology flow in the same direction), firms can get access to new technological knowledge by investing in a technological leading country. Empirical studies, however, find little support for the technology-sourcing motive of FDI.

[174] See e.g. Sachwald (1995), Teece (1992b), DeMeyer (1993), Cantwell (1995), Florida (1997) and the contributions in Granstrand et al. (1992).

[175] Data on R&D of foreign firms in the United States show that R&D growth between 1987 and 1994 correlates positively with growth in gross product (Belitz, Beise 1999, p. 97). Japanese firms are observed to establish integrated innovation-production complexes abroad (Florida, Kenney 1994).

industries positive externalities exist between R&D and manufacturing (Kümmerle 1996). Process innovations are often improvements of the existing production facilities. This requires that firms establish R&D functions on the production site. Often close interaction and communication between the staff of product development and the staff of prototype production is also essential for firms' competitiveness, especially if R&D determines the manufacturing costs of new products.[176] The knowledge about what determines production costs is mostly incorporated in the experience of the production staff. Communication between R&D and production can also be crucial for shorter time to market and lower defect rates in production (Kümmerle 1996, p. 24). In addition, in companies without independent R&D sites, the production staff or even the entrepreneur performs some R&D functions. R&D is often a real by-product because the foreign activities of a company often start with distribution and end later with the set up of foreign production activities without any R&D (international product life cycle). After production is well established R&D functions are added to the production site because it is easier to augment production facilities with R&D in order to share auxiliary departments and service functions than to build up stand-alone R&D labs. Also, local management can sometimes decide independently from the headquarters (Garnier 1982) and establish R&D functions to support local production, react to local innovation opportunities or simply to increase prestige within the multinational corporation or within their local community (Behrman, Fisher 1980). Leroy (1976, p. 83) observed that foreign affiliates started R&D activities, because local management just wanted it.[177]

It seems striking that in earlier studies the proximity of R&D to foreign markets seems apparent but is not considered important anymore as a valuable strategy for the R&D of multinational firms. Recent empirical studies about the choice of location for R&D and the recent political discussion about firms shifting R&D abroad seems to favour the technology-sourcing hypothesis of knowledge spillover from external research as the main determinant for location decision as well as the best strategy. Spillovers from scientific sources, as formulated in the technology-sourcing thesis, are frequently considered more important than knowledge spillover from customers. When the country of most advanced technology development and the high-end markets vary (Bartlett, Ghoshal 1995), literature tends to

---

176 Leroy (1976, p. 79) reports that R&D and production of electronic instruments of Hewlett-Packard were located in the same foreign affiliate, because its highly complex required close contact between the development centre and the production centre.

177 The empirical analysis of the hypotheses, however, can be difficult, because of multicolinearity between local production and local market attractiveness. Product-life-cycle theory suggests that foreign production activities are closely related to local market volume. To include foreign production volume and foreign market volume as exogenous variables could potentially lead to an unidentifiable regression matrix. Most of the earlier studies that include variables for production activities in the host country in their statistical analyses find a positive relationship to R&D activities.

favour that R&D is to be placed in the technology rich country. Implicitly included in the scientific knowledge spillover hypothesis is the assumption that innovations and technological progress are based on recent scientific findings. Innovation is becoming more "science-based" (Narin et al. 1997). Yet the importance of scientific findings for innovations is far from being quantitatively assesses. Some scholars argue that science is based as much on technology as technology is on science (Brooks 1984; Kline, Rosenberg 1986; Stephan 1996). Another argument that seems to speak in favour of the technology-sourcing hypothesis is the homogenisation of demand preferences. If demand preferences are converging worldwide, it would be reasonable to shift R&D to the location where the best engineers and the most current scientific knowledge is accessible. In the technology-sourcing concept, R&D is mostly seen as a function in the firm that is unrelated to local markets. The critical interface between marketing and R&D is not taken into consideration.

While firms expect to access new technologies in high-tech regions like Silicon Valley or Boston, there is no valid evidence, apart from the anecdotal evidence, to suggest that regional spillover potential can be used successfully and turned into a technological advantage. The next section reviews the statistical evidence of the location determinants of foreign R&D.

5.3.3 A critical review of the empirical literature on foreign R&D

This section reviews studies on the behaviour of multinational firms when they allocate R&D internationally in order to identify the prevailing motive for foreign R&D. Studies on foreign R&D of multinational firms first appeared in the 1970s in the United States (Cordell 1973; Creamer 1976; Ronstadt 1977; Ronstadt, Kramer 1982; Terpstra 1977; Behrman, Fisher 1980, Lall 1979). At that time it became known that US multinational firms were not only shifting production abroad but were also performing R&D in their foreign affiliates to a considerable extent.[178] For European and Japanese firms foreign R&D seemed to play no role yet. In the 1960s and 1970s, the United States were technological leaders in almost every industry and US multinationals were seen as a threat to European companies.[179] Technology-sourcing could hardly be a motive of US firms for foreign R&D. Instead, all studies agree that it was the willingness of US firms to penetrate overseas markets that made foreign R&D advantageous. Because of differences in market conditions, close contact of local R&D with the large overseas markets and manufacturing units was considered necessary. Although at least in the 1980s the situation changed somewhat with the United States losing its clear technological lead over European and Japanese firms in several industries (e.g. chemicals), the foreign share of foreign R&D of the United States remained at

[178] This foreign R&D activity was documented for the first time in the US direct investment statistic for the year 1966 published in 1970, see Creamer (1976).

[179] See, for instance, the notorious book by Servan-Schreiber (1968).

10 %.[180] While the technological gap between the United States on the one side and Europe and Japan on the other side was closing, the share of R&D performed by foreign-owned firms in the United States grew from 5 % in the mid-1970s to almost 15 % in 1997.[181] This too contradicts the technology-sourcing hypothesis.

Another strand of literature on the determinants of international allocation of R&D by multinational firms emerged from regional science. The regional pattern of R&D sites within countries can expose the importance of technology-sourcing as a location factors for R&D as well. There are several studies, beginning with Malecki (1980), that analyse the regional pattern of R&D activities of firms within a country.[182] More relevant for the internationalisation of R&D are studies that limit the analysis to foreign R&D activities, because the regional determinants of R&D in the home country and in foreign countries can be quite different. The observed co-location of foreign R&D laboratories and universities, public R&D labs and other R&D performing firms suggests that technology-sourcing is a relevant motive for foreign research centres (Dalton, Serapio 1995). On the other hand, firm surveys reveal that closeness to product and labour markets are the main location factors for R&D (e.g., Dalton, Serapio 1993, Florida, Kenney 1994, Jetro). Florida and Kenney (1994) find that the main motive for Japanese firms are closeness to markets and production sites, albeit most R&D laboratories are located in research intensive regions. The proximity of R&D to educational institutions could also reflect the need for scientists and engineers, whom the foreign firm usually expects to find near universities and other firms, once it has selected the United States as a location for R&D for reasons other than technology-sourcing, for instance market size. This talent seeking component of firms' behaviour is the main result of Florida (1997). Florida (1997) studies the geographical factors by questioning foreign-owned R&D units in the United States. He interprets the responses as that foreign affiliates are becoming more technology-oriented as compared to

---

180 The annual fluctuations in the share of foreign R&D of US firms are almost entirely due to varying exchange rates. The share of foreign R&D and the exchange rate of the German Mark to the US-$ for the years from 1960 to 1995 correlate with a coefficient of $r = 0.88$.

181 These figures were computed with data from the United States Department of Commerce (foreign R&D) and the National Science Foundation (R&D financed and performed by industry in the United States).

182 The early studies of Malecki (1980), Howells (1984), Feldman (1994), Legler (1994) are merely descriptive, demonstrating a regional concentration of R&D activity in metropolitan areas. More recent studies such as Anselin, Varga, Acs (1997) are mostly concerned with the question of whether spillovers from public research to firms occur. Cowan and Cowan (1998a) present a rare theoretical model of regional clustering of R&D sites. Beise, Gehrke et al. (1998) provides a review of the theoretical argument, indicators of the regional dispersion of innovation activities and empirical results for Germany in comparison to other countries. Recent data collecting activities of the European Commission (1997b) promises a revival of studies on regional pattern of R&D activities.

market-oriented. The study, however, has serious shortcomings that cast doubt on the conclusion made by the author. First, the survey includes stand-alone laboratories only, not R&D associated with manufacturing activities. This selection biases the study on location motives, because the motive determines the organisational form of R&D. It can be assumed that the regional pattern of R&D activities coupled with other activities depend much more on the local factors for these other activities, e.g. proximity to markets. Furthermore, respondents declare the item "developing new product ideas" as the most important activity. And these "ideas" were mostly initiated by customers and to a much lesser degree by scientific sources (only 16 % of the respondents rate universities as a very important source of new product ideas). This is even the case for R&D in biotechnology and drugs, which is considered as a science-based industry. That would imply, that foreign affiliates' R&D is focussed on the local market, not the local science system. Overall, regional studies show that firms not only conduct adaptive work but already generate innovations in foreign affiliates and that external technological knowledge is an important complement for foreign R&D. They find little evidence that technology-sourcing is the prevailing motive for shifting R&D abroad, but reveal evidence that local markets are an important input for innovations of foreign affiliates.

The number of studies on the internationalisation of R&D has increased rapidly over the last decade in the United States, Europe and in Japan. A second body of empirical literature was established at the University of Reading in the mid-1980s. These studies are based on the theory of industrial location, which Dunning influenced greatly. Pearce (1989) and Pearce and Singh (1992) and Casson and Singh (1993) prepared several in-depth studies about the determinants of foreign R&D activities. There is also a tradition of studies on both German (Jungnickel et al. 1977; Wortmann 1990; Pausenberger 1982; Gerpott 1990; Brockhoff, Böhmer 1993; Böhmer 1996; Beckmann 1996) and Swedish multinational firms (Håkanson 1981; Håkanson, Nobel 1993; Zander 1997).

The main proposals of the early case studies were the arrangements of varying motives of foreign R&D in a taxonomy of foreign R&D units. More recent studies have refined these typologies (for a review, see Niosi 1999). Foreign R&D units in these typologies correspond to the three main hypotheses of location advantage summarised above. For instance, multinationals created science-based or knowledge augmenting units (Kümmerle 1996) to access knowledge in foreign countries. Support of technology transfer or knowledge-exploiting units is located close to production units and markets in order to transfer and adapt innovations to foreign market conditions (Kümmerle 1996). The taxonomies of R&D units confirm the relevance of all three hypotheses. It is difficult, however, to evaluate the weight each type has for the success of foreign R&D units.

Although case studies and small sample studies of multinational firms' international R&D activities are conducted extensively, statistically valid tests of the determinants of foreign R&D, and especially the role of host country-specific variables are less frequent. Most studies collect data about R&D sites from a rather small number of multinational firms.[183] Another body of literature uses the direct investment statistic of the United States Department of Commerce. The annual database covers R&D activities of US multinational firms outside the United States and the R&D of affiliates of non-US multinational firms in the United States since 1989 on an industry level.[184] Recently, some authors used patent data matched with information on capital holdings of multinational firms.[185] Patent data reveal the location of invention and the patent assignee, which is either the firm or the affiliate. Together with data on the names of the affiliated firms of a multinational company the locations of a multinational firms' patented inventions can be identified for a long time. Patent data have the additional advantage that technological fields can be identified as well.[186] In summarising these studies, some conclusions can be drawn from the empirical literature. Five stylised facts can be inferred as follows:

1. R&D abroad is not new.[187] US companies already started foreign R&D activities in the 1920s; most European firms followed after the Second World War in the 1960s and Japanese companies developed a massive expansion of foreign R&D in the mid-1980s. During the emergence of multinational firms in the nineteenth century, foreign activities were clearly confined to manufacturing the iden-

---

183 These are studies such as Boehmer (1996), Kümmerle (1996), Gerybadze, Reger (1999). These studies of samples of firms are insightful but problematic. First, they are not representative for the industry, because there is always a selection bias towards multinational firms with large foreign R&D activities. There are, however, many large companies without considerable foreign R&D such as Boeing or Microsoft. Second, foreign R&D is not always the result of a strategic decision. Mergers ensue large R&D units at globally dispersed locations, e.g. the merger between Daimler-Benz and Chrysler. In this case, empirical models test the merger behaviour rather than the foreign R&D behaviour. Also, studies are highly influenced by the industries they investigate. Industries vary in their degree of internationalisation of R&D but also in their most important driving factors. For instance, the science-based pharmaceutical industry has a high degree of internationalisation of R&D and many foreign research labs can be observed but national regulation requires some R&D in local markets as well.

184 Hewitt (1980), Lall (1979), Hirschey, Caves (1981), Mansfieled et al. (1979), Mansfield, Romeo (1984).

185 Barré (1995), Cantwell (1995), Patel (1995), Patel, Vega (1999), Zander (1999), Cantwell, Janne (1999).

186 Despite the common disadvantages of patent data, a preliminary test showed that patents are excellent indicators for the location of R&D activities by multinational firms (Beise, Belitz, Grenzmann 1998).

187 The first studies of foreign R&D activities of US multinational firms showed that US firms already spent more than 6 % of their R&D expenditures abroad in the 1960s (Creamer, 1976). In this statistic, US firms reported 1,445 foreign affiliates with R&D activities. Extensive case studies were conducted in the 1970s, e.g. Ronstadt (1977), Terpstra (1977), Behrman, Fisher (1980), which showed how a variety of R&D activities gained market share in foreign countries.

tical product that was developed and designed at the headquarters. Yet innovation activity took place at the first foreign affiliates, albeit occasionally.[188] The patent statistics compiled by Cantwell (1995) show that in the second half of the 1920s the share of patents invented outside the home country of the largest nationally owned industrial firms was already about 6 % for US companies and 5 % for German firms. These shares increased (with a break in Germany after World War II) to two digit levels in the 1990s.

2. Foreign R&D is a typical activity of large multinational firms. The majority of foreign R&D is concentrated in a few large companies (Patel, Pavitt 1992). Empirical studies indicate that very few firms besides the largest multinational firms still do foreign R&D at a larger volume compared to domestic R&D. The size of the firm has been a significant determinant of the share of foreign R&D in most studies on the firm level (e.g., Mansfield et al. 1979, Pearce 1989). This suggests that there are large economies of scale in R&D contrasting the regional dispersion of R&D.

3. Mergers and acquisitions have become the main driving force for the internationalisation of R&D. Mergers and acquisitions (M&As) are responsible for most of the growth of foreign R&D between 1979 and 1990 (Patel 1995). International M&As increased rapidly during the 1980s and again from 1991 onwards.[189] Foreign acquisitions of large firms ensues a sharp growth of foreign R&D of the acquiring firm, because most large firms conduct R&D in their home countries. Although R&D is rarely the main reason for the acquisition, local R&D activities are normally devoted to keeping the knowledge stock of the foreign affiliate and avoiding the resistance of foreign management, which regards its own R&D activities as prestigious, a matter which distinguishes it from production platforms.[190]

---

[188] Although Mira Wilkins, the leading historian on multinational firms, does not specifically indicate any foreign innovation activities of the emerging multinationals before 1914, she suggests how refinement activities of foreign affiliates of U.S. firms filled foreign requirements before 1914 (Wilkins 1970). Adapting existing products to foreign environments was the most likely innovation activity of foreign affiliates. Sophisticated foreign R&D activities emerged in the 1920s. Probably the first industrial research laboratory abroad was set up by the US company Kodak in Harrow, England in 1928 (Wilkins 1974, p.84).

[189] See Unctad (var. years), in contrast to the prevalence of greenfield investments in the 1950s and 1960s, M&As have become the major means of entering foreign markets since the 1980s. The Uctad estimates that on average over the last two decades 50 % of all foreign direct investments of the world are cross-border mergers and acquisitions (64 % in 1998). The share is much higher for investments in developed countries, for instance almost 90 % for investments in the United States, where most of foreign R&D is conducted.

[190] See the empirical studies for German corporations by Pieper (1998), Süverkrüp (1992) and Gerpott (1995). For US firms, Lichtenberg (1992, p. 54-55) confirms the finding of Hall (1988) that mergers do not ensue significant reductions in R&D spending.

4. Foreign R&D activities are conducted by European, US and Japanese firms in the United States, in Europe and to a lesser degree in Japan (Pearce 1989; Böhmer, Brockhoff, 1994; Pausenberger 1982). Developing countries and newly developed countries are recipients of few R&D funds. A comparison between R&D intensities of domestically owned and foreign owned firms shows that most countries attract as many investments in R&D as domestic firms do R&D, compared to physical investments from foreign sources (OECD 1998; Beise, Belitz 1997).

5. There are differences from industry to industry. The chemical industry and the pharmaceutical industry in particular seem to be frontrunners in the internationalisation of R&D, whereas the aircraft industry concentrates R&D in the home country (Creamer 1976). International consolidation and the M&A boom let other industries catch up fast. Besides industry specifics, firms conduct R&D in technical fields in which the home country has an international advantage (Patel, Vega 1999; Barré 1995). For instance, in Germany the chemical and electrical machinery industries are the frontrunners of the trend towards foreign R&D activities (Beise, Belitz 1998; Beckmann, Fischer 1994).

The historical perspective and especially the last fact contradicts the technology-sourcing hypothesis and supports the market-orientation of foreign R&D. To conclude, there is little statistical evidence – besides anecdotal evidence – to indicate that the behaviour of firms has shifted from market orientation to technology-sourcing in the global allocation of R&D.[191] Although some firms have already created science-based R&D units in regional research clusters around the world, their share and importance for global R&D is still rather small. The overall conclusion is that foreign R&D is still conducted mostly as a response to local market differences. Large multinational firms aim to penetrate all markets in the triad. Different preferences pressure them to carry out local R&D. Furthermore, mergers and acquisitions and the firms' own responsibilities for foreign affiliates foster foreign R&D activities. Therfore, a global concept for the international allocation of R&D by multinational firms is needed.

5.3.4 The need for an international allocation strategy of R&D

In this section I argue that the lead market concepts can be used as the basis of a global strategy of the international R&D activities of a firms in product lines in

[191] The main problem in evaluating the technology-sourcing hypothesis is to find an indicator for the technology knowledge advantage of a country. Most studies use the revealed comparative advantage indicator suggested by Balassa (1965). Yet this is an indicator for the comparative advantage and not the absolute advantage. Technology gaps are absolute advantages. The only studies that estimate the use the 'reverse' technology transfer from foreign subsidiaries' R&D at home are Mansfield and Romeo (1984) and Fors (1997). Although the former study finds a positive inflow of technology from foreign sources for U.S. MNEs, the latter does not support foreign technology-sourcing for Swedish MNEs.

which lead markets exist. In the 1990s foreign R&D reached considerable shares of worldwide R&D expenditures – as much as 50 % in pharmaceutical firms (Beckmann 1997) – so that the international allocation of R&D resources in the multinational firm became an increasingly important task for the headquarters.[192] Foreign R&D activities are often not based on a global strategy. Over time, many foreign affiliates in developed markets have established their own R&D resources not only in order to respond to local innovation opportunities but also just to lose their cheap production image. Several studies find that a typical evolutionary process of foreign R&D originates from simple local technical support towards indigenous R&D for the firm's own product development (Ronstadt 1977, Behrman, Fisher 1980, Beckmann 1997). The affiliates' own financial responsibilities foster the increase of foreign R&D capabilities. These local R&D activities are indeed mostly suitable to increasing local market penetration. They are, however, often not included in the *global* innovation strategy of a multinational firm aiming at globally standardised products and processes. In addition, after large mergers and acquisitions firms have to restructure their R&D organisations, avoiding redundant activities that appear in various laboratories and exploiting economics of scale in R&D. Yet, R&D activities are normally not concentrated in one location, because the merged firm would lose knowledge stock embodied in human capital or because of the resistance of local management.

This evolutionary and often uncoordinated growth of global R&D networks contrasts the aim of multinational firms to generate globally standardised innovations and calls for a strategic approach to the international allocation of resources among the R&D sites. An internationally dispersed net of R&D sites does not only need co-ordination and international factor allocation to prevent parallel R&D. The globalisation of markets through the convergence of per-capita-income in the triad countries and the emergence of European and Japanese multinational firms have created a new competitive environment, calling for the globalisation of corporate strategy (Levitt 1983; Ohmae 1985; Kotabe 1992). Multinational firms cannot rely on national markets alone. They must develop a transnational approach, leveraging local opportunities for global markets (Bartlett and Ghoshal 1989). A clear global concept of international R&D allocation is necessary, which will take the new environment of global market dynamics and global technological advance into account. For the reasons given in section 5.2, increasing R&D costs and the emergence of globally dominant designs, a multinational firm must

---

[192] The management survey conducted by Arthur D. Little (1997) found that 'Managing R&D in a global world' grew rapidly during a 10-year period as a priority issue in Technology and Innovation Management. 'Multiplying and managing transnational projects', 'Tapping local competencies and building capabilities worldwide' and 'Managing R&D across different cultures to build synergy' were associated as issues of this item. In contrast, the annual survey of the Industrial Research Institute finds that among the top ten problems industry leaders face, the item "Managing global R&D" lost importance in 1998 and 1999 after a climax in 1997 (Blake 1999).

participate early in the development and adoption of the coming global dominant design.[193]

The lead market concept presented in this study offers a solution to the problem of the international allocation of R&D in product ranges and technological fields in which lead markets exist or can be expected to exist. The lead market concept is predominantly a strategy of assigning innovation projects to existing R&D units. The concept suggests that R&D should respond to the users in the lead markets and that R&D tasks should be assigned to R&D units in the lead market.[194]

5.3.5 Three case studies

In an in-depth research project, Reger, Beise and Belitz (1999) studied the international distribution of R&D by the 15 largest multinational firms in each of three high-technology industries: pharmaceuticals, semiconductors and telecommunications equipment. The study encompassed interviews with the 45 multinationals and an analysis on the location of their patented inventions. In this section I will report the findings of this study on the existence and pertinence of lead markets to multinational firms. Although the examined high-tech industries are frequently described as science-based industries, the study found evidence for lead markets in each industry and it found that some firms already allocate resources to R&D units in these markets precisely as a result of their lead function. Lead markets, however, are important only in different segments or phases of the innovation process in these industries. In these phases of the innovation process, information on demand preferences and the close interaction with customers are especially important for market entry, for reducing time-to-market and for the technological refinement process.

---

[193] In a seemingly rather mature technology like telecommunication, which has existed for almost 150 years, everything seems to be open now. Digitalisation, mobile cellular technology, satellite communication and the internet offer a diverse range of technical alternatives for verbal, video and data communication, so that even the market trend of the next 5 years is not easy to forecast. On the other hand, it is likely that cost advantages and network economics will lead to the convergence of technological alternatives, or more likely to the dominance of one alternative technology or standard. A firm's success and often its survival depend on its ability to bet on "the right horse", i.e. to choose the technological design of its innovation which will become the global dominant design.

[194] Recent literature suggests new forms of global co-ordination of R&D activities (Gassman 1997; Gerybadze, Meyer-Krahmer, Reger 1997; Beckmann 1997; Reger 1998). It is not necessary to review all the proposed concepts of international R&D. This thesis derives a new concept of international assignment of R&D tasks from the lead market theory. The lead market phenomenon was included in Gerybadze et al. (1997) in part, but few other authors have incorporated the market interaction potential of lead markets into their concepts.

Pharmaceuticals

In the matter of pharmaceuticals, the United States and the UK were described by multinationals as lead markets in clinical research. First, time-to-market of a new pharmaceutical product after the pre-clinical phase is crucial because patent life starts after the active substance was found. Thus, efficient interaction with clinics and doctors is essential. Efficient interaction is determined by the skills and professional attitude of the clinic personnel in carrying out clinical tests as well as their ability and incentive to co-operate with pharmaceutical firms. Specialised study nurses who work in accordance with the good clinical practices (GCP) make clinics in the United States and the UK attractive as research locations in the clinical phase. Second, good co-operation with the national approval office, transparency of approval conditions and short or at least foreseeable approval times are advantages of a country for a lead in the market entrance of new pharmaceuticals. The lead effect of a market is even more pronounced in the case of a reference approval. Approval procedures of the US food and drugs agency (FDA) became standard for clinical tests. Once a new treatment has been authorised in the United States it is easier for a firm to get the approval in other countries as well. The procedures for authorising medical products in the EU by the European approval office (EMEA) in London are based upon the principle of mutual recognition of national authorities. A country with efficient approval procedures therefore acts as a lead market since it is most attractive as the first market to introduce a new medical product. Third, the United States is not only the largest market but also the fastest growing market and it has the highest per capita spending for health products according to the market research consultant IMS Health. Per capita spending is highly dependent on the health care security set up by governments. When compulsory social security was first introduced in Germany it created a large and leading market for pharmaceuticals (Vernon 1971). In the 1990s high regulation and price controls to dampen increasing costs of health care led to lagging dynamic compared to the United States.

Semiconductors

In the semiconductor industry the vast majority of integrated circuits (ICs) are designed for special applications in other industries. These customised applications require intense interaction between the producer and the user during the design phase. Here lead markets follow the value chain. Once a market is a lead market in a product range, the market also constitutes a lead market for supplier industries that innovate in close interaction with their customers. Semiconductor firms have been locating their design centres close to the leading markets of specific application, so as to participate in prevailing trends of the application technology. Important user industries are, for instance, telecommunications equipment, auto electronics and computers. Lead markets of the customer industries are frequently the United States and Germany. Silicon valley, where almost all of the 15 largest semiconductor firms have located an R&D site, is not only attractive because of its universities and vast supply of qualified labour, but because it is the most dynamic, competitive and standard-setting regional market. Ideas are continuously generated and the time of commercialising the ideas is much shorter than in other countries and regions. The proximity to a large number of customer industries facilitates the co-operation necessary to commercialise a new semiconductor application. Germany is especially important in semiconductor applications for automotive electronics, telecommunications and smart cards. The market for these application industries is demanding and firms are keen and able to integrate microelectronics in their products. At the same time, the market is a good test market, since customers of these industries are neither too conservative to accept built-in electronics, nor do they demand technical gimmicks which will fail to attract the world market.

Telecommunications equipment

For a long time the telecommunication equipment industry was constrained by regulation in the telecommunication service industry. International R&D was a prerequisite of an access to national markets. Deregulation, first introduced in the UK and the United States, enabled competition between equipment supplier and service providers, the globalisation of the industry and facilitates global lead markets. New entrants competed against the old established service provider with lower prices, inducing high growth of demand for services, and new services enabled by new technologies. Both increased the incentives for producers to innovate. In Germany, although the service provider was a monopoly before deregulation, competition in the supply industry had already been introduced in the 1980s, when the public provider opened the procurement of public switches to competitive bids and included foreign suppliers in its procurement of network electronics. It also facilitated the development of two public digital switches in Germany that subsequently became highly successful worldwide. Fierce competition between different suppliers constituted a lead market. As a result of early competition in telecommunications among equipment suppliers and later among service providers on the one hand, and among a variety of alternative technologies for telecommunication on the other, a market dynamic unfolded which dominated the direction of technical progress. With Japan locked-in to idiosyncratic standards and the vertically integrated US telecommunications industry, deregulation and investments in internationally successful standards made Germany the largest and most dynamic market in Europe. This made almost all of the 15 largest multinational firms locate R&D units in Germany (Beise 1999).

In interviews, Reger et al. (1999) found that some of the largest companies of the three studies are already aware of the role of lead markets. In all three technologies, companies feel the mounting pressure to introduce global products because of large and increasing R&D costs. International consolidation is a main reaction of high-tech industries to these pressures. Mergers and acquisitions in turn add to the international spread of R&D sites within multinational corporations. Most multinationals began to reduce the dispersion of regional R&D and concentrate the R&D tasks for each product line in a single location, sometimes called 'com-

Table 5-1: Location factors for foreign R&D in three high-tech industries

	Pharmaceuticals		Semiconductors		Telecommunications equipment	
Importance of proximity to ...	Pre-clinical	Clinical	Process	Product	Hardware	Software
Lead market	Low	Very high	Low	Very high	High	Very high
Science system	Very high	High	High	Low	Low	Low
Production	Low	Low	High	Low	High	Low

Source: Reger, Beise, Belitz (1999)

petence centres'. These competence centres are mandated with the responsibility for the main R&D-phase of a global product. These entities are disease groups in pharmaceuticals, technical standards in telecommunications equipment and chip applications in semiconductors. Table 5-1 presents an assessment of the importance of location factors perceived by the management responsible for location decisions. Lead markets are seen as the decisive factor for location of as least one R&D entity. Proximity to the science system like universities and public research institutes was especially important for biotechnological pre-clinical research, but of lesser importance (within the triad countries) for the other two rather mature technologies. Lead markets were, however, ill defined and were selected by experience and belief. Analytical tools to assess the lead factor of a regional market were totally absent.

5.3.6 Discussion

The concentration of R&D in the lead markets for each particular range of products or technology is an R&D strategy for technical fields with high technology and market uncertainty. Even if companies hardly know what technologies will prevail to be dominant on the world market, they will probably have a better idea as to *where* this selection in going to take place. Multinationals do not have to be insiders in all key markets, but they do have to be insiders in the lead market. Contrary to the technology-sourcing hypothesis, the location selection for R&D will not be based upon the maximisation of local scientific excellence, but on the maximisation of the lead effect of a regional market. In the lead market concept, local availability of scientists and engineers becomes a simple pre-condition. The open question of the lead market concept is whether sufficient talent is available in the lead market or can be shifted to the R&D unit in the lead market.

The lead market concept assumes that external technology can be better accessed and used without being close to where it is generated than relevant market information. Although it can be often observed that globally successful innovations are not developed in countries where the invention or the basic technology was generate, the counter-argument is that access to talent has often been an important motive for firms to establish R&D sites abroad. In this thesis I argue that for the choice of location of R&D not the technological excellence of the local human capital in the local labour market should be maximised but the propensity that the local market demands and adopts an technological design that can be commercialised worldwide. The main reason for this statement is that the national market conditions are a more important success factor than technological excellence. This hypothesis will not be evaluated further in this thesis but it is the hypothesis to be falsified to disprove the concept of locating R&D in the lead market.

Furthermore, there are several problems with locating R&D tasks in the lead market. If the firm does not run an R&D unit in the country that is expected to be the lead market, the firm must decide whether to assign the R&D task to one of the established R&D units other than the lead market, or to establish a new R&D facility in the lead market, but risk losing some of the internal knowledge stock as the experienced R&D staff resists moving to the new location. It is not easy to derive optimisation between advantages of internal knowledge bound to the locations of the R&D units and the external market interaction potential. The assignment of R&D tasks solely on the basis of the lead market concept will therefore be confined to innovations of technological discontinuities that do not rely heavily on the experience of the existing R&D units, which are not located in or cannot be shifted to the lead market. In this case, lead market information can still be used. The next section discusses alternatives to locating R&D in the lead market.

5.4 Alternatives to R&D in Lead Markets

A firm is not always capable to develop an innovation in the lead market. If a firm's resources are constrained, it has additional options to include the lead market in its product strategy. It is important that a firm's innovation resources such as marketing and R&D are devoted to demand in the lead market and oriented to the conditions in the lead market, whether they are located in the lead market or not. Cooperation with firms in the lead market can become a bridging institution. At least, lead market can serve as test markets. Although most of the costs of innovation development have already been spend, the global rollout of an innovation is costly as well and can be avoided when market entry in the lead market signals a worldwide failure.

5.4.1 Participating in the lead market

Bartlett and Ghoshal (1990) suggest that multinational firms can take advantage of lead markets by locating market and technological "sensing resources" in them, using their output as input in the innovation process. These sensing resources can be small in size but have the task to collect information on local design preferences, habits and the adoption of new technologies. For instance multinational firms have already located design centres in markets that lead the trends in specific automobile segments.

Furthermore, cooperations with lead market insiders can be a powerful means of participating at the lead market dynamics without devoting many resources to the lead market. In co-operating with suppliers, competitors or customers that are insiders in the lead market a firm can link up with the technological adoption path of the lead market. Co-operation partners supply the lead market intelligence necessary for its own innovation projects. They know the specification and configuration of new products and processes favoured in the lead market. Cooperations and alliances are also a means of overcoming exclusion strategies of lead market firms against outsiders. For instance, the Japanese telecommunications equipment company NEC developed a new standard for mobile telephony (W-CDMA) together with Ericsson of Sweden, the market leader for mobile telephony equipment with headquarters in the lead market. NEC like other Japanese firms were effectively disadvantaged by European firms in cross-licensing agreements for the globally successful GSM standard. The joint development ensures that the standard employed in Japan will be the same as the one employed in the Nordic countries, the lead markets for mobile telephony. The more resources the company already has in the lead market, the less necessary are co-operation partners in the lead market and vice versa. If a company does not know the domestic market context of the potential lead market, co-operation partners that are insiders in the lead market become more important. These partners can be multinational firms active in the lead market or firms established in the lead market.

If the lead market is characterised mainly by a market structure advantage and in particular by its entrepreneurial dynamic, it is probably not efficient for a large firm to locate majority-owned affiliates in the lead market. The turbulence in the lead market causes a high degree of uncertainty. For instance, high-technology agglomeration such as Silicon Valley (Saxenian 1994) or Richardson near Dallas (Beise 1999, p. 132) cultivated a competitive environment that made it difficult for large firms, especially foreign multinational firms, to become insiders without abandoning their traditional formal organisation. Investing in a wide range of newly founded start-ups would maximise the likelihood of gaining access to the technology that prevails in the lead market or "betting on the many horses in the right course". By investing risk capital in lead market firms the entrepreneurial spirit of the lead market can be harnessed. How lead markets are best embedded in the strategy of a multinational firm therefore depends on the characteristic advantage of the particular lead market.

5.4.2 Lead markets as test markets

As noted above, concentrating R&D in the lead markets is not always possible or it causes large tangible and intangible costs such as losing human capital when engineers are not willing to move into the lead market. In this case, market research should be concentrated on the lead market in order to assess demand preferences. Depending on the goods, market research methods such as household scanning panels, conjoint measurement and several methods of pre-marketing (Möhrle 1995) can be focussed on the lead market. Test marketing becomes irrelevant in the lag markets, which makes market research for global innovations much less expensive. But not only demand preferences are important to incorporate into the development of the innovation. The lead market is the global reference market. Innovation development must focus on the conditions of the lead market such as factor prices and availability of complementary assets.[195]

Another problem of the R&D in the lead market strategy is that for many products, especially high technology products, data on customer preferences are difficult to assess prior to market entry (Urban et al. 1996). Some innovations are even found in a firm's laboratory serendipitously and not derived from customers' needs at all (Hauschildt 1993, p. 153). The more "science-based" a product is the fewer customer preferences are included during the development phase. Kotabe and Helsen (1998) cite a new toothpaste with a new antibacterial formula. In this case, and if the knowledge stock accumulated by research and development activities cannot be shifted to the lead market, companies can still invest substantially to penetrate them. Companies willing to introduce an innovation globally use the country of initial entry as a test market to "learn more about customers and competitors and to adapt the marketing program as sales results flow in" (Johansson 200, 374). Test marketing is a common method of assessing the market response to a new product (Urban, Hauser 1993, p. 495). Test markets are supposed to be markets that are representative for the targeted market (Nieschlag, Dichtel, Höschgen 1985, p. 722). Because they are similar to most other markets they are expected to reveal demand preferences that exist in other markets as well but are not transparent.

A lead market can be used as a test market. A lead markets as test market have even more advantages than traditional test markets. Lead markets as test markets are representative for future needs. They are characterised by either anticipatory demand or the ability to leverage domestic success through large cost advantages and the ability to influence other markets' demand preferences. The argument for the lead market as test market is that if you can sell it there you can sell it everywhere later. Takeuchi, Porter (1986, p. 130) report that Procter and Gamble tested its new line of improved disposal diapers in Japan because Japanese demand is most demanding. According to Swasy (1993, p.269), P&G developed the internationally successful thin diaper "Ultra Pampers" to match the Japanese demand for disposable diapers that take less storage space in Japanese flats.

[195] Conditions in other markets are only incorporated in the innovation development in the case of a strong export advantage. The other lead market advantages suggest that the lead market conditions will be transferred to the other countries over time.

Demand in the lead market, however, is sophisticated enough to already take part in the development process and can give feedback for improving and refining a product. Traditionally, test markets are often selected because of their isolated situations in order to avoid interference with non-resident customers. Hong Kong and formerly Western Berlin are such ideal test markets. Isolation, however, supports idiosyncratic demand. Dense inter-regional communication, which facilitates worldwide diffusion of innovations and the influx of outside market information, is one of the features of the lead market. The traditional criteria of test market selection should therefore not be applied to lead markets. On the contrary, a lead market concept can be a powerful method to *select* test markets.

5.4.3 Lead market strategy and global market entry

Global market entry is another issue ensued by the lead market concept. Traditionally, innovations were introduced first in the home market and later in markets that were most similar to the home market. Over time refined innovation was introduced in other foreign markets. This strategy is called the "waterfall" model of global market entry.[196] It is considered as the right strategy to develop the world market if market conditions differ internationally (Kalish et. al. 1995). From the observation that countries do adopt new products and processes at different times because of their socio-economic characteristics, Dekimpe et. al. (1998b) infer that a firm should launch a product country by country and not immediately on a global basis. They only offer a rule of thumb, however, which is product unspecific and rather useless: wealthy, culturally homogenous countries with a highly concentrated population should be used as first markets to enter. Yet if global products are developed by the universal segment approach and market preferences are equal globally, or if there are large economies of scale or imitation of innovation is rampant, simultaneous market introduction has advantages over the waterfall strategy (Kreutzer 1989, pp. 241-246).

The sprinkler model of triad market penetration advocated by Ohmae (1985) suggests that multinational firms should "attack the key markets simultaneously" by introducing a new product in all triad markets at the same time. This, however, requires large financial and marketing resources. Kreutzer (1989, pp. 250-251) presents combined methods of global market entry that try to use the advantages of both models. A firm can derive a global market strategy from experiences in the first country. The presence of lead markets supports such a combined approach. If the innovation handed over from the R&D lab is not a totally refined and standardised product, which has to be forced through a homogeneous world market, the lead market concept suggests a two-stage model of world market entry. The lead market concept suggests developing and introducing the innovation in one

[196] Fundamental for the global market entry is the empirical study by Davidson and Harrigan (1977) and the strategy proposed by Ayal and Zif (1979). Ohmae (1985, p. 33) called this traditional strategy 'waterfall'.

Figure 5-2: Three different global market entry strategies

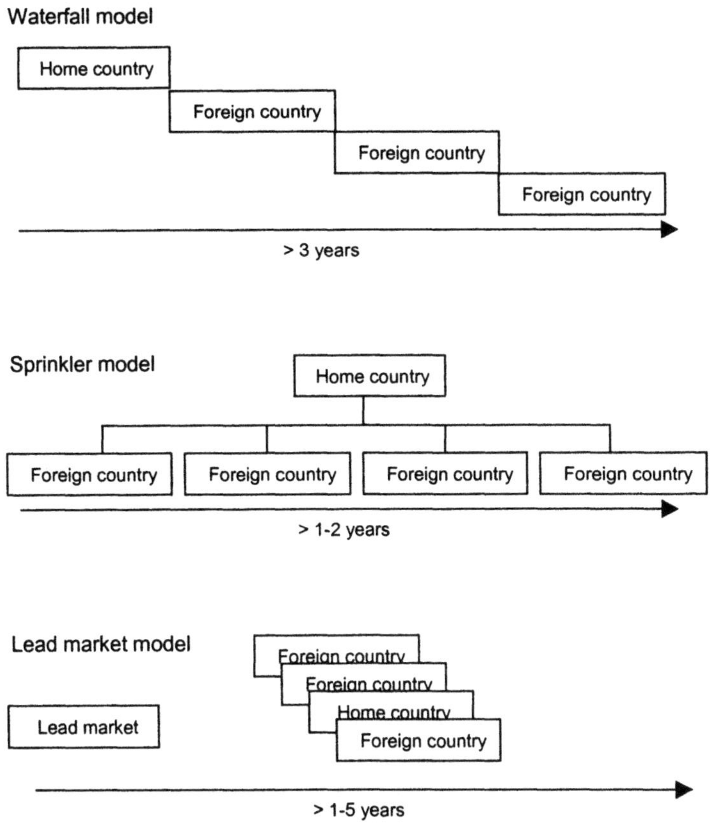

Source: Waterfall/sprinkler model: Riesenbeck and Freeling (1991); lead market model: author

specially selected market, the lead market. The role of local customers in the lead market is to give feedback in the refinement and standardisation of new innovations. The proximity to the lead market in the first market entry phase gives the organisation the assurance that the feedback it receives from the local market leads the process of development and refines the innovation in the "right" direction towards a final design that finds global acceptance. Later the innovation can be introduced in *all* other markets in order to reap the benefits of global market penetration. The time lag depends on the refinement and standardisation process and the time lag of the transfer of conditions from the lead market to the lag markets. Figure 5-2 depicts the three basic models. While the home market still stands out in both the waterfall and the sprinkler model, it can be the lead market as well as the lag market in the lead market concept of market entry.

5.5 Organisation of Lead Market Innovations

In the international corporation with worldwide R&D activities, two new types of innovation strategy have emerged to face the challenge of the global market: globally-linked and locally-leveraged innovations (Bartlett, Ghoshal; 1990). Lead market innovations and product and process development in these markets are locally-leveraged innovations. They are locally developed but can be commercialised worldwide. An innovation strategy of firms with global R&D networks are globally-linked innovations: all R&D units work together in an innovation project to bring together all local advantages. In the next section I will argue that locally leveraged innovations are more efficient than globally-linked innovations.

5.5.1 The prospect of globally-linked innovations

Globally-linked innovations follow the aim of worldwide close collaboration between the internationally dispersed R&D units. In this framework, an innovation should be achieved by diving the innovation project into specific parts and assigning each task to the R&D units that has the highest qualification for the particular technology. According to Bartlett and Ghoshal (1990, p. 217): "each unit contributes its own unique resources to develop a truly collaborative response to a globally perceived opportunity". In most cases, globally-linked innovations are either based on globally dispersed R&D activities that are mainly caused by acquisitions in order to achieve instant market entry, or they are based on the assumption of technology-sourcing. The technology-sourcing, in turn, is aimed at regionally varying technological knowledge or competence, i.e. information, knowledge and ability, and at neglecting the technological importance of regionally-specific demand conditions. In the first case, it is not based on an explicit innovation strategy, but it is rather an outcome of a market strategy without daring to close R&D units out of consideration for local management. The latter is based solely on the assumption of regional knowledge spillover.

One successful example is Nortel's GSM cellular phone, which was developed jointly in Canada, Germany and France. The dispersed R&D units were the result of acquisitions of European firms. This project however had a clear definition: to develop a standard that already became a global standard and the product could be introduced in an established worldwide market. If the global standard is unclear the questions is what national preferences to follow and what standard to chose, if there is no globally homogeneous demand. The crux of the globally linked approach, however, is not only to perceive a global opportunity, but also to prevent R&D units from being biased towards their own local environments. On the other hand, a global collaboration project might support the global market orientation of an R&D project. Globally-linked innovations might supposed to take into consideration all regional environment-specific differences, with each R&D unit supplying its local requirements.

Yet globally-linked innovations are no guarantee for the development of a global product. Firms find it hard to design global products that can be introduced in all markets simultaneously. Often there is absolutely no knowledge of what the "global product" should look like, but lots of information on how *local* products should vary from the prototype. Even for mature products that contain almost the same principal technical specifications internationally and vary only in auxiliary parts and design features, such as is the case for automobiles, the advantage of lead-markets over globally designed products can remain. Ford's challenge to develop a "global car", developed jointly by R&D units in Germany, Britain and the United States and named metaphorically 'Mondeo', was nowhere received well. They did not achieve a true global design because none exists. German luxury cars, Italian sports cars, US all-purpose-vehicles and Japanese small cars are still more successful internationally than cars of no local origin.[197]

Another problem is inefficient communication between R&D units. Firms also strive to work continuously on the same research or development task by using the time window of each R&D unit and by periodically transferring the research project to the next unit. This approach relies heavily on new communication technologies like video-conferencing and the Internet. These ambitious plans have not yet proven to be more efficient than concentrating R&D in one location, mainly because face-to-face communication is still the most efficient communication mechanism (Casson, Singh 1993; DeMeyer 1993; Gerybadze et al. 1997).

5.5.2 The leverage-effect of lead markets

Originally, the traditional starting points for locally-leveraged innovations are local-for-local innovations, which are designed locally and take the environment of the local market as the sole reference in which innovations have to satisfy demand and then introduce these innovations in foreign countries. Locally-leveraged innovations have been called innovations that offer an opportunity for foreign market entry through incidental awareness or conscious screening of local product portfolios by attentive managers.

---

[197] So-called ethnic products that sell everywhere do not contradict global homogenisation but confirm it (Levitt 1983, p. 187). Also, the image of country-of-origin plays a part in overseas marketing success. Haucap et al. (1997a) argue that in R&D-intensive goods, this is based on the customer's belief in high product quality made in a high-cost country. A more convincing explanation is that customers judge product quality by the local market's sophistication. Haucap et al. (1997b) confirm a country-of-origin effect empirically by observing a higher willingness of consumers to pay for a car that was made in Germany compared to a car of the same company that was made in and for overseas markets. This signals that the product was downgraded somewhat; see also Han and Terpstra (1988) for a US car company with an R&D unit in Germany. The market in Germany where the lack of a general speed limit on highways has the same effect, (Porter 1990, p. 91; Johansson 2000, p. 108).

Lead market innovations are planned locally-leveraged innovations. In contrast to globally-linked innovations, locally-leveraged innovations avoid communication inefficiencies because all R&D tasks are concentrated in one country. National biases of R&D staff are no problem but a purpose. Locally-leveraged innovations respond to local innovation opportunities, but can subsequently be transferred to lead similar trends in other locations (Bartlett, Ghoshal, 1990, p. 221). In these cases the company can leverage its worldwide innovative resources. A lead market serves as a global platform (Porter 1986) in that it provides an environment that yields an advantage to successfully compete outside the regional market. It is straightforward that locally-leveraged innovations are more efficient than all other types of innovations once they have been made possible. The higher efficiency results mainly from the higher communication efficiency of regionally concentrated R&D activities as opposed to regionally dispersed R&D activities.

Even for multinational firms it is hard to innovate without substantial demand in their home country. Even though foreign affiliates may become true insiders, especially those who have been acquired and can respond to local needs, it "is a daunting task to communicate [foreign buyer needs] to headquarters", as Porter (1990, p. 87) points out. Though decisions on innovation projects of large multinational firms should depend on the perspectives of *world* market potential, it would be a strong obstacle to innovate if there is no potential demand in the home market. Japanese firms, as explicitly quoted already by Linder (1961), have never exported products for which they were not inspired by a strong home market (see also Ohmae 1985, p. 90). Nowadays, as pointed out by a director of an R&D lab of a Japanese firm in Germany, it is still almost impossible to innovate without being backed up by Japanese customers.

The strategy of locally-leveraged innovation, however, is not entirely new. Indeed, Edison saw a future for facsimile machines in Japan as Japanese characters could not be telegraphed by alphanumeric codes, which motivated his research on fax machines (Coopersmith 1993). Siemens concentrated its development activities for sea cables in its British subsidiary in the 1860s because the local market was most dynamic and competition most fierce (Siemens 1961).[198] Although most European firms lacked the capital and the ownership advantage to invest in the United States directly after the Second World War, there is an early example of a European firm taking advantage of the lead market role of the US market, constituted by its high per capita income. The British-Dutch food corporation, Unilever, used the local market experience of its US affiliate, founded in the 1920s by its

198 Siemens Brothers in England started their own innovation activity because of the ambition of Wilhelm Siemens, who headed the English affiliate and was an inventor himself. He first invented a water meter responding to the emerging British public water utilities (Siemens 1961, p. 36). Later he gained responsibility over Siemens' sea cable business. Affiliates' innovation successes were exceptions, because the German headquarters were unwilling to integrate the affiliates innovations in the firm's product line.

British branch Lever Brothers Co., to develop and test new products which could be introduced in Europe in the future. In the words of the company's biographer the company "enjoyed the entrée to a homogenous market, offering unique opportunities for experiment which in turn could serve as a base for further aggression into foreign markets," (Wilson 1969, p.231). Today, Unilever operates 71 innovation centres in key markets for consumer goods innovations for local and regional markets in highly local food products and locally-leveraged innovations in the international brand ranges like personal care products. On the other side, many US firms have given European affiliates a global leadership role for a particular product (Lehrer, Asakawa 1999, p. 283), a "world product mandate" strategy, that is summarised in the next section.

5.5.3 World product mandates of subsidiaries in lead markets

Porter (1990) emphasis the "home" base of a firm as a determinant of the competitiveness of firms: Firms are competitive because the country of the "home"-base has competitive advantages. Porter defines the "home" base of a firm not as the country where the firm was founded but "where strategy is set, core product and process development takes place, and the essential and proprietary skills reside" (Porter 1990, p. 69). Consequently, Porter argues that companies can move their "home"-base abroad: "If the circumstances in the home nation do not support the innovation required for competitive advantage and cannot be improved a firm must shift its home base to a nation that better catalyzes and provides the needed tools for international success" (Porter 1990, p. 614). Porter (1990) includes other functions than R&D as well to be shifted and emphasis that a firm can have different home bases for each distinct businesses. This is the "ultimate act of global strategy" (Porter 1990, p. 615).

Lead market configuration of worldwide activities means concentrating and accumulating resources of each product line in the respective lead market. The concept of concentrating development, production and the development of a global marketing strategy of a new product in a foreign subsidiary of a multinational company has previously been called a *world product mandate* (WPM).[199] The assignment of global mandates to subsidiaries has host-country-specific as well as

[199] The concept of global product mandates of foreign subsidiaries originates from Canadian studies, e.g. Rugman, Bennett (1982), Poynter, Rugman (1982), Etemad (1983), and has been refined in a number of studies, see Bartlett, Ghoshal (1986), Raffée, Kreutzer (1989), Roth, Morrison (1992) and Birkinshaw, Morrison (1995). The concept of the world product mandate is a slightly different organisational approach compared to Porters strategy of international configuration of a firm's "home bases" for distinct product lines. Porters idea is more similar to "division headquarters" (Forsgren, Holm, Johanson 1995). Locating division headquarters seems less temporary and to include a larger range of lines of products than world product mandates or a lead market strategy which is about assigning responsibilities for the development and management of single innovation projects to foreign affiliates.

firm-specific reasons: for instance, technological capabilities of the subsidiary, greater motivation of subsidiaries staff, avoiding centralisation in headquarters and greater acceptance on strategies in other subsidiaries (Schröder 1996, p. 184)[200]. Only few studies such as Bartlett, Ghoshal (1986) stress the potential of innovations induced by the local environment. In contrast, subsidiary mandates are even criticised because the subsidiary is too biased towards the local market environment (Schröder 1996, p. 185). In addition, WPM has been criticised for increasing risk and uncertainty to the MNC (Paliwoda 1993, p. 223, Rugman 1983). These argument do not hold in the case of mandates for lead market subsidiaries.

In the presence of lead markets, product mandates make sense because the advantages of global mandates can be reaped and their disadvantages avoided. Subsidiaries in the lead market are supposed to be biased towards their local market context. It is the purpose of the subsidiary to react to the local demand and market dynamic. When a lead market is identified for a particular product line or innovation idea, assigning a world product mandate to the subsidiary in the market has advantages over mere scanning functions in the lead market based on communication, cost and standardisation efficiency. First, the efficiency of world product mandated subsidiaries derives form the efficiency of close personal communication between marketing, research and development and production and interactive learning. Second, the concentration of product development of local market conditions is cheaper than including units in different countries in the market research and R&D process. Third, the simplification and standardisation of product and marketing strategy proves consistency advantages like the image of a global product and communication across national boundaries. World product mandates are most often confined to single products or narrow product lines rather than whole product ranges or technologies (Raffée, Kreutzer 1989).[201]

When assigning a world product mandate to the subsidiary in the lead market, responsiveness and integration match in the lead market. The lead market subsidiary has a clear world market task while concentrating all functions on the feedback from the local market. The disadvantage of a world product mandate of the subsidiary in the lead market is the risk that the lead market was erroneously selected. If the host country turns out to be an idiosyncratic market rather than a lead

[200] As a result of this variety of motivations to assign product mandates, multinational firms often have an incoherent strategy of mandate assignment based on host country environment.

[201] In the pharmaceutical industry a product line is a disease group such as cancer or Alzheimer's; in the automobile industry a product line would be a vehicle class like a compact, a sedan or a pick-up; in telecommunications equipment, standards such as GSM or ISDN constitute a product line (Reger et al. 1999). New technologies are used for a wide range of products and are seldom exclusively used for one product alone. Biotechnology for instance is applicable for a variety of disease groups for which the lead market could differ. It is therefore not reasonable to concentrate a technology in one location, like the technology-sourcing hypothesis suggests.

market, the MNC would have problems commercialising the product worldwide and would miss the real bandwagon. It would bet on the best horse in the wrong course. When it becomes clear that the presumed lead market has actually no lead function, the multinational corporation has to react by either abandoning the lead market concept in favour of a decentralised R&D programme or by shifting the world product mandate to subsidiary the new country that is now expected to be a lead market. This would be associated with considerable cost as well as resistance from the subsidiary that would lose its global mandate.

In the lead market concept WPM are local market oriented not local technology oriented. Again, a WPM has been suggested to be assigned to the subsidiary that offers the best technical capabilities. And again empirical evidence for such an assignment behaviour as well as for the success of technology-resource based global mandates of subsidiaries is scarce. Roth and Morrison (1992) find no support for global product mandates based on independent R&D activities. Birkinshaw (1996) studied how Canadian subsidiaries of multinational firms gained (and lost) product mandates. He observed that full-scope world product mandates were mostly gained by rather autonomous subsidiaries that responded to opportunities for new business lines initiated by sophisticated local customers. Less frequent were cases in which the mandate was gained because the subsidiary offered the most attractive set of resources or capabilities. This suggests that the local market environment is already at least as important for a lead role of a subsidiary within the multinational corporation.

5.5.4 Transnational mentality

An international dispersion of world product mandates is a challenge to multinational firms with traditional centric or polycentric organisations. However, it is neither the task of this thesis to formulate a lead market organisation in detail nor to present a roadmap for the organisational transition towards it. There is certainly much further research to be done in order to elaborate the management of a lead market oriented R&D network. At this point, only a brief note should draw attention to this field of research important for the successful implementation of a lead market strategy.

Literature emphasis that there are internal preconditions for successful locally-leveraged innovations generated in foreign subsidiaries. There are several barriers to the international diffusion of innovations within a multinational organisation that must be overcome. Local country managers will strongly emphasise differences of their country and the need to accumulate their own resources to modify and develop country specific solutions (Porter 1986). On the other hand, the headquarters are reluctant to loose its power and ability to set the global strategy. Bartlett and Ghoshal (1990) regard "transnational mentality" as the most important management qualification of the multinational firm. This is when the management of foreign subsidiaries does not primarily identify with the local environment, but instead is simultaneously locally sensitive and globally conscious. Porter (1990, p. 615) recommends that personnel in the headquarters must be motivated to adopt a supporting role when the product mandate for a new product is shifted to a foreign affiliate. The headquarters must regard the organisation's worldwide capabilities as an opportunity for stimulating innovations that meet global market demand.

Leveraging innovations from each lead market requires an organisation that has the ability to transfer standardised innovations within the multinational firm. Affiliates need to accept adopting innovations without much change from other affiliates, although they have built up their own R&D resources and their own tight focus on the local market environment in their respective lead market product lines. On the other hand, the lead market concept enhances the market awareness of foreign affiliates since R&D funds are allocated regionally according to lead market potential. Scientific expertise is not enough; the affiliate has to document the lead function of its host market in order to gain funds from the headquarters.

5.6 Predicting Lead Markets: A Preliminary Approach

It is certainly hard to predict which design is going to dominate in the world market. Externality models such as the one by Arthur (1989) make small historical events responsible for the choice of the dominant technology lowering the possibility of predicting the dominant design. As for the concept of the lead market, we are not predominantly interested in *what* technology is finally chosen, but *where* this choice is being made. This is because even in a lead market nobody might be able to foresee what technology finally prevails. There are many examples of leading experts in the lead market having the wrong expectations for the prospect of a technology (e.g. the mainframe computer, fax, PC, the Internet). A firm might have a better idea, however, at which market and in what country the selection process is going to be fought out between competing technologies. Being close to the lead market means being the first to realise which will become the dominant design. In this section I discuss the identification of lead markets and how it would be possible to predict a lead market *ex ante,* that is before the lag markets adopt the innovation design of the lead market. At the end a first approach to develop a method for predicting potential lead markets is presented. First, it is necessary to discuss whether an *ex post* defined lead market can at all be identified *ex ante* (Harhoff 1999, p. 125).

5.6.1 When can a lead market be identified?

First, I consider the different time periods of the international diffusion of innovation designs (Figure 5-3). In the international diffusion of an innovation three periods can be differentiated. The invention is assumed to occur in t=0. In t_1, the adoption of a specific innovation-design takes off in the lead market. In t_2, the take-off period of this special design in the lag markets begins. After t_2 the first country to adopt the innovation can be recognised as the lead market. At this time a multinational firm especially out side the lead market can still gain an international competitive advantage by quickly shifting resources to the lead market and by adopting the technological design preferred by the lead market.[202] This is analog to a fast follower strategy of market entry.[203]

Identifying lead market *ex ante* means identifying a lead market before t_2. In the pre take-off period, experts know about the innovation and early users are toying around with different designs, but a mass market has not yet emerged. Between t_1 and t_2 the innovation design that becomes the globally dominant design has been adopted in one country only; it is unclear whether other countries will follow suit. This is the question the lead market concept deals with: what country has the highest lead or leverage effect, i.e. what country is most likely to be followed.

Before t_1 it is not clear whether the innovation will be adopted at all. This uncertainty is an additional problem that is actually not tackled by the lead market concept. The lead market concept makes expectations about the likelihood that an innovation design preferred by a country can become an internationally dominant design and not whether an innovation design is a market success somewhere at all. Between t_1 and t_2 a lead market analysis is based on the certainty that the innovation is a success in a market and would ask whether this local market success can be transferred to other countries.

The first phase between the basic invention of an innovation and the first take-off (t_1) includes the uncertainty of preferences in country markets.[204] Before t_1 the lead market analysis would make conditioned expectations such as: *if* the country adopts an innovation, the design preferred has the potential to be adopted worldwide. The lead market concept requires a firm to find out what designs countries

---

202 International diffusion patterns of cellular telephony, the facsimile machine and the personal computer indicated the lead markets years before lag market firms invested in idiosyncratic technologies such as personal satellite communications, telex and non-US PC-standards.

203 Fast followers have even some advantages compared to pioneers, because they can learn from the mistakes of the pioneer and use the dominant technology at a lower cost, see e.g., Lieberman, Montgomery (1988).

204 The first phase, however, can be long compared to the other phases of an innovation life cycle (Gort, Klepper 1996). As we have seen in the case study, the first phase of cellular telephony lasted almost 40 years. Although one can expect that the period between invention and market decision will decrease, it is still long enough for the identification of a lead market to be beneficial for firms. The phase between take-off in the lead market and take-off in the lag market can be long as well. The globalisation of markets, however, suggests that this lag will decrease as well and is already relatively small today. The examples presented in this thesis show international adoption lags between one year or shorter (steel processes) and three (cellular telephony, semiconductors, PC) to four years (fax).

Figure 5-3: The phases of the international diffusion of an innovation

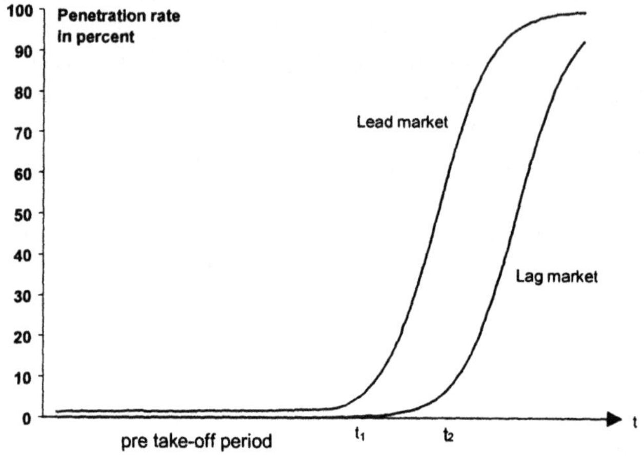

would prefer. This might be a result of market intelligence or test marketing in the lead market after the potential lead market has been identified. It follows that a lead market analysis would be most beneficial before an innovation project has completely the innovation design. The innovation should be designed in order to be successful in the lead market.

Lead markets, however, do not exist for all innovations. In many technologies and product lines it is possible that national standards continuously coexist, for instance if several competing designs break even and survive in different parts of the world (t_2 is infinite). Therefore, for each innovation project, a lead market analysis requires first, a diagnosis of whether lead markets are likely to exist at all for the innovation. Lastly, there is the question whether a lead market can be predicted at all before t_2. If a lead market emerges by chance it cannot be predicted. It has been argued in this thesis, however, that there are nation-specific factors that support the lead market role of a country, i.e. that other countries follow a lead market *if* the lead market adopts an innovation. In many cases these factors do play a higher role than chance in explaining the worldwide success of an innovation design first adopted in one country. In general the higher the influence of chance in the outcome, the lower the predictability of lead markets. If the lead of a market for a particular product results mainly from historic coincidences because the lead factors are highly volatile over time or systematic differences from country to country are small, the lead market strategy of a firm is confined to quickly refocusing attention and resources on the lead market once it becomes apparent.

5.6.2 Approaches to identifying potential lead markets

Part of the difficulty in identifying the lead market comes from the multitude of mechanisms that can explain lead markets, reflected in the assortment of lead market factors. The focus on a single national advantage or internationalisation mechanism is not valid as a method of predicting lead markets.[205] Former approaches to identify the best market to enter first with an innovation are mostly confined to single nation-specific attributes such as size. In practise, firms tend to select countries as the first to enter with an innovation where the developed innovation design has the highest benefit. This might maximise the success of the innovation in that country, but not necessarily the international success. I call this the "Need but no lead" problem of first market entry.[206]

Another approach is trend spotting. This is part of the lead-user analysis. In his lead-user concept, v. Hippel (1988) formulates a method to identify lead-users. For the lead-user analysis an important market or technical trend and users at the front of the trend must be identified. As Urban and v. Hippel (1988) and Herstatt (1991) demonstrate, one can often find general market trends, such as trends towards decreasing product size, higher speed, lower energy consumption, environmentally friendlier products and so on. If a trend can be identified, then the lead market, analogous to the lead-user, is the market where users are at the front of the trend, the most demanding, highly sophisticated. Cvar (1986), for instance, reports that a pet food company that was faced with seemingly different needs in each country market discovered through historical analysis that a country market normally evolves from the use of scraps as pet food, to fresh forms of food, to processed products, and finally toward premium food for pets viewed as companions. This corresponds to the stage of economic development of a country. This global trend was most advanced in France, which the company used as the first market to enter. The identification of a universal trend offers a valuable first step towards the identification of lead markets, even in cases where there is no independent single lead user. In this case the lead market reveals the tastes of the mass-market audience, i.e. the knowledge about future global needs is intrinsically embedded in the local market dynamic.

---

205 It was suggested, for instance, that "lead countries can be easily identified as those in which the most important product or process innovations occur" (Yip 1992, p. 226). Lead markets as defined in this thesis are, however, those markets in which global innovations were first thoroughly *adopted* and refined through user-producer interaction, not those in which they were first *invented*. The fax machine was invented in the United States and in Germany, but achieved the breakthrough and its final design in Japan. GSM was jointly developed by German, US and Swedish companies and started its success story in Finland. According to the Boston Copmputer Museum the first PC was invented in France, however, the mass market for PCs emerged in the US.

206 An example is based on the study by Beise and Cleff (2000) on remote diagnosis and maintenance of commercial trucks, which will be reviewed in more detail below. The truck manufacturing company that intended to introduce a remote system for truck maintenance initially argued that the best countries to introduce the technology to first would be countries with low coverage of maintenance infrastructure. Low coverage on the other hand is a signal for low demand for service. Contrary, an existing high level of demand for services is an indicator for a lead market.

The lead market examples presented in this thesis, however, show that frequently a single market trend is difficult to identify. What is the future trend of television or telephony? Is it going to be transmitted through the Internet, through satellite receivers, through cable or wireless operators? There is probably a technical trend and a lead market in satellite technology, one in cable and one in wireless communication resulting from different environments. For telecommunication companies, however, the question is what future means and standards of communication will prevail globally. Furthermore it may even be hard to identify a trend in one product range. Which trend led to the fax machine? The actual question is often whether or not a new product can substitute other technologies. When technologies compete in different countries with different national environments, one technical alternative sometimes becomes the global standard due to standardisation and cost advantages. In such cases there is neither a market trend nor a market whose particular environment favours the successful technology, therefore it does not really foreshadow global demand conditions. This is the moment when the lead market analysis must go beyond the simplicity of the lead-user analysis. Even if one cannot identify a trend, one can probably identify a market where the future trend is going to be created.

If a theoretical concept of the identification of lead markets is not applied, it is prone to follow stereotypes that can be misleading. Miniaturisation and integration are attributes often assigned to Eastern cultures (Albach 1993, p. 81). Japanese manufacturers did succeed in commercialising VCRs for a mass market by transforming the larger first video recorder designed by the US-firm Ampex into a smaller one suitable for use in private homes (Rosenbloom, Cusmanano 1987; Prahalad, Doz 1987). On the other hand, Japan did not constitute a lead market for other products, for which miniaturisation was also a main success factor. Cellular phones, for instance, are a masterpiece of miniaturisation and integration, but despite their strengths, Japanese firms are not the world leaders in cellular phone manufacturing. Instead two Scandinavian companies and one American company are the world leaders. These are countries hardly notorious for their miniaturisation skills (Economist 1995, p. 60). It is necessary to have a detailed analysis for each single product and every lead market factor. In addition, in a lead market analysis the competitive advantage of national companies is rather irrelevant. The analysis has to focus on the lead attributes of local demand, not on the international advantages of producers in these markets.

Finally, one might argue that a long-time producer simply knows the lead markets of its products. Apart from many obvious errors made by firms that do not respond to lead markets, firms must innovate in product lines that they do not know entirely. As Schumpeter (1911) observed, innovation is a process of creative destruction. Other products and processes become obsolete in the process. Examples of lead markets suggest that the destruction can originate geographically from less familiar countries such as Finland. An early warning tool about newly emerging lead markets can therefore be vital for keeping a firm's competitive advantage. In the next section I will suggest a methodology that uses country indicators for the set of lead market advantages derived in Chapter 3 to compare the lead market potential of countries.

5.6.3 A suggested methodology to predicting lead markets

As argued above, one must evaluate all possible lead market factors for each innovation project and each country. The analysis suggested here follows an indicator-based approach to the theoretical mechanisms. The method for identifying potential lead markets has several steps. After a discussion on whether one can expect a lead market to exist at all, one must derive the lead market factors specific to the innovation project. Third, one must find quantitative indicators for the lead market factors for every country that could be a lead market. Fourth, the values of the indicators for each country shall be aggregated into a small set of factor values. Finally, the set of factor values should lead to a ranking of countries according to their lead market potential. Figure 5-4 depicts the structural model of the lead market theory and the empirical model. The lead market theory derived in this thesis suggests that all five lead market factors can have an autonomous influence on the lead market role of a country. The correlation between each lead market factor and the lead market role might vary from innovation to innovation. The lead market factors correspond to the parameters of the theoretical model, such as the cost reduction potential of innovation designs adopted in countries, the competition intensity of country markets and the degree of similarity or dual-usability of the designs. The lead market factors are all relative variables and not absolute variables, because the lead market potential results from the relative advantage of a country compared to other countries. For instance, the relative cost reduction potential is more important than the absolute cost reduction potential. Because the lead market factors are not expected to be quantifiable directly, they are treated as latent variables. The endogenous empirical model constructs indicators that should correlate highly with the latent lead market factors.

The endogenous side of the model is the lead market potential. The lead market potential is the ability of a county to shape the global dominant design by its domestic preferences and market conditions. The country with the largest lead market potential is expected to become the lead market. The lead market potential is a true latent variable because the lead market potential of countries that finally follow the country that has the largest lead market potential is not observable. The empirical model of the international diffusion of an innovation is that one market leads and all others follow suit. In the lead market theory there is no further distinction within countries that follow, whether they follow earlier or later. There are probably determinants for fast and slow followers but these are not investigated in this thesis. Therefore observation of the exogenous variable would be 1 for the lead market and 0 for all countries that follow. This observation pattern makes it impossible to estimate the influence of the lead market factors on the lead market role of countries unless a sufficient number of *ex post* lead market cases have been

Figure 5-4: Structural and Empirical Models of the Lead Market Analysis

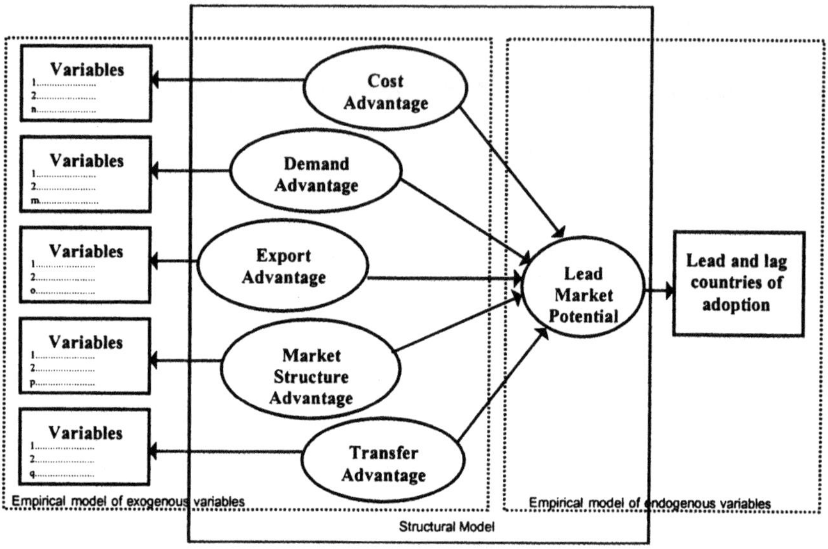

collected. In the current situation, one must make an analysis of potential lead markets for new innovation ideas without knowledge about the significance of the determinants. In effect that is a prognosis without past data that can "train" the prognosis model.

In the *ex ante* prognosis of potential lead markets for new innovation projects, only the empirical model of exogenous variables is available. Since the significance and power of the lead market factors on the lead market potential is unknown, the aggregation of the factors into the lead market potential in the structural model has to be based on plausibility. Below I will return to this problem. The main practical challenge of the empirical model of the exogenous variables is to find country data on indicators that can be used as proxies for the lead market factors. Table 5-2 gives an overview of a set of possible variables for the five lead market factors. Beise and Cleff (2000) uses this schema in their study, in which they filled the sheet during a discussion with the project teams of an automobile firm that intended to identify potential lead markets for two telematic innovations. The analysis starts with the specification of the innovation and the competing technological designs: the header in the sheet. The first column resumes the main lead market factors and their sub factors as described in Chapter 3. For these factors variables are specified that are able to quantify the lead effect per country for the specific innovation project. The variables are either directly country-specific such as factor costs prevailing in a country or they are attributes of the technical design of an innovation preferred by the country such as the cost reduction potential of the design most suitable for the country.

Table 5-2: A concordance of lead market factors, variables and examples of proxies

Innovation: Product/Industry class.:		Competing technologies:
Potential Markets		Former experience, failures
Theoretical argument Sub-attributes	**Ideal variables**	**Available Indicators by country** [M]etric, [O]rdinal, [N]ominal
Cost advantage		
Cost reduction potential of design nationally preferred	Cost reduction per production and accumulated production volume	[M] Market Size [M] Market size of early adopters
Nat. stock adjustment	Vintage of capital	[M] Market growth
Anticipatory factor costs in the country	Trend of factor costs	[M] Recent prices of factor costs (+/- if the prices increase/decrease)
Demand advantage		
Global Trend	Trend variables	[M/O/N] Trend indicators
User budget	Spending budget of users	[M] Per-capita-income of potential users
Anticipatory availability of complementary goods	Trend of availability of complementary goods	[M/O/N] Stock of complementary goods
Export advantage		
Sensibility to global needs	Global problem variables	[O/N] Mass media coverage, lobbying, demand for problem related products
Export orientation	Usability of nationally preferred designs abroad	[M] Export share [M] Comparative trade advantage
Similarity to foreign markets	Average distance to foreign countries of demand parameters	[M] Distance measures of technical parameters relevant for the specification of innovation design (e.g., climate, speed, size, quality)
Market structure advantage		
Competition	Degree of competition, e.g. market power	[M] Market concentration indicators of industry and user industry, price-cost ratios
Contestability	Entry barriers	[M] Investments that are sunk costs
Firm formation	Firm formation rate	[M] Firm formation rate
Transfer advantage		
International demonstration	International communication links	[O] Media coverage, availability of trial information, export promotion of government
Risk reduction	Risk Opinion leaders	[M] Gross investments, subsidies [N] Former failures of former designs
Global externalities	Degree of global increasing returns of adoption	[O] Importance of learning by using [O] Network dependency [O] usability of complementary assets for users in foreign countries
Multinational firms	Standardisation of technology employed in MNU	[M] Direct investment rate [M] Number of MNU dom. headquartered
International mobility of users	Transfer mediators	[M] Travel intensity of users, e.g. spending of consumers for tourism
Propriety of technology	Patent protection of nat. preferred design	[O] Licensing fees for technological design
Structure/sophistication of demand	User know-how	[M] Share of industry or user industry [O/N] Trade journals, lead users,
Government influence	Research programs, state-owned users	[M/O/N] Research subsidies, [M] Share of demand from government

Table 5-3: Overview on complementary goods

Energy as input factor
Fuel
Natural sources (Water, Sun)
Batteries
Complementary goods
Used together with innovation (e.g. razors)
Increases variability (e.g. video cassettes)
Software
Infrastructure
Energy
Electronic Networks
Telecommunications
Traffic infrastructure
Repair/ Maintenance
Complementary Knowledge
Know-how of previous innovations
Additional know-how
Basic education (e.g. language)

If known, each country could be characterised by the design it would prefer because these designs are competing on the world market for the dominant design. For the demand effect and the anticipatory factor price effect a trend must be identified first. The trend is required as the international diffusion mechanism. After the trend is specified, the country that leads the trend has to be assigned the largest value of the trend variable. For instance, a decreasing factor price trend means that the country with the lowest factor price is the country with the highest lead effect, the prices must therefore be transformed into negative values.

Since these are ideal variables it can be expected that country data is not available for most of them. For instance the cost reduction potential of a design is available only after a detailed study is done to estimate the experience curve (Henderson 1980). Assuming the same cost reduction potential of different designs leads to the national market size as a proxy for the price effect. In the third column indicators are listed that can be used as proxies for the "ideal" variables and that are possible to quantify. Country data can be found in a range of databases published by international organisations such as the OECD, IMF, Worldbank or United Nations. However, some indicators wont be available. In this case indicators can be derived by questioning experts.

Normally, these surveys generate only ordinal or nominal scaled data. An additional possibility of a large multinational firm is to ask market researchers of the foreign affiliates. This has the advantage, that the R&D department does not have to disclose the innovation project to experts outside the company. The indicators must be quantified for a set of countries that can be expected to be possible lead markets. Possible countries are not only industrialised countries but newly industrialised countries as well (Brazil, Singapore, South Africa). The set of countries should be representative to all environments and should include the expectations of all project team members about the lead markets, for better internal acceptance of the result. If these countries are not included in the analysis members might oppose the result because of the exclusion.

Availability and variety of complementary goods and complementary goods determine the benefit of an innovation. Anticipatory availability and the prices of complementary goods must are included in the lead market factors. It is especially important to quantify complementary goods. An additional table can be used to check all possible infrastructure assets and complementary goods relevant to the innovation project (Table 5-3). After a collection of variables for the lead market factors has been found, the lead market factors can be quantified. In order to derive a ranking of countries by the lead market potential, the set of quantified indicators must the aggregated. In a first step, indicators for each lead market factor can be reduced to one or more main components by factor analysis. The aggregation of all lead market factors into an lead market index depends on weighing each lead market factor. A theoretically-based weighting scheme for the lead markets has not yet been derived. The resulting ranking is the less sensitive to the weighting scheme the less the lead market factors correlate to each other. If all lead market factors positively correlate, the result of a ranking of most promising lead market will be robust.

In the study by Beise and Cleff (2000) the indicators for each lead market factor were first aggregated by a main component analysis. This process standardises the lead market factors. Only the distribution pattern of the lead market factors over the countries is variable from factor to factor. They argue that the value of the countries for each factor depends on the skewness of the distribution. The more skewed the distribution is, the higher the values of the extreme countries. Since it has been argued that the lead potential is a *relative* variable and not an absolute one, the skewness of the distribution of lead market factors over the countries could be used as a weighting factor for the impact of each lead market factor. The skewness of a component indicates the distribution from a normally distributed variable. The higher the skewness, the larger the likelihood that a single country will lead other countries on a technical path, i.e. the possibility of becoming a lead market. A high positive skewness reveals that one or few countries have very large values, i.e. a large lead market advantage, while the majority of countries have lower values. This is a typical lead market situation. A negative skewness value indicates that the majority of countries cluster around the maximum value. For this lead market component, no country has a real lead market advantage.

5.6.4 First experiences with the lead market analysis

The first experience with the identification of potential lead markets will be reported at the end of this thesis. Beise and Cleff (2000) tested the methodology in an exploratory study for DaimlerChrysler AG. The multinational firms' lorry division planned to develop two specific telematic services for which the technology was not selected yet. Two innovation projects were specified and the task was to identify potential lead markets based on the lead market method suggested in this thesis. The first innovation project was an automated guiding system for lorries for automated transport applications. The second innovation project was a remote diagnosis system for lorries of haulage firms. In a first step, variables were defined for the five lead market factors applied to the specific innovations. This identification process was completed together with project staff from Daimler-

Chrysler. The majority of variables could not be quantified directly; they were latent variables. Other variables had to be found that correlate with the latent variables. These were proxies for the lead market advantages of countries. For instance, the degree of competition in an industry in a country is indicated by the concentration of lorry sales in the country's markets. A special concentration index called Herfindahl was used to quantify the concentration degree. Altogether a set of 32 and 29 indicators respectively were used in the analysis.

The most difficult and time-consuming work involved finding the appropriate databases that contained the comparable country data for the selected indicators. The researchers used general as well as industry-specific databases. Some databases could be purchased on CD-Rom, some were published on paper only, others had to be constructed based on individual data (e.g. container turnover per country was generated by adding container turnover per port). During this screening process, the researchers found that some indicators were not collected by national or international organisations or they were not published. Data belonging to commercial research firms were not used because of the high charges. For these variables the researchers had to find other indicators which could be used as proxies, albeit weaker ones.

A limited group of countries was included in the analysis. This group consisted of all OECD countries and those non-OECD countries which were deemed as being relevant as first adopters of automated vehicles, especially countries with large ports (Taiwan) or large road infrastructures (China, Brazil). In total, 30 countries were included. For these countries the indicators were quantified. In the computations they were imputed with country means which neutralised their impact for those countries in the final ranking. In order to reduce the complexity of the whole set of indicators, indicators of each lead market factor were combined using a factor analysis. In the first innovation project (automated guided truck) the factor analysis resulted in the reduction of the price advantage to three main components, which can be interpreted as a size, cost and unemployment component of the price advantage. The demand advantage could be reduced to two components, roughly interpreted as traffic density and automation penetration. The indicators of the other three lead market factors could be reduced to one component each. As a result, a matrix of factor values of eight main components for 30 countries was generated. In the second innovation project the factor analysis resulted in two main components for each of the five lead market factors. The values of the components were compounded into a single index for each country.

To reduce the set of lead market components to a country ranking, several country ranking methods are used to test for robustness of the result against the ranking method: the mean of all component values, the mean without the biggest value of each county, the mean without the size component, the median, the number of top 10 rankings of a country for each component, and the number of last 10 rankings. Although the ideal ranking has not been found yet. The skewness interpretation given above suggests that mean is a good ranking method because the skewness of an indicator is already included in the factor value due to the standardisation.

The exploratory test of the method showed that the result is sufficiently robust to weighting. In both cases, different ranking methods did not alter the country with the highest lead market potential. In addition, it showed that country data on lead market factors can be found but that this is the most time consuming work. Data not available could be derived from expert interviews. Third, the case study results did not confirm the expectation of the firm's engineers. After the presentation of the indicators, however, they agreed with the lead market result. The data analysis demonstrated that their perception was biased towards particular lead market factors or even factors that are not related to the international diffusion of an innovation. Expectations for the best entry market are often biased toward countries that have are supposed to gain the highest utility of an innovation. This confirms that the lead market analysis with all the shortcomings can be an import information source for multinational firms' innovation strategy.

6 Discussion, Limitations and Further Research

In this chapter I shall summarise the hypotheses presented in this thesis and critically discuss the validity of the concept of lead markets. Lead markets were defined as regional markets that are characterised by market-specific attributes which support the innovation design that is adopted in the domestic market to become the globally dominant design. In order to do so lead market designs have to substitute other designs that might be or would have been initially preferred by users in other countries.

The lead market hypothesis is based on the three assumptions

(1) that the stimuli for the adoption of innovations such as demand preferences, income and local externalities varies from country to country,

(2) that particular characteristics of local markets increase the probability that locally adopted innovations are finally adopted worldwide,

(3) that location-specific demand preferences and the local market context can be perceived more efficiently by domestic firms and suitable innovations better developed by local R&D activities.

A theoretical discussion showed that the mechanisms by which an innovation design preferred originally in one lead market diffuses internationally is composed of price, income and demand lead effects. Further analysis suggest that these lead effects can be facilitated by relative price reductions for the lead market design, anticipation of factor prices, high per-capita-income of users in the lead market, anticipation of needs in the lead market, transfer effects that increase the benefit of lead market designs in lag markets, incentives for including foreign preferences in the local innovation design and by a high degree of competition in the lead market supporting the selection of superior innovation designs.

The conclusion from these hypotheses for technology management is that for a multinational firm it is important to gear new products or process development towards the lead market context provided a lead market exists. If it is possible that there is a lead market, knowledge of lead market characteristics of regional markets is vital for a firm to develop globally successful innovations. Regional proximity facilitates access to knowledge about the lead market context. What is important for firms is the responsiveness and proximity of innovators to users in lead markets, not to users in lag markets. The most efficient means of harnessing lead markets is to locate R&D activities in the lead market, which helps to match designs with lead market needs, and to facilitate instant feedback and close collaboration with local customers in that market.

Lead markets are not just an opportunity for multinational firms, they are also a threat to a firm's competitive position. Firms that do not participate in lead markets, but respond to the demand in other markets either see the commercialisation of their innovations hampered or risk committing themselves to idiosyncratic demand and locking-in to a technology which is well received in the domestic market, but will not succeed worldwide.

Several counter-arguments, however, limits the support for the lead market hypotheses. First of all, it can be argued that differences between country market contexts are diminishing. Globalisation is accompanied by the homogenisation of demand preferences: new products in particular are demanded everywhere (Roth 1979 as cited by Kreutzer 1989, p. 245); the world is turning into "a global village where market opportunities frequently emerge simultaneously on a regional or global basis" (Keegan, Green 1997, p. 39). Because users remain heterogeneous in terms of adoption stimuli, e.g. size of firm, R&D intensity, risk-taking, etc., individual-specific rather than region-specific factors would determine the adoption of innovations. In a globalised world as such the phenomenon of lead markets could become less pronounced. It would not be a regional market that leads the adoption of innovations, but certain segments of users that can be found in many countries, e.g. lifestyle groups, businessmen, the largest multinational firms that take the lead. Therefore, multinational firms would have to develop innovations focussing on global user segments. So far, however, this *globalisation-cum-user-heterogeneity* argument has been a weak one, simply because it does not explain the pattern of cross-border diffusion of innovations still observable for many modern innovations, but suggests that the pattern of country-specific adoption of innovations is diminishing more and more. So far there are still countries leading the adoption of innovations with every segment of users (early adopters, majority, laggards) adopting the innovation first worldwide.

Second, it can be claimed that technological sophistication is the most important advantage of innovation design in the international competition among technologies. Cases where technologically inferior alternatives prevail are more or less the exception to the rule.[207] Furthermore, it has been argued that technological prog-

[207] The market failure hypothesis, which is based on seemingly inferior designs that became dominant, has been challenged, see for instance Utterback' s review of the disputed inferiority of the typewriter keyboard (Utterback 1994, pp. 5-7).

ress is increasingly dependent on scientific findings (e.g. Narin et al. 1997). Together, this would suggest that it is crucial for a firm to gain access to scientific findings at an earlier stage than its competitors. Early access to scientific findings could be achieved through cooperations and research agreements with public and private research laboratories. Since it was argued that interaction efficiency increases with proximity, firms would be advised to locate their R&D close to regions of scientific excellence. This idea is problematic. First of all, the assumption that in high-technology industries technological progress is solely driven by scientific advances and not by local markets has yet to be empirically proven. What can be said is that new innovations increasingly refer to scientific findings and not that they become more independent from market interaction. Second, for the argument to hold, a close correlation between scientific superiority and the cost-benefit relationship of an innovation design for users needs to be demonstrated, which is not an easy task. Technologically "inferior" designs can become the globally dominant designs because they are more *economically* beneficial (e.g. can be offered at lower prices). In addition, it must be shown that when market contexts differ, the ranking of technological "superiority" of designs is the same in each country, so that each country selects the most "superior" design. A third argument casting doubt on the technological superiority argument is that the benefit of a design depends on the adoption and it is likely that this adoption dependency will gain in importance, since technological complexity and data exchange are increasingly making learning and network economies more important for the functionality of a product compared to technological core performance. It follows from technical models including externalities that the larger the increasing returns of adoption, the higher the probability of an inferior design becoming the dominant design.

In addition, regional distribution of scientific advances and demand are related. Often regions of cutting-edge scientific competence are also lead markets. This is because a demanding environment provides incentives to firms to do R&D with the objective, for example, to solve the most serious problems in the region, thus maximising the benefit for customers in all the other regions. Moreover, in this region publicly funded research will focus more on this task than in all the other regions. Sophistication and the volume of local demand therefore support local scientific excellence.

Third, sometimes it appears that dominant firms play a more important role in the adoption of innovations than admitted in this thesis. For instance, Microsoft has been pictured as a monopolist able to impose innovation designs on world markets together with its latest software releases. Yet, even multinational firms respond to local demand and do not ignore it, and even large firms are biased towards home markets. The lead market attribute has been an explanation of the international success multinational firms enjoy since Vernon's international product life cycle theory.

It can further be argued that globalisation leads to increased international coordination, whether it is standardisation agencies becoming more effective in setting standards or multinationals realising that when it comes to setting a globally dominant design. "Going it alone" means running the risk of losing the whole market and that therefore they are better off agreeing on industry standards. The efficiency of international standard setting mechanisms is indeed a topic that has been given short shrift in this thesis. Again, this is a matter for further research. Yet, the case study showed that despite international standards for certain products (satellite communications, pagers, cellular phones), there are still competing standards for different products within a single product domain (mobile telephony).

An argument against the lead market hypothesis that carries greater weight is that lead market attributes are endogenously reversing the causality of lead markets. It is possible that the international diffusion of an innovation is triggered by other factors such as historical coincidences, direct political intervention or international commitment to standard setting. The attributes of lead markets presented in this thesis could actually be a result of this international adoption process and not the determinants of the process. The adoption of an innovation can indeed cause prices to drop, exports to surge, international attention to increase and competition to intensify. As a result, the first country to adopt an innovation design that is later adopted by other countries (for other reasons) would appear to be the country with the lowest prices, the highest exports, etc. In the end, the endogeneity of the factors regarded as exogenous to the international diffusion process can only be refuted by empirically valid tests. Yet, the case study on cellular mobile telephony showed that the international distribution of lead market attributes was not caused by high penetration rates, rather it preceded the adoption. Apart from this case, I found no evidence that lead market factors were a mere by-product of the international diffusion of innovations.

Another limitation of the lead market model can be illustrated with the following scenario: An innovation design is adopted in a large country with low penetration rate. The large market size helps to realise a large cost reduction potential of the design and to become a globally dominant design. Yet, a small country adopted this design with a high penetration rate earlier but because the country market is low could not trigger the cost reduction before. The small country, however, would appear as a lead market despite the fact that the price effect was caused by the adoption in the large country, that looks like a lag market. I found no example for this scenario but it limits the theoretical relation of the lead market factors to the country with the highest penetration rate.

One last argument questioning the value of the lead market theory is that chance plays a major role in the international success of innovation designs. Even if internationalisation mechanisms are behind the observed pattern of international innovation diffusion, chance could have so large an impact on the selection of a lead market that predictions about lead markets have little predicting power. Since there are so many possible mechanisms, one can not know *ex ante* what mechanism will finally prevail and what country will finally set the globally dominant design. A prediction would require that so many variables for so many countries be forecast that the uncertainties associated with the individual variables would add up to a high forecasting uncertainty and thus the prediction would be of limited persuasiveness for the location decisions related to innovation projects. I would argue, that even if chance plays a major role, any information about possible lead effects would help support the location decisions.

Finally, it can be argued that proximity of users to innovators is declining in importance. The rise of the Internet and the "global village"-nature of international business could imply that information about foreign market preferences is easily available. This argument does not question the existence of lead markets, but counters the home market theory according to which a firm's innovation development is biased towards the local context, and the conclusion from the lead market concept to locate R&D in the lead market. Internationally varying adoption stimuli are a prerequisite for lead markets. The efficiency of proximity of innovators and adopters has not been empirically proven in this thesis, it has solely been based on literature. There has been no empirical evidence so far showing that the impact of proximity on communication efficiency has vanished.

Apart from listing these counter arguments against the basic lead market concept, some qualifications regarding the lead market strategy have to be made. First of all, the lead market concept is not a universal concept for a firm's international strategy, but part of a product-specific strategy to develop a globally standardised innovation. It does not imply a standardised marketing strategy encompassing packaging, advertising, pricing, and distribution channels. Market positioning issues and the market segments the product is targeting may still differ from country to country (as in the diverse segment strategy, see Takeuchi, Porter 1986). Furthermore, because there are not lead markets for all new products and processes local-for-local innovations and globally-linked-innovations will always be necessary for firms seeking to penetrate world markets in all lines of business they are in. The need to adapt innovation strategies arises partly from insurmountable international differences in demand specifics such as region-specific standards, which lead mechanisms cannot compensate for and which persist over time. In such cases there is no market from which an innovation can spread to other markets. Instead, a single innovation has to be designed to meet all the requirements in the different markets. It is indeed a major challenge for the multinational firm "of designing an organization that can facilitate all three innovation processes simultaneously" (Ghoshal 1986).

Most multinational firms will carry on developing local innovations or conducting adaptive R&D in large foreign markets, just to achieve a large market share, even if there is only a small likelihood of introducing these local innovations into other markets. Some large markets with idiosyncratic demand in certain product lines are simply too important to be left aside. Especially the United States is so vast a market that for almost all innovations even in high technology fields, it is large enough to justify developing an innovation for the US context. If an innovation is successful in the United States, US sales will likely pay back R&D investments. Only on foreign markets such as Europe and Asia do US producers have a hard time selling their US products if the United States is not the lead market. Often when the United States is not the lead market, the US market remains a large and profitable market for an idiosyncratic innovation and does not follow the lead market in adopting their preferred innovations. US firms are thus not pressured too hard to apply the lead market concept. This is because the lead market concept will shift attention away from the home market if the home market does not correspond to the lead market. Therefore, the innovation will not perfectly fit market conditions in the United States, and will be inferior to innovations from other domestic producers that focus entirely on the US market. Only if foreign market innovations threaten US innovations and squeeze them not only out of foreign markets but also out of the home market, is the lead market concept the right strategy for US firms as well.

Of course, the success of firms cannot be totally explained by the fact that they are headquartered in the lead market. There are firms located in lag markets that have successfully commercialised the globally dominant design (e.g. Alcatel of France is a successful global player in cellular mobile telephony equipment). On the other hand, there is evidence that even firms that pioneered the globally dominant design are not immune to losing their first mover advantage (CAT scanner, pocket calculator, see Teece 1992a). As statistical tests are unavailable, the lead markets' explanatory power (variance explained) for firms' international success is unknown, but expected to be significant. This lack of statistical validation and of some form of quantification of the lead market advantage is certainly the most significant shortcoming of this thesis and a task for further research.

The analysis of lead market attributes is only part of the system of the competitiveness of nations and therefore of locations for R&D activities of multinational firms. I do not offer a comprehensive understanding of the system as a whole, only one (vital) element. The way multinational firms build their strategies and make the decisions required, however, depends on the evaluation of the entire system. This complex task cannot be accomplished by a single thesis. My task was to deepen the understanding of a part of Porter's diamond, the demand side factor, which in my view is underestimated in terms of its significance and has been less frequently studied than the other parts, which are nevertheless important, too.

Undoubtedly, the task ahead consists in deriving a better methodology to validate the lead effect in industries and product lines, and to assess the lead potential of national markets.

7 Epilogue: Implications for National Policies[208]

Suddenly, it seems, the sovereign states are feeling naked
RAYMOND VERNON (SOVEREIGNTY AT BAY, 1971)

Government policy does affect national advantage, both positively and negatively
MICHAEL E. PORTER (COMPETITIVE ADVANTAGE OF NATIONS, 1990)

Lead market ability constitutes an international competitive advantage for a nation, because it strengthens domestic firms and facilitates exports. In contrast, an idiosyncratic market is a disadvantage for domestic firms, since preference is given to innovation designs that cannot be easily exported and even risk being squeezed out of the home market. Therefore, it is of vital interest to governments that the domestic market is a lead market and not an idiosyncratic or lag market.

To start with, a country that is the first to adopt a globally dominant innovation boosts the pioneer advantages of domestic firms; it "catalyzes" the firms' international success (Porter 1990, p. 614). Local adoption encourages domestic firms to invest in R&D and provides the necessary market information that guides firms towards global products that can be commercialised worldwide. A lead market gives domestic firms a head start in terms of learning, economies-of-scale, quality improvements, setting up distribution systems, access to supplies, brand loyalty and international reputation, product line differentiation and long-term market share. Furthermore, a lead market is able to lure direct investments from multinational companies into the country and is attractive to high-income and skill-intensive R&D activities. Most leading firms will find it necessary to participate in the lead market in order to get access to market information required for global competition. Third, lead markets attract direct investments even if they do not offer any cost advantage. Instead, it is possible to set national wages at premium

[208] Section 7.2 of this chapter was prepared while I was a visiting researcher at the Multimedia University, Cyberjaya, Malaysia. I am grateful to Dr. Avvari Mohan for graciously hosting me.

levels, because lead markets open up the prospect of global success. Lead markets can even reverse a comparative disadvantage in input factors costs, for high factor prices that lead global price trends induce globally successful innovations.[209] And lastly, the presence of highly competitive firms in the lead market competing to set the local standard supports the availability of the latest technology and brings prices down. Consumers and industrial users enjoy a high consumer's surplus.

Hence it would make sense for a country to support not only the generation of scientific knowledge and inventions, but also the adoption of new technologies and innovations. Porter (1990, p. 644) notes that the government of a country affects demand conditions "in many often unintentional and counterproductive ways because it has an incomplete view of what determines competitive advantage". A government's task is to be aware of these influences and to adjust them in order to strengthen demand conditions. Porter suggests that governments can ensure there is early sophisticated demand for innovations. The crux of demand side policies is that the innovation design adopted locally also has to be adopted in other countries in order to generate an international competitive advantage. Two policy options will be discussed in this chapter. First, a government can attempt to support the lead market role of a country. Second, a government can concentrate public support on industries in which the country has lead market potential. The effectiveness of the first option will be briefly addressed in this section, the prospects of the second policy are outlined in the following section on Southeast Asian countries.

7.1 Towards a Lead Market Technology Policy

Research policy is mainly focussed on the supply side, the production of technological knowledge and infrastructure, because knowledge spillover effects suggest that private research investments are below the social optimum.[210] Research policy assumes that technological advances generated by publicly funded research support the technological superiority of domestic firms. The lead market theory suggests that it is not a national technological lead, but a national adoption lead that gives domestic firms an international advantage. Diffusion technology policies support the diffusion of new technologies. These demand side technology policies can be subdivided into specific and unspecific instruments. Specific in-

---

209 For example, poor growing conditions in Israel have prompted local farmers to demand innovations regarding irrigation and cultivation techniques (Porter 1986), making Israel a lead market in agricultural technologies (Takeuchi, Porter 1986). In Germany high labour cost have spurred the international success of its automation technology. High energy costs in Denmark fostered a pilot market for highly energy-efficient refrigerators (Jänicke et al. 1999).

210 The theoretical foundation of the rationale for public research was laid by Arrow (1962a); for a review of supply side policy instruments see Lyden, Link (1991).

struments support a specific technology. Specific policies increase the incentives to adopt a specific innovation, for instance by subsidising new technologies, through mandatory adoption of a specific end-of-pipe technology (e.g. catalytic converters for motor vehicles), or by setting up demonstration centres. Within national technology policy, public procurement has often been used to support domestic demand for advanced technologies, accelerating their development and nurturing sophistication (Mowery 1995, p. 535). For example the German public telecommunications operator like many other PTTs pursued a national procurement strategy which was supposed to stimulate R&D investments and innovations made by equipment firms. The creation of infrastructure that is a complementary asset of a particular technology increases the benefit of an innovation and thus the rate of adoption. *Specific policies* implies that governments have to select a specific design that they sponsor. Unspecific instruments support the ability of firms to adopt innovations, but are not biased towards a particular technology or innovation design. Unspecific demand side policies include the tax treatment of investments in new equipment or lowering emission limits for motor vehicles.

How are these policies related to the lead market role of a country? Supporting knowledge generation and the adoption of new technology policies do not automatically facilitate a lead market. First of all, research findings are likely to be rapidly available to foreign firms. Publicly funded research activities do not support the adoption of an innovation in a country. Diffusion policies, in contrast, promote the adoption of innovations. However, it is not certain that a design first adopted by one country will be adopted by other countries as well, if preferences vary from country to country. In order to promote exports, a government has to support the adoption of the design that will become the globally dominant design. Predicting the innovation design that will become not only domestically dominant but also globally dominant is a task that is likely to fail (Utterback 1994). What kind of policy promotes the adoption of the global design? In a first attempt to answer this question, the impact of government policies on the five lead market factors will be sequentially discussed.

7.1.1 Price advantage

Early adoption of an innovation design lowers its cost through learning economies and economies-of-scale. Public support for the adoption of an innovation intensifies the price reduction effect of the international diffusion of innovations. In industries and technologies in which the cost reduction effects of an adoption are considerable, governmental sponsorship seems to be able to support the lead market role of a country. In order to leverage domestic technologies internationally, a government could sponsor the adoption of the design with the largest cost reduction potential. Sponsorship can be achieved through subsidies, public procurement, favourable product approval or legislation that pressures firms to adopt a specific design (e.g. for health reasons or to protect the environment).

The problem with this policy is that the price reduction potential of certain designs is not known. Only projections and estimations can be made. In addition, not all designs are actually known. To decide which design is to be sponsored, the relative cost reduction potential needs to be estimated for a variety of designs that could be introduced in certain countries. Furthermore, this technology policy approach of strengthening the lead market role of a country is only effective in large countries. In small countries the quantities demanded are too small to enable large cost reduction effects resulting from learning curves and mass production, if these countries cannot export the design at the same time.

7.1.2 Demand advantage

A demand advantage means leading a global trend. Is a government able to position a country at the front of a global trend? First, governments have to identify global trends. Second, they can become early users themselves or via state-owned firms simulating demanding users, or pressure private users in a country to adopt an innovation that responds to future global needs. The question is whether governments are good at choosing innovation designs that are suitable for private users as well and whether users that are pressured by governments to adopt an innovation are as good as users that adopt innovations without experiencing pressure to select the "right" innovation design, i.e. the one that will turn into the globally dominant design in a competitive market.

Governments differ from private users, because they neither maximise profits nor are they threatened by losses. One could argue that they can overcome the myopic attitude of the market and are free to maximise social welfare with an appropriately low discount rate. Yet, this lack of profit orientation proves to be counterproductive in the case of lead markets, because it is private firms that are the potential adopters and are supposed to take their cue from the government. It is safe to say that governments are not good at simulating private firms and at choosing the design private firms would choose if they were at the front of the trend. Governments do not have any customers that are constantly driving them towards more competitive prices, they do not feel any pressure from the market driving them to higher efficiency. Instead, official agencies are subject to legal restrictions, for example they have to treat national citizens equally. In short, governments have less information on what a competitive technological design should look like.

However, in some industries governments are able to shift the national contexts towards the front a global trend. For instance, negative environmental externalities can be corrected by assigning a price to environmental risks, water pollution and emissions into the atmosphere.[211] Worldwide environmental statistics reveal a global trend. Sometimes international agreements determine the road most countries will go down in the future. The Kyoto Agreement on worldwide climate change laid down the CO_2 reduction targets for the participating countries. Since the agreement is binding once it has been ratified, it provides some certainty that demand for energy-efficient industrial processes and appliances will grow over the next few years. By pressuring domestic companies to innovate to improve energy efficiency ahead of the timetable included in the agreement, governments would ensure a head start which would foster a lead market for energy-efficient appliances and CO_2 reducing processes. Denmark already enjoys a reputation for energy-efficient household appliances like refrigerators due to energy taxes and regulation (Jänicke et al. 1999). However, national regulations are likely to create idiosyncratic conditions if the conditions created by law do not exactly anticipate future conditions in other countries. In the CO_2 emission reduction example this is guaranteed through the international agreement.

Another policy commonly pursued is to support the creation of infrastructure and complementary goods. Again, if the infrastructure is created in other countries as well irrespective of the adoption of an innovation, governments can support the lead market role of a country. However, often the infrastructure is design-specific and a prerequisite for the adoption of a specific design. For instance, the tracks for magnetic levitation trains do not represent complementary goods in the sense of a demand advantage. Building a design-specific infrastructure does not boost the demand advantage. Only if an infrastructure can be used universally, is it possible for public funds to directly (without any other advantages) promote the adoption of a globally dominant design.

7.1.3 Export advantage

Governmental policies can strengthen local firms' export orientation. Export orientation can be strengthened by making information on foreign market preferences available, setting regulation that is similar to other countries' regulations and a procurement policy that prefers technologies and innovations that can be exported and avoids highly nation-specific designs. National legislation and regulation tend to focus on domestic needs and the local environmental context. Often this policy does promote the adoption of technologies that fit domestic context best regardless of the benefit for other countries. Porter (1990) stresses that government specifications "should be set with an eye to what will be valued in other advanced nations". By actively anticipating the requirements for the context of foreign markets and including them in national regulations, idiosyncratic country-specific innovations can be avoided.

---

211 The relationship between environmental regulation and innovation has been addressed by Porter and van der Linde (1995). They suggest that governments can create market conditions that support first mover advantages.

The case study of the is thesis showed that government agencies can help firms to develop innovations that fit foreign market contexts. For instance, state-owned firms and government agencies can demand that firms develop exportable innovations instead of demanding innovations that fit the national context perfectly. Promoting the export orientation of domestic firms can mean sponsoring a design that takes account of demand preferences abroad. Supplying information on foreign demand preferences is another policy option that supports export orientation.

It has been argued that countries that are sensitive to global problems facilitate a lead market. The political system can support the responsiveness of firms to global problems. Political systems can be more or less sensitive to problems by strengthening the political and social values that foreshadow global needs, e.g. all the problems arising from the growing share of elderly people, the rising cost of the health care system, or increasing individual mobility and public transportation. On the supply side, governments can promote technologies that tackle global problems.

Supporting export orientation seems to be the best policy option for small countries with an idiosyncratic environmental context. Export promotion is vital to increase incentives for firms to invest in R&D. Local competition is often severely limited as the small home market does not allow many firms to survive. Low trade barriers increase competition and expose domestic firms to the world market.

7.1.4 Transfer advantage

The transfer advantage is one of the traditional reasons for a national diffusion policy. Public sponsorship of the first adoption of an innovation supports the international demonstration effect, reduces the risk of subsequent foreign users of the same design, increases international attention and boosts the reputation as a country where high technology is tested. If public agencies and state-owned firms adopt innovations, the risk facing other early adopters is reduced. The risk inherent in the adoption of a new technology is socialised, shifted from early private adopters to the public. The nuclear reactor case reviewed in chapter 2 is an international success story of government sponsorship of national technologies.

However, the effectiveness of policies focussing on the transfer advantage has to be questioned. State sponsorship of technologies can have the opposite effect. Potential foreign users could be suspicious of the benefits of technologies that have to be pushed by national governments. Nationalistic arguments are used to oppose the adoption of technologies that are government-sponsored to increase world market share and support domestic firms. Foreign firms start calling for the same support from their governments and even for trade restrictions.

New technologies are often characterised by increasing returns. Increasing returns result from growing networks and post-invention improvements. Most network effects, however, seem to be greatest within a region or country, and are small internationally. For instance, a communications technology does not increase the benefit for customers in foreign countries, because very few potential users communicate across borders, and interface technology is mostly able to convert communications signals at international switching centers. Post-invention improvements can increase the benefit of a domestic technology abroad, but are often confined to perfecting features preferred in the domestic market.

At the same time, increasing returns compound the complexity of the government's decision on the technological design it will sponsor. The dominant design is not necessarily the design which is initially the best design. The market mechanism could lock-in to an inferior technology, leaving superior technologies untested. Competition ceases too early in the process for technologies that are better in the long run to demonstrate their superiority (Cowan 1991a, Arthur 1989). In this case a central planner, that anticipates the future merits of several technologies by means of discounting the learning effects of adoption, would lead to a better outcome than the market. A government wishing to support the lead market function of local demand could then try to identify the (theoretically) superior technology and support its domestic development and adoption. Next, it could intervene in market selection by supporting the allegedly superior technology, e.g. through selective subsidies. This way even a larger, but less innovative country, e.g. with slower or lagging diffusion, that adopts and locks in to the superior technology could become the one to set the global standard, precisely because it is able to demonstrate the superiority of its technology.

There are two problems with this policy. The first is that government agencies need to know the benefits and learning curves of the alternative technologies not only in one environment, but in all environments. Cowan (1991a) showed that if government agencies are unable to predict technological progress accurately even with the help of appointed expert bodies, it is possible to lock-in to an inferior technology. If the technology which the government agency believes to be the best is supported too early, private investment may be misled at the expense of learning more about other technologies. Second, even if government agencies manage to predict the superior technology (because it was theoretically proved that a given technology is more efficient than the others), the optimal policy need not be to support this technology. The right policy depends on what technology other countries adopt. An inferior technology could nevertheless become the globally dominant design, if it diffuses in other large countries with high adoption rates and gains a lead in learning. The outcome of the international innovation race toward the global design is still open even if one country adopts the superior technology. The country that adopted the superior technology could still lose the world market if the inferior technology gains so much support from other countries that its benefits outweigh those of the superior technology through increasing returns of adoption. Then it would be advantageous for all countries that intend to adopt a given technology next to prefer the inferior to the superior technology. This is especially true when large countries do not intervene and the market selects one out of several technologies with increasing returns.

Again, nuclear reactor technology is given as an example. While it was recognised early on that light water reactors were inferior, they were ultimately used in about 80 % of the world's reactors (International Atomic Energy Agency as cited by Cowan 1990). France and Britain spent a lot of public funds on the superior gas-graphite reactor, pushed it in their protected domestic markets, but did not manage to export much of the technology abroad. While the German government funded research at public research institutions on different reactor types, the choice of the prevailing reactor was ultimately left to the private utilities (Keck 1980), which chose the internationally standardised light water reactor, causing Germany's nuclear industry to become highly competitive internationally.

A last transfer advantage is sophisticated demand that increases the benefit. To simulate sophisticated and demanding buyers, state-owned firms often demand higher quality than private firms.[212] Even without orders from the government to create high-tech demand, Rovizzi and Thompson (1992) argue on the basis of the model of Bös and Peters (1988) that public monopolies could offer products at a higher quality level than the socially optimal quality. This is because the cost of achieving higher levels of quality is not fully taken into account, since for example state-owned firms have bureaucratic structures not included in cost optimisation. If German technologies tend to be over-engineered, it is partly because state-owned firms or public regulators are over-ambitious to get the best solutions on technical criteria alone that could prove to be uncompetitive in the world market, because the high quality cannot fully justify the high prices. Deutsche Telekom, for example, demanded the highest possible quality from its telephone equipment supplier before being privatised, because it rented telephone sets to customers. However, the cost of this quality level seems to have exceeded the optimal quality in the investment function. Thus these telecommunications products did not match the optimal price-quality relationship, which a competitive market would have led to. Other examples are the utilities and the German Railway.

7.1.5 Market structure advantage

As argued above, markets reveal which technological design best satisfies user needs. The „knowledge" about future applications of new technology is in the market. Fierce competition and innovative users that try out several alternatives reveal this knowledge. According to models of the selection process in markets such as evolutionary models of technological change there are two major instru-

[212] Theoretically, it is not clear what the quality of products from monopolistic supply is like compared to the competitive market situation (see Tirole 1988, p. 102). It depends on the ratio of the willingness to pay for quality of marginal customers to that of average customers.

ments of technology policy. First, government policy can help to exploit technological opportunities through publicly funded research and second it can support the selection mechanisms (Metcalfe 1995). The former includes publicly funded research which preserves technological variety to prevent the market from prematurely selecting a technology. One precondition is the existence of several inventors with competing technological alternatives. With a monopolist as the supplier there are no alternatives for users to choose a technology from. Low entry barriers for new competitors are essential for competition in technologically dynamic sectors (Audretsch 1995). Open markets for foreign competitors enhance the variety of technologies even more. Publicly funded research could within limits substitute for insufficient research by competitors into alternative technologies in the form of so-called place-marker research. A case in point is semiconductor material. When the dominant German electronics firm decided to concentrate on silicon as the basic material for all its electronic components, the government should not have seen its main task in supporting this decision by similarly concentrating publicly funded research on silicon. On the contrary, it should have supported research activities revolving around alternatives like germanium to keep this option alive in case it not only proves to be the more efficient semiconductor material in the long run, but is also adopted by international competitors as the global standard.

In sum, the lead function of a market means that it does not always choose the best technology, but the one which finally dominates the global market. Room for intervention would thus be limited to keeping the alternatives for adoption open and to preventing a rapid lock-in of the local market before a globally dominant design emerges, the choice of technology should be left to the market. Since markets will under-supply experimentation (Cowan 1991a), publicly funded research could compensate by experimenting with technologies which were not adopted during the first stage. Although this policy does not directly support the lead function other than by maintaining competition, it does prevent local firms from becoming niche suppliers in the global marketplace on account of locking-in to an idiosyncratic technology. In addition local lock-ins to idiosyncratic technologies result in high changeover cost for local customers when they switch to the globally dominant design.

This example leads to the second policy approach which limits the instruments to improve the technology selection mechanism in general. In the absence of increasing returns on adoption, a close correlation between technology and competition policy becomes even more obvious (Metcalfe 1995). Even policymakers often try to support the diffusion and adaptation of a technology. To push the diffusion of what the government believes to be the best technology, the rate of adoption of a new technology can be increased by paying subsidies to adopters. Yet, evolutionary theory warns precisely of a policy approach characterised by a „picking national winners" strategy or a static optimisation policy in general. A support bias in favour of the diffusion of a particular technology has the same effect. It could lock the national economy in to a technological alternative which may not become the global standard, in the words of Cowan (1990) it would be like „backing the wrong horse". An example is Minitel in France, a locally successful information retrieval service in France. When the socialists came to power in 1980, France adopted an even more interventionist industrial policy than before. They nationalised the electronics and telecommunications industries and merged them into a few large corporations. R&D expenditures rose and a new technology was introduced and publicly subsidised to spur adoption. The General Telecommunication Agency (DGT) sought new forms of communication and new products. Possible offspring from the marriage between telecommunications and computing like teletex, electronic mail, pay-TV, telepayment, and home banking were supposed to be pursued and adopted early in France. It was thought that the technological advances in France would make it possible to impose French technology on Europe and the rest of the world.

Minitel was one of the technologies implemented by French governmental agencies where the adoption was highly subsidised. Yet, corresponding systems in other European countries (like BTX in Germany) were not successful either. Instead the Internet became the globally dominant design for information systems. Minitel's early lead even turned out to be a disadvantage for France, because for a long time the adoption of the Internet was very slow in France (DTI 1999, p. 28). As late as 1997 France only had 4 Internet hosts per thousand inhabitants compared to an OECD average of 15 and the figure was much lower than in most industrialised countries (OECD 1997a, p. 58).

7.1.6 Discussion

In sum, policies for the early adoption of a specific innovation design suffer from general problems. The foremost problem for a government is that it knows even less about consumer preferences, price reduction potentials and international trends than firms do. Unless these variables of the international diffusion of innovations are known, sponsorship of designs can easily lead to "backing the wrong horse". Governmental technology choices, expressed either by monopolising a technology or through domestic price distortions, tend to be biased towards the technology that would have normally been neglected in favour of an alternative technological variant. If the latter is finally introduced in other countries it will become the globally dominant design, leaving the first country internationally isolated, which not only hinders exports but entails other disadvantages, too. Only if the early adoption of a technology leads to a dramatic improvement in the technology due to the knowledge gained from using it, can the initially greater benefit of the alternative technology be offset.

Second, other governments interpret this adoption policy as an unfair strategic trade policy and may choose to counteract it by imposing some restrictions on the domestic adoption of the government-sponsored design or sponsor their own design. The problem with a guiding technology policy can be demonstrated with the help of game theory. Companies from other countries regard this political intervention as active trade policy and ask their governments to respond in kind. This either leads to competing international subsidies or to a trade war, where a government reacts with trade restrictions to the interventions of another country. US-Japanese and US-European Union trade relations abound in examples of the latter.

Another consequence is international competition in R&D subsidies. With global designs a country has only limited possibilities of international rent-shifting through R&D subsidies (Brander, Spencer 1985), because if a nation's innovation system is confrontational in nature, the possibility of setting global standards decreases. Other countries would not accept the innovation of a country as a global standard if the government uses public funds or supports its firms otherwise precisely to achieve the advantage inherent in being the country that sets the global standard. In addition, governments would fiercely support their domestic firms' technologies, too, and erect non-tariff barriers like approval procedures to avoid having to adopt the foreign system and weaken their own industry. They would thus again risk supporting country-specific technologies. One example, which shows just how sensitive countries are to interference from foreign governments, is the digital transmission system for mobile phones. While European, often state-owned telecom providers developed and successfully implemented the GSM system, giving European equipment companies an advantage from „being there", American firms are eager to push their own CDMA system in their home market to remain competitive on foreign markets. Japan does not accept foreign systems in the first place. In connection with global designs the most promising approach for national governments is thus to promote international collaboration between firms, in particular in the triad nations, for them to agree on global standards.

Lastly, the main argument of this thesis is that a lead market is a lead market and a lag market is a lag market due to their specific contexts. The transformation of a lag market into a lead market requires institutional changes that governments cannot possibly bring about, such as changes in demand preferences and changes in the environmental context. Although governments are capable of influencing the adoption incentives for domestic users, they cannot change the domestic context entirely. For instance, in a lead market context, the user-producer interaction is crucial in guiding producers to refinements which anticipate usage in other countries. Competition is a characteristic of lead markets when they test several alternatives before choosing the most beneficial. Government policies, however, frequently distort markets (Christensen 1997, p. 192).

Research and technology policies are mostly concerned with the allocation of public research funds to private and public institutions, and with research topics and technological fields. A possible approach in a lead-lag market environment is to support the industry or the technological fields in which a country context facilitates an international lead market role without a government's manoeuvring. Instead of asking how their country can become a lead market in a potentially successful technology, governments would ask (1) For which technology can the country become a lead market due to its environment and context? And (2) For which technology is the country likely to remain a lag market? The first question will be addressed in the next section for the newly industrialised countries in South-East Asia. The last section discusses policies for industries in which a country is a lag market.

7.2 A Lead Market Oriented Policy for Southeast Asian NICs

When a government decides to support research and technology development in its country it has to allocate a limited research fund on technological fields. Limited public budgets imply a priority setting (National Academy of Science 1995). In most industrialised countries and in many newly industrialised countries alike national industry and technology policies are focused on fostering and strengthening the strategic high-technology industries. Strategic or critical industries are considered important for all of a nation's economic growth (e.g., Council on Competitiveness 1991; Teece 1991; OECD 1991). The main argument for this is that once a country loses its price competitiveness based on low labour cost, it has to be competitive in knowledge-based industries. R&D-intensive industries are the most visible knowledge-based industries because a large share of sales has to be invested in research and development. The most advanced newly industrialised countries in Southeast Asia already experience the price competition from neighbouring countries when foreign manufacturing firms shift their production across the border, witness the move of labour-intensive production from Singapore to Malaysia and from there to Vietnam. R&D-intensive industries are based on the knowledge and skills of the employees and are therefore not as footloose as labour-intensive industries.

The local demand side, however, has often received less attention from national research and technology policy compared to publicly funded research programmes. Gerybadze (1999) notes that especially western European countries follow mostly a national technology leader strategy and insufficiently a national need leader strategy he proposes. This is even more apparent in newly developed countries because local demand is not considered more demanding than the demand in industrialised countries. Market penetration of consumer goods is much lower in Asia compared to the United States and Northern Europe. A high penetration of one good often induces demand for other complementary goods. Local demand is often experienced as a disadvantage of newly industrialised countries in contrast to advanced countries. Technology policy is therefore mostly export oriented and aims to serve the markets of industrialised countries.

For instance, Southeast Asian countries are eager to develop an Internet and multimedia industry because this is seen as a fast-growing industry. But local demand for e-commerce is lower in Asia than in the United States because fewer people have credit cards, which is the main means of payment via the Internet. This lead in credit card and Internet use makes the United States a lead market in e-commerce because credit card use grows with per capita income and Internet hosts are on an exponential growth path in almost every country. For a country that lags the penetration in both Internet and credit card use to adopt multimedia innovations, such as new authorisation protocols or smart cards, in order to avoid credit card payments, which will later be adopted by US customers, seems to be odd because it opposes the worldwide trend and mirrors only the context of a lag country.

Raising the effectiveness of technology policy should take local demand side factors into consideration. This section will present anecdotal evidence that demand in newly industrialised countries can be characterised as the most sophisticated and of high quality. This demand of high quality can be found in industries that are not R&D intensive or not considered strategic. Non-price competitiveness is based on innovations, for which a higher price can be charged than for standardised products. Innovations, however, are not only characteristic of high-technology industries but of many other industries with middle or low R&D intensity as well. Policy to foster national competitiveness should therefore broaden the range of industries to consider beyond only high-tech industries.

As was discussed in Chapter 5, identifying lead market potential is not an easy task. I have tentatively identified several potential lead markets for Southeast Asian countries by applying the lead market factors derived in this thesis.[213] In this chapter I will discuss these industries and the relevant lead market factors which could make Southeast Asian countries internationally competitive.

7.2.1 Container ports and airports

Singapore's port and airport are the leaders in the region. Both have the potential to set the world standards in port services and port equipment as well. The port of Singapore (PSA) is the world leader in port efficiency and the utilisation of port technology.[214] It is the world's biggest container port with a turnaround of 15 Mio. TEUs (Twenty-foot equivalent units). Singapore is strategically located in the traditional European-Asian trading straight between the Asian mainland and the Indonesian archipelago. The British colonialists built Singapore as their main trading post in substitution of the older Portuguese trading post Malacca. Over time Singapore became the dominant transhipment port of Southeast Asia. Around 80 % of the container volume is reloaded to other ships. Large container vessels either collect the containers from smaller vessels from other countries in Asia and

[213] These industries have been found in literature and through interviews with company officials during my research stay in Malaysia.

[214] Porter (1990, p. 75) already mentioned Singapore as a leading country for port services.

ship these to the Americas, Europe and the Middle East or containers from these regions are distributed to Asian countries via Singapore.

Demand advantage: Singapore is at the front of the international trend in transportation and unfolds anticipatory demand. With international trade increasing steadily, cargo turnover at ports and airports is growing in many countries. This is especially true for Asia, where industries are shifting to international production because of the growing Asian population, rising per-capita-income and lower labour cost. The increasing size of container vessels illustrates the trend towards few regional hubs, where containers are reloaded to smaller vessels and distributed to their final destinations within the region.

Singapore port employs the newest technology in cranes, transport vehicles, automation and electronic data exchange. It does so because it benefits early from new technology and it can procure equipment at a cheaper price. Port volumes in transhipment hubs are growing worldwide; container turnaround in the largest ports increased by 14 % annually from 1998 to 1999. As a result, the technology that is profitable to employ in Singapore now will, over time, become profitable in other ports too.

Cost advantage: Equipment employed in Singapore has a relatively large cost reduction potential. Turnover of containers in the Singapore port is threefold the turnover in the largest European, American and Japanese ports. Since equipment is not standardised, cost of equipment is likely to decrease after it is adopted in Singapore.

Singapore has anticipatory costs inducing the employment of equipment that can later be employed in other ports or airports. As a result of its large size, Singapore port has the lowest cost-per-container due to high fix investments and small marginal cost. Compared to Asia the labour cost in Singapore is high and Singapore is eager to become more independent of skilled labour from abroad. In addition, Singapore port enjoys rebates on equipment because of its reputation as a pilot customer, while overall prices for port equipment decrease. The worldwide growing port turnover, increasing labour costs and the downward price trends of equipment supports the adoption of technology employed in Singapore, such as automated cranes and vehicles by other ports.

Market structure advantage: Competition between ports increase with proximity. Although competition in the region lagged the competitive situation in Europe somewhat because of the dominating position of Singapore, new ports in Malaysia and Indonesia will stimulate competition in the region. Malaysia's Westport in the Klang valley near the capital city Kuala Lumpur was recently upgraded to a transhipment container port. Just 25 km across the border to Malaysia a new transhipment port, Tanjung Pelepas, opened in March 2000 aiming at a share of Singapore's load. Traditionally, public authorities manage most of the ports in the world. The international privatisation trend of state assets is slowly beginning to include ports. Singapore port was incorporated in 1998 as the PSA Corp. and will be listed publicly in 2000. The new Malaysian ports are also publicly listed corporations, while most large European ports are still governmental bureaucracies. If the privatisation of ports succeeds, European countries are likely to follow in order to become more competitive.

Transfer advantage: Multinational port operating companies emerge along with privatisation. PSA Corp. started investing in foreign port terminals to use its know-how lead internationally and is now one of the largest port companies in the world. PSA bought licences for container terminals in China, India, the Middle East and Portugal. These foreign ports had a container turnaround of about 1.5 million TEUs (Twenty feet Equivalent Units). This figure it planned to increase to 10 Mio. TEUs in 2007. The transformation from a port authority into a multinational firm facilitates a potent transfer advantage: Singapore port started to transfer its management officers to its foreign ports where they will implement Singapore's management system. Technology that has been adopted in Singapore will, over time, be transferred to the subsidiaries of the Singapore port corporation when the international standardisation within the multinational operations offers sufficient economies of scale and advantages from the transfer of the know-how ownership advantage to its subsidiaries. Using a standard technology worldwide is economically justified if these advantages can compensate for the disadvantages of employing a technology that fits the context in Singapore but is inferior to the context of the foreign subsidiary.

Beyond its multinational operations, Singapore's reputation as a world leader is renowned. Singapore is a demanding and sophisticated customer of equipment. First, Singapore has demanding conditions because of limited space available. Second, the country invests in training and human capital and its know-how and management system is considered the best in the world. Technology employed in Singapore is proven technology that reduces the risk of adoption. Singapore has a reputation of being the most efficient port in the world and the risk of failure of new technology employed is high, since the reliability of a port is the most important competition factor. Shipping lines, too, could push a standard technology employed in ports worldwide. Ports depend on the few large shipping lines to ensure the base load. These shipping lines therefore have the power to request a specific technology that allows them to save time and become more efficient. The test dive and refinement of such a new technology is likely to happen in Singapore on the base of its reputation as the most advanced and competent port and its long time relationship with shipping lines.

Export Advantage: Singapore's disadvantage is limited space and high skill labour shortage. This special context makes Singapore prone to adopt idiosyncratic technological solutions. Yet Singapore is also becoming export oriented to level its own context with the foreign context. Singapore authorities fund national R&D centres that focus on automation and transport communication systems and they support the transfer of indigenous technological designs abroad. Together with the DSO National laboratories and CET Technologies, PSA has developed a navigation system for automated guided vehicles (AGVs) that it intends to commercialise to other ports and also in combination with other application of AGVs.

7.2.2 Health care

A lead market can be a market that offers new service innovations that are demanded worldwide. Trade in services means that the service is done in Asia for foreign customers. Providing high quality health care and related convenience services in the hospital for patients with acute health problems or check up services during holiday trips are growing business opportunities. Private hospitals see patients as customers and offer services to foreign and domestic patients. Although they began as the preferred health centre for expatriate residents, private hospitals in Southeast Asia discovered the demand for better accommodation service among wealthy non-residents. Packages with airport transfer and first class accommodations offer foreign customers an alternative to domestic public hospitals.

For instance, Thailand's Bumrungrad hospital, with 554 beds one of the largest private hospitals in Southeast Asia, offers foreign patients medical treatment and health screening. Health care vacations will be introduced by travel agents and airlines will be aimed at the business traveller market.

Demand advantage: Increasing income will shift preferences towards more service in health care and disease prevention, which general insurance will not cover. Increasing standards of living and a growing middle and upper class not bounded to mandatory medical insurance, the increasing share of elderly people and the progress of health care technology have created a large and growing demand for private health care worldwide. The US Health Industry Manufacturer Association (HIMS) estimates a growth rate of 14 % per year. In contrast to advanced nations a service-oriented demand for personal care is most advanced in Southeast Asia. Cultural traditions, a high inequality of income and the lack of state-managed health insurance facilitate a large segment of private heath care demand.

In addition, the increasing global mobility of people lowers the reluctance to receive medical treatment abroad. The deregulation and liberalisation of the health care business put pressure on insurance companies for better cost efficiency and better incentives for trade in health services. The globalisation of medical insurance companies provides the financial backing for global health care. In addition to western medicine, doctors in China practise Chinese medicine, which is increasingly popular in western countries as an alternative to western orthodox medicine. In Asian hospitals, service personnel may practise acupuncture and teach traditional Chinese exercises like *nei gong*, which can bring relief from insomnia, back pain, asthma and arthritis.

Transfer advantage: Southeast Asia is not a home for many multinational firms. Yet several private multinational firms in the hospital business have emerged in Southeast Asia. One of the largest firms, Parkway group Healthcare, headquartered in Singapore and listed on the stock exchange, operates three hospitals in Singapore, two in Malaysia, three in Indonesia, one in India and one in Britain. It employs the newest medical technology and offers priority service to local and foreign patients. Malaysia's Sime Darby Group owns and operates Subang Jaya Medical Centre. The Landmark group owns a substantial share in Australia's hospital care. Thailand and Malaysia are renowned as service intensive countries. If these countries can add a reputation for high quality medical treatment, a considerable transfer advantage could be built up over time.

Cost advantage: Health care in Southeast Asia holds a strong anticipatory cost advantage. World travel costs will fall, whereas cost of health care will increase. Air travel prices fall in general and especially for long-haul flights because competition is much higher among international flights than among domestic flights in most countries. Today, it is already almost as expensive to travel from Europe to Southeast Asia as it is to travel within Europe. In contrast, health costs are likely to increase steadily because of raising labour costs for intensive personal care and technical progress in medical equipment. As a result, the cost advantage of Southeast Asian countries will increase over time.

Export advantage: A worldwide standardisation of medical equipment and skills ensures that medical services in Asia will match the same high quality levels necessary to attract patients from advanced countries. Medical treatment in newly industrialised countries is shifting more and more from diseases typical for developing countries to diseases caused by civilisation, which prevail in most advanced countries. Training doctors and medical personnel in western countries fosters knowledge about common western diseases and makes good English language skills necessary. This adds to the export orientation of hospitals, i.e. the orientation of demand for medical treatment in advanced countries.

Market structure advantage: Competition in the medical industry is much more intense in Southeast Asian countries than in western countries, where hospitals are state-owned and most of the health care sector is highly regulated. In Asia private hospitals are common and preferred by high-skilled doctors and nurses. Even public hospitals are competitive. Competition comes from medical centres run by entrepreneurial doctors. In Europe private hospitals are rare and mandatory medical insurance prevents competition between health institutions, leaving few incentives for hospitals to provide additional nursing and related convenience services.

7.2.3 Skin and hair care products

The skin and hair care industry is growing in Southeast Asia and many local companies compete successfully in their domestic markets against the largest multinational firms despite large financial and technological resources and a long tradition of market presence of western multinationals such as Unilever and Procter & Gamble in Asia. Asian producers of personal care products are successful with local products that respond to highly demanding customers and not with a low price advantage. While western multinationals promote global standardised brands induced by western demand, local firms can adapt products to the local specific consumer preferences. For instance, some herbs are traditionally used as personal care throughout Southeast Asia. Herbal remidies have a particularly long tradition in China and Indonesia as health and beauty products. Jakarta based Mustika Ratu produces a variety of goods from domestic herbs. Herbs are used as ingredients for shampoos and other hair treatment products in Thailand, Malaysia and the Philippines. Asian firms, however, have not been able to leverage their products worldwide. The reason seems to be mostly the lack of financial resources and market entry barriers of advanced countries. Unlike labour-intensive industries, Asian countries have no cost advantage but still have to compete with innovative products. Although Asian herbs have been successfully introduced in western countries, the country-of-origin effect tends to be a disadvantage for the Asian personal care industry. Only Japanese firms have been able to introduce new formulas for problematic hair treatment worldwide.

On the other hand, Western multinational firms started to use Asian markets as test markets for new shampoo formulas (cf., Czinkota, Ronkainen 1998, p. 549). Unilever introduced its new shampoo Organics in Thailand before it started the global roll out (Kilburn 1997). Colgate uses the Philippines as a global platform for new products like Noriché, which failed the local market test and was taken off the market (Geddes 1994, p. 1-22). Later the new brand Naturals/Plantanics entered the East Asian market. This product has still not been introduced in other markets.

Demand advantage: There are temporary trends in the personal care industry. Western countries tend to be more responsive to functional and high-tech products. As a result, new products are marketed more as innovations resulting from technological progress. Another strong trend in the personal care industry towards natural ingredients such as herbal remedies and vitamins (Source: Euromonitor) opposes the technical products. The trend towards products with a "natural" label is apparent in many food and consumer products. The natural trend is not generally led by one country, but depends on the product. Natural pharmaceuticals such as phytomedicine are strongly demanded in Germany, whereas vitamins are consumed in the United States. The global trend towards natural personal care products has developed most strongly in Southeast Asian countries. Southeast Asian countries are traditionally responsive to new herbal ingredients. This trend could guide local firms to the world market.

Export advantage: Countries with multi-ethnic populations can gain an export and demand advantage when they respond to the preferences of local ethnic groups that share their preferences with culturally related populations of large foreign markets.[215] Malaysia not only hosts a strong Malay ethnic population but also Indian and Chinese minorities; Malays make up only 60 % of the population. Malaysia is used as a test market by a German hair care company because of the Indian and Chinese population that acts as a springboard for the vast Indian and Chinese market.[216] The export advantage derives from a combination of characteristics in one technological design preferred by a mixture of users. Malaysia has a unique society of people of Malay, Chinese and Indian descent. Islamic culture is another export advantage. Malaysia has a considerable Islamic population that is devoted to Islamic rules. Malaysian personal care producers have responded to the market with a range of *halal* products that are sensitive to Islamic rules, i.e. no ingredients from pork and no alcohol. This opens export opportunities for export to Middle Eastern countries. Malays themselves are close to the Thais and the Indonesians in their cultural preferences. All three ethnic groups, the Indians, the Chinese and the Malays, in Malaysia have a higher average income than their cultural relatives outside Malaysia do. Since China and India are expected to maintain a strong growth in per-capita income, Malaysia could be a forecasting laboratory for consumer goods for the markets in South and East Asia.

Cost advantage: Southeast Asian countries still have a cost disadvantage in the personal care industry. Western multinational firms have built up large cost efficient production facilities throughout the world. In addition, the import taxes of many Southeast Asian countries prevent firms in Southeast Asia from building plants of sufficient size from exports to other Asian countries. Taxes for trade within Asian countries, however, are scheduled to be reduced by 2002, allowing firms to export to other Southeast Asian countries and lower their production costs. It is likely that the import tax reductions may have a larger cost effect on domestic Southeast Asian firms than on multinational firms that already operate large facilities. Therefore Asian firms can catch up to the production cost of western firms.

Market structure advantage: The large number of local producers spur competition and maintain a constant flow of innovations. In Malaysia more than 100 small firms operate in the hair care sector. As a result, the variety of products is much higher and the discovery of new consumer trends is more likely in these countries than in the oligopolistic markets in Europe, the United States and Japan. A few large firms dominate the personal care business and the consumer distribu-

---

215 Ohmae (1995) suggests that firms in countries with multi-ethnic populations can respond to a variety of cultural preferences and thus develop innovations that can be exported to their home countries. Singapore is one prominent example for Ohmae. He expects that this multi-ethnic agglomeration can help the local industry create products that can be exported to the vast markets of India and China. This could strengthen two lead market advantages, namely demand anticipation and an export advantage of multi-usage innovations.

216 Personal communication with Wella AG.

tion system in the advanced countries, making market entry costly. Few multinational firms in the personal care industry aim at large market shares with certain brand products and where existing brands are protected by large marketing budgets. More innovations are tested on the Southeast Asian market because market entry is cheaper than elsewhere; the *contestability* of markets is higher.

Transfer advantage: There is a sophisticated demand for personal care in Southeast Asian countries, especially for hair care, because hair has a high status and is washed daily, sometimes several times a day. Dark Asian hair requires more treatment and is not easily coloured than blond hair, which challenges even large western firms that are competent in hair treatment products and operate large research laboratories. This challenge led several firms to establish R&D sites specialised in Asian hair treatment in Southeast Asia.

They still have a transfer disadvantage in many respects, however. Asian multinational firms have not emerged in the personal care industry and the reputation is low for most products compared to France, which is regarded by consumers as the leader in high-quality hair care products. Yet a reputation for quality can be built up over time. The herbal tradition in Asia and the trend towards natural and herbal ingredients in personal care products can be leveraged into a global penetration of new natural products from Asia. The quality perception of consumers depends on their former experience with goods and the image of the country-of-origin. This can vary from product to product regarding the image of the country in the particular product range. In less developed countries technical products like auto vehicles are considered to be of higher quality than the domestic brand if foreign companies build them. On the other hand, consumers often stick to domestic brands of food and beverages because they are adapted to the local taste and regarded as high in quality. Malaysia's effort to develop a domestic motor vehicle will require import duties on foreign models for a long time since the image of domestic cars in comparison to foreign cars will change only over time. On the other hand, domestic products in the food and personal care industries have high market shares without the protection of tariff and non-tariff import restrictions. This indicates that the home market in these industries can be used as a springboard for foreign products if the worldwide reputation can be actively fostered.

7.3 Lag Market Policies

A lag market adopts a technological design that was adopted before in other countries. A lag market can be the result of an overall low "innovativeness" of the local users or of idiosyncratic demand. Idiosyncratic demand leads to the adoption of a technological design that is not adopted by other countries and is even abandoned later in favour of the lead market's dominant design because the lead market design has gathered advantages that compensate the disadvantage of a foreign design in the domestic environment. As a result, a lag market with idiosyncratic demand for innovations is likely to induce technologies that cannot be exported and may become import intensive when domestic users switch to the lead market design.

National technology policies in lag countries are prone to worsen the competitive disadvantage of a lag market. In a lag country, the government often feels obliged to sponsor the development and adoption of domestic innovations. This is so either because it perceives that the domestic lack of demand for innovations may weaken the national technological base or because it feels the reluctance of multinational firms to respond to the idiosyncratic domestic need for innovations. Nevertheless, even if local users adopt indigenous technologies, the context of a lag country has no leverage advantage to lead the worldwide adoption and diffusion process. The government's policy is likely to face an uphill battle against the lead market design. A lag market government that attempts to lead the adoption of innovation tends to misguide local firms into adopting idiosyncratic technological designs than adopting the globally dominant design. The adoption of idiosyncratic technological design can weaken related industries as well, such as firms that produce complementary goods. Idiosyncratic technologies are likely to induce demand for idiosyncratic complementary goods and weaken the demand for globally dominant complementary goods.

A policy option of a country with an idiosyncratic innovative market is to change the idiosyncratic context if the idiosyncratic context is related to governmental regulation or institutions. Another option of technology policy in a lag market is to not be preoccupied with supporting the country in its quest to become a lead market but to consider the prospect of being an efficient lag market. Lag market technology policies can even be more important than lead market policies. First of all, most countries will be lag markets for most products and technologies, since there are only a few lead markets. Second, it seems unlikely that governments can change a national lag market context into a lead market context.

In contrast, an efficient technology policy of a lag country would be to facilitate and support a fast follower strategy for domestic firms.[217] Domestic firms in a lag country can gain a competitive advantage if they quickly follow a lead market, adopt the innovation design favoured in the lead market, transfer technology from the lead market, receive the knowledge generated in the early learning processes of the pioneer companies and imitate the lead market design. Technology policy can pro-actively follow the lag market prospect by supporting the country's users

[217] There are a variety of additional marketing strategies for companies in lag markets. Firms in lag markets can acquire or establish manufacturing plants in the lead markets in order to re-import to lag markets to use the country-of-origin effect and use the image of the lead market. Or they can simply name and present their own brands as if they came from the lead market. For instance, a fragrance firm in Malaysia, Unza, gave its perfumed personal care products French product names, its split-hair treatment products a Japanese brand name and its male fragrance line an Italian brand name.

and manufacturers to swiftly follow the lead market and by lowering the responsiveness of local firms to the local idiosyncratic demand. Governmental policies, regulation and procurement can strengthen the lead market orientation of local firms. Regulation and public procurement should be opened or even biased to foreign technological designs. National technology policy can encourage cooperation between domestic firms and firms in the lead market.

Lag market policies can support the adoption of the foreign lead market designs if the lead market can be identified. Often a lead market is apparent by the highest penetration rates of an innovation or complementary good worldwide. But the lead market is unknown for innovations that have not been introduced in the market. However, it is probably easier to identify a lag market than the lead market. For instance, if a country lags in the construction of infrastructure or the availability of complementary goods is low compared to other countries then domestic policy can follow a lag market approach of learning and technology transfer. If the market context is very different from other markets' contexts and is not at the front of a global trend, domestic policy should not support the development of domestic technologies and instead should support the adaptation of foreign designs to the domestic context. A government can even actively support the compensation of the disadvantage of foreign design compared to domestic designs. This policy is somewhat counter-intuitive and a domestic (non-multinational) firm would oppose this policy. In the long run, however, the adoption of a dominant design through licenses or cross-border cooperations seems to be more successful in terms of exports and participation in the globally prevailing technology path than trying to impose a domestic (lag market) design on the world market as a globally dominant design.

7.4 Conclusions

Besides their resource-based competitiveness, countries can successfully foster domestic new technologies in which they hold a potential lead market advantage. I have argued in this thesis that although a government cannot actively create local demand that leads to exports by local firms, it can support a lead market potential in creating an environment that supports competition, innovation, adoption and demand preference transparency. On the other hand, lag market countries need a different policy approach. Lag countries with idiosyncratic demand are prone to lock-in to idiosyncratic technical designs that cannot be exported and are likely to be abandoned later altogether. The technology policy of lag markets should support a fast follower strategy of local firms instead of sponsoring the development of indigenous technologies. Support of the export orientation is important for both lead market and lag market technology policies.

Lead market policies are not confined to advanced countries. The market context in newly industrialised countries can conceal lead market advantages as well.

Technology policies for newly developed countries are considered to be more effective if they are focused on industries in which the countries have lead market advantages. But it is more difficult for newly industrialised countries to leverage their demand advantages in the world market because domestic firms face tough competition from established multinational firms of advanced countries in the triad. In these industries the infant industry argument[218] holds because established multinational firms have the power to squeeze small domestic firms in less developed countries. Market entry in highly developed countries is expensive and multinational firms protect their home market ground. The infant industry argument does not seem to be promising in industries in which the country is a lag market and is likely to remain one. Because the industry in a lag market will always be disadvantaged by the domestic lag market context after the catch up process, the domestic firms will continue to pressure the government to keep the import protection, R&D subsidiaries and other support programmes.

[218] The infant industry argument has existed since the 19th century as a policy to foster domestic industry and protect it from international competition. Asian countries such as Japan and Korea are said to have established internationally successful industries because of these protectionism policies (Mowery, Nelson 1999).

Appendix

History of GSM in Brief

1979	World Administrative Radio Conference (WARC) set aside 900 MHz band for mobile telephony in Europe, not available in the USA, instead: 800 MHz.
1982	CEPT working group on pan-European cellular system initiated by Scandinavian and Dutch PTTs Chairman Thomas Haug, Telecom Sweden. CEPT comprised the telecoms administrations of twenty six European countries. Not exciting, not the decisive step: many working group were not successful.
1984	French PTT decides to invest in analog interim system Radiocom 2000. German-French analog cellular proposal rejected at French-German political level. Bilateral agreement to develop digital system for the 1990s. Formation of group special mobile (GSM)
1985	Italy and UK joins bilateral agreement. Cooperation of GSM group with CEPT working group. Heavy R&D investments by German, French PTTs and firms for digital systems.
1986 Jun.	Formation of permanent nucleus of GSM in Paris Preparation of invitation of tender for a GSM system
Nov.-Jan 87	Test in Paris of eight proposals for a GSM system
1987 Feb.	Madeira: on technical level proposal for narrowband GSM against French-German wideband solution (technical superiority of broadband against economic and frequency economy advantages of narrowband) Narrowband was better in basic parameters
1987 Mai	In Bonn Ministerial level accepts compromise of narrowband solution.
1987 Jun.	GSM conference in Brüssel agrees narrowband compromise with no exception.
1987 Sept.	Memorandum of Understanding (MoU) of 13 European countries.
1988 Feb.	Invitation-to-tender by operators of all 13 MoU countries
1989	Dti paper: "Phones on the move" personal communication no car application only, mass market beyond vehicles, substitution of fixed line access possible; but PCN leads to DCS 1800 and GSM 1800 only, because GSM achieves the same idea.
1992	First GSM service offered in Finland

References

Abernathy, William J., James M. Utterback, 1978, Patterns of Innovation in Industry, *Technology Review* 80 (7), 40-47.

Abramowitz, Moses, 1986, Catching up, Forging Ahead and Falling Behind, *Journal of Economic History* 46 (2), 385-406.

Acs, Zoltan, David Audretsch, Maryann Feldman, 1992, Real Effects of Academic Research: Comment, *American Economic Research* 82, 363-367.

Äkermarck, Mikael, 1999, Telecommunications in Finland – A Statistical Overview, Paper presented at the 2nd World Telecommunication Indicators Meeting, 29-31 March, Geneva.

Albach, Horst, 1993, *Culture and Technical Innovation: A Cross-Cultural Analysis and Policy Recommendations*, Akad. d. Wiss. zu Berlin, Working Group Culture and Technical Innovation, Berlin: de Gruyter.

Albach, Horst, Diana de Pay, Raul Rojas, 1989, Der Innovationsprozeß bei kulturspezifisch unterschiedlich innovationsfreudigen Konsumenten, *Zeitschrift für Betriebswirtschaft* Ergänzungsheft (1), 109-129.

Alberts, Sönke, 1999, Adoption und Akzeptanz von Nutzungsinnovationen im Bereich der Neuen Medien, Paper presented at the Ersten Fachtagung der Kommssion Technologie- und Innovationsmanagement, October 29th, Cottbus.

Altshuler, Alan A., M. Anderson, D. T. Jones, D. Roos, J. Womack, 1984, *The Future of the Automobile: The Report of MIT's International Automobile Program*, London: Allen & Unwin.

Amin, Ash, Nigel J. Thrift (eds.), 1994, *Globalization, Institutions, and Regional Development in Europe*, Oxford: Oxford University Press.

An, Mark Y., Nicholas M. Kiefer, 1995, Local Externalities and Societal Adoption of Technologies, *Journal of Evolutionary Economics* 5, 193-117.

Anand, Jaideep, Bruce Kogut, 1997, Technological Capabilities of Countries, Firm Rivalry and Foreign Direct Investment, *Journal of International Business Studies* 28 (Third Quarter), 445-465.

Anderson, Esben Sloth, Bent Dalum, Gert Villumsen, 1981, International Specialisation and the Home Market – an Empirical Analysis, Industrial Development Research Series No. 19, Research Report, Aalborg University Press.

Anderson, Philip, Michael L. Tushman, 1990, Technological Discontinuities and Dominant Designs: A Cyclical Model of Technological Change, *Administrative Science Quarterly* 35 (December), 604-633.

Andersson, Fredrik, 1992, The International Diffusion of New Drugs: A Comparative Study of Seven Industrialized Countries, *Journal of Research in Pharmaceutical Economics* 4 (2), 43-62.

Anselin, Luc, Attila Varga, Zoltan Acs, 1997, Local Geographic Spillovers Between University Research and High Technology Innovations, *Journal of Urban Economics* 42, 422-448.

Anthony, Julie M., 1993, Family Feud, *Cellular Business* 10 (10), 20.

Anthony, Julie M., 1994, Digital Status Report, *Cellular Business* 11 (6), 44.

Antonelli, Christiano, 1986, The International Diffusion of New Information Technologies, *Research Policy* 15, 139-147.

Antonelli, Christiano, 1998, The Dynamics of Localized Technological Changes: The Interaction Between Factor Costs Inducement, Demand Pull and Schumpeterian Rivalry, *Economics of Innovation and New Technologies* 6, 97-120.

Armstrong, Mark, 1997, Competition in Telecommunications, *Oxford Review of Economic Policy* 13 (1), 64-82.

Arrow, Kenneth, 1962a, Economic Welfare and the Allocation of Resources for Invention, in: R. Nelson (ed.), *The Rate and Direction of Inventive Activity: Economic and Social Factors*, Princeton: Princeton University Press, 609-702.

Arrow, Kenneth, 1962b, The Economic Implications of Learning by Doing, *Review of Economic Studies* 29, 155-173.

Arthur D. Little, 1997, *Priority Issues in Technology and Innovation Management*, ADL Inc.

Arthur, Brian, 1989, Competing Technologies, Increasing Returns and Lock-In by Historical Events, *Economic Journal* 99, 116-131.

Arthur, Brian, 1990, Positive Feedbacks in the Economy, *Scientific American* 262 (February), 80-85.

Atal, B. S., J. R. Remde, 1982, A New Model of LPC Excitation for Producing Natural-Sounding Speech at Low Bit Rates, Proceedings of the International Conference on Acoustics Speech and Signal Processing, 614-617.

Audretsch, David B., 1995, *Innovation and Industry Evolution*, Cambridge: The MIT Press.

Audretsch, David B., 1996, International Diffusion of Technological Knowledge, in: G. Koopmann, H.-E. Scharrer (eds.), *The Economics of High-Technology Competition and Cooperation in Global Markets*, Baden-Baden: Nomos, 107-135.

Ayal, Igal, Jehiel Zif, 1979, Market Expansion Strategies in Multinational Marketing, *Journal of Marketing* 43 (Spring), 84-94.

Ayu, Asando, 1999, Mobile Nation, *Look Japan*, October, 7-12.

Balassa, Bela, 1965, Trade Liberalisation and "Revealed" Comparative Advantage, *The Manchester School of Economic and Social Studies* 33 (2), 99-123.

Barré, Raymond, 1995, Relationships Between Multinational Firms' Technology Strategy and National Innovation Systems, in: OECD (ed.), *Innovation, Patents and Technological Strategies*, Paris, 201-222.

Barro, Robert J., 1991, Economic Growth in a Cross Section of Countries, *Quarterly Journal of Economics* 106, 407-444.

Bartlett, Christopher A., Sumantra Ghoshal, 1986, Tap Your Subsidiary for Global Reach, *Harvard Business Review* 64 (November-December), 87-94.

Bartlett, Christopher A., Sumantra Ghoshal, 1989, *Managing the Global Firm: The Transnational Solution*, Cambridge: MIT Press.

Bartlett, Christopher A., Sumantra Ghoshal, 1990, Managing Innovation in the Transnational Corporation, in: Bartlett, Ch., Y. Doz, G. Hedlund (eds.), 215-255.

Bartlett, Christopher A., Sumantra Ghoshal, 1995, *Transnational Management: Textes, Cases and Readings in Cross-Border Management*, 2. ed., Chicago et al.: Irwin.

Bartlett, Christopher A., Yves Doz, Gunnar Hedlund (eds.), 1990, *Managing the Global Firm*, London: Routledge.

Bass, Frank M., 1969, A New Product Growth Model for Consumer Durables, *Management Science* 15 (5), 215-227.

Baumol, William J., John C. Panzar, Robert D. Willig, 1982, *Contestable Markets and the Theory of Industry Structure*, New York: Harcourt Brace Jovanovich.

Beckmann, Christoph, 1997, *Internationalisierung von Forschung und Entwicklung in multinationalen Unternehmen*, Aachen: Shaker Verlag.

Beckmann, Christoph, Joachim Fischer, 1994, Einflußfaktoren auf die Internationalisierung von Forschung und Entwicklung in der deutschen Chemischen und Pharmazeutischen Industrie, *Zeitschrift für betriebswirtschaftliche Forschung* 46 (7/8), 630-657.

Behrman, Jack N., William A. Fischer, 1980, *Overseas R&D Activities of Transnational Companies*, Cambridge, Mass.: Oelgeschlager, Gunn & Hain.

Beise, Marian, 1999, Internationalisierung technologischer Kompetenzen in der Telekommunikationstechnik, in: G. Reger, M. Beise, H. Belitz (eds.), 109-140.

Beise, Marian, Birgit Gehrke, et al., 1998, *Zur regionalen Konzentration von Innovationspotentialen in Deutschland*, ZEW-Dokumentation 98-09, Mannheim.

Beise, Marian, Heike Belitz, 1997, *Internationalisierung von Forschung und Entwicklung in multinationalen Unternehmen*, Report submitted to the Federal ministry of Research and Technology, Berlin, Mannheim.

Beise, Marian, Heike Belitz, 1998, Trends in the Internationalisation of R&D – The German Perspective, *DIW Vierteljahrsheft* 67 (2), 67-85.

Beise, Marian, Heike Belitz, Christopher Grenzmann, 1998, *Indicators for R&D Investments of Multinational Enterprises*, Paper presented at the Joint NESTI/TIP/GSS Workshop "New S&T Indicators for a Knowledge-based Economy", June 17 1998, Paris, Room Document No. 10.

Beise, Marian, Thomas Cleff (2000), Predicting Lead Markets for Innovations, mimeo, Mannheim.

Belitz, Heike, Marian Beise, 1999, Trends in the Internationalisation of R&D – The German Perspective, in: R. Barell, N. Pain (eds.), *Innovation, Investment and the Diffusion of Technology in Europe German Direct Investment and Economic Growth in Postwar Europe*, Cambridge: Cambridge University Press, 89-119.

Bennett, Colin J., 1991, Review Article: What is Policy Convergence and What Causes it? *British Journal of Policy Studies* 21, 21-233.

Bennett, Colin J., 1997, Understanding Ripple Effects: The Cross-National Adoption of Policy Instruments for Bureaucratic Accountability, *Governance* 10 (3), 213-233.

Benvignati, Antia M., 1982, Origin and Diffusion of Industrial Innovation, *Economica* 49, 313-323.

Berresford, John W., 1989, The Impact of Law and Regulation on Technology: The Case History of Cellular Radio, *Business Lawer* 44, 721-735.

Binswanger, Hans, Vernon Ruttan, 1978, *Induced Innovation: Technology, Institutions, and Development*, Baltimore, London: John Hopkins University Press.

Birkinshaw, Julian, 1996, How Multinational Subsidiary Mandates are Gained and Lost, *Journal of International Business Studies* 27 (3), 467-495.

Birkinshaw, Julian, Allen J. Morrison, 1995, Configurations of Strategy and Structure in Subsidiaries of Multinational Corporations, *Journal of International Business Studies* 26 (4), 729-753.

Blake, Gary, 1999, Ten 'Biggest' Problems Technology Leaders Face, *Research Technology Management* 42 (6), 13-14.

Böhm, Manfred, 1980, Der bewegliche Teilnehmer – ein Stiefkind der Kommunikation, *VDE-Fachberichte*, Band 31, 146-156.

Böhm, Manfred, 1987, Chancen und Risiken des paneuropäischen digitalen Mobiltelefons, mimeo.

Böhmer, Alexander von, 1995, *Internationalisierung industrieller Forschung und Entwicklung: Typen, Bestimmungsgründe und Erfolgsbeurteilung*, Wiesbaden: DUV.

Bös, Dieter, Wolfgang Peters, 1988, Privatisation, Internal Control, and Internal Regulation, *Journal of Public Economics* 36, 231-258.

Bowers, Raymond, Alfred M. Lee, Cary Hershey (eds.), 1978, *Communications for a Mobile Society: An Assessment of New Technology*, Beverly Hills, London: Sage.

Brander, James A., Barbara Spencer, 1985, Export Subsidies and International Market Share Rivalry, *Journal of International Economics* 18, 83-100.

Brezis, Elise S., Paul Krugman, Daniel Tsiddon, 1993, Leapfrogging in International Competition: A Theory of Cycles in National Technological Leadership, *American Economic Review* 83 (5), December, 1211-1219.

Brockhoff, Klaus, 1990, *Stärken und Schwächen industrieller Forschung und Entwicklung: Umfrageergebnisse aus der Bundesrepublik Deutschland*, Stuttgart: Poeschel.

Brockhoff, Klaus, 1992, *Forschung und Entwicklung: Planung und Kontrolle*, 3rd Ed., München, Wien: Oldenbourg.

Brockhoff, Klaus, 1998, *Der Kunde im Innovationsprozess*, Joachim Jungius-Gesellschaft der Wissenschaften, Göttingen: Vandenhoeck und Ruprecht.

Brockhoff, Klaus, Alexander v. Böhmer, 1993, Global R&D Activities of German Industrial Firms, *Journal of Scientific & Industrial Research* 52, 399-406.

Brooks, Harvey, 1994, The Relationship Between Science and Technology, *Research Policy* 23, 477-486.

Buhrmann, Michael, 1997, D-AMPS: The Quiet Global Success Story, *Telecommunications* 31 (10), 48-60.

Buzzell, Robert D., 1968, Can You Standardize Multinational Marketing? *Harvard Business Review* 46 (Nov./Dec.), 102-113.

Calhoun, George, 1988, *Cellular Mobile Radio Telephony*, Norwood, MA: Artech House.

Camagni, Roberto (ed.), 1991, *Innovation Networks: Spatial Perspectives*, London: Belhaven.

Cantwell, John, 1995, The Globalisation of Technology: What Remains of the Product Life Cycle? *Cambridge Journal of Economics* 19 (1), 155-174.

Cantwell, John, Odile Janne, 1999, Technological Globalisation and Innovative Centres: The Role of Corporate Technological Leadership and Locational Hierarchy, *Research Policy* 28 (2/3), 119-144.

Casson, Mark, Satwinder Singh, 1993, Corporate Research and Development Strategies: The Influence of Firm, Industry and Country Factors on the Decentralisation of R&D, *R&D Management* 23 (2), 91-107.

Cattaneo, Gabriella, 1994, The Making of a Pan-European Network as a Path Dependency Process: The Case of GSM Versus IBC Network, in: G. Pogorel (ed.), *Global Telecommunications Strategies and Technical Change*, Amsterdam: Elsevier, 59-79.

Cave, Martin, Peter Williamson, 1996, Entry, Competition, and Regulation in UK Telecommunications, *Oxford Review of Economic Policy* 12 (4), 100-121.

Chandler, Alfred D., 1990, *Scale and Scope*, Cambridge: Harvard University Press.

Chemical Week, 1996, Competing Software Muscles in on SAP, Vol. 158 (32), 28.

Chen, Yu-Min, Hirokazu Takada, 1994, Estimating the Geographical Diffusion of the Video Cassette Recorder Market, *Empirical Economics* 19, 451-472.

Cheng, Joseph L.C., Douglas S. Bolon, 1993, The Management of Multinational R&D: A Neglected Topic in International Business Research, *Journal of International Business Studies* 24 (First quarter), 1-18.

Chou, Chien, Oz Shy, 1990, Network Effects Without Network Externalities, *International Journal of Industrial Organisation* 8, 259-270.

Christensen, Clayton M., 1997, *The Innovator's Dilemma: When New Technologies Cause Great Firms to Fail*, Boston, Mass.: Harvard Business School Press.

Clark, Kim B., 1985, The Interaction of Design Hierarchies and Market Concepts in Technological Evolution, *Research Policy* 14, 235-251.

Cooper, Robert G., Elko J. Kleinschmidt, 1987, Success Factors in Product Innovation, *Industrial Marketing Management* 16, 215-223.

Coopersmith, Jonathan, 1993, Facsimile's False Starts, *IEEE Spectrum*, February, 46-49.

Cordell, Arthur J., 1973, Innovation, the Multinational Corporation: Some Implications for National Science Policy, *Long Range Planning* 6 (3), 22-29.

Cornish, Susan L., 1997, Product Innovation and the Spatial Dynamics of Market Intelligence: Does Proximity to Markets Matter? *Economic Geography* 73 (2), 143-165.

Council on Competitiveness, 1991, *Gaining New Ground: Technology Priorities for America's Future*, Washington, D.C.

Council on Competitiveness, 1998, *Going Global: The New Shape of American Innovation*, Washington, D.C.

Cowan, Robin, 1990, Nuclear Power Reactors: A Study in Technological Lock-In, *Journal of Economic History* 50 (3), 541-567.

Cowan, Robin, 1991a, Tortoise and Hares: Choices Among Technologies of Unknown merit, *Economic Journal* 101, 801-814.

Cowan, Robin, 1991b, Technological Variety and Competition: Issues of Diffusion and Intervention, in: OECD, *Technology and productivity: The Challenge for Economic Policy*, Paris, 509-521.

Cowan, Robin, John H. Miller, 1998, Technological Standards With Local Externalities and Decentralized Behaviour, *Journal of Evolutionary Economics* 8 (3), 285-296.

Cowan, Robin, William Cowan, 1998a, On Clustering in the Location of R&D: Statics and Dynamics, *Economics of Innovation and New Technology* 6, 201-229.

Cowan, Robin, William Cowan, 1998b, Technological Standardization With and Without Borders in an Interaction Agents Model, mimeo.

Craig, Samuel C., Susan P. Douglas, Andreas Grein, 1992, Patterns of Convergence and Divergence Among Industrialized Nations: 1960-1988, *Journal of International Business Studies* 23, Fourth Quarter, 773-787.

Craig, Samuel C., Susan P. Douglas, 2000, *International Marketing Research*, 2nd Ed., Chichester et al.: Wiley.

Crandall, Robert W., 1988, Surprises From Telephone Deregulation and the AT&T Divestiture, *AEA Papers and Proceedings* 78 (2), 323-327.

Creamer, Daniel, 1976, *Overseas Research and Development by United States Multinationals, 1966-1975*, Report No. 685, New York: The Conference Board.

Cvar, Marquise R., 1986, Case Studies in Global Competition: Patterns of Success and Failure, in: M. E. Porter (ed.), *Competition in Global Industries*, Boston: Harvard Business School Press, 483-516.

Czinkota, Michael R., Ilkaa A. Ronkainen, 1998, *International Marketing*, 5th Ed., Fort Worth, Philadelphia et al.: Dryden Press.

Dalton, Donald H., Manuel G. Serapio Jr., 1993, *U.S. Research Facilities of Foreign Companies*, U.S. Department of Commerce, Washington, D.C.

Dalton, Donald H., Manuel G. Serapio Jr., 1995, *Globalizing Industrial Research and Development*, U.S. Department of Commerce, Washington, D.C.

Davelaar, Evert Jan, Peter Nijkamp, 1997, Spatial Dispersion of Technological Innovation: A Review, in: C. S. Bertuglia, S. Lombardo, P. Nijkamp (eds.), *Innovative Behaviour in Space and Time*, Heidelberg: Springer, 17-40.

David, Paul A., 1975, *Technical Choice, Innovation and Economic Growth*, Cambridge: Cambridge University Press.

David, Paul A., 1985, Clio and the Economics of QWERTY, *American Economic Review* 75, 332-337.

David, Paul A., 1993, Path-Dependencies and Predictability in Dynamic Systems With Local Externalities: A Paradigm for Historical Economics, in: D. Foray, C. Freeman (eds.), *Technology and the Wealth of Nations: The Dynamics of Constructed Advantage*, London: Pinter, 208-231.

David, Paul A., Dominique Foray, Jean-Michel Dalle, 1998, Marshallian Externalities and the Emergence and Spatial Stability of Technological Enclaves, *Economic Innovation of New Technologies* 8, 147-182.

David, Paul A., Dominique Foray, 1994, Dynamics of Competitive Technology Diffusion Through Local Network Structures: The Case of EDI Standardisation, in: L. Leydesdorff, P. Van den Besselaar (eds.), *Evolutionary Economics and Chaos Theory: New Directions in Technology Studies*, London: Pinter, 63-78

Davidson, William H., Richard Harrigan, 1977, Key Decisions in International Marketing: Introducing New Products abroad, *Columbia Journal of World Business* 12, Winter, 15-23.

Davies, Stephen, 1979, *The Diffusion of Process Innovations*, Cambridge: Cambridge University Press.

Deaton, Angus, John Muellbauer, 1980, *Economics and Consumer Behavior*, Cambridge, Mass: Cambridge University Press.

Dekimpe, Marnik G., Philip M. Parker, Miklos Sarvary, 1998a, Staged Estimation of International Diffusion Models: An Application to Global Cellular Telephone Adoption, *Technological Forecasting and Social Change* 57, 105-132.

Dekimpe, Marnik G., Philip M. Parker, Miklos Sarvary, 1998b, "Globalisation": Modeling Technology Adoption Timing Across Countries, INSEAD working paper No. 98/69/MKT.

Dekimpe, Marnik G., Philip M. Parker, Miklos Sarvary, 1998c, Multi-Market and Global Diffusion, INSEAD working paper No. 98/73/MKT.

DeMeyer, Arnoud, 1993, Internationalizing R&D Improves a Firm's Technical Learning, *Research Technology Management* 36 (2), 42-49.

Department of Trade and Industry (DTI), 1999, *Moving into the Information Age: An International Benchmarking Study 1999*, London.

Dertouzos, Michael L., Richard K. Lester, Robert M. Solow, 1989, *Made in America: Regaining the Productivity Edge*, Cambridge, Mass.: MIT Press.

Dichter, Ernest, 1962, The World Customer, *Harvard Business Review* 40 (4), 113-122.

Dolowitz, David, David Marsh, 1996, Who Learns What from Whom: A Review of the Policy Transfer Literature, *Political Studies* 44, 343-357.

Dörrenbächer, Christoph, 1999, *Vom Hoflieferanten zum Global Player*, Berlin: Ed. sigma.

Dosi, Giovanni, 1982, Technological Paradigms and Technological Trajectories: A Suggested Interpretation of the Determinants and Directs of Technical Change, *Research Policy* 11, 147-162.

Dosi, Giovanni, 1988, Sources, Procedures and Microeconomic Effects of Innovation, *Journal of Economic Literature* 26, 1120-1171.

Dosi, Giovanni, Keith Pavitt, Luc Soete, 1990, *The Economics of Technical Change and International Trade*, New York et al.: Harvester Wheatsheaf.

Douglas, Susan P., Yoram Wind, 1987, The Myth of Globalisation, *Columbia Journal of World Business* 22, Winter, 19-29.

Doz, Yves, 1986, *Strategic Management in Multinational Companies*, Oxford.

Drexel, Michael, 1999, Japan Set to Play Leading Role in Mobile Market, *Computerworld Hong Kong*, April 19th.

Dunning, John H., 1979, Explaining Changing Patterns of International Production: In Defence of the Eclectic Theory, *Oxford Bulletin of Economics and Statistics* 41, 269-295.

Dwyre, Douglas, 1998, New Satellite Services to Bridge the Gap, *Telecommunications* 32 (12), 47-49.

Echikson William, 1994, Nokia: How to Win Markets Fast, *Fortune* 129 (11), 114.

Economist, 1995, Hello Japan? Are you There?, August 12th, European Edition, 60.

Economist, 1996, Germany Drops the Drivers, Dec 7th, International edition, 57-58.

Economist, 1998, Will it Play in Penang?, May 2nd, European Edition, 65-66.

Economist, 1999a, America is Going Soft, April 3rd, European Edition, 81-82.

Economist, 1999b, Fuel Cells Hit the Road, April 24th, European Edition, 91-92

Economist, 1999c, Survey Telecommunications, European edition, October 9th.

Economist, 2000a, The Formula That Drives Formula One, European edition, February 26th, 109-110.

Economist, 2000b, Battle of the Airwaves, European Edition, July 29th, 61-62.

Edquist, Charles, Staffan Jacobsson, 1988, *Flexible Automation. The Global Diffusion of New Technology in the Engineering Industry*, Oxford: Basil Blackwell.

EITO, 1997, *European Information Technology Observatory 97*, Frankfurt.

Etemad, Hamid G., 1983, World Product Mandating in Perspective, in: A. Rugman (ed.), *Multinationals and Technology Transfer: The Canadian Experience*, New York: Praeger.

European Commission, 1997a, *Telecommunications Equipment*, The Single Market Review Subseries I: Impact on Manufacturing, Vol. 8, Luxembourg.

European Commission, 1997b, *Second European Report on Science and Technology Indicators*, Luxembourg.

Fagerberg, Jan, 1995, User-Producer Interaction, Learning and Comparative Advantage, *Cambridge Journal of Economics* 19, 243-256.

Fagerberg, Jan, 1988, International Competitiveness, *Economic Journal* 98, 355-374.

Fagerberg, Jan, 1992, The Home Market Hypothesis Re-Examined: The Impact of Domestic User-Producer Interaction on Export Specialisation, in: B.-A. Lundvall (ed.), *National Systems of Innovation,* London, New York: Pinter, 226-239.

Fagerberg, Jan, 1994, Technology and International Differences in Growth Rates, *Journal of Economic Literature* 32, 1147-1175.

Farell, Joseph, Garth Saloner, 1985, Standardisation, Compatibility, and Innovation, *Rand Journal of Economics* 16, 70-83.

Farley, Tom, 1999, *Digital Wireless Basics*, http://www.privateline.com/PCS/history.htm

Fayerweather, John, 1969, *International Business Management: A Conceptual Framework*, New York: McGraw-Hill.

Feder, Barnaby J., 2000, Lacking Buyer, Iridium is Set to Shut Down, *The New York Times*, March 18th, C.1.

Feldman, Maryann P., 1994, *The Geography of Innovation*, Dordrecht: Kluwer.

Findlay, Ronald, 1978, Relative Backwardness, Direct Foreign Investment, and the Transfer of Technology: A Simple Dynamic Model, *Quarterly Journal of Economics* 62 (1), 1-16.

Flichy, Patrice, 1991, *Une histoire de la communication moderne: espace public et vie privâee*, Paris: Ed. la Découverte.

Florida, Richard, 1997, The Globalisation of R&D: Results of a Survey of Foreign-Affiliated R&D laboratories in the USA, *Research Policy* 26 (1), 85-103.

Florida, Richard, Martin Kenney, 1994, The Globalisation of Japanese R&D: The Economic Geography of Japanese R&D Investment in the United States, *Economic Geography* (October), 344-369.

Fors, Gunnar, 1997, Utilization of R&D Results in the Home and Foreign Plants of Multinationals, *Journal of Industrial Economics* 45 (2), 341-358.

Forsgren, Mats, Ulf Holm, Jan Johanson, 1995, Division Headquarters go Abroad – A Step in the Internationalisation of the Multinational Corporation, *Journal of Management Studies* 32 (4), 475-491.

Forward Concepts, 1999, North American Digital Cellular Technologies & DSP Market Opportunities, Research report, Arizona.

Frank, Björn, 1992, *Internationale Entwicklungsmuster zellularen Mobilfunks*, WIK Diskussionsbeiträge Nr. 83, Bad Honnef.

Franko, Lawrence G., 1976, *The European Multinationals*, London: Harper & Row.

Fransman, Martin, 1992, Japanese Failure in a High-Tech Industry? The Case of Central Office Telecommunications Switches, *Telecommunications Policy* 16 (3), 259-276.

Fransman, Martin, 1995, *Japan's Computer and Communications Industry: The Evolution of Industrial Giants and Global Competitiveness*, Oxford: Oxford University Press.

Freeman, Chris, Luc Soete, 1997, *The Economics of Industrial Innovation*, Cambridge: MIT Press.

Freiberger, Paul, Michael Swaine, 1984, *Fire in the Valley: The Making of the Personal Computer*, Berkeley: Osborne/MCGraw-Hill.

Frey, Jeffrey, Alfred Lee, 1978, Technologies for Land Mobile Communications 900 MHz Systems, in: Bowers et al. (eds.), 35-65.

Fudenberg, Drew, Jean Tirole, 1985, Preemption and Rent Equalisation in the Adoption of New Technology, *Review of Economic Studies* 52, 383-401.

Funk, Jeffrey L., 1997, The Competition Between Regional Standards and the Success and Failure of Firms in the World-Wide Mobile Communication Market, *Kobe Economic & Business Review* 42, 137-161.

Gabor, André, Clive Granger, 1966, Prices as Index of Quality – Report on an Inquiry, *Economica* 33, 43-70.

Galbraith, Michael, 1993, Japan Courts Asia With Renamed Digital Cellular Standard, *Telephony* 224, March 22nd, 9.

Ganesh, Jaishankar, V. Kumar, Velavan Subramaniam, 1997, Learning Effects in Multinational Diffusion of Consumer Durables: An Exploratory Investigation, *Journal of the Academy of Marketing Science* 25 (3), 214-228.

Garnier, Gerard H., 1982, Context and Decision Making Autonomy in the Foreign Affiliates of U.S. Multinational Corporations, *Academy of Management Review* 25, 893-908.

Garrett, John, 1984, TACS: the U.K. Standard for Cellular Radio, *Telephony*, July 23rd, 58-64.

Gassmann, Oliver, 1997, *Internationales F&E-Management*, München, Wien: Oldenbourg.

Gatignon, Hubert, Jehoshua Eliashberg, Thomas S. Robertson, 1989, Modelling Multinational Diffusion Patterns: An Efficient Methodology, *Marketing Science* 8 (3), 231-247.

Geddes, Andrew, 1994, Colgate Tries Thai for Global Entry, *Advertising Age International*, May 16th, I-22.

Gehrke, Birgit, Hariolf Grupp, 1994, *Innovationspotential und Hochtechnologie: Technologische Position Deutschlands im internationalen Wettbewerb*, 2. A., Heidelberg: Physica.

Gemünden, Hans Georg, 1981, *Innovationsmarketing: Interaktionsbeziehungen zwischen Hersteller und Verwender innovativer Investitionsgüter*, Tübingen: Mohr/Siebeck.

Gemünden, Hans Georg, Peter Heydebreck, Rainer Herden, 1992, Technological Interweaverment: A Means of Achieving Innovation Success, *R&D Management* 22 (4), 359-376.

Gerdes, Olle, 1991, From Wireless Telegraph to Mobile Telephone, *Dædalus*, Yearbook of the Technical Museum, Stockholm.

Geroski, Paul, David Thompson, Saadet Toker, 1989, Vertical Separation and Price Discrimination: Cellular Phones in the UK, *Fiscal Studies* 10, 83-103.

Gerpott, Thorsten J., 1990, Globales F&E-Mangement, *Die Unternehmung* 44 (4), 226-246.

Gerpott, Thorsten, 1995, Successful Integration of R&D Functions After Acquisitions: An Exploration Empirical Study, *R&D Management* 25 (2), 161-178.

Gertler, Meric, 1995, "Being There": Proximity, Organisation, and Culture in the Development and Adoption of Advanced Manufacturing Technologies, *Economic Geography* 71, 1-26.

Gerybadze, Alexander, 1996, Technologische Vorhersagen, in: W. Kern et al. (eds.), *Handwörterbuch der Produktionswirtschaft*, Stuttgart: Schäffer-Poeschel, 2027-2040.

Gerybadze, Alexander, 1999, Multinationale Unternehmen und nationale Innovationssysteme: Konflikt oder Komplementarität?, In: Otto G. Mayer (ed.), *Internationale Unternehmensstrategien und nationale Standortpolitik*, Baden-Baden: Nomos, 103-122.

Gerybadze, Alexander, Frieder Meyer-Krahmer, Guido Reger, 1997, *Globales Management von Forschung und Innovation*, Stuttgart: Schäffer-Poeschel.

Gerybadze, Alexander, Guido Reger, 1999, Globalization of R&D: Recent Changes in the Management of Innovation in Transnational Corporations, *Research Policy* 28 (2-3), 251-274.

Ghoshal, Sumantra, 1986, *The Innovative Multinational: A Differentiated Entwork of Organizational Roles and Management Processes*, unpublished DBA, Harvard University.

Gibson, Stephen W., 1987, *Cellular Mobile Radiotelephones*, Englewood Cliffs NJ: Prentice-Hall.

Gierl, Heribert, 1997, Neue Technologien und Leap-Frogging der Nachfrager, *Zeitschrift für Betriebswirtschaft* 67 (10), 1073-1091.

Ginarte, Juan C., Walter G. Park, 1997, Determinants of Patent Rights: A Cross-National Study, *Research Policy* 26, 283-301.

Golder, Peter, Gerard J. Tellis, 1993, Pioneer Advantage: Marketing Logic or Marketing Legend? *Journal of Marketing Research* 30, 158-170.

Gort, Michael, Steven Klepper, 1982, Time Paths in the Diffusion of Product Innovations, *Economic Journal* 92, 630-653.

Götzke, Gudrun, 1991, Mobilfunk-Entwicklung in Europa, Diskussionspapiere des Instituts für Industrie- und Gewerbepolitik der Universität Hamburg, Nr. 45, Hamburg.

Granstrand, Ove, Lars Håkanson, Sören Sjölander (eds.), 1992, *Technology Management and International Business*, Chichester et al.: Wiley.

Granstrand, Ove, Lars Håkanson, Sören Sjölander, 1993, Internationalization of R&D – A Survey of Some Recent Research, *Research Policy* 22, 413-430.

Green, James R., David J. Teece, 1998, Four Approaches to Telecommunications Deregulation and Competition: The USA, the UK, Australia and New Zealand, *Industrial and Corporate Change* 7 (4), 623-635.

Green, Paul E., Yoram Wind, 1975, New Way to Measure Consumers' Judgements, *Harvard Business Review* 53 (4), 107-117.

Griliches, Zvi, 1957, Hybrid Corn: An Exploration of the Economics of Technological Change, *Econometrica* 25 (4), 501-522.

Grimes, Christopher, 2000, Doomed Iridium is all Set to Go Into Free-Fall, *Financial Times* March 18th , 10.

Grubel, Herbert G., Peter J. Lloyd, 1975, *Intra-Industry Trade: The Theory and Measurement of International Trade in Differentiated Products*, London: Macmillan.

Gruber, Harald, 1992, Persistence of Leadership in Product Innovation, *Journal of Industrial Economics* 40 (4), 359-375.

Gruber, Harald, Frank Verboven, 2001, *The Diffusion of Mobile Telecommunications Service in the European Union*, European Economic Review 45, 577-588.

Gruner, Kjell E., Christian Homburg 1997, *Customer Interaction as a Key to New Product Success*, mimeo, Vallendar/Koblenz.

Grupp, Hariolf, 1990, Japan, in: Grupp, H., Th. Schnöring (eds.), *Forschung und Entwicklung für die Telekommunikation – Internationaler Vergleich mit zehn Ländern*, Band I, Berlin: Springer Verlag, 141-240.

Grupp, Hariolf, Shlomo Maital, 1998, Interpreting the Sources of Market Value in a Capital Goods Market: R&D Management in Industrial Sensors, *R&D Management* 28 (2), 65-77.

Hagenauer, Joachim, 1998, Ein europäisches System auf dem Weg zum globalen Erfolg, in: K. Pinkau, M. Popp, Ch. Stahlburg (eds.), *Der Universitäts- und Forschungsstandort Deutschland im globalen Markt*, Stuttgart: S. Hirtzel, 59-66.

Hägerstrand, Torsten, 1973, *Innovation Diffusion as a Spatial Process*, Chicago, London: University of Chicago Press.

Håkanson, Lars, 1981, Organisation and Evolution of Foreign R&D in Swedish Multinationals, *Geografisker Annaler* 63B, 47-57 (reprinted in: Mark Casson (ed.), Multinational Corporations, Aldershot: Edward Elgar).

Håkanson, Lars, Robert Nobel, 1993, Determinants of Foreign R&D in Swedish Multinationals, *Research Policy* 22, 397-411.

Håkansson, Håkan (ed.), 1987, *Industrial Technological Development – A Network Approach*, London: Croom-Helm.

Hall, Bronwyn H., 1988, The Impact of Takeover Activities on Corporate Research and Development, in: A. J. Auerbach (ed.), *Corporate Takeovers: Causes and Consequences*, Chicago: University of Chicago Press, 69-96.

Han, Min C., Vern Terpstra, 1988, Country-of-Origin Effects for Uni-National and Bi-National Products, *Journal of International Business Studies* 19, 235-255.

Hardman, Kenneth, 1982, A Primer on Cellular Mobile Telephone Systems, *Federal Bar News & Journal* 29 (11), 385-391, cited in Calhoun (1988), 50-54.

Harhoff, Dietmar, 1995, Agglomerationen und regionale Spillovereffekte, in: B. Gahlen, H. Hesse und H. J. Ramser (eds.), *Standort und Region. Neue Ansätze zur Regionalökonomik*, Schriftenreihe des Wirtschaftswissenschaftlichen Seminars Ottobeuren, Bd. 24, Berlin: Duncker & Humblot, 83-115.

Harhoff, Dietmar, 1999, Korreferat zu Alexander Gerybadze: Multinationale Unternehmen und nationale Innovationssysteme: Konflikt oder Komplementarität?, in: O. G. Mayer (ed.), *Internationale Unternehmensstrategien und nationale Standortpolitik*, Baden-Baden: Nomos, 123-128.

Harhoff, Dietmar, 2000, R&D Spillovers, Technological Proximity, and Productivity Growth – Evidence From German Panel Data, *Schmalenbach business review (Zfbf)* 52 (3), 238-260.

Harrigan, Kathryn Rudie, 1984, Innovation Within Overseas Subsidiaries, *Journal of Business Strategy* 4 (4), 47-55.

Haucap, Justus, Christian Wey, Jens Barmbold, 1997a, Location Choice as a Signal for Product Quality, *Journal of Institutional and Theoretical Economics* 153 (3), 510-531.

Haucap, Justus, Christian Wey, Jens Barmbold, 1997b, *Location Choice and Implicit Franchise Contracts*, Paper presented at the Jahrestagung des Vereins für Socialpolitik, September 23-26th, Bern.

Hauschildt, Jürgen, 1993, *Innovationsmanagement*, München: Vahlen.

Hayek, Friedrich August, 1945, The Use of Knowledge in Society, *American Economic Review* 35, 519-530.

Hecker, Silke, 1997, *Kommunikation in ökologischen Unternehmenskrisen: Der Fall Shell und Brent Spar*, Wiesbaden: DUV.

Helsen, Kristiaan, Kamel Jedidi, Wayne S. DeSarbo, 1993, A New Approach to Country Segmentation Utilizing Multinational Diffusion Patterns, *Journal of Marketing* 57, October, 60-71.

Henderson, Bruce, 1980, *Perspectives on Experience*, by the Staff of The Boston Consulting Group, Ann Arbor, Mich.

Herbig, Paul A., Fred Palumbo, 1994, The Effect of Culture on the Adoption Process: A Comparison of Japanese and American Behavior, *Technical Forecasting and Social Change* 46, 71-101.

Herstatt, Cornelius, 1991, *Anwender als Quellen für die Produktinnovation*, Zürich.

Hewitt, Gary, 1980, Research and Development Performed Abroad by US Manufacturing Multinationals, *Kyklos* 33, 308-327.

Hicks, John R., 1932, *The Theory of Wages*, London: Macmillan.

Hill, Jill, 1986, *Deregulating Telecoms: Competition and Control in the United States, Japan and Britain*, London: Frances Pinter.

Hill, John S., Richard R. Still, 1984, Adapting Products to LDC Tastes, *Harvard Business Review* 62, March/April, 92-101.

Hills, Jill, 1986, *Deregulating Telecoms: Competition and Control in the United States, Japan and Britain*, London: Pinter.

Hines, James R. Jr., 1994, No Place Like Home: Tax Incentives and the Location of R&D by American Multinationals, in: J. M. Poterba (ed.), *Tax Policy and the Economy*, No. 8, National Bureau of Economic Analysis, Cambridge, Ma: MIT Press, 65-104.

Hippel, Eric v., 1976, The Dominant Role of Users in the Scientific Instrument Innovation Process, *Research Policy* 5, 212-239.

Hippel, Eric v., 1986, Lead Users: A Source of Novel Product Concepts, *Management Science* 32 (7), 791-805.

Hippel, Eric v., 1987, Has a Customer Already Developed Your New Product?, in: E. B. Roberts (ed.), *Generating Technological Innovations*, New York, Oxford: Oxford University Press, 105-116.

Hippel, Eric v., 1988, *Sources of Innovation*, New York: Oxford University Press.

Hippel, Eric v., 1999, Explorations of the Impact of "Sticky" Local Information on the Locus Innovation Marketing: A Progress Report, in: N. Franke (ed.), *Innovationsforschung und Technologiemanagement: Konzepte, Strategien, Fallbeispiele;* [Symposium zum Gedenken an Prof. Dr. Stephan Schrader am 2. Juli 1998], 275-284.

Hippel, Eric v., Stefan Thomke, Mary Sonnack, 1999, Creating Breakthroughs at 3M, *Harvard Business Review* 77, September-October, 47-57.

Hirschey, Robert C., Richard E. Caves, 1981, Research and Transfer of Technology by Multinational Enterprises, *Oxford Bulletin of Economics and Statistics* 43 (2), 115-130.

Hirschman, Elizabeth C., 1980, Innovativeness, Novelty Seeking, and Consumer Creativity, *Journal of Consumer Research* 7 (December), 283-295.

Hofstede, Geert H., 1980, *Culture's Consequences: International Differences in Work-Related Values*, Beverly Hills: Sage Publ.

Howells, Jeremy, 1984, The Location of Research and Development: Some Observations and Evidence From Britain, *Regional Studies* 18 (1), 13-29.

Hufbauer, Gary C., 1966, *Synthetic Materials and the Theory of International Trade*, London: Gerald Duckworth & Co.

Huggins, Robert, 1997, Competitiveness and the Global Region: The Role of Networking, in: J. Simmie (ed.), *Innovation, Networks and Learning Regions?,* London: Kingsley, 101-123.

Hultén, Staffan, Bengt G. Mölleryd, 1995, Mobile Telecommunications in Sweden, in: Karl-Ernst Schenk, Jürgen Müller, Thomas Schnöring (eds.), *Mobile Telecommunications: Emerging European Markets*, Boston: Artech House, 1-28.

Ihde, Olaf, 1996, *Internationale Diffusion von Mobilfunk*, Wiesbaden: DUV.

International Telecommunications Union (ITU), 1999, *World Telecommunication Development Report 1999*, Geneva.

Jaffe, Adam, 1989, Real Effects of Academic Research, *American Economic Research* 79, 957-970.

Jaffe, Adam, Manuel Trajtenberg, Rebecca Henderson et al., 1993, Geographic Localization of Knowledge Spillovers as Evidenced by Patent Citations, *Quarterly Journal of Economics* 198, 577-598.

Jänicke, Martin, 2000, *Ökologische Modernisierung als Innovation und Diffusion in Politik und Technik: Möglichkeiten und Grenzen eines Konzepts*, FFU-report 00-01, Berlin.

Jänicke, Martin, Lutz Mez, Pernille Bechsgaard, Börge Klemmensen, 1999, Innovationswirkungen branchenbezogener Regulierungsmuster am Beispiel engergiesparender Kühlschränke in Dänemark, in: P. Klemmer (eds.), *Innovationen und Umwelt*, Berlin: Analytica, 57-80.

Japan External Trade Organisation (Jetro), various years, *Survey on the Operations of Japanese-Affiliated Manufacturing Companies in Europe and Turkey*, mimeo.

Johanson, Jan, Jan-Eric Vahle, 1977, The Internationalisation Process of the Firm – A Model of Knowledge Development and Increasing Foreign Market Commitments, *Journal of International Business Studies* 8 (1), 22-32.

Johansson, Johny K., 2000, *Global Marketing: Foreign Entry, Local Marketing, & Global Management*, Boston et al.: Irwin McGraw Hill.

Johansson, Johny K., Thomas W. Roehl, 1994, How Companies Develop Assets and Capabilities: Japan as a Leading Market, in: S. Beechler, A. Bird (eds.), *Research in International Business and International Relations: Emerging Trends in Japanese Management*, Vol. 6, Greenwich, Connecticut: JAI Press, 139-160.

Jung, Volker, Hans-Jürgen Warnecke (eds.), 1998, *Handbuch für die Telekommunikation*, Berlin: Springer.

Jungmittag, Andre, Guido Reger, Thomas Reiss (eds.), 2000, *Changing Innovation in the Pharmaceutical Industry: Globalization and New Ways of Drug Development*, Berlin et al.: Springer.

Jungnickel, Rolf, Henry Krägenau, Matthias Lefeldt, Manfred Holthus, 1977, *Einfluß multinationaler Unternehmen auf Außenwirtschaft und Branchenstruktur der Bundesrepublik Deutschland*, Hamburg: Weltarchiv.

Kalish, Shlomo, Vijay Mahajan, Eitan Muller, 1995, Waterfall and Sprinkler New-Product Strategies in Competitive Global Markets, *International Journal of Research in Marketing* 12, 105-119.

Karshenas, Massoud, Paul Stoneman, 1995, Technological Diffusion, in: P. Stoneman (ed.), 265-297.

Katz, Ralph, 1988, *Managing Professionals in Innovative Organisations: A Collection of Readings*, Cambridge, MA.: Ballinger.

Katz, J. Sylvan, 1994, Geographical Proximity and Scientific Collaboration, *Scientometrics* 31 (1), 31-43.

Katz, Michael L., Carl Shapiro, 1985, Network Externalities, Competition and Compatibility, *American Economic Review* 75 (3), 424-440.

Keck, Otto, 1980, Government Policy and Technical Choice in the West German Reactor Programme, *Research Policy* 9, 302-356.

Keegan, Warren J., 1969, Multinational Product Planning: Strategic Alternatives, *Journal of Marketing* 33 (1), 58-62.

Keegan, Warren J., Mark C. Green, 1997, *Principles of Global Marketing*, Upper Saddle River, NJ: Prentice-Hall.

Kennedy, Carol, 1992, How Nokia is Going High Tech, *Long Range Planning* 25 (2), 16-25.

Kennedy, Richard, 1999, History of GSM, www-server of GSM MoU: www.gsm.org .

Kern, Kristine, Helge Jörgens, Martin Jänicke, 2000, Die Diffusion umweltpolitischer Innovationen: Ein Beitrag zur Globalisierung von Umweltpolitik, *Zeitschrift für Umweltpolitik & Umweltrecht* (4), 507-546.

Kilburn, David, 1997, Thai Recipe for Hair-Care Growth, *Marketing Week*, April 10th, London.

Klemperer, Paul, 1987, The Competitiveness of Markets With Switching Costs, *Rand Journal of Economics* 18 (1), 138-150.

Klepper, Steven, 1996, Entry, Exit, Growth and Innovation Over the Product Life Cycle, *American Economic Review* 86 (3), 562-583.

Kline, Stephen J., Nathan Rosenberg, 1986, An Overview of Innovation, in: R. Landau, N. Rosenberg (eds.), *The Positive Sum Strategy: Harnessing Technology for Economic Growth*, National Academy, WA, 275-305.

Kotabe, Masaaki, 1992, *Global Sourcing Strategy: R&D, Manufacturing, and Marketing Interfaces*, New York: Quorum.

Kotabe, Masaaki, Kristiaan Helsen, 1998, *Global Marketing Management*, New York: Wiley.

Kotler, Philip, 1978, *Marketing Management*, Englewood Cliffs: Prentice-Hall.

Kravis, Irving B., Robert E. Lipsey, 1971, *Price Competitiveness in World Trade*, New York: National Bureau of Economic Research.

Kreutzer, Ralf, 1989, *Global Marketing – Konzeption eines länderübergreifenden Marketing: Erfolgsbedingungen, Analysekonzepte, Gestaltungs- und Implementierungsansätze*, Wiesbaden: DUV.

Krugman, Paul, 1979, A Model of Innovation, Technology Transfer and the World Distribution of Income, *Journal of Political Economy* 87 (2), 253-265.

Krugman, Paul, 1994, Location and Competition: Notes on Economic Geography, in: R. Rumelt, D. Schendel, D. Teece (eds.), *Fundamental Issues in Strategy: A Research Agenda*, Boston: Harvard Business School Press, 463-493.

Kumar, Brij, 1982, Die multinationale Unternehmung und das Grundbedürfniskonzept, in: E. Pausenberger (ed.), *Entwicklungsländer als Handlungsfelder internationaler Unternehmungen*, Stuttgart: Poeschel, 153-178.

Kumar, V., Jaishankar Ganesh, Raj Echambadi, 1998, Cross-National Diffusion Research: What Do We Know and how Certain are We?, *Journal of Product Innovation Management* 15, 255-268.

Kümmerle, Walter (1996), *Home Base and Foreign Direct Investment in Research and Development – An Investigation Into the International Allocation of Research and Activity by Multinational Enterprises*, unpublished DBA thesis, Harvard University.

Laffont, Jean-Jacques, Jean Tirole, 2000, *Competition in Telecommunication*, Harvard: MIT Press.

Lall, Sanjaya, 1979, The International Allocation of Research Activities by US Multinationals, *Oxford Bulletin of Economics and Statistics* 41 (4), 313-331.

Lancaster, Kelvin, 1981, *Modern Consumer Theory*, Aldershot: Edward Elgar.

Langloise, Richard, Edward Steinmueller, 1999, The Evolution of Competitive Advantage in the Worldwide Semiconductor Industry, 1947-1996, in: D. Mowery, R. Nelson (eds.), *Sources of Industrial Leadership*, Cambridge: Cambridge University Press, 19-78.

Lee, Chol, 1990, Determinants of National Innovativeness and International Market Segmentation, *International Marketing Review* 7 (5), 39-49.

Lee, James A., 1966, Cultural Analysis and Overseas Operation, *Harvard Business Review* 44 (2), 106-114.

Lee, William C. Y., 1989, *Mobile Cellular Telecommunications Systems*, New York et al.: McGraw-Hill.

Legler, Harald, 1994, Regionale Verteilung industrieller Forschungskapazitäten in Westdeutschland, *ZEW Wirtschaftsanalysen* 2 (4), 415-434.

Lehrer, Mark, Kazuhiro Asakawa, 1999, Unbundling European Operations: Regional Management and Corporate Flexibility in American and Japanese MNCS, *Journal of World Business* 34 (3), 267-286.

Lerner, Josh, 2000, *150 Years of Patent Protection*, NBER Working paper No. 7478, Washington.

Leroy, Georges, 1976, *Multinational Product Strategy: A Typology of Worldwide Product Innovation and Diffusion*, New York et al.: Praeger.

Leser, Conrad E. V., 1963, Forms of Engel Functions, *Econometrica* 31, 694-703.

Levinthal, Daniel A., 1998, The Slow Pace of Rapid Technological Change: Gradualism and Punctuation in Technological Change, *Industrial and Corporate Change* 7 (2), 217-247.

Levitt, Theodore, 1983, The Globalisation of Markets, *Harvard Business Review* 61 (3), 92-102.

Licht, Georg, 1994, Gemeinsam forschen: Motive und Verbreitung strategischer Allianzen in Europa, *ZEW Wirtschaftsanalysen* 2 (4), 371-399.

Lichtenberg, Frank, 1992, *Corporate Takeovers and Productivity*, Cambridge: MIT Press.

Lichtenberg, Frank, Bruno van Pottelsberghe de la Potterie, 1996, *The Channels of International R&D Spillovers*, Paper prepared for the OECD-Conference on the NEW Indicators for the Knowledge based Economy, 19th -21st June, Paris.

Lieberman, Marvin B., David B. Montgomery, 1988, First Mover Advantages, *Strategic Management Journal* 9 (Summer), 41-58.

Lindbeck, Assar, 1981, Industrial Policy as an Issue in the Economic Environment, *The World Economy* 4 (4), 391-405.

Linder, Staffan Burenstam, 1961, *An Essay on Trade and Transformation*, Uppsala: Almqvist & Wiksells.

Link, Frederik, 1997, *Diffusion Dynamics and the Pricing of Innovations*, Lund Studies in Economics and Management No. 39, Lund: Lund University Press.

Littlewood, Bev, Lorenzo Strigini, 1992, The Risks of Software, *Scientific American* 267 (5), 62-63.

Livingstone, James M., 1989, *The Internationalization of Business*, Houndmills: Macmillan.

Lundvall, Bengt-Åke, 1988, Innovation as an Interactive Process – From User-Producer Interaction to the National System of Innovation, in: G. Dosi et al. (eds.), *Technical Change and Economic Theory*, London: Pinter, 349-369.

Lundvall, Bengt-Åke, 1993, User-Producer Relationships, National Systems of Innovation and Internationalisation, in: Daniel Foray, Chris Freeman (eds.), *Technology and the Wealth of Nations: The Dynamics of Constructed Advantage*, London: Pinter, 277-300.

Lyden, Dennis P., Albert N. Link, 1991, *Government's Role in Innovation*, Dordrecht: Kluwer.

Lynn, Michael, Betsy Gelb, 1996, Identifying Innovative National Markets for Technical Consumer Goods, *International Marketing Review* 13 (6), 43-57.

Maddala, Gangadharrao S., Peter T. Knight, 1967, International Diffusion of Technical Change: A Case Study of the Oxygen Steel Making Process, *Economic Journal* 77 (Sept.), 531-558.

Mahajan, Vijay, Eitan Muller, Frank M. Bass, 1990, New Product Diffusion Models in Marketing: A Review and Directions for Research, *Journal of Marketing* 54, 1-26.

Majone, G, 1991, Cross-National Sources of Regulatory Policy Making in Europe and the United States, *Journal of Public Policy* 11, 79-106.

Malecki, Edward J., 1980, Dimensions of R&D Location in the United States, *Research Policy* 9, 2-22.

Mansfield, Edwin, 1961, Technical Change and the Rate of Imitation, *Econometrica* 2, 741-766.

Mansfield, Edwin, 1963, The Speed of Response of Firms to New Techniques, *Quarterly Journal of Economics* 77, 290-311.

Mansfield, Edwin, 1968, *Industrial Research and Technological Innovation: An Econometric Analysis*, New York: Norton.

Mansfield, Edwin, 1989, The Diffusion of Industrial Robots in Japan and the United States, *Research Policy* 18, 183-192.

Mansfield, Edwin, Anthony Romeo, 1984, 'Reverse' Transfer of Technology from Overseas Subsidiaries to American Firms, *IEEE Transactions on Engineering Management* EM-31 (3), 122-127.

Mansfield, Edwin, David Teece, Anthony Romeo, 1979, Overseas Research and Development by US-based Firms, *Economica* 46, 187-196.

Marshall, Alfred, 1920, *Principles of Economics*, 8th Ed., Philadelphia: Porcupine Press.

Maslow, Abraham H., 1970, *Motivation and personality*, 2. Ed., New York : Harper Row.

Mason, Charles F., 1991, Cellular Power to the People, *Telephony* 220 (25), 36.

Mason, Charles F., 1993a, Cellular Industry Inches Closer to Seamless Roaming, *Telephony* 224 (7), 18.

Mason, Charles F., 1993b, Ameritech Drops TDMA, Says Technology is Inferior to Analog, *Telephony* 225 (4), 8.

McClelland, Stephen, 1991, Finland, *Telecommunications* 25 (10), 95.

McIntyre, Shelby H., 1988, Market Adaptation as a Process in the Product Life Cycle of Radical Innovations and High Technology Products, *The Journal of Product Innovation Management* 5 (2), 140-150.

McKinsey Global Institute, 1997, *Removing Barriers to Growth and Employment in France and Germany*, Frankfurt et al.

Metcalfe, Stan, 1995, The Economic Foundations of Technology Policy: Equilibrium and Evolutionary Perspectives, in: P. Stoneman (ed.), 409-512.

Midgley, David F., Grahame R. Dowling, 1978, Innovativeness: The Concept and Its Measurement, *Journal of Consumer Research* 4 (March), 229-242.

Miller, Merton H., 1991, *Financial Innovations & Market Volatility*, Cambridge, MA: Blackwell.

Millman, Sidney (ed.), 1984, *A History of Engineering and Science in the Bell System: Communications Science 1925-1980*, Indianapolis, Ind.: AT&T Bell Labs.

Möhrle, Martin, 1995, *Prämarketing: Zur Markteinführung neuer Produkte*, Wiesbaden: Gabler.

Mölleryd, Bengt G., 1997, *The Building of a World Industry – The Impact of Entrepreneurship on Swedish Mobile Telephony*, Via Teldok 28e, Stockholm.

Montefiore, Neil, 1996, Telepoint in Asia, in: Turtlebee (ed.), 59-70.

Mowery, David, 1995, The Practice of Technology Policy, in: P. Stoneman (ed.), 513-557.

Mowery, David, Nathan Rosenberg, 1979, The Influence of Market Demand Upon Innovation: A Critical Review of Some Recent Empirical Studies, *Research Policy* 8, 102-153.

Mowery, David, Richard Nelson, 1999, Introduction, in: D. Mowery, R. Nelson (eds.), *Sources of Industrial Leadership*, Cambridge: Cambridge University Press, 1-18.

Nabseth, Lars, George F. Ray (eds.), 1974, *The Diffusion of New Industrial Processes: An International Study*, London: Cambridge University Press.

Nadel, Mark V., Robert E. Glanville, Philip L. Bereano, 1978, Land Mobile Communications and the Regulatory Process, in: R. Bowers et al. (eds.), 66-95.

Nagle, Thomas T., Reed Holden, 1995, *The Strategy and Tactics of Pricing: A Guide to Profitable Decision Making*, 2nd ed., Englewood Cliffs, NJ: Prentice-Hall.

Nakata, Cheryl, K. Sivakumar, 1996, National Culture and New Product Development: An Integrative Review, *Journal of Marketing* 60 (1).

Narin, Francis, K.S. Hamilton, D. Olivastro, 1997, The Increasing Linkages Between US Technology and Public Science, *Research Policy* 26, 317-330.

National Academy of Science, 1995, *Allocating Federal Funds for Science and Technology*, Washington, D.C.: National Academy Press.

Nelson, Richard, 1990, Capitalism as an Engine of Progress, *Research Policy* 19, 193-214.

Nelson, Richard, Gavin Wright, 1992, The Rise and Fall of American Technological Leadership, *Journal of Economic Literature* 30 (4), 1931-1964.

Nelson, Richard, Sydney Winter, 1982, *An Evolutionary Theory of Economic Change*, Cambridge, Mass.: Harvard University Press.

Neven, Damien, Georges Siotis, 1996, Technology Sourcing and FDI in the EC: An Empirical Evaluation, *International Journal of Industrial Organization* 14, 543-560.

Newbery, David M., 1997, Privatisation and Liberalisation of Network Utilities, *European Economic Review* 41, 357-383.

Nieschlag, Robert, Erwin Dichtl, Hans Hörschgen, 1985, *Marketing*, 14th Edition, Berlin: Duncker & Humblot.

Niosi, Jorge, 1999, The Internationalization of Industrial R&D – From Technology Transfer to the Learning Organization, *Research Policy* 28, 107-117.

Nohria, Nittin, Robert G. Eccles, 1992, Face-To-Face: Making Network Organisations Work, in: N. Nohria, R. G. Eccles (eds.), *Networks and Organizations: Structure, Form and Action*, Boston, MA: Harvard University Press, 288-308.

O'Grady, Shawna, Henry W. Lane, 1996, The Psychic Distance Paradox, *Journal of International Business Studies* 27 (2), 309-320.

O'Keefe, Susan, 1997, GSM Carriers Ally, but Still Face Challenges, *Telecommunications* 31 (11), Americas edition, 17-18.

OECD, 1968, *Gaps in Technology: General Report*, Paris.

OECD, 1991, *Strategic Industries in a Global Economy: Policy Issues for the 1990s*, Paris.

OECD, 1997a, *Communications Outlook 1997*, Vol. 1, Paris.

OECD, 1997b, *OSLO manual*, Paris.

OECD, 1997c, *Reforming Environmental Regulation in OECD Countries*, Paris.

OECD, 1998, *Internationalisation of Industrial R&D: Patterns and Trends*, Paris.

OECD, 1999, *Communications Outlook 1999*, Paris.

Ogbuehi, Alphonso, Ralph A. Bellas, 1992, Decentralized R&D for Global Product Development: Strategic Implications for the Multinational Corporation, *International Marketing Review* 9 (5), 60-70.

Ohmae, Kenichi, 1985, *Triad Power*, New York: Free Press.

Ohmae, Kenichi, 1995, *The End of the Nation State: The Rise of Regional Economies*, New York: Free Press.

Päch, Susanne, 1994, *Die D2-Story: Mobilkommunikation; Aufbruch in den Wettbewerb*, Düsseldorf et al.: Econ.

Paetsch, Michael, 1993, *The Evolution of Mobile Communications in the U.S. and Europe: Regulation, Technology, and Markets*, Boston, London: Artech House.

Paliwoda, Stanley, 1993, *International Marketing*, 2. Edition, Oxford: Butterworth-Heinemann.

Parker, Philip M., Lars-Hendrik Röller, 1997, Collusive Conduct in Duopolies: Multimarket Contact and Cross-Ownership in the Mobile Telephony Industry, *Rand Journal of Economics* 28, 304-322.

Patel, Pari, 1995, Localised Production of Technology for Global Markets, *Cambridge Journal of Economics* 19, 141-153.

Patel, Pari, Keith Pavitt, 1992, Large Firms in the Production of the World's Technology: An Important Case of Non-Globalisation, in: Granstrand, O., L. Hakanson, S. Sjölander, (eds.), 53-74.

Patel, Pari, Manuel Vega, 1999, Patterns of Internationalisation of Corporate Technology: Location Versus Home Country Advantages, *Research Policy* 28, 145-155.

Pausenberger, Ehrenfried, 1982, Technologiepolitik internationaler Unternehmungen: Eine empirische Untersuchung über Forschung und Entwicklung, Technologietransfer und Technologieanpassung in internationalen Unternehmen, *Zeitschrift für Betriebswirtschaftliche Forschung* 34, 1025-1053.

Pavitt, Keith, 1984, Sectoral Patterns of Technical Change: Towards a Taxonomy and a Theory, *Research Policy* 13, 343-373.

Pearce, Robert, 1989, *The Internationalisation of Research by Multinational Enterprises*, London: Macmillan.

Pearce, Robert, Satwinder Singh, 1992, *Globalizing Research and Development*, Houndmills: Macmillan.

Pehrsson, Anders, 1996, *International Strategies in Telecommunications: Model and Applications*, London: Routledge.

Pemple, T.J., 1978, Land Mobile Communications in Japan: Technical Developments and Issues of International Trade, in: R. Bowers et al. (eds.), 317-343.

Perlmutter, Howard V., 1969, The Tortuous Evolution of the Multinational Corporation, *Columbia Journal of World Business* 4, Jan/Feb., 9-18.

Perrino, Albert C., James W. Tipping, 1989, Global Management of Technology, *Research Technology Management* 32 (3), 12-19.

Peters, Guy, 1997, Policy Transfer Between Governments: The Case of Administrative Reform, *West European Politics* 20, 71-88.

Peterson, M.J., 1995, The Emergence of a Mass Market for Fax Machines, *Technology in Society* 17 (4), 469-482.

Pieper, Ute, 1998, *Wirkungen von Unternehmensakquisitionen auf Forschung und Entwicklung*, Wiesbaden: DUV.

Plettner, Bernhard, 1994, *Abenteuer Elektrotechnik: Siemens und die Entwicklung der Elektrotechnik seit 1945*, München, Zürich: Piper.

Polany, Michael, 1966, *The Tacit Dimension*, New York: Doubleday & Co.

Pollack, Andrew, 1998, Toyota's Gas/Electric Hit: A Success at Home, Hybrid Cars Heads for U.S., *International Herald Tribune* Aug. 5th, p. 1/8.

Porter, Michael E., 1986, Changing Patterns of International Competition, *California Management Review* 28 (2), 9-40.

Porter, Michael E., 1990, *The Competitive Advantage of Nations*, New York: Free Press.

Porter, Michael E., 1998, Competing Across Locations: Enhancing Competitive Advantage Through a Global Strategy, in: Michael E. Porter, *On Competition*, Boston: Harvard Business School Press, 309-348.

Porter, Michael E., Claas van der Linde, 1995, Towards a New Conception of the Environment-Competitiveness Relationship, *Journal of Economic Perspectives* 9 (4), 97-118.

Porter, Michael, Örjan Sölvell, 1998, The Role of Geography in the Process of Innovation and the Sustainable Competitive Advantage of Firms, in: A. Chandler Jr., P. Hagström, Ö. Sölvell (eds.), The Dynamic Firm: The Role of Technology, Strategy, Organisation and Regions, Oxford: Oxford University Press, 440-457.

Posner, Michael V., 1961, International Trade and Technical Change, *Oxford Economic Papers* 30, 323-341.

Poynter, Thomas, Alan M. Rugman, 1982, World Product Mandates: How Will Multinationals Respond? *Business Quarterly* (Autumn), 54-61.

Poznanski, Kazimierz Z., 1983, International Diffusion of Steel Technologies: Time Lag and the Speed of Diffusion, *Technological Forecasting and Social Change* 23, 305-323.

Prahalad, Coimbatore K., Yves L. Doz, 1987, *The Multinational Mission: Balancing Local Demands and Global Vision*, New York: Free Press.

Putsis, W.P., S. Balasubramanian, E.H. Kaplan, S. Sen, 1997, Mixing Behavior in Cross-Country Diffusion, *Marketing Science* 16, 354-369.

Raffée, Hans, Ralf T. Kreutzer, 1989, Organisational Dimensions of Global Marketing, *European Journal of Marketing* 23 (5), 43-57.

Redmond, William H., 1994, Diffusion at Sub-National Levels: A Regional Analysis of New Product Growth, *Journal of Product Innovation Management* 11, 201-212.

Reger, Guido, 1998, Changes in the R&D Strategies of Transnational Firms: Challenges for National Technology and Innovation Policy, *STI Review* No. 22, OECD, 234-276.

Reger, Guido, Marian Beise, Heike Belitz, 1999, *Innovationsstandorte multinationaler Unternehmen: Internationalisierung technologischer Kompetenzen in der Pharmazie, der Halbleiter- und Telekommunikationstechnik*, Schriftenreihe des FhG-ISI, Band 37, Heidelberg: Physica.

Reger, Guido, Sybille Hinze, 1999, Internationalisierung technologischer Kompetenzen in der Pharmazeutik, in: G. Reger, M. Beise, H. Belitz (eds.), 43-80.

Reinganum, Jennifer, 1981, Market Structure and the Diffusion of New Technology, *Bell Journal of Economics* 12, 618-624.

Riesenbeck, Hajo, Anthony Freeling, 1991, How Global are Global Brands? *McKinsey Quarterly* (4), 3-18.

Riley, John J., 1958, *A History of the American Soft Drink Industry: Bottled Carbonated Beverages*, Washington, D.C.: American Bottlers of Carbonated Beverages.

Robertson, Thomas S., Yoram Wind, 1980, Organisational Psychographics and Innovations, *Journal of Consumer Research* 7, 24-31.

Robinson, William, Claes Fornell, 1985, Sources of Market Pioneer Advantage in Consumer Goods Industries, *Journal of Marketing Research* 22, 305-317.

Rogers, Everett M., 1995, *Diffusion of Innovation*, 4th Edition, New York: Free Press.

Romer, Paul M., 1990, Endogenous Technical Change, *Journal of Political Economy* 98 (5), 71-101.

Ronstadt, Robert, 1977, *Research and Development Abroad by U.S. Multinationals*, New York: Praeger.

Ronstadt, Robert, Robert J. Kramer, 1983, Internationalization Industrial Innovation, *Journal of Business Strategy* 3 (3), 3-15.

Rose, Richard, 1993, *Lesson-Drawing in Public Policy: A Guide to Learning Across Time and Space*, Chatham, New Jersey: Chatham House.

Rosenberg, Nathan, 1982, *Inside the Black Box: Technology and Economics*, Cambridge: Cambridge University Press.

Rosenbloom, Richard S., Michael A. Cusamano, 1987, Technological Pioneering and Competitive Advantage: The Birth of the VCR Industry, *California Management Review 29* (1), 51-76.

Roth, Kendall, Allen J. Morrison, 1992, Implementing Global Strategy: Characteristics of Global Subs, *Journal of International Business Studies* 23 (4), 715-736.

Roth, R. F. (1979): Creative Guidelines for Transnational Advertising, In: Oak Broak III, 416-419.

Rothbarth, Erwin, 1946, Causes of the Superior Efficiency of the U.S.A. Industry as Compared With the British Industry, *Economic Journal* 56 (September), 383-390.

Rothwell, Richard, Christopher Freeman, A. Horseley, V.T.P. Jervis, J. Townsend, 1974, Sappho Updated – Project Sappho Phase II, *Research Policy* 3, 204-225.

Rovizzi, Laura, David J. Thompson, 1992, The Regulation of Product Quality in the Public Utilities and the Citizen's Charter, *Fiscal Studies* 13 (3), 74-95.

Rugman, Alan M., 1983, Multinational Enterprises and World Product Mandates, in: A.M. Rugman (ed.), *Multinationals and Technology Transfer: The Canadian Experience*, New York: Praeger, 73-90.

Rugman, Alan M., Jocelyn Bennett, 1982, Technology Transfer and World Product Mandating in Canada, *Columbia Journal of World Business* 17 (4), 58-62.

Ruttan, Vernon W., 1997, Induced Innovation, Evolutionary Theory and Path Dependence: Sources of Technical Change, *Economic Journal* 107, 1520-1529.

Sachwald, Frederique, 1995, *The Organization of Technological Activities Within Firms and Between Countries: The Consequences of Globalization*, Tokyo Club Papers No. 8, Tokyo Club Foundation for Global Studies.

Sahal, Devendra, 1981, *Patterns of Technological Innovation*, Reading, Mass.: Addison-Wesley.

Saxenian, Anne, 1994, *Regional Advantage: Culture and Competition in Silicon Valley and Route 128*, Cambridge: Harvard University Press.

Scheele, Peter, 1992, *Mobilfunk in Europa*, 2. Ed., Heidelberg: v. Decker.

Scherer, Frederic M., 1992, *International High-Technology Competition*, Cambridge: Harvard University Press.

Scherer, Frederic M., David Ross, 1990, *Industrial Market Structure and Economic Performance*, Boston: Houghton Mifflin.

Scherler, Patrik, 1996, *Kommunikation mit externen Anspruchsgruppen als Erfolgsfaktor im Krisenmanagement eines Konzerns*, Basel, Frankfurt a. M.: Helbing & Lichtenhain.

Schmookler, Jacob, 1962, Changes in Industry and the State of Knowledge as Determinants of Industrial Invention, in: R. Nelson (ed.), *The Rate and Direction of Inventive Activity: Economic and Social Factors*, Princeton: Princeton University Press, 195-232.

Schmookler, Jacob, 1966, *Invention and Growth*, Cambridge, Mass.: Harvard University Press.

Schoder, Detlef, 1995, Diffusion von Netzwerkgütern: Modellierung auf Basis des Mastergleichungsansatzes der Synergetik, *Marketing ZFP* (1), 18-28.

Schröder, Hans-Ulrich, 1996, *Globales Produktmanagement: eine empirische Analyse des Instrumenteeinsatzes in ausgewählten Branchen der Konsumgüterindustrie*, Frankfurt a. M.: Lang.

Schumpeter, Joseph A., 1911, *Theorie der wirtschaftlichen Entwicklung: eine Untersuchung über Unternehmergewinn, Kapital, Kredit, Zins und den Konjunkturzyklus*, Berlin: Dunker&Humblot.

Servant-Schreiber, Jean-Jacques, 1968, *The American Challenge* (org. Le Défi Américain), London: Hamish Hamilton.

Shan, Weijian, Jaeyong Song, 1997, Foreign Direct Investment and the Sourcing of Technological Advantage: Evidence From the Biotechnology Industry, *Journal of International Business Studies* 28 (Second Quarter), 267-284.

Siemens, Georg, 1961, *Der Weg der Elektrotechnik: Geschichte des Hauses Siemens*, Band I: 1847-1910, Freiburg: Verlag Karl Alber.

Soete, Luc, 1991, National Support Strategies for Strategic Industries: The International Implications, in: OECD (ed.), *Strategic Industries in a Global Economy: Policy Issues for the 1990s*, Paris, 51-80.

Solow, Robert M., 1956, A Contribution to the Theory of Economic Growth, *Quarterly Journal of Economics* 70, 65-94.

Sonnenfeld, David A., 2000, Contradictions of Ecological Modernisation: Pulp and Paper Manufacturing in South-east Asia, in: A. Mol, D. Sonnenfeld (eds.), *Ecological Modernisation Around the World: Perspectives and Critical Debates*, London, Portland, OR: Frank Cass, 235-256.

Steenkamp, Jan-Benedict, Frenkel ter Hofstede, Michel Wedel, 1999, A Cross-National Investigation Into the Individual and National Cultural Antecedents of Consumer Innovativeness, *Journal of Marketing* 63 (2), 55-69.

Stephan, Paula, 1996, The Economics of Science, *Journal of Economic Literature* 34, 1199-1235.

Stigler, George J., Gary S. Becker, 1977, De Gustibus Non Est Disputandum, *American Economic Review* 67, 76-90.

Stolcke, Ariane, 1991, *Bedarfsanalyse für Mobilkommunikation: Entwicklungstendenzen im Bereich mobiler Telefone, Cityruf und Euromessage*, München.

Stoneman, Paul, 1980, The Rate of Imitation, Learning and Profitability, *Economic Letters* 6, 375-388.

Stoneman, Paul, 1989, Technological Diffusion and Vertical Product Differentiation, *Economic Letters* 31, 277-280.

Stoneman, Paul, 1991, Copying Capabilities and Intertemporal Competition Between Joint Input Technologies: CD vs. DAT, *Economies of Innovation and New Technology* 1, 233-241.

Stoneman, Paul (ed.), 1995, *Handbook of the Economics of Innovation and Technological Change*, Oxford: Blackwell.

Storper, Michael, 1993, Regional 'World' of Production, Learning and Innovation in the Technology Districts of France, Italy and the USA, *Regional Studies* 27 (5), 433-455.

Süverkrüp, Christian, 1992, *Internationaler technologischer Wissenstransfer durch Unternehmensakquisitionen: eine empirische Untersuchung am Beispiel deutsch-amerikanischer und amerikanisch-deutscher Akquisitionen*, Europäische Hochschulschriften, Bd. 1352, Frankfurt: Lang.

Swan, Philip L., 1973, The International Diffusion of an Innovation, *Journal of Industrial Economics* 23 (1), 61-69.

Swasy, Alecia, 1993, *Soap Opera: The Inside Story of Procter & Gamble*, New York: Times Books.

Sweeny, Dan, 1993, Bird Watching, *Cellular Business* 10 (7), 22.

Takada, Hirokazu, Dipak Jain, 1991, Cross-National Analysis of Diffusion of Consumer Durable Goods in Pacific Rim Countries, *Journal of Marketing* 55, April, 48-54.

Takeuchi, Hirotaka, Ikujiro Nonaka, 1986, The New New Product Development Game, *Harvard Business Review* 64 (1), 137-146.

Takeuchi, Hirotaka, Michael E. Porter, 1986, Three Roles of International Marketing in Global Strategy, in: M. E. Porter (ed.), *Competition in Global Industries*, Boston: Harvard Business School, 111-146.

Teece, David, 1977, Technology Transfer by Multinational Firms. The Resource Cost of Transferring Technological Know-How, *Economic Journal* 87 (2), 242-261.

Teece, David, 1986, Profiting From Technological Innovation: Implications for Integration, Collaboration, Licensing and Public Policy, *Research Policy* 15, 285-305.

Teece, David, 1992a, Strategies for Capturing the Financial Benefits From Technological Innovation, in: N. Rosenberg, R. Landau, D. Mowery (eds.), *Technology and the Wealth of Nations*, Stanford, 175-205.

Teece, David, 1992b, Foreign Investment and Technological Development in Silicon Valley, *California Management Review* (Winter), 88-106.

Terpstra, Vern, 1977, International Product Policy: The Role of Foreign R&D, *Columbia Journal of World Business* 12 (4), 24-32.

Terpstra, Vern, Kenneth H. David, 1991, *The Cultural Environment of International Business*, 3rd Ed., Cincinnati, Ohio: South-Western Publications.

Tether, Bruce S., David J. Storey, 1998, Smaller Firms and Europe's High Technology Sectors: A Framework for Analysis and Some Statistical Evidence, *Research Policy* 26, 947-971.

Teubal, Morris, Tamar Yinnon, Ehud Zuscovitch, 1991, Networks and Market Creation, *Research Policy* 20, 381-392.

Thirtle, Colin G., Vernon W. Ruttan, 1987, *The Role of Demand and Supply in the Generation and Diffusion of Technical Change*, Fundamentals of Pure and Applied Economics, Vol. 21, Chur: Harwood Academic.

Tilton, John, E., 1971, *International Diffusion of Technology: The Case of Semiconductors*, Washington, D.C.: The Brookings Institution.

Tirole, Jan, 1988, *The Theory of Industrial Organisation*, Cambridge, Mass.: MIT Press.

Törnroos, Jan-Åke, 1991, Relations Between the Concept of Distance and International Industrial Marketing, in: S. J. Palowoda (ed.), *New Perspectives on International Marketing*, London, New York: Routledge, 126-139.

Turtlebee, Walter H.W., 1996, *Cordless Telecommunications Worldwide: The Evolution of Unlicensed PCS*, London: Springer.

Unger, Renate, Ursula Lachnit-Fixson 1993, Die Entwicklung der "Pille" (Oral Contraceptives), in: H. Albach (ed), *Culture and Technical Innovation*, Berlin: de Gruyter, 922-1012.

United Nations Conference of Trade and Development (Unctad), var. years, *World Investment Report*, Geneva.

Urban, Glen L., Theresa Carter, Steven Gaskin, Zofia Mucha, 1986, Market Share Rewards to Pioneering Brands: An Empirical Analysis and Strategic Implications, *Management Science* 32, 645-659.

Urban, Glen L., John R. Hauser, 1993, *Design Marketing of New Products*, 2. Ed., Englewood Cliffs: Prentice-Hall.

Urban, Glen L., Eric v. Hippel, 1988, Lead-User Analysis for the Development of New Industrial Products, *Management Science* 34 (5), 569-582.

Urban, Glen L., Bruce D. Weinberg, John Hauser, 1996, Premarket Forecasting of Really-New Products, *Journal of Marketing* 60 (January), 47-60.

Utterback, James M., 1994, *Mastering the Dynamics of Innovation*, Boston: Harvard Business School Press.

Utterback, James M., Fernando F. Suárez, 1993, Innovation, Competition, and Industry Structure, *Research Policy* 22, 1-21.

Utterback, James M., William J. Abernathy, 1975, A Dynamic Model of Process and Product Innovation, *Omega* 3 (6), 639-656.

Valletti, Tommaso M., Martin Cave, 1998, Competition in UK Mobile Communications, *Telecommunications Policy* 22 (2), 109-131.

Vernon, Raymond, 1966, International Investment and International Trade in the Product Cycle, *Quarterly Review of Economics* 88, May, 190-207.

Vernon, Raymond, 1971, *Sovereignty at Bay: The Multinational Spread of U.S. Enterprises*, New York, London: Basic Books.

Vernon, Raymond, 1979, The Product Cycle Hypothesis in a New International Environment, *Oxford Bulletin of Economics and Statistics* 41 (4), 255-267.

Verspagen, Bart, 1993, *Uneven Growth Between Interdependent Economies: A Evolutionary View on Technology Gaps, Trade and Growth*, Aldershot: Avebury.

Wakabayashi, Hideki, 1994, Japan's Revolution in Wireless Communications, *NRI Quarterly* (Autumn), 22-57.

Walsh, Vivien, 1988, Technology and the Competition of Small Countries: Review, in: C. Freeman, B.-Å. Lundvall (eds.), *Small Countries Facing the Technological Revolution*, London: Pinter, 37-66.

Whitelock, Jeryl M., 1987, Global Marketing and the Case for International Product Standardisation, *European Journal of Marketing* 21 (9), 32-44.

Wilkins, Mira, 1970, *The Emergence of Multinational Enterprise: American Business Abroad From the Colonial Era to 1914*, Cambridge, Mass.: Harvard University Press.

Wilkins, Mira, 1974, *The Maturing of Multinational Enterprise: American Business Abroad From 1914 to 1970*, Cambridge, Mass.: Harvard University Press.

Wilkins, Mira, 1989, *The History of Foreign Investment in the United States to 1914*, Cambridge, Mass.: Harvard University Press.

Wilson, Charles, 1969, *Unilever 1945-1965: Challenge & Response in the Post-War Industrial Revolution*, London: Cassell.

Woeckener, Bernd, 1995, Industrieökonomik für die Informationsgesellschaft: Vom Hotelling- zum Mastergleichungs-Ansatz, in: A. Wagner, H.-W. Lorenz (eds.), *Studien zur Evolutorischen Ökonomik* III, Berlin: Duncker&Humblot, 117-141.

Wong, Kar-yiu, 1995, *International Trade in Goods and Factor Mobility*, Cambridge, Mass.: MIT Press.

Workman, John Jr., 1993, Marketing's Limited Role in New Product Development in One Computer Systems Firm, *Journal of Marketing Research* 30 (November), 405-421.

Wortmann, Michael, 1990, Multinationals and the Internationalization of R&D: New Developments in German Companies, *Research Policy* 19, 175-183.

Yip, George S., 1992, *Total Global Strategy: Managing for Worldwide Competitive Advantage*, Englewood Cliffs: Prentice-Hall.

Yoffie, David B. (ed.), 1997, *Competing in the Age of Digital Convergence*, Boston, Mass.: Harvard Business School Press.

Young, W.R., 1979, Advanced Mobile Phone Service: Introduction, Background, and Objectives, *Bell System Technical Journal* 58 (1), 1-14.

Zander, Ivo, 1997, Technological Diversification in the Multinational Corporation – Historical Evolution and Future Prospects, *Research Policy* 26, 209-227.

Index of Figures

Index of Tables